The Generation of Edward Hyde

Jay Bland

The Generation of Edward Hyde

The Animal within, from Plato to Darwin to Robert Louis Stevenson

PETER LANG

Oxford · Bern · Berlin · Bruxelles · Frankfurt am Main · New York · Wien

Bibliographic information published by Die Deutsche Nationalbibliothek.
Die Deutsche Nationalbibliothek lists this publication in the Deutsche Nationalbibliografie;
detailed bibliographic data is available on the Internet at <http://dnb.d-nb.de>.

A catalogue record for this book is available from the British Library.

Library of Congress Cataloguing-in-Publication Data:

Bland, Jay, 1945-
  The generation of Edward Hyde : the animal within, from Plato to
Darwin to Robert Louis Stevenson / Jay Bland.
     p. cm.
  Includes bibliographical references and index.
  ISBN 978-3-0343-0135-0 (alk. paper)
  1. Stevenson, Robert Louis, 1850-1894. Strange case of Dr. Jekyll and
Mr. Hyde. 2. Stevenson, Robert Louis, 1850-1894--Characters--Edward
Hyde. 3. Hyde, Edward (Fictitious character) 4. Plato--Influence. 5.
Darwin, Charles, 1809-1882--Influence. 6. Bible--Influence. 7.
Evolution (Biology) in literature. 8. Human evolution in literature. 9.
Literature and science--Great Britain--History. I. Title.
  PR5485.B58 2009
  823'.8--dc22

                    2009045004

ISBN 978-3-0343-0135-0

© Peter Lang AG, International Academic Publishers, Bern 2010
Hochfeldstrasse 32, CH-3012 Bern, Switzerland
info@peterlang.com, www.peterlang.com, www.peterlang.net

Printed in Germany

Contents

Acknowledgments

The present work has grown out of a doctoral thesis which I undertook at Flinders University in Adelaide. It is no exaggeration to say that this project could never have begun without the generosity of the Royal Society for the Blind, whose Low Vision Centre in Adelaide gave me a reading machine. My studies could not have continued without the support of the Flinders Library staff. To single out one would be to insult the rest, but I must mention Ian McBain who looked to my technical needs, as did the university's disability liaison officer Paula Williams. My research could not have borne fruit without the guidance and advice of my supervisor Professor Graham Tulloch, whose name may one day be proverbial for patience. Thanks are also due to my co-supervisor Associate Professor Peter Morton who came late to the project, and to Associate Professor Robert Phiddian who advised on my chapter on *Gulliver's Travels*.

I would like to thank Flinders University for its financial support towards the cost of publication; and the Richard Llewellyn Arts and Disability Trust of Arts S.A. for its financial support during the preparation of the MS.

My greatest thanks, however, must go to my wife Janet for her love, her encouragement, and her constant care.

CHAPTER ONE

Introduction

One evening in September 1885, after 'a copious supper of bread and jam',[1] Robert Louis Stevenson had the nightmare which gave him the inspiration for his *Strange Case of Dr Jekyll and Mr Hyde*.[2] The next morning he wrote a hasty first draft of the story, over which he and his wife Fanny disagreed; and he burned it. According to Fanny, Stevenson had missed the allegory underlying his own creation, and had written a simple horror story. Stevenson then wrote another draft, correcting his oversight and adding the necessary allegorical layer to the existing framework.[3] With what, then, did Stevenson begin?

In 'A Chapter on Dreams' (1888) Stevenson reveals that he 'had long been trying to write a story [...] of man's double being',[4] and that during a time of financial embarrassment he had a dream:

> I dreamed the scene at the window. And a scene afterwards split in two, in which Hyde, pursued for some crime, took the powder and underwent the change in the

---

1 Andrew Lang, letter to *The Athenaeum*, 3507 (12 January 1895), 49, in *The Letters of Robert Louis Stevenson*, ed. by Bradford A. Booth and Ernest Mehew, 8 vols (New Haven and London: Yale University Press, 1995), V, 150, n2. (Hereafter *RLS Letters*.)

2 For a detailed account of the work's composition and publication, see *Strange Case of Dr Jekyll and Mr Hyde*, ed. by Richard Dury (Edinburgh: Edinburgh University Press, 2004), pp. 174–83. (Hereafter Dury, *Jekyll*.)

3 Frank McLynn writes of 'the absurdity of the suggestion that RLS missed the point of *Jekyll and Hyde* in the first draft until alerted to it by Fanny' (*Robert Louis Stevenson: A Biography* (New York: Random House, 1993), p. 257). Nevertheless, something in their dispute must have persuaded him to burn the first draft.

4 *The Works of Robert Louis Stevenson*, Vailima edition, 25 vols (New York: AMS Press, 1974), XII, 231–49 (p. 247). (Hereafter *Works*.)

presence of his pursuers. [...] All that was given me was the matter of three scenes, and the central idea of a voluntary change becoming involuntary.[5]

And the rest?

All the rest was made awake, and consciously, [...]. The meaning of the tale is therefore mine, [...]; indeed, I do most of the morality, [...]. Mine, too, is the setting, mine the characters.[6]

At no point does Stevenson suggest that Hyde's appearance formed part of his dream; so it is safe to assume that he consciously and deliberately chose all of Hyde's physical details – in particular, his apishness. Hyde is specifically referred to as monkey-like,[7] and ape-like (47; 96; 97); his hands are 'thickly shaded with a swart growth of hair' (88); and he walks about 'chattering' to himself (94) – a behaviour traditionally associated with apes and monkeys.

Why did Stevenson make Hyde ape-like and – as will be argued in a later chapter – take such pains to make him authentically ape-like? For a possible explanation, one might look no further than a *Punch* cartoon of December 1884. The cartoon shows a monkey-like figure wearing a large placard on which is written: 'The Maniac-Man-Monkey. New Sensational Christmas Story by B. Bones'.[8] Katherine Linehan writes:

This cartoon may include among its targets the *Pall Mall Gazette*'s method of advertising Stevenson's 'The Body Snatcher' on the streets of London shortly before Christmas 1884: Sidney Colvin reports that the tale was publicized 'by sandwich men carrying posters so horrific that they were suppressed, if I remember aright, by the police'.[9]

---

5   *Works*, XII, 248. The 'scene at the window' is the scene in which Utterson and Enfield talk with Jekyll while he sits at the window at the back of his establishment.
6   *Works*, XII, 248.
7   *Dr Jekyll and Mr Hyde and Other Stories*, ed. and intro. by Jenni Calder (London: Penguin, 1979), p. 68. Further references from this edition will be given after quotations in the text. The chattering tradition will be explained in a later section.
8   *Punch*, 87 (27 December 1884), 305.
9   Robert Louis Stevenson, *Strange Case of Dr Jekyll and Mr Hyde*, ed. by Katherine Linehan (New York and London: Norton, 2003), p. 121. (Hereafter Linehan, *Jekyll*.)

Stevenson's letter of November 1884 to Charles Morley[10] shows that he was aware of the sandwich men before the event; so it is highly likely that he became aware of the *Punch* cartoon as well; and, given that his sensational Christmas story for the following year featured a maniac-man-monkey, one would be hard put to argue for the workings of coincidence.[11]

Stevenson had a mischievous sense of humour. When he was a child he would run through his grandfather's flower beds, then make his footprints bigger in order to throw suspicion on his older cousin.[12] During his time at Edinburgh University he and his friend Charles Baxter played many pranks and practical jokes, both within the university and on the general public.[13] In Samoa he was amused to hear of the rumour that his step-daughter Belle Strong was his illegitimate daughter by 'a Morocco woman', a rumour which he then actively encouraged.[14] It would not have been out of character for him to have carried on the joke from *Punch*.

But one should also bear in mind Stevenson's attitude towards the process in which he was involved.[15] He had hopes for himself as a serious

---

Colvin's reminiscence appears as a headnote to Stevenson's letter of 15 November 1884 to Edmund Gosse, in the Edinburgh Edition of Stevenson's Letters (I, 339) (Linehan, *Jekyll*, p121). See the letter also, without the headnote, in *RLS Letters*, letter 1332, 5, 33. Mehew quotes the Colvin passage in relation to Stevenson's letter of November 1884 to Charles Morley of the *Pall Mall Gazette*, q.v., *RLS Letters*, letter 1336, 5, 35, n1.

10   *RLS Letters*, letter 1336, I, 35.

11   *Jekyll and Hyde* was intended for the Christmas market of 1885, but was held over until January 1886. For details see Roger G. Swearingen, *The Prose Writings of Robert Louis Stevenson* (Hamden, Connecticut: Archon, 1980), pp. 98–102.

12   Mrs Dale, 'Fresh Side-Lights on R.L.S.', *I Can Remember Robert Louis Stevenson*, ed. by Rosaline Masson (Edinburgh and London: Chambers, 1922), pp. 6–12 (p. 8).

13   McLynn, pp. 44–45.

14   *RLS Letters*, letter 2550 to J.M. Barrie, 2 or 3 April 1893, VIII, 44–48 (p. 45). In a letter to Charles Stoddard of 21 [February] 1893, Belle writes: 'Louis was delighted with the idea. ... Introduces me as his daughter, and when he talks about old days in Morocco he is magnificent. He tells me long tales about my mother which invariably wind up with "She was a damned fine woman!"' (45, n5).

15   Here I am indebted to:– Patrick Brantlinger and Richard Boyle, 'The Education of Edward Hyde: Stevenson's "Gothic Gnome" and the Mass Readership of Late-

writer, yet found himself surviving by contributing to what James Ashcroft Noble in a review of *Jekyll and Hyde* refers to as 'a class of literature familiarity with which has bred in the minds of most readers a certain measure of contempt'.[16] Stevenson's publishers Longmans, apparently above embarrassment in such matters, had been wanting him to write them a 'shilling shocker'. Dr Thomas Scott, who was at that time Stevenson's physician, recalls that the suggestion was 'much against his inclination'.[17] Patrick Brantlinger and Richard Boyle observe the conflict in Stevenson's mind:

> Producing a 'shilling shocker' for Longmans might disagree with his sense of the higher aims of literature, but it agreed with his desire for financial independence and popularity.[18]

The word 'popularity' here contains its own contradictions. In a letter of 2 January 1886 (precisely one week before *Jekyll and Hyde* went on sale), Stevenson wrote to Edmund Gosse a cynical and bitter letter expressing contempt for both the great unwashed public and their lack of taste, and for himself for pandering to it. He begins with what was to prove a most prophetic utterance, given the success of *Jekyll and Hyde* and the speed of its composition:

> That is the hard part of literature. You aim high, and you take longer over your work; and it will not be so successful as if you had aimed low and rushed it. [...]
> Let us tell each other sad stories of the bestiality of the beast whom we feed. [...] I do not like mankind; but men, and not all of these – and fewer women. As for respecting the race, and above all that fatuous rabble of burgesses called 'the public',

---

Victorian England', in *Dr Jekyll and Mr Hyde after One Hundred Years*, ed. by William Veeder and Gordon Hirsch (Chicago: University of Chicago Press, 1988), pp. 265–82 (hereafter *100 Years*); and to Stephen D. Arata, 'The Sedulous Ape: Atavism, Professionalism, and Stevenson's *Jekyll and Hyde*', *Criticism*, 37 (1995), 233–59.

16   *Academy*, 29 (23 January 1886), 55. Reprinted in *Robert Louis Stevenson: The Critical Heritage*, ed. by Paul Maixner (London: Routledge & Kegan Paul, 1981), pp. 203–05 (p. 203).

17   Masson, p. 213.

18   *100 Years*, p. 265.

God save me from such irreligion; that way lies disgrace and dishonour. There must be something wrong in me, or I would not be popular.[19]

Stevenson's Puckish sense of humour alone could have provided the impetus for his decision to carry on the joke from the *Punch* cartoon. In that case the decision would not have been directed towards anybody. But Stevenson may have been hurt by the cartoon. His attitude towards his material and his audience suggests that he felt the genre deserved nothing better than a maniac-man-monkey, and neither did his readership. At the same time his self-disgust would have left him vulnerable to any taunts by others. Thus at one stroke he thumbs his nose at his mockers in *Punch* by effectively using their idea against them; he stands aloof from his story by treating it as a joke; and he shows his contempt for the burgesses by giving them the kind of rubbish that they both demand and deserve.

Be that as it may, Stevenson's treatment of his maniac-man-monkey transcended the shilling shocker genre, and turned Hyde into a cultural icon. But did Stevenson simply come upon him by a happy accident; or was his appearance determined by other factors? Could such a potent mythic figure have arisen simply from a one-line gag in a cartoon? Even if that were the case, Stevenson deliberately and methodically added layer upon layer of meaning to Hyde, drawing upon a rich and extensive litera-ture dealing with apes, Wild Men, and other grotesque embodiments of sin and evil. The question then becomes not, What does Hyde do?, or, Why does he do it?; but, What is he?, Why does he look like that?, and, How does he come to be there in Jekyll? My intention is to answer these questions by examining works which may not necessarily have influenced

19 *RLS Letters*, letter 1510, V, 170–72 (p. 171). This letter provides a good example of Stevenson's tendency to invoke other authors: '[L]et us sit upon the ground/ And tell sad stories of the death of kings' (*Richard II*, III, ii, 155–56); 'I hate and detest that animal called man, although I hartily [*sic*] love John, Peter, Thomas, and so forth' (*The Correspondence of Jonathan Swift*, ed. by Harold Williams, 5 vols (Oxford: Clarendon Press, 1963–65), III, 103); 'O! that way madness lies' (*King Lear*, III, iii, 21).

Stevenson directly, but which, taken together, provide a context in which to view the figure of Hyde.

Readers and reviewers at the time of the book's publication typically addressed its universal implications. Andrew Lang, for example, writes:

> Mr Stevenson's idea, his secret (but a very open secret) is that of the double personality in every man.[20]

He goes on:

> It is not a moral allegory, of course; but you cannot help reading the moral into it, and recognizing that [...] every Jekyll among us is haunted by his own Hyde.[21]

James Ashcroft Noble expands on Lang's statement. He writes:

> [*Jekyll and Hyde*] is a marvellous exploration into the recesses of human nature; and though it is more than possible that Mr Stevenson wrote with no ethical intent, its impressiveness as a parable is equal to its fascination as a work of art.[22]

Another anonymous reviewer begins with the particular, referring to Jekyll and

> this delineation of a feeble but kindly nature steadily and inevitably succumbing to the sinister influences of besetting weaknesses.[23]

But he then immediately goes on to give Jekyll's story a universal application:

> [Stevenson] works out the essential power of Evil, which, with its malignant patience and unwearying perseverance, gains ground with each casual yielding to temptation, till the once well-meaning man may actually become a fiend, or at least wear the reflection of the fiend's image.[24]

---

20 *Saturday Review*, 61 (9 January 1886), 55–56. Quoted in Maixner, pp. 199–202 (p. 200). The review was unsigned. Maixner attributes it to Lang.
21 Maixner, p. 201.
22 Maixner, pp. 204–05.
23 *The Times* (25 January 1886), 13. Reprinted in Maixner, pp. 205–07 (p. 207).
24 Maixner, p. 207.

Julia Wedgwood's review offers the most penetrating response:

> Mr Stevenson represents the individualizing influence of modern democracy in its more concentrated form. Whereas most fiction deals with the relation between man and woman (and the very fact that its scope is so much narrowed is a sign of the atomic character of our modern thought), the author of this strange tale takes an even narrower range, and sets himself to investigate the meaning of the word *self*.[25]

Over the years, however, as we have moved further away from the latter end of the nineteenth century, commentators have begun to regard *Jekyll and Hyde* as a document which informs us about either Stevenson's psychology, or the tensions within the society of his day, or simply as a text which can be deconstructed. We find a striking illustration of the range of modern scholarly approaches to the text in the Introduction to Veeder and Hirsch's much-cited collection *Dr Jekyll and Mr Hyde after One Hundred Years*:

> The principal enterprise of our volume is critical. Eight essays reflect in their diverse interests and tactics the breadth of appeal that has made *Jekyll and Hyde* a force in our culture for one hundred years. The essays employ such divergent methodologies as deconstruction, feminism, psychoanalysis, intellectual and cultural history, and genre study, as well as close textual analysis. They evoke diverse theorists: Bakhtin, Barthes, Derrida, and Foucault; Marx, Lukacs, and Jameson; Freud, Lacan, and Kristeva (xiv).

Commentators have also moved away from a fascination with Hyde, to a fascination with Jekyll as representing the hypocrisy and double standards of his period. With this shift has come a tendency to analyze the characters from a very twentieth-century viewpoint. Claire Harman writes: 'Many – indeed, most – modern critics have interpreted the novel as a psycho-sexual allegory.'[26] And of course, wherever there is a psycho-sexual allegory,

---

25 *Contemporary Review*, 49 (April 1886), 594–95. Reprinted in Maixner, pp. 222–24 (p. 223).

26 *Robert Louis Stevenson: A Biography* (London: Harper Collins, 2005), p. 304. See, e.g., Stephen Heath, 'Psychopathia Sexualis: Stevenson's *Strange Case*', *Critical Quarterly*, 28 (1986), 93–108.

a psycho-homosexual allegory is never far away. Elaine Showalter writes that *Jekyll and Hyde* is

> a case of male hysteria, not only that of Henry J. but also of the men in the community around him. It can most persuasively be read as a fable of *fin de siècle* homosexual panic, the discovery and resistance of the homosexual self. [It is] a story about communities of men.[27]

Among those who use the text to explore Victorian society at large we find William Veeder:

> *Jekyll and Hyde* dramatizes the inherent weakness of late-Victorian social organization, a weakness that derives from unresolved pre-oedipal and oedipal emotions and that threatens the very possibility of community.[28]

He goes on to observe that Stevenson's attention is on

> late-Victorian patriarchy; the focus of the story is less on Jekyll's attitude toward Hyde than on the way that the Jekyll/Hyde relationship is replicated throughout Jekyll's circle (108).

He refers to this circle as 'an emblematic community, a relational network'. He continues:

> This network marks a psychological condition as a cultural phenomenon. The cultural and psychological come together in Stevenson's famous statement of the theme: 'that damned old business of the war in the members'.[29] Because members of the psyche

---

27 *Sexual Anarchy: Gender and Culture at the Fin de Siècle* (New York: Viking, 1990), p. 107. Showalter also refers to Stevenson as 'the *fin-de-siècle* laureate of the double life' (106).

28 'Children of the Night: Stevenson and Patriarchy', in *100 Years*, pp. 107–60 (p. 107). On this theme, see also Irving S. Saposnik, *Robert Louis Stevenson* (Boston: Twayne, 1974), pp. 88–101. Veeder's partly Freudian approach complements Barbara Hannah's Jungian analysis of Stevenson and *Jekyll and Hyde* in *Striving Towards Wholeness* (London: Allen & Unwin, 1972), chap. 3.

29 Letter to J.A. Symonds, March 1886, *RLS Letters*, letter 1571, V, 220–22. Stevenson writes: '*Jekyll* is a dreadful thing, I own, but the only thing I feel dreadful about is that damned old business of the war in the members. This time it came out; I hope

are at war, other members must be – family members, members of society, genital members. The resulting casualty is not simply Jekyll/Hyde but culture itself (108).

Richard Gaughan also declares for this approach to the tale:

> The very fragmentation and inconclusiveness of the narrative, then, parody Jekyll's desire to find purity [of personality] and tempt the reader to repeat Jekyll's mistake by trying to find a single key to the mysteries of the story. The easiest, and most treacherous, way to do this is to follow Jekyll's lead and read the story as an allegory.[30]

Gaughan acknowledges the allegorical presence, but denies its validity:

> Throughout the novel Stevenson tempts the reader with allegory, but he just as consistently frustrates any simple allegorical reading (187).

Furthermore, Gaughan limits Hyde's potency as an embodiment of evil:

> Jekyll repeatedly refers to Hyde as his evil side. This 'evil' side, however, is nothing more than a slightly exaggerated form of that part of Jekyll that has always chaffed [*sic*] under the constraints of conventional respectability and Jekyll's imperious desire to be seen as superior in the eyes of all men. Hyde is less evil than he is the embodiment of pride or, more generally, impersonal will. Read in this way, the story of Dr Jekyll and Mr Hyde is not a moral allegory but a study of the relationship between will and the various structures (social, psychological, and intellectual) that both express and confine will (187).

And he determinedly redirects the reader's attention from the universal to the particular:

> In this respect, Jekyll's story is the story of the same ambiguity of human forces that forms the basis of tragedy. But, Jekyll is not a tragic hero. The conflict Jekyll experiences is of a very special kind. The manifestation of will in Hyde is largely determined by Jekyll's hypocrisy and his desire to master himself by externalizing himself into

---

it will stay in, in future' (220). Stevenson is alluding to a passage in St Paul's letter to the Romans, which will be quoted later in this chapter.

30   'Mr Hyde and Mr Seek: Utterson's Antidote', *Journal of Narrative Technique*, 17 (1987), 184–97 (p. 187).

a series of pure personalities. Hyde is the impersonal will to externalize everything, to bring everything under the control of pride and intellect.

Consequently, Hyde cannot be a universal Dionysian urge to destroy constraints. Hyde is only Jekyll's ambition stripped of all sentimentality (187).

A comparison of the immediate responses by reviewers with the passages from the later commentators shows that in the tendency to concentrate on Jekyll's psychology; his sexuality; his relationship with his father; the dynamics of his social circle; on the societal structure which he inhabits – in the tendency to focus on these, commentators have in fact not broadened the scope of their analysis, but narrowed it. They have narrowed it from an examination of the human condition, to an examination of one man in a particular socio-economic milieu at a particular point in history.

Obviously these are legitimate and illuminating areas of inquiry, but do they, in themselves, do justice to the work as a whole, and, in particular, to Stevenson's intentions? Surely a profounder understanding of *Jekyll and Hyde* lies not so much with the homosexual,[31] drug-addicted[32] onanist[33] Jekyll, or his undignified pleasures (for which one need look no further than Stevenson's own extra-mural activities while he was at Edinburgh University),[34] but with Hyde – or, rather, with the fact of Hyde's existence. Gaughan's assertion that 'Hyde is only Jekyll's ambition stripped of all sentimentality' would be well enough if Hyde looked normal. But he does not; and there is enough emphasis on the fact to make it significant. His deformity and hairiness signify something; and since the text is insistent on this point, one must assume that they signify evil. Jekyll, in fact, is quite specific:

> The drug had no discriminating action; it was neither diabolical nor divine; it but shook the doors of the prisonhouse of my disposition; and, like the captives of

---

31   Showalter, Veeder, *et al.*

32   Daniel L. Wright, '"The Prisonhouse of my Disposition": A Study of the Psychology of Addiction in *Dr Jekyll and Mr Hyde*', *Studies in the Novel*, 26 (1994), 254–67.

33   *The Strange Case of Dr Jekyll and Mr Hyde*, ed., intro. and notes by Robert Mighall (London: Penguin, 2002; repr. 2003), pp. 154–56; 177. (Hereafter Mighall, *Jekyll*.)

34   These consisted of low dives, lower company, and prostitutes with hearts of gold. See, e.g., McLynn, chap. 2.

Philippi, that which stood within ran forth. At that time my virtue slumbered; my evil, kept awake by ambition, was alert and swift to seize the occasion; and the thing that was projected was Edward Hyde. Hence, although I had now two characters as well as two appearances, one was wholly evil (85).[35]

The reader should take this passage seriously as an accurate reflection of Stevenson's intentions, regardless of Jekyll's reliability as a witness, since Stevenson himself corroborates it, giving his assessment of Hyde in a letter to the American journalist John Paul Bocock:

The harm was in Jekyll, because he was a hypocrite – not because he was fond of women; he says so himself; but people are so filled full of folly and inverted lust, that they can think of nothing but sexuality. The hypocrite let out the beast Hyde – who is no more sensual than another, but who is the essence of cruelty and malice, and selfishness and cowardice: and these are the diabolic in man.[36]

This thing that has been prowling around in Jekyll's consciousness, although not an ape, is sufficiently ape-like to suggest not simply evil, but ancient, primitive, timeless evil; an enduring evil which has resisted mankind's rise to civilization; an evil which in Stevenson's day had been given a new and disturbing origin by the writings of Charles Darwin, whose *Origin of Species* appeared in 1859, when Stevenson was nine years old.

Darwinism and the Bible

When Stevenson was growing up, and as each new scientific discovery contradicted the account of the Creation given in Genesis, every thinking Christian was having to redefine what it meant to be human. Since the eighteenth century, geologists had continued to push the age of the Earth far

---

35   Note that although Jekyll's evil was kept awake by ambition, it was the evil that was projected, not the ambition.

36   *RLS Letters*, letter 1939, November 1887, VI, 56–57 (p. 56). See also Maixner, p. 231.

back before the time of Adam and Eve. Bones of extinct animals had been unearthed; and fossilized sea shells had been found in the peaks of mountain ranges. Charles Darwin's grandfather Erasmus Darwin (1731–1802) entered the lists with *Zoonomia, or the Laws of Organic Life* (1794–96) and *The Temple of Nature* (1803). In 1844 the anonymous *Vestiges of the Natural History of Creation* appeared to a shocked and horrified public.[37] This 'atheistical and blasphemous'[38] work, which, to many readers, advocated 'a new theory of creation, and one which was in direct opposition to the account given in the Word of God'[39] – namely, that the apes gave rise to humans – created a storm far beyond its scientific merits.

> It was denounced from the pulpit, abused in the Press, laughed at by superior persons anxious to exhibit their own scientific knowledge; it was the theme of conversation in fashionable drawing-rooms and in devout religious assemblies; so that even those who had not read it knew something of its theory and purpose.[40]

But not all who read it were horrified. Many young people, 'in revolt against a too rigid religious creed that had ruled their upbringing',[41] embraced it – too uncritically for the then nineteen-years-old Thomas Henry Huxley, who was offended by its lack of scientific scholarship.[42]

Despite its shortcomings, *Vestiges* prepared the ground for the publication of Charles Darwin's *Origin of Species* (1859) and *Descent of Man* (1871).

---

37 For an account of the controversy see Amy Cruse, *The Victorians And Their Books* (London: Allen & Unwin, 1962), chap. 5. The author of *Vestiges* was subsequently found to be Robert Chambers, 'the younger of the two brothers who, in 1832, had begun the publication of *Chambers's Journal*, a valuable educational periodical for working men' (Cruse, p. 86).

38 Cruse, p. 84.

39 Cruse, p. 84.

40 Cruse, p. 85.

41 Cruse, p. 87.

42 Cruse, p. 87. He was still offended thirty-four years later when, in 'Evolution in Biology', he referred to it as 'that particularly unsatisfactory book' (T.H. Huxley, *Darwiniana, Collected Essays,* 9 vols (London: Macmillan, 1894–95), II, 187–226 (p. 222)). (Hereafter *Collected Essays.*) The offence retained its potency; see 'Science and Pseudo-Science', *Science and Christian Tradition, Collected Essays,* V, 90–125 (pp. 108–10).

These two books, tirelessly championed by Huxley, provided the scientific ammunition for an assault on Church dogma which has continued to this day.

Unfortunately this war also drew in the members of the Stevenson household. G.K. Chesterton says:

> It is an obvious truth that Stevenson was born of a Puritan tradition, in a Presbyterian country, where still rolled the echoes, at least, of the theological thunders of Knox; and where the Sabbath was sometimes more like a day of death than a day of rest.[43]

The lad Louis, who as a child had been 'a tiny religious maniac'[44] who had wanted the Bible read to sheep and horses,[45] later found himself 'at the particular modern moment to catch the first fashion and excitement of Darwinism'.[46] J.C. Furnas is more explicit:

> [Stevenson] was still in skirts when Darwin and [Alfred Russell] Wallace published the explosive works that would revolutionize the thinking he grew up with and provide a bitter idiom for reciprocally disembowelling battles between himself and his father.[47]

This is no exaggeration. After one nasty episode in September 1873 Stevenson wrote to Mrs Fanny Sitwell, with whom he was in love at the time, quoting his father Thomas's words:

> I have made all my life to suit you [...] and the end of it is that I find you in opposition to the Lord Jesus Christ. I find everything gone. I would ten times sooner see you lying in your grave than that you should be shaking the faith of other young men and bringing ruin on other houses as you have brought it on this.[48]

---

43   G.K. Chesterton, *Robert Louis Stevenson* [1927], 3rd edn (London: Hodder and Stoughton, 1929), p. 63.
44   McLynn, p. 15.
45   McLynn, p. 16.
46   Chesterton, p. 55.
47   J.C. Furnas, *Voyage to Windward: The Life of Robert Louis Stevenson* (London: Faber, 1952), p. 38.
48   *RLS Letters*, letter 143, 22 September 1873, I, 311–13 (p. 312). Quoted in Furnas, p. 78.

Although Stevenson was desperately unhappy with himself for distressing his parents, he could not submit his reason to the yoke of their orthodoxy. He writes in the notebook which he kept during his time at Edinburgh University:

> Faith means holding the same opinions as the person employing the word. It is faith to agree with Dr Orthodoxy; but it is unbelief to believe in the persistence of force.[49]
>
> [...]
>
> The presently orthodox have a nasty way of using the word *theory*. [...] Mr Darwin is a theoriser; very well, but what are those that adhere so stoutly to the contrary view? merely theorisers also. This sounds very trivial; but it is a great truth for all that, and a much neglected truth into the bargain.[50]

The wretched youth Stevenson would have derived much comfort from the following observations by Northrop Frye:

> The Bible is the supreme example of the way that myths can, under certain social pressures, stick together to make up a mythology. A second look at this mythology shows us that it actually became, for medieval and later centuries, a vast mythological universe, stretching in time from creation to apocalypse, and in metaphorical space from heaven to hell. A mythological universe is a vision of reality in terms of human concerns and hopes and anxieties: it is not a primitive form of science. Unfortunately, human nature being what it is, man first acquires a mythological universe and then pretends as long as he can that it is also the actual universe. [...]
>
> The secession of science from the mythological universe is a familiar story. The separating of scientific and mythological space began theoretically with Copernicus, and effectively with Galileo. By the nineteenth century scientific time had been emancipated from mythological time.[51]

---

49   *Works*, XXV, 28. 'Persistence of force' is a term used by Herbert Spencer in *First Principles* (1867). See Herbert Spencer, *First Principles*, 2 vols (London: Williams and Norgate, 1910), I, 154. Persistence of force was central to Spencer's conception of the principles underlying evolution. See *First Principles*, II, 323.

50   *Works*, XXV, 36.

51   Northrop Frye, *The Secular Scripture* (Cambridge, Massachusetts, and London: Harvard University Press, 1976), p. 14.

And – he might have said – with the arrival of the theory of natural selection, man had been emancipated from the Fall. The down-side was that he was now just a sophisticated monkey – or, as Stevenson put it, an 'ennobled lemur'.[52] It is ironic, and rather sad, that the physical energy and the mental drive which led to the confidence and hubris of Victorian England should have produced the scientists and philosophers whose discoveries and insights left their fellows, not the lords of creation, but beasts of the field.

Stevenson, realizing his parents' distress, did not abandon his deeply ingrained religious beliefs overnight. Nor, when he had relaxed his grip on the doctrine, did he let go of the poetry and literature that sprang from it. Nor, as he matured, could he entirely let go of the God who had inspired it. In his twenty-seventh year he writes a conciliatory letter to his father, although it begins on an equivocal note:

> Christianity is, among other things, a very wise, noble, and strange doctrine of life. [...] I speak of it as a doctrine of life, and as a wisdom for this world. [...] I feel every day as if religion had a greater interest for me; but that interest is still centred on the little rough-and-tumble world in which our fortunes are cast for the moment. I cannot transfer my interests, not even my religious interests, to any different sphere.[53]

But at least he now acknowledges the fountainhead of his religion:

> I have a good heart and believe in myself and my fellow men and the God who made us all (241).

And he ends with an observation much in keeping with the views of Charles Kingsley, one of the authors to be discussed later:

---

52   'Pulvis et Umbra' [1888], *Works*, XII, 283–92 (p. 290). Stevenson's phrase may derive from a sentence towards the end of *The Origin of Species*: 'When I view all beings not as special creations, but as the lineal descendants of some few beings which lived long before the first bed of the Cambrian system was deposited, they seem to me to become ennobled' (*The Origin of Species and The Descent of Man* (New York: The Modern Library, 1927), p. 373).

53   *RLS Letters*, letter 511, 15 February 1878, II, 240–42 (p. 240).

There is a fine text in the Bible, I don't know where, to the effect that all things work together for good to those who love the Lord. [footnote: Romans 8.28.] Indeed, if this be a test, I must count myself one of those. Two years ago, I think I was as bad a man as was consistent with my character. And of all that has happened to me since then, strange as it may seem to you, everything has been, in one way or another, bringing me a little nearer to what I think you would like me to be. 'Tis a strange world, indeed, but there is a manifest God for those who care to look for him (241).

Thus Stevenson progressed through an enthusiastically Christian childhood and a turbulently agnostic youth, to return in manhood to the fold, albeit with an individualized belief. John Kelman sums up Stevenson's belief, beginning with a quotation from *The Merry Men*:

A generous prayer is never presented in vain; the petition may be refused, but the petitioner is always, I believe, rewarded by some gracious visitation. The horror, at least, was lifted from my mind; I could look with calm of spirit on that great bright creature, God's ocean.[54]

Kelman adds:

In these words two things are plain. There is the belief in a direct and personal contact with the Divine; and there is the vision of God through Nature.[55]

Elsewhere Kelman observes that Stevenson's belief in God

was so far removed from any reasoned metaphysical conclusion, that we have described it as the highest form of a spirituality which belongs rather to the Religion of Sentiment than to the Religion of Dogma (265).

However, Stevenson's passage through the dark night of doubt, and his repudiation of dogma, in no way diminished his love of the Bible. Biblical phrases and references sparkle in his writings – including *Jekyll and Hyde*;

---

54   *Works*, XI, 11–87 (p. 49). This quotation, like most in Kelman's book, has no reference.
55   *The Faith of Robert Louis Stevenson* (Edinburgh and London: Oliphant Anderson and Ferrier, 1907), p. 150. The vision of God through Nature is a recurring theme in *The Faerie Queene*, *The Water-Babies*, and 'Olalla'.

and the many quotations in his letters from such religious-minded writers as Spenser and Milton – whose works both inform and illuminate *Jekyll and Hyde* – show that they too were never far below the surface of his thought.

But the Bible was one thing, and modern science was another. God may have made us all; but He made us all through a scientifically observable biological process; and man's biological origins were, in Stevenson's word, 'appalling'. In 'Pulvis et Umbra' he leaves his readers in no doubt as to where they stand in the scheme of things:

> We behold space sown with rotary islands, suns and worlds and the shards and wrecks of systems: some, like the sun, still blazing; some rotting, like the earth; others, like the moon, stable in desolation. All of these we take to be made of something we call matter: a thing which no amount of analysis can help us to conceive; to whose incredible properties no familiarity can reconcile our minds. This stuff, when not purified by the lustration of fire, rots uncleanly into something we call life; seized through all its atoms with a pediculous malady; swelling in tumours that become independent, sometimes even (by an abhorrent prodigy) locomotory; one splitting into millions, millions cohering into one, as the malady proceeds through varying stages. This vital putrescence of the dust, used as we are to it, yet strikes us with occasional disgust [...] the moving sand is infected with lice [...].
>
> In two main shapes this eruption covers the countenance of the earth: the animal and the vegetable: one in some degree the invasion of the other: the second rooted to the spot; the first coming detached out of its natal mud, [...] a thing so inconceivable that, if it be well considered, the heart stops.[56]

Ironically, in the debate which raged over the origins of this quintessence of dust, both sides were in agreement on one point: it had indeed *been* dust. The main argument was over what had *animated* it. On the one hand there was the Word of God:

> And the Lord God formed man of the dust of the ground, and breathed into his nostrils the breath of life; and man became a living soul (Genesis 2.7).

56 *Works*, XII, 283–85. This passage is a reworking of a section in 'Lay Morals' (written in 1879, but not published until after Stevenson's death), in which he also uses the word 'appalling' to describe the Earth as a place of residence (*Works*, XXIV, 198–99).

On the other there was T.H. Huxley who, on 8 November 1868, when Stevenson was in his second year at Edinburgh University, came to that place and delivered, in 'the most publicised event of 1868',[57] a lecture called *On the Physical Basis of Life*.[58] William Irvine describes what happened on the night:

> Appearing before a large audience with a bottle of smelling salts and other familiar, commonplace articles, Huxley declared that he had before him the essential ingredients of protoplasm – the physical basis of life. All life, from the amoeba up to man, is composed of this single substance, which uniformly exhibits the same properties and the same functions. Plants are distinguished from animals by the ability to generate organic matter from inorganic, but as there is no sharp distinction between simple plants and animals, so there is no distinction between simple protoplasm and non-living matter except in a certain arrangement of molecules. In fact, mind itself is but 'the result of molecular forces' in 'the protoplasm which displays it'. Man is therefore [...] brother not only to the monkey, but to the amoeba, even to the molecule and the atom.[59]

The similarities between *On the Physical Basis of Life* and 'Pulvis et Umbra' are too close to be accidental, regardless of whether or not the transmission from Huxley to Stevenson was direct. The affinity between 'Pulvis et Umbra' and *Jekyll and Hyde* will be examined later.

57   Cyril Bibby, *Scientist Extraordinary: The Life and Scientific Work of Thomas Henry Huxley* (Oxford: Pergamon Press, 1972), p. 63.

58   Stevenson was not there. He was home in bed, ill. See *RLS Letters*, letter 72, 17 November 1868, I, 167–72. However, the lecture was published in the following year; so Stevenson could have read it. Bibby writes that 'it carried *The Fortnightly* into seven printings' (63).

59   *Apes, Angels and Victorians* (London: Readers Union, Weidenfeld and Nicholson, 1956), pp. 192–93. Huxley's words were: '[A]ll vital action may [...] be said to be the result of the molecular forces of the protoplasm which displays it. And if so, it must be true, in the same sense and to the same extent, that the thoughts to which I am now giving utterance, and your thoughts regarding them, are the expression of molecular changes in that matter of life which is the source of our other vital phenomena' ('On the Physical Basis of Life', *Method and Results, Collected Essays*, I, 130–65 (p. 154)). It is tempting to link this passage with the line in Stevenson's *Macaire* (1885): 'What are Ideas? the protoplasm of wealth' (*Works*, VI, 285).

In the debate between evolution and the Church, the stakes were high on both sides. Cardinal Manning voiced the position of the Roman Catholic Church when he attacked Darwinism as 'a brutal philosophy—to wit, there is no God, and the ape is our Adam'.[60] This point is central to the concerns of all the Churches. It was all very well for biologists to declare disingenuously that they were merely describing a process in nature, and that no theological inferences should be drawn from it,[61] but the implications were profound: if man was descended from some ape-like ancestor, then there was no Adam. If there was no Adam, then there was no Fall. If there was no Fall, then the Incarnation of Jesus and his death on the cross were meaningless, and there was no Salvation. The Church's doctrine was outlined by St Paul in his letter to the Romans:

> But God commendeth his love toward us, in that, while we were yet sinners, Christ died for us.
> [...]
> Wherefore, as by one man sin entered into the world, and death by sin; and so death passed upon all men, for that all have sinned:
> [...]
> Nevertheless death reigned from Adam to Moses, even over them that had not sinned after the similitude of Adam's transgression, who is the figure of him that was to come.
> [...]
> For if by one man's offence death reigned by one; much more they which receive abundance of grace and of the gift of righteousness shall reign in life by one, Jesus Christ.
> [...]
> That as sin hath reigned unto death, even so might grace reign through righteousness unto eternal life by Jesus Christ our Lord (Romans 5.8–21).

St Paul's letter to the Romans in fact provides the cornerstone for Henry Jekyll's Statement, something which has already been alluded to by Veeder – the war in the members. St Paul writes:

60 Quoted in Cruse, p. 95.
61 See Northrop Frye, *Myth and Metaphor: Selected Essays, 1974–1988*, ed. by Robert D. Denham (Charlottesville and London: University Press of Virginia, 1990), p. 142.

But I see another law in my members, warring against the law of my mind, and bringing me into captivity to the law of sin which is in my members (Romans 7.23).

Henry Jekyll writes:

And it chanced that the direction of my scientific studies [...] reacted and shed a strong
light on the consciousness of the perennial war among my members (81–82).

This biblical reference was of course obvious to contemporary readers;
and a contemporary reviewer of *Jekyll and Hyde* in a Christian magazine
took it as the text for his sermon:

It is an allegory based on the two-fold nature of man, a truth taught us by the Apostle
PAUL in Romans vii., 'I find then a law that, when I would do good, evil is present
with me' [7.21]. We have for some time wanted to review this little book, but we have
refrained from so doing till the season of Lent had come, as the whole question of
temptation is so much more appropriately considered at this period of the Christian
year, when the thoughts of so many are directed to the temptations of our Lord.[62]

The reviewer, naturally, finds a universal message in the story:

How many men live out two distinct characters? To the outer world they are the
honourable, upright men, with a good professional name, holding a respectable
position in society, looked up to and spoken well of by their neighbours. Within,
however, the inner sanctum of their own hearts they are conscious of another self, a
very different character. So far this is more or less common to all (225).

The reviewer then locates this situation within its Judaeo-Christian context:

62   From an unsigned review, 'Secret Sin', *The Rock* (2 April 1886), 3. Reprinted in Maixner,
      pp. 224–27 (p. 224). Maixner writes: '"Jekyll and Hyde" became a popular topic
      in the pulpit. The following review gives some idea of what sermons based upon it
      must have been like. The "Rock" (London) was an organ of the Unified Church of
      England and Ireland' (224). *Jekyll and Hyde* remained a popular topic in the pulpit for
      some time. In September 1886, eight months after the story's publication, Stevenson's
      mother went to hear the Revd W.W. Tulloch preach on it. See 'Notes about Robert
      Louis Stevenson from his Mother's Diary', *Works*, XXVI, 285–366 (p. 345).

It is a result of the Fall of Man that we have ever present a lower nature struggling to get the mastery (225).

Not content with explaining the presence of evil, the reviewer has earlier undertaken to explain the presence of good. Note the use of the term 'primitive man', a term which in the 1880s would usually evoke images of Darwinian primitive man, that is, primitive man who has not fallen from a higher condition, but who has risen from some kind of small furry animal. The reviewer therefore deliberately equates primitive man with God's Creation, as a provocative rebuke to evolutionary theory:

> Of the best of men it can always be said that there is about them an element of evil, whereas with the worst of men there is, if we can only discover it, an element of good – doubtless a relic of primitive man 'made in the image of God' before the fall of our ancestors (225).

Curiously, in a review which shows an awareness of the evolution question, the reviewer appears to find nothing Darwinian in *Jekyll and Hyde*:

> Though there is nothing distinctively Christian about it, we hope none will suppose that we mean to imply that there is anything antagonistic to Christianity (224).

There were some, however, who at the time not only saw the moral allegory, but also recognized Hyde's Darwinian implications. And for those who did, in the acrid and unsettling climate generated by the theory of natural selection, Stevenson's decision to make Hyde ape-like was confronting to say the least. Among the confronted was Stevenson's friend the scholar John Addington Symonds (1840–93), who writes to Stevenson:

> At last I have read Dr Jekyll. It makes me wonder whether a man has the right so to scrutinize 'the abysmal deeps of personality'. It is indeed a dreadful book, most dreadful because of a certain moral callousness, a want of sympathy, a shutting out of hope. [...]
> The fact is that, viewed as an allegory, it touches one too closely.[63] Most of us at some epoch of our lives have been upon the verge of developing a Mr Hyde.

---

63 Commentators interpret this sentence as a reference to Symonds's struggle to conceal his homosexuality. See, e.g., Claire Harman, p. 214.

Physical and biological Science on a hundred lines is reducing individual freedom to zero, and weakening the sense of responsibility. I doubt whether the artist
should lend his genius to this grim argument. It is like the Cave of Despair in the
Faery Queen.

I had the great biologist Lauder Brunton with me a fortnight back. He was talking about Dr Jekyll and a book by W.O. [*sic*] Holmes, in wh [*sic*] atavism is played
with. I could see that, though a Christian, he held very feebly to the theory of human
liberty; and these two works of fiction interested him, as Dr Jekyll does me, upon
that point at issue.[64]

Symonds's intent becomes clearer when the preceding letter is compared with one which he wrote to the American scholar Thomas Sergeant
Perry (1845–1928), after reading the latter's *From Opitz to Lessing*:

Are you really prepared to deny any scope for individuality, origination, creative-
ness? Are we naught but the creatures of circumstance? If you really hold this view
of art and literature, you must a fortiori apply it to conduct and morality. It seems
true that you, with a great many present thinkers, accept Darwin's hypothesis too
absolutely as proved. [...]

That theory always strikes me as a most suggestive method for investigation; but
by no means as yet demonstrated so irrefragably as to justify its logical conclusions—
which involve absolute negation of free will.[65]

Symonds's letter to Perry shows that his 'point at issue' in his letter to
Stevenson is that, if we are God's creatures, then we have God-given free

---

64   *The Letters of John Addington Symonds*, ed. by Herbert M. Schueller & Robert L.
     Peters, 3 vols (Detroit: Wayne State University Press, 1967–69), letter 1522, 3 March
     1886, III, 120–21. This letter is also quoted in Maixner, pp. 210–11. According to
     Maixner, Symonds is probably referring to *Elsie Venner* (1861) by Oliver Wendel
     Holmes, whose eponymous subject grows up with glittering dark eyes, sharp teeth
     and a hypnotic malevolent presence, having been *in utero* when her mother was
     bitten by a rattlesnake. Linehan (*Jekyll and Hyde*, p. 99) also suggests that Symonds
     may be referring to Holmes's *The Guardian Angel* (1867).

65   Symonds, *Letters*, II, 969, letter 1433, 18 November 1884. Perry's book was published
     in 1885; perhaps he sent Symonds an advance copy. Perry was what Donald Pizer
     calls an 'evolutionary critic' – one who applied evolutionary theory to the study of
     culture and literature. See 'Evolutionary Ideas in Late Nineteenth Century English
     and American Literary Criticism', *Journal of Aesthetics and Art Criticism*, 19 (1961),
     305–10.

will to behave justly or unjustly. If we are no more than a highly developed animal, then we always have been, now are, and always will be slaves to our animal nature. The impersonal forces of Nature – not we ourselves – determine our actions. Hyde, representing our animal nature, testifies to our moral doom.

St Paul provides the theological framework for Jekyll's war in the members. Darwinism provides a contemporary scientific framework for Hyde's ape-like appearance. But what is the mechanism which projects him? James Ashcroft Noble writes in his review of *Jekyll and Hyde*:

> The fateful drug acts with its strange transforming power upon the body as well as the mind; for when the first dose has been taken the unhappy victim finds that 'soul is form and doth the body make', and that his new nature, of evil all compact, has found for itself a corresponding environment.[66]

Soul is form. What is form? A form is an archetypal pattern which exists in the realm of Ideas, and has the power to impose itself on matter. According to Socrates, forms (or, in Jowett's translation, ideas),

> are, as it were, patterns fixed in nature, and other things are like them and resemblances of them—what is meant by the participation of other things in the ideas, is really assimilation to them.[67]

Noble's choice of quotation is both accurate and ironic: accurate, because it identifies the philosophical source behind Jekyll's transformation into Hyde; ironic, because the line is taken from Edmund Spenser's 'An Hymne In Honour Of Beautie' – the second of *The Fowre Hymnes*, his 'most overtly Neoplatonic work',[68] – and Hyde is far from beautiful. Spenser writes:

66 Maixner, p. 204.
67 *The Dialogues of Plato*, translated in English with analyses and introductions by Benjamin Jowett, [1871] 4 vols, 4th edn (Oxford: Clarendon Press, 1953), *Parmenides*, 132d. All quotations from Plato's Dialogues are taken from this edition.
68 John Roe, 'Italian Neoplatonism and the Poetry of Sidney, Shakespeare, Chapman and Donne', in *Platonism and the English Imagination*, ed. by Anna Baldwin and Sarah Hutton (Cambridge: Cambridge University Press, 1994; repr. 2004), pp. 100–16 (p. 100).

For of the soule the bodie forme doth take:
For soule is forme, and doth the bodie make.   (132–33)[69]

Here, then, is the third great pillar on which Stevenson has rested his
story: Platonism.

The Platonic Tradition

The Platonic tradition begins – obviously enough – with the Greek philosopher Plato (429–347 BC). At the beginning of the Christian era some
of his concepts concerning the mind and the soul were incorporated in
the writings of St John and St Paul, and have remained part of the foun-
dations of Christianity to this day. In the third and fifth centuries AD certain philosophers – most notably Plotinus (205–270) in Alexandria, and
Proclus (?412–485) in Alexandria and Athens – interpreted and enlarged
upon Plato's writings, with an especial emphasis on the metaphysical areas
of his work.

During the Renaissance Plato enjoyed a renaissance of his own. But,
just as he had been enlarged upon in Alexandria, so he and his Alexandrian
commentators were interpreted again by Italian scholars in the fifteenth
century; and, by the sixteenth century, in England, according to Lilian
Winstanley, 'When [Edmund] Spenser proceeded to Cambridge in 1569,
[...] all that was intellectual in the University was Platonist.'[70] Spenser's own
Platonism derives mainly from the Continental commentators.[71] Spenser's
influence extends from his immediate successors – notably Henry More

---

69   *Edmund Spenser: The Fowre Hymnes*, ed. by Lilian Winstanley (Cambridge:
       Cambridge University Press, 1907). All quotations from *The Fowre Hymnes* are
       taken from this edition.
70   *Fowre Hymnes*, p. x.
71   Cf. Thomas Bulger, 'Platonism in Spenser's *Mutabilitie Cantos*', in Baldwin and
       Hutton, pp. 126–38.

and John Milton – through eighteenth-century writers such as Jonathan Swift (whose *Gulliver's Travels* is the subject of a later chapter); to such nineteenth-century writers as Thomas Love Peacock (who will also appear later), Charles Kingsley, and Stevenson himself. Indeed, it would be hard to overestimate Spenser's importance as a poet in the Platonic tradition. Herbert Agar writes, in his study on Milton:

> During his youth, Milton had been strongly influenced by Spenser, in whose poetry the Renaissance variety of Platonism reaches its high-water mark for England. [72]

So enduring was Spenser's legacy, that there are at least three separate references to his work by those discussing *Jekyll and Hyde* at and around the time of the book's publication. Significantly, none is explained; therefore their familiarity and meaning are assumed. The first, from J.A. Symonds's letter to Stevenson, likens the story to the Cave of Despair in *The Faerie Queene*. The second, the quotation from *The Fowre Hymnes*, used by James Ashcroft Noble, is specifically employed in order to provide a context within which to understand Hyde. The third – by Stevenson himself, also from *The Faerie Queene* – cleverly reprises the Platonic image of the soul putting on a body fit for its own nature and purpose. This will be discussed in the next chapter.

In the Age of Reason people turned away from Plato's metaphysics, and especially away from that of his later adherents and commentators, who had extended his speculations. Plato remained acceptable as a political and ethical theorist, but little more than that. Towards the end of the eighteenth century the Romantic movement reawakened interest in Platonic spirituality. But leading thinkers were hostile to this drift away from rationalism, and in the 1830s scholars began to use the term 'neo-Platonism' to distinguish between Plato's writings and those of the Alexandrian school and their Renaissance successors. Since then, the distinction has continued,

---

72 *Milton and Plato* (Gloucester, Mass.: Smith, 1928; repr. 1965), p. 30. Agar continues: 'Hence in his early poems Milton conformed to the seventeenth century type of Platonism. The whole of *Comus* is permeated with this Spenserian Platonism' (30). *Comus* will play a part in the following chapter.

although it can at times be blurred. Charles Kingsley, for example – a man not known for his consistency of thought – while owning an edition of Plato's works, and referring to himself as a Platonist, and dismissing Alexandrian neo-Platonism as irrelevant to the concerns of everyday life, nevertheless in *The Water-Babies* draws heavily on Spenser and neo-Platonic theories of the soul and its relationship to the body.

What were the Platonic influences on Stevenson? The deepest and earliest lay in the religion which played such a large part in his childhood. Dean William Inge observes Platonic influences in the Johannine and Pauline writings. Of Paul he says, 'his psychology of body, soul, and spirit, in which, as in the Platonists, Soul holds the middle place, and Spirit is nearly identical with the Platonic Νοῦς [...] show[s] that Christianity no sooner became a European religion than it discovered its natural affinity with Platonism.'[73] In another work Inge says, 'Other examples may be given of St Paul's affinity with Plato. The use of νους in Romans vii, 23 ("I see another law in my members, warring against the law of my mind [νους]") is Platonic.'[74] Therefore the cornerstone of *Jekyll and Hyde*, previously seen as biblical, is now found to be Platonic as well.

This interweaving of Platonic and Christian thought can still be seen clearly in the writings of modern commentators on *Jekyll and Hyde* when they come to discuss Utterson's response to his first encounter with Hyde. Utterson concludes that Hyde's awful ugliness is 'the mere radiance of a foul soul that thus transpires through, and transfigures, its clay continent' (40), which is a Platonic concept. Jerrold Hogle writes that Utterson has to explain Hyde to himself, and 'therefore fixes on the old Platonic *and Christian* [my emphasis] notion of a "foul soul" emanating its nature toward and into its bodily enclosure'.[75] Stephen Arata, however, describes the 'foul

73 William Ralph Inge, *The Philosophy of Plotinus*, 2 vols, 3rd edn (London: Longmans, Green, 1948), I, 11. (Hereafter *Plotinus*.)

74 William Ralph Inge, *The Platonic Tradition in English Religious Thought* (London: Longmans, Green, 1926), p. 12.

75 'The Struggle for a Dichotomy: Abjection in Jekyll and His Interpreters', in *100 Years*, pp. 161–207 (p. 192).

soul' concept as 'familiar Christian imagery' (234), without linking it to its Platonic origins.

Stevenson undertook an intensive study of Philosophy as part of his Law course at Edinburgh University, during which time he read *Lectures on Greek Philosophy* by James Frederick Ferrier (1808–64). This was one of several books which he read outside the course because 'he wanted to know Philosophy enough to disagree with his friend James Walter Ferrier'.[76] Although he was reading Classics and Philosophy, Stevenson was no Greek scholar. He enrolled in a Greek class, but honoured it more in the breach than the observance. Shortly afterwards, he lost his Greek dictionary and felt no need to replace it. He could, of course, have read Plato in translation, which he did in later life (see below), but given his religious and literary background, it would have been possible for him (as it had been for others) to absorb the Platonic tradition without ever approaching it at its source: Stevenson would have found Platonic thoughts and images among such poets as Spenser, Milton, Pope, Blake, Coleridge, Shelley, Tennyson and Wordsworth; and among such prose writers as Ruskin and Emerson.[77]

Of the authors appearing in this work, Henry More was one of the so-called Cambridge Platonists; Swift was interested in Plato, and drew on him (negatively) for Gulliver's voyage to the land of the Houyhnhnms; Peacock owned books by Thomas Taylor 'the Platonist' (1758–1835) – whose translation of Plato's works (1804) contained mainly neo-Platonic annotations – and counted him among his closest friends;[78] Kingsley was not only a committed Platonist from his days at Cambridge (his mentor

---

76 Reverend Archibald Bisset, 'Personal Reminiscences of the University Life of Robert Louis Stevenson', in Masson, ed., pp. 48–56 (p. 51). Revd Bisset tutored Stevenson in Classics and Philosophy.

77 Baldwin and Hutton include such Platonist writers as: Chaucer; Sir Thomas More; Sir Philip Sidney; Shakespeare; Chapman; Donne; Spenser; the Cambridge Platonists; Milton; Marvell; Vaughan; Traherne; Blake; Coleridge; Wordsworth; Shelley; Carlyle; Arnold.

78 George Mills Harper, *The Neoplatonism of William Blake* (Chapel Hill: University of North Carolina Press, 1961), pp. 13; 26; 15; 28.

Frederick Denison Maurice was also a Platonist), but a devoted reader of
Spenser and Milton.

Interest in Plato had waned during the eighteenth century. Although
the Romantics took him up through the writings of Thomas Taylor, and
although there was much enthusiasm for Hellenic thought and culture
during the first half of the nineteenth century, serious scholarship on Plato
was both limited and of varying competence. This began to change in
the mid-century; and in 1871 Benjamin Jowett's *Dialogues of Plato* were
published. Did Stevenson read any of them? He may have done. He spent
two winters in the Swiss health resort of Davos, where he passed many an
hour discussing literature with the consumptive John Addington Symonds.
Symonds had studied under Jowett at Oxford; and was himself a classicist. Jowett visited Symonds at Davos, on one occasion missing Stevenson by several days. In April 1886, having missed the Stevensons on yet
another occasion, Jowett invited them to Oxford, but Stevenson eventually
declined.[79] Stevenson's loose association with Jowett through Symonds
may have provided the motivation for Stevenson to read the *Dialogues*.
Symonds could have lent them to him during one of his stays in Davos.
On the other hand, Stevenson's failure to meet with Jowett when invited
could equally suggest that he had not read them.[80]

The mid-century also saw a revival in Plato as an ethicist and social
theorist – and, unexpectedly, as the main target of Charles Darwin's *Origin
of Species*.[81] This is highly ironic, given that Darwin's grandfather Erasmus
looked to Plato's disciples for inspiration in his studies. Henry Fairfield
Osborn writes:

> As to the origin of life [Erasmus] drew from the Greeks, especially from Aristotle,
> limiting spontaneous generation, however, to the lowest organisms; they also gave

---

79 See *RLS Letters*, letters 1598; 1622. Claire Harman (290) claims that Stevenson did
    meet Jowett, but does not cite a source.
80 In a letter from Samoa Stevenson tells Sidney Colvin that he is reading 'a crib to
    Phaedo'; which unfortunately leaves us little the wiser. See *RLS Letters*, letter 2357,
    October 1891, VII, 178–83 (p. 179).
81 See Frank M. Turner, *The Greek Heritage in Victorian Britain* (New Haven and
    London: Yale University Press, 1981), chap. 8.

him the fundamental idea of Evolution, for he says, 'This idea of the gradual forma-
tion and improvement of the Animal world seems not to have been unknown to
the ancient philosophers.'[82]

Erasmus's embattled grandson, however, had to contend not only
with outraged Christian creationists but also – and in particular – with an
important prevailing scientific opinion, passed down through history from
Plato to Aristotle; to Plotinus and the other neo-Platonists; to Carl Linnæus; to the French biologist Georges Cuvier and his intellectual disciple
Louis Agassiz; and to the great English opponent of Darwin and Huxley,
Sir Richard Owen. This received wisdom stated that each species is the
physical expression of a form that was conceived by the Creator in the
world of Ideas. Therefore each species is, as James Moore puts it, 'a discrete
act of the divine intellect and, as such, none can be related to another by
physical descent.'[83] According to Moore:

> The belief in fixity, likewise of pre-Christian origin, persisted in the post-Darwinian
> period largely as an amalgam of biblical literalism and neo-Platonism, the latter
> deriving from German romantic philosophy through the idiosyncratic and widely
> influential teaching of Louis Agassiz [at Harvard. ...] The anti-Darwinian element
> in Christian Anti-Darwinism may thus in fact have had little to do with Christian
> doctrines. Perhaps, after all, what conflicted with Darwinism were the philosophical
> assumptions with which the Christian faith had been allied (215).

So pervasive was the Platonic belief in fixity, and so entrenched, that the
anti-Platonic Darwin's energies were directed as much against countering
it, as against the theological attacks on his theory by the Church.[84]

---

82 *From the Greeks to Darwin: An Outline of the Evolution Idea* (New York and London:
    Macmillan, 1894), p. 142.
83 James R. Moore, *The Post-Darwinian Controversies: A Study of the Protestant Struggle
    to come to Terms with Darwin in Great Britain and America 1870–1900* (Cambridge:
    Cambridge University Press, 1979), p. 208.
84 See Walter F. Cannon, 'Darwin's Vision in *On the Origin of Species*', in *The Art of
    Victorian Prose*, ed. by George Levine and William Madden (New York, London,
    Toronto: Oxford University Press, 1968), pp. 154–76 (pp. 159–60).

The attack on Platonic science did not begin with Darwin. In October 1858 – a year before the publication of *The Origin of Species* – Herbert Spencer writes:

> In so far as his theory of the skeleton is concerned, Professor Owen is an avowed disciple of Plato. At the conclusion of his *Archetype and Homologies of the Vertebrate Skeleton*, he quotes approvingly the Platonic hypothesis of ιδεα, 'a sort of models, or moulds in which matter is cast, and which regularly produce the same number and diversity of species.' The vertebrate form in general [...], or else the form of each kind of vertebrate animal [...], Professor Owen conceives to exist as an 'idea' – an 'archetypal exemplar on which it pleased the Creator to frame certain of his living creatures'.[85]

Spencer goes on to argue that Owen 'carries the Platonic hypothesis much further than Plato does' (550). And he condemns Owen for subscribing to a theory which would later provide the intellectual background to *Jekyll and Hyde*. In Owen's writing, claims Spencer, there is

> implied the belief that the typical [i.e., the 'ideal'] vertebra has an abstract existence apart from actual vertebræ. It is a form which, in every endoskeleton, strives to embody itself in matter (551).

In other words, archetypal forms existed before matter, and express themselves in matter which they mould after their own shape. The next chapter will explore the world of Ideas.

In Stevenson's day there existed no greater threat to the sense of self than the theory of evolution. It confused and disturbed the individual, estranged families and provided an intellectual justification for great social

---

85   'A Criticism on Prof. Owen's Theory of the Vertebrate Skeleton', *British & Foreign Medico-Chirurgical Review* (October 1858). Repr. in Herbert Spencer, *The Principles of Biology*, 2 vols, rev. and enlarged (London: Williams and Norgate, 1898), II, 548–66 (p. 550). Revd Bisset recalls that Stevenson had read this work of Spencer's (along with his *First Principles* and *Theory of Evolution*) by the time that their sessions began. See Masson, p. 52.

ills. Stevenson grew up in and reflected this turmoil. He wrote *Jekyll and Hyde* in a Darwinian intellectual environment; but he also wrote it in the still-foaming wake of Renaissance neo-Platonism and Platonic Romanticism, during the middle of the Victorian Platonic revival. With *Jekyll and Hyde* he articulated not only his personal vision of mankind, but, by weaving into it a strange antagonistic blend of Darwinian, Platonic, and biblical imagery, raised it from the personal to the biological and finally to the cosmic.

And yet, if he had written it one, two, or three centuries earlier, his readers would have interpreted Hyde in the same way. Hyde is a traditional, pre-Darwinian figure whose origins stretch back to Classical Greece. His appearance in a Darwinian landscape obliges the reader to take Darwinism into account, but that may be ultimately incidental to Stevenson's purpose. Although evolution is implicit in the text, Stevenson is not making a point about mankind's origins, but about mankind's capacity for evil. Stevenson knew his Darwin; he would have been well aware of the fundamental differences between Platonism and Darwinism. Hyde may be apish, but Stevenson's language consistently presents him as a Platonic expression of the evil element in Jekyll's soul; and Darwinism does not concern itself with questions of good and evil.

At the same time, however, there is a strong Darwinian theme in the story: not Hyde's apishness, but Jekyll's revelation – in his famous 'slime of the pit' passage (95) – about inherited characteristics. Darwin was talking about inherited physical characteristics and behaviour; Stevenson's writings show him grappling with the problem of inherited sin and evil. In his essays he jokes about primitive memories and instincts lingering in the minds of modern people, one of whom was his grandfather, the Reverend Lewis Balfour:

> What sleeper in green tree-tops, what muncher of nuts, concludes my pedigree? Probably arboreal in his habits. ...
>
> And I know not which is the more strange, that I should carry about with me some fibres of my minister-grandfather; or that in him, as he sat in his cool study, grave, reverend, contented gentleman, there was an aboriginal frisking of the blood that was not his; tree-top memories, like undeveloped negatives, lay dormant in his mind; tree-top instincts awoke and were trod down; and Probably Arboreal (scarce

to be distinguished from a monkey) gambolled and chattered in the brain of the old divine.[86]

But even in his moods of apparent lightness, Stevenson raises the spectre of biological determinism which so worried J.A. Symonds. He describes:

> a certain low-browed, hairy gentleman, at first a percher in the fork of trees, next (as they relate) a dweller in caves, and whom I think I see squatting in cave-mouths, of a pleasant afternoon, to munch his berries—his wife, that accomplished lady, squatting by his side: his name I never heard, but he is often described as Probably Arboreal, which may serve for recognition. Each has his own tree of ancestors, but at the top of all sits Probably Arboreal; in all our veins there run some minims of his old, wild, tree-top blood; our civilised nerves still tingle with his rude terrors and pleasures; and to that which would have moved our common ancestor, all must obediently thrill.[87]

And in *Jekyll and Hyde* and 'Olalla' (written almost immediately after)[88] he approaches his theme with an almost biblical sense of doom. In *Jekyll*

86   'The Manse' [1887], *Works*, XII, 84–93 (p. 93). 'Probably arboreal' is a term used by Charles Darwin, who writes: 'By considering the embryological structure of man,— the homologies which he presents with the lower animals,—the rudiments which he retains,—and the reversions to which he is liable, we can partly recall in imagination the former condition of our early progenitors; and can approximately place them in their proper place in the zoological series. We thus learn that man is descended from a hairy, tailed quadruped, probably arboreal in its habits, and an inhabitant of the Old World' (*The Descent of Man*, p. 911). Darwin goes on to trace the origin of all vertebrata back to a marine animal 'like the larvæ of the existing marine Ascidians' – a possible literary ancestor of the flopping thing in the dying ocean shallows of *The Time Machine*. Note also Stevenson's use of 'chatter' for both his own primitive ape-like ancestor's language, and that of Hyde when agitated.

87   'Pastoral' [1887], *Works*, XII, 72–83 (pp. 81–82). 'Common ancestor' is another term used by Darwin. See *The Origin of Species*, p. 86.

88   *Jekyll and Hyde* was written in September–October 1885. Andrew Lang writes: 'as to the date of this work, Mr Charles Longman informs me that his letter to Mr Stevenson, acknowledging the MS., was written on October 31st, 1885' (Letter to *The Athenaeum*, 3511 (9 February 1895), 187). Stevenson then began 'The Misadventures of John Nicholson', but laid it aside. By the first week of November 1885 he had begun work on 'Olalla', which appeared in the Christmas 1885 edition of the *Court and Society Review*. For details see Swearingen, pp. 102–03.

and Hyde it is not stated clearly; but in 'Olalla', as we shall see, it is quite explicit.

There are three major influences bearing on *Jekyll and Hyde*: Platonism, Christianity, and Darwinism. To view the text through the lens of one of these alone is to risk misinterpreting the figure of Hyde, because Hyde is drawn from all three. However, where these influences are concerned, *Jekyll and Hyde* scholarship has tended to neglect the first and, to a lesser degree, the second, and focus on the third. Irving Saposnik sees Hyde as a 'creature of primitive sensibilities'.[89] Julia Briggs sees man as a 'descendant of the beasts', with a 'bestial inheritance within him which he must learn to sublimate and restrain'.[90] David Punter sees Jekyll's transformation into Hyde as 'the reversion of the species'.[91] Ed Block, drawing our attention to the friendship between Stevenson and the evolutionary psychologist James Sully, interprets the tale as a 'depiction of psychological aberration treated in evolutionist terms'.[92] Stephen Heath interprets Hyde as being symbolic of Jekyll's hidden animal (i.e., sexual) urges which surface in times of extreme emotional stress, and express themselves in violent perverted acts. He refers to Jekyll's use of the term 'ape-like' as 'Stevenson's evolutionary reference word'.[93] Veeder notes Stevenson's interest in Darwin and other scientific thinkers. He writes:

> That Jekyll's chemical tastes liberate Hyde's animality (beast as ape, [...]) is revelatory not only of the doctor and the patriarchy but of late-Victorian society as well. In this period arise the sciences of anthropology and psychology. Darwin's tracing of human anatomy back to animal origins is complemented by anthropological and

89   *Robert Louis Stevenson* (Boston: Twayne, 1974), p. 98.
90   *Night Visitors: The Rise and Fall of the English Ghost Story* (London: Faber, 1977), p. 20.
91   *The Literature of Terror: A History of Gothic Fictions from 1765 to the Present Day* (London: Longmans, 1980), p. 244.
92   'James Sully, Evolutionist Psychology, and Late Victorian Gothic Fiction', *Victorian Studies*, 25 (1982), 443–67 (p. 458). (Hereafter Block, *Sully*.)
93   'Psychopathia Sexualis', p. 103.

psychological attributions of social practices and emotional states to comparably archaic sources.[94]

Donald Lawler writes that Hyde 'represents pre-evolved man in his atavistic, degenerated physical and psychological state', and he regards the novella as a 'case study of degeneration'.[95] Christine Persak discusses the text in the light of Herbert Spencer's doctrine of moral evolution, which saw man evolving psychologically and morally as well as physically. She equates Hyde's appearance with that of Spencer's Primitive Man.[96] Robert Mighall sees Hyde as 'the physical expression of moral lowness according to Post-Darwinian thought'.[97] Julia Reid describes the tale as representing 'the atavism unveiled by evolutionist psychiatry, which focused on the survival of primitive elements in human consciousness'.[98]

Fewer commentators address the biblical theme. William Veeder devotes a section in his essay to an examination of 'what critics have never discussed – Stevenson's manifold allusions to Genesis';[99] Larry Kreitzer discusses *Jekyll and Hyde* in the light of the Bible, in particular St Paul's 'war in the members' passage in his letter to the Romans;[100] Kevin Mills also discusses Jekyll and St Paul;[101] Katherine Linehan explores Stevenson's various intertextual allusions. Linehan writes: 'The best-developed and

---

94   *100 Years*, pp. 121–22.
95   'Reframing *Jekyll and Hyde*: Robert Louis Stevenson and the Strange Case of Gothic Fiction', in *100 Years*, pp. 247–61 (p. 252).
96   'Spencer's Doctrines and Mr Hyde: Moral Evolution in Stevenson's "Strange Case"', *Victorian Newsletter*, 86 (1994), 16–18 (p. 16). Stevenson mentions Spencer's Primitive Man in a letter of 18 January 1875 to Fanny Sitwell. See *RLS Letters*, letter 355, II, 109.
97   Mighall, *Jekyll*, p. xxiv.
98   *Robert Louis Stevenson, Science, and the Fin de Siècle* (Basingstoke and New York: Palgrave Macmillan, 2006), p. 97.
99   *100 Years*, p. 137.
100 'R.L. Stevenson's *Strange Case of Dr Jekyll and Mr Hyde* and Romans 7.14–25: Images of the Moral Duality of Human Nature', *Journal of Literature and Theology*, 6 (1992), 125–44.
101 'The Stain on the Mirror: Pauline Reflections in *The Strange Case of Dr Jekyll and Mr Hyde*', *Christianity and Literature*, 53 (2004), 337–48.

least appreciated set of orchestrated references revolves around the many biblical echoes in the tale.'[102] As for Platonism, Mills also notes the Platonic element in Paul's (and, by implication, Jekyll's) duality which has already been mentioned by Dean Inge;[103] and refers to 'a Platonic-Pauline tone in the description' of the effect of Jekyll's drug.[104] Aaron Perkus equates Jekyll's permanent transition into Hyde with the Platonic movement of the soul from man to beast. He also argues that Hyde represents Jekyll's feminine nature, and likens Jekyll to Adam, and Hyde to Eve.[105] Hogle mentions 'the old Platonic and Christian notion of a "foul soul" emanating its nature toward and into its bodily enclosure'.[106] This mention, however, is simply about Utterson's attempts to define Hyde, and no reference is made to Jekyll's specific Platonic assessment of Hyde. Hogle also examines the tension in Jekyll's Statement between Jekyll's 'religious' rhetoric and his 'evolutionary' rhetoric (by which means Jekyll tries to distance himself from his ape-like other half), and thereby at least mentions Plato, the Bible and Darwin in his essay.[107] Douglas Thorpe, one of the few who examine both the scientific and religious ingredients, anticipates the thrust of this treatise, but does not include Platonism in his examination. 'Hyde', he writes, 'has a complex pedigree and it should be clear that it is no simple matter to tag *the* source for Stevenson's conception.' Hyde 'is born of chemicals, Calvinism, folklore, myth, and the scientific speculations of the Industrial age [to which] the controversy surrounding evolution adds the blurring

---

102 "The Devil Can Cite Scripture: Intertextual Hauntings in *Strange Case of Dr Jekyll and Mr Hyde*', *Journal of Stevenson Studies*, 3 (2006), 5–32 (p. 6). (Hereafter Linehan, *Devil.*)

103 See Inge, *Plotinus*, I, 11.

104 Mills, p. 343.

105 'Dr Jekyll Hydeing in the Garden of Eden', *Mythos*, 6 (1996), 35–43. The article is a revised chapter from Perkus's 'Where the Wild Things Are: The Male Uterus and the Creation of Monsters' (unpublished doctoral dissertation, Binghamton University, 1994). I shall argue that Stevenson deliberately invokes Milton's Adam and Eve, but not for the reason given by Perkus, i.e., that Hyde represents Jekyll's feminine nature (Perkus, p. 36).

106 *100 Years*, p. 192.

107 *100 Years*, pp. 182–85.

of animal and human nature'.[108] There would seem to be an overall lack
of scholarly research in the biblical and Platonic contribution to *Jekyll
and Hyde*. This review is an attempt to remedy the imbalance. However,
just as Stevenson scholarship has moved on to contemporary concerns,
and away from the subjects of humanity's place in the natural world and
humanity's relationship to God, so scholarship in other authors has done
so as well. Accordingly the present work, in examining the authors who
precede Stevenson, will frequently turn to earlier commentators who were
dealing with these fundamental concerns. The argument thus on the one
hand looks back to some well ploughed scholastic fields, and on the other
hand looks forward in order to provide a much needed synthesis of the
three identified themes in *Jekyll and Hyde*.[109]

As the Darwinian commentaries listed above suggest, the Darwinian
analysis necessarily leads to questions of degeneration, devolution, and
reversion; but such an approach serves only to answer part of the riddle that
is Hyde. Although Jekyll may appear to degenerate, devolve, or revert to a
more primitive form, in fact he does not; he first encourages, then unsuc-
cessfully tries to resist, then finally succumbs to the true expression of the
evil within him – and that is not a Darwinian process. Indeed Stevenson's
language reveals the weight which he gives to his various influences. Hyde
is referred to as ape-like three times (47, 96, 97), and monkey-like once
(68). He chatters (like a monkey or ape) once (94). He is associated with
an animal twice (69, 92); and is referred to as a brute once (94). So much
for the Darwinian aspect. His diabolical side is mentioned more often. He
is a devil (90, 93); and Satanic (32, 40); and his evil is mentioned fourteen
times (56, 68, 82, 84, 84, 84, 84, 85, 85, 85, 87, 90, 91, 92). He is referred to
as deformed on no less than seven occasions (34, 34, 40, 50, 66, 84, 95).

---

108 'Calvin, Darwin, and the Double: The Problem of Divided Nature in Hogg,
     MacDonald, and Stevenson', *Newsletter of Victorian Studies Association of Western
     Canada*, 11.1 (Spring 1985), 6–22 (p. 18). Thorpe does not address the issue of the
     Platonic blurring of animal and human nature.
109 In order to maintain a consistent focus on works which preceded *Jekyll and Hyde*, I
     have drawn exclusively on translations which were published before 1885, e.g., Jowett's
     translation of Plato; Pope's translation of the *Iliad*.

Deformity is not a Darwinian concept, but, as the following chapters will show, has a Platonic association with spiritual and moral delinquency. Stevenson employs it in this traditional manner. Towards the end of his Statement Jekyll writes:

> I became, in my own person, a creature eaten up and emptied by fever [...] and solely occupied by one thought: the horror of my other self. [...] I would leap almost without transition [...] into the possession of a fancy brimming with images of terror, a soul boiling with causeless hatreds, and a body that seemed not strong enough to contain the raging energies of life. The powers of Hyde seemed to have grown with the sickliness of Jekyll. And certainly the hate that now divided them was equal on each side. With Jekyll, it was a thing of vital instinct. He had now seen the full deformity of that creature (95).

Obviously, then, Hyde's physical deformity (which no one can specify) reflects his moral deformity (which is transparent to Jekyll because they share 'some of the phenomena of consciousness').

The aim of this work is to locate Edward Hyde within the strand of the history of ideas that deals with mankind's origins and mankind's relationship to the beasts. Modern commentators are inclined to regard the hairy ape-like Hyde as an embodiment of early mankind, and, having invoked the name of Darwin, continue their inquiries within that theoretical framework. For them, Hyde thus represents the primitive beastly urges which present-day humanity is yet to overcome. Others interpret Jekyll's duality within the context of the biblical 'war in the members' addressed by St Paul in his letter to the Romans. A few give passing mention of the Platonism underlying Hyde's hateful effect on those around him.

This work will argue that, while the Darwinian interpretation is inescapable, Stevenson's concerns with human duality are far deeper and far more complicated, investigating not just mankind's origins, but mankind's enduring capacity to sin. Mankind is a highly evolved ape, but man is also a biblically fallen creature, the understanding of whose soul owes as much to Platonic philosophy as to Judaeo-Christian theology. This does not imply a rejection of the Darwinian interpretation, so much as an enrichment by showing how it interacts with this other much older tradition. There is, moreover, an important distinction which should be borne in mind:

the Darwinism is making one point (human origins), and the Platonism is making another (the evil soul). Stevenson employs them both because they both apply and are inseparable in his vision of mankind.

The conceit of one man swallowing a potion and turning into another came to Stevenson in a dream; Edward Hyde did not. Every aspect of Hyde's appearance and character – especially the explanation for his existence – arises from a conscious intellectual choice by Stevenson, each choice being informed and determined by Stevenson's cultural inheritance. The task, then, is to explore that cultural heritage and show how Stevenson drew on it for his portrait of Hyde.

This exploration will examine earlier literature involving apes or ape-like creatures, thereby revealing a tradition which deals with mankind's burden of evil; a tradition in which evil is portrayed in ugly, deformed, and beastly bodies; a tradition which explores and questions the origins of mankind – theological, philosophical, and scientific – in an attempt to account for the presence of our lower impulses; a tradition which links humanity with the beasts – very often, although not exclusively, with the apes. The chosen texts will show that, as time passes and knowledge of the natural world increases through exploration and scientific learning, earlier ways of looking at the world, instead of being replaced by new ideas, come to serve as a mythic or poetic way of accommodating such new ideas, absorbing the new and incorporating it into the old mythological framework.

Accordingly, we shall begin with an examination of some Platonic poetry by Spenser, Henry More, Milton, and Donne dealing with the nature of the soul; its relationship to the physical body; the soul's progression from form to form; the accumulation of sin; moral degeneration; and its deforming influence on the body.

The Platonic relationship between soul and body having been established, the discussion will then move on to *Gulliver's Travels* (1726) and in particular the Yahoos, the most notorious example of deformed and degraded humanity. These bizarre creatures are likened to various animals, especially to apes. Swift draws on a variety of sources for his portrait, ranging from the Old Testament, to Classical authors, to travellers' tales of primitive peoples, to scientific treatises on apes. Swift's debt to Plato is apparent in both his description of the Houyhnhnms' society, and his portrayal of the Yahoos' physical deformities.

Another source which Swift draws on is the Wild Man tradition. This tradition, which dates back at least as far as ancient Mesopotamian legends, continued on, unchanged in some aspects, and constantly evolving in others, until by Stevenson's day it had developed three co-existing but physically distinct representatives: the Wild Man, the Noble Savage, and the Child of Nature. The figure of the Wild Man, and the imagery surrounding him, play an important and ongoing role in representations of apes, including the ape-like Edward Hyde.

Thomas Love Peacock's *Melincourt* (1817) brings together the ape, the Wild Man, the Noble Savage and the Child of Nature, together with Classical mythology, Platonism, more travellers' tales, and late-eighteenth-century theories of evolution. *Melincourt* shows a progression of the debate as more scientific information becomes available; and offers a satiric inversion of values, in which the ape – now represented as the original man – is physically and morally superior to the degenerate specimens of modern humanity about him. However, as the ape's links with mankind become more firmly established, the imagery surrounding him, instead of becoming more scientific and prosaic, draws even more heavily on ancient myth and Wild Man lore. Sir Oran Haut-ton in his natural goodness and chivalrous wrath corresponds not only to the relaxed and amicable anthropoids who begin Stevenson's family tree in his essays, but also to Spenser's gentle Salvage Man in *The Faerie Queene*, who, when roused, displays a terrible fierceness. Sir Oran's contemplative nature and customary benignity, however, militate against a purely Darwinian interpretation of Hyde's ape-like viciousness.

Charles Kingsley's *The Water-Babies* (1862) prefigures Stevenson's method in *Jekyll and Hyde*. Kingsley was a scientifically trained clergyman, writing at the height of the excitement generated by Darwin's theory of natural selection, as scientists, philosophers and theologians struggled to come to terms with humanity's place in the universe. *The Water-Babies* brings together Platonism, Christianity and Darwinism in an attempt to harmonize them all in one grand theory. Yet again it is clear that traditional language and imagery not only survive the shock of Darwinism, but within their own larger narrative manage to incorporate Darwinism as no more than a mechanism of God's design, mediated through a Christiano-Platonic system described by Spenser at the end of *The Faerie Queene* – a mechanism, moreover, which also turns lazy, self-indulgent humans back into apes.

These texts and their sources provide a context within which to examine Hyde: firstly within the Wild Man tradition; then from a Darwinian viewpoint; next within a biblical framework; and finally as a Platonic expression of Jekyll's soul.

Jekyll and Hyde demonstrates that there is within mankind a duality which can be explained theologically, philosophically, and scientifically; that down through history it has been portrayed in much the same way; and that mankind's relationship to the ape has always been a matter of unease and inquiry. *Jekyll and Hyde* is, however – as the many commentaries testify – an oblique and elusive text, and does not provide enough information within itself for an adequate understanding of one of its key expository passages – the 'slime of the pit' passage (95). This understanding is provided by 'Olalla', in which Stevenson more transparently deals with the themes of degeneration and the inheritance of evil which play such a fundamental role in his more famous story. Yet again one finds images of the Wild Man and the Child of Nature; yet again, biblical language and imagery; yet again, Platonic sentiment; and yet again, the theme of degeneration, which can be either Darwinian (as expressed by Kingsley), or pre-Darwinian (as expressed by Swift). Written one after the other, *Jekyll and Hyde* and 'Olalla' form a complementary pairing, each illuminating an understanding of the other. 'Olalla' clarifies the presence of Hyde in Jekyll; and *Jekyll and Hyde* gives a shape to the evil which lurks within Olalla's pure soul.

By the time he came to write *Jekyll and Hyde*, Stevenson had a cultural heritage at his disposal which stretched all the way back from the most recent scientific discoveries, to God's command to Let there be light. Stevenson's story, dealing as it does with the timeless theme of evil within the human soul, employs language and imagery from this heritage; language and imagery which were familiar and accessible to the educated readers of his day, but which have become increasingly remote and unrecognizable with the passage of time. The object of the present work is to provide a literary background from which to interpret the figure of Edward Hyde, and his importance as a traditional emblem of evil; and to offer an interpretation of his role which brings together that literary background and the more commonly recognized Darwinian element in order to provide a fuller and more complex reading of the text.

PART ONE

Body and Soul. Sin and Deformity

CHAPTER TWO

Platonic Evolution, Spenser, More, Milton, Donne

The previous chapter introduced Spenser's phrase from his *Fowre Hymnes*, 'soule is forme, and doth the bodie make'. This chapter will explore the soul's relationship to the physical body. In so doing, it will examine works by Spenser, More, Milton, and Donne, which deal with this theme. (Although Milton's contribution to this chapter is slight, he will come to play an important role in the final reading of *Jekyll and Hyde*.) The writings of Spenser, More, Milton, and Donne reveal a fusion of Platonism and Christianity which continues on through English literature and finds ongoing expression in the writings of Stevenson. Moreover, both Platonic and Christian thought provide an ancient and traditional explanation for the bestial presence of Hyde in Henry Jekyll. Let us begin with the author of the phrase 'soule is forme'.

Edmund Spenser

Edmund Spenser (1552–99) was a Cambridge man. Lilian Winstanley writes that:

> Cambridge represented for sixteenth century England both the most ardent spirit of the Reformation and the most zealous study of Plato. When Spenser proceeded to Cambridge in 1569, the religious enthusiasm in the University was almost wholly Puritan in tone and certainly all that was intellectual in the University was Platonist; the identification of Cambridge with Platonism lasted, in fact, for well over a century.[1]

---

1   *Fowre Hymnes*, p. x.

What does it mean to say that Spenser was a Platonist? According to Einar Bjorvand and Richard Schell:

> Elizabethans like Spenser commonly derived their knowledge of Plato through two channels: medieval Neoplatonism and the Florentine Neoplatonists [of the fifteenth century]. The antiquity of Neoplatonic ideas in Spenser's time and milieu and his apparent unconcern with scholarly precision renders unwise the naming of any one source for what Spenser may have found in several places. In most cases the more popularly read sources would be the most likely.[2]

However, scholars are more specific about the provenance of particular works. Thomas Bulger writes:

> Given the subject matter and phrasing of the *Fowre Hymnes*, it is virtually certain that Spenser read [Marsilio] Ficino's commentary on Plato's *Symposium*, the well known *De Amore* [1469]; and it may well be that Spenser read Ficino's 1492 translation of the *Enneads* [by Plotinus], thus making Spenser one of the first English authors to read Plotinus directly.[3]

The Fowre Hymnes is based on the proposition that the soul, when it comes into the natural world, takes on a body which represents and exemplifies the soul's beauty. Spenser writes in his 'Hymne In Honour Of Beautie':

> Thereof it comes, that these faire soules, which have
> The most resemblance of that heavenly light,
> Frame to themselves most beautiful and brave
> Their fleshly bowre, most fit for their delight,
> And the grosse matter by a soveraine might
> Tempers so trim, that it may well be seene,
> A pallace fit for such a virgin Queene.

2   *The Yale Edition of the Shorter Poems of Edmund Spenser*, ed. by William A. Oram
     (New Haven: Yale University Press, 1989). (Hereafter *Yale Spenser*.) Introduction
     to *The Fowre Hymnes* by Einar Bjorvand and Richard Schell, p. 685.

3   Baldwin and Hutton, p. 127.

> So every spirit, as it is most pure,
> And hath in it the more of heavenly light,
> So it the fairer bodie doth procure
> To habit in, and it more fairely dight
> With chearefull grace and amiable sight.
> For of the soule the bodie forme doth take:
> For soule is forme, and doth the bodie make. (120–33)[4]

The beauty of the beloved's soul may therefore be inferred from her outward appearance; and the true lover dwells on her external form in loving contemplation of the divine spark within.

Hyde of course provokes the opposite reaction. People dwell on his external form in loathing of the foul soul within (40). His pallor, his dwarfishness, his hairiness, his unexpressed deformity, are not mere physical shortcomings, but, as Socrates says, a sign, because the body is 'the index of the soul, because the soul gives indications to [...] the body'.[5] Similarly Plato's unnamed Athenian says:

> that the soul is in all respects superior to the body, and that even in life what makes each one of us to be what we are is only the soul; and that the body follows us about in the likeness of each of us.[6]

This raises the question – how does one come by such an unattractive soul? Socrates explains that, just as the body is ravaged by sin and abuse, so is the soul. He goes on:

> [W]hen the soul is stripped of the body, everything in it is laid open to view—all its natural features and all the characteristics it has acquired in each of its various activities. And when they come to the judge, as those from Asia come to Rhadamanthus, he stops them and inspects them one by one quite impartially, not knowing whose the soul is: often he may lay hands on the soul of some king or potentate such as the Great King, and discerns no soundness in him, but a soul marked with the whip,

---

4   Spenser is playing with two meanings of the word *form*. The body takes its form (i.e., its shape) from the soul, which is form (i.e., the creative principle).

5   *Cratylus*, 400c. Jowett offers an alternative translation: – 'Or: "gives indications with the body"'.

6   *Laws*, XII, 959a.

and full of the scars of perjuries and crimes with which each action has stained him, and all crooked with falsehood and imposture, and without straightness, because he has lived without truth. Him Rhadamanthus beholds, full of the deformity and disproportion which is caused by licence and luxury and insolence and incontinence, and dispatches him ignominiously to his prison, and there he undergoes the punishment he deserves.[7]

Henry Jekyll begins his Statement by describing his 'certain impatient gaiety of disposition', his 'pleasures', which have led to 'a profound duplicity of life'. However, they then become 'irregularities', and we are told at last that they occurred when he 'laid aside restraint and plunged in shame' (81). Here is a soul warped by deception, and distorted and ugly from private licence and public arrogance. This duplicity has in fact begun to stamp itself upon his body as well. In his introductory scene he is described as 'a large, well-made, smooth-faced man of fifty, with something of a slyish cast perhaps' (43). Even the smooth face is a bad sign; Hyde's housekeeper in Soho has 'an evil face, smoothed by hypocrisy' (49).

In his other writing Stevenson continues to link Jekyll and Hyde with Platonic thought, in particular, the soul assuming the appropriate form. In 'A Chapter on Dreams' he writes:

> I had long been trying to write a story on this subject, to find a body, a vehicle, for that strong sense of man's double being which must at times come in upon and overwhelm the mind of every thinking creature. [...] The meaning of the tale is therefore mine, and had long pre-existed in my garden of Adonis, and tried one body after another in vain.[8]

Stevenson is being highly specific in his allusion. John Cooper explains that 'Gardens of Adonis were pots or window boxes used for forcing plants during the festival of Adonis'.[9] Stevenson thus presents the image of himself desperately attempting to force the flowering of his muse; but his primary meaning – as the mention of bodies shows – derives from the Garden of

7   *Gorgias*, 524d–525a.
8   *Works*, XII, 247–48.
9   Plato, *Complete Works*, ed., intro. and notes by John M. Cooper (Indianapolis: Hackett, 1997), p. 553, n67.

Adonis in Spenser's *Faerie Queene*, in which souls continually incarnate and reincarnate in form after form.[10] Here then is the third Spenserian reference in association with *Jekyll and Hyde*, the first two being by Symonds[11] (the Cave of Despair in *The Faerie Queene*), and James Ashcroft Noble[12] ('soul is form' from *The Fowre Hymnes*).

A likely source for Spenser's Garden may be the tale told by Er, the son of Armenias, in Plato's *Republic*. Er died in battle, but revived after several days, and related what he had seen in the other world:

> He said that when his soul left the body it went on a journey with a great company, and that they came to a mysterious place at which there were two openings in the earth; they were near together, and over against them were two other openings in the heaven above. In the intermediate space there were judges seated, who commanded the just [...] to ascend by the way up through the heaven on the right hand; and in like manner the unjust were bidden by them to descend on the lower way by the left hand [...]. Then he beheld and saw on one side the souls departing at either opening of heaven and earth when sentence had been given on them; and at the other two openings other souls, some ascending out of the earth dusty and worn with travel, some descending out of heaven clean and bright (*Republic*, X, 614c–d).

The souls are taken on a long journey, finally being brought into the presence of the Fates, where they are addressed by a speaker who tells them, 'Mortal souls, behold a new cycle of life and mortality' (*Republic*, X, 617d). The souls are then given lots to determine the order in which they will choose their next lives. The speaker

> placed on the ground before them the patterns of lives; and there were many more lives than the souls present, and they were of all sorts. There were lives of every animal and of man in every condition. [...] The disposition of the soul was not, however, included in them, because the soul, when choosing a new life, must of necessity become different (*Republic*, X, 618a–b).

---

10   Stevenson also dropped quotations from *The Faerie Queene* into his correspondence. See *RLS Letters*, vol. III, letters 681; 910.
11   *Letters*, letter 1522, 3 March 1886, III, 120–21. Maixner, pp. 210–11.
12   *Academy*, 29 (23 January 1886), 55. Maixner, p. 204.

No one elects to continue in their former condition. Men become women; women become men; humans become birds; birds become human:

> And not only did men pass into animals, but I must also mention that there were animals tame and wild who changed into one another and into corresponding human natures—the righteous into the gentle and the unrighteous into the savage, in all sorts of combinations (*Republic*, X, 620d).

The souls then proceed to the Plain of Forgetfulness and camp beside the River of Unheeding, whose waters they must drink:

> and each one as he drank forgot all things. Now after they had gone to rest, about the middle of the night there was a thunderstorm and earthquake, and then in an instant they were driven upwards in all manner of ways to their birth, like stars shooting (*Republic*, X, 621a–b).

In the Garden of Adonis Spenser depicts the incarnating souls as naked babies, waiting to be clothed in flesh before being sent out into the world:

> In that same Gardin all the goodly flowres,
>   Wherewith dame Nature doth her beautifie,
>   And decks the girlonds of her paramoures,
>   Are fetcht: there is the first seminarie
>   Of all things, that are borne to liue and die,
>   According to their kindes. Long work it were,
>   Here to account the endlesse progenie
>   Of all the weedes, that bud and blossome there;
> But so much as doth need, must needs be counted here.
>
> It sited was in fruitfull soyle of old,
>   And girt in with two walles on either side;
>   The one of yron, the other of bright gold,
>   That none might thorough breake, nor ouer-stride:
>   And double gates it had, which opened wide,
>   By which both in and out men moten pas;
>   Th'one faire and fresh, the other old and dride:
>   Old *Genius* the porter of them was,
> Old *Genius*, the which a double nature has.

He letteth in, he letteth out to wend,
   All that to come into the world desire;
   A thousand thousand naked babes attend
   About him day and night, which doe require,
   That he with fleshly weedes would them attire:
   Such as him list, such as eternall fate
   Ordained hath, he clothes with sinfull mire,
   And sendeth forth to liue in mortall state,
Till they againe returne backe by the hinder gate.   (III.6.30–32)[13]

In keeping with the principle of metempsychosis the naked babes don all kinds of fleshly weeds:

Infinite shapes of creatures there are bred,
   And vncouth formes, which none yet euer knew,
   And euery sort is in a sundry bed
   Set by it selfe, and ranckt in comely rew:
   Some fit for reasonable soules t'indew,
   Some made for beasts, some made for birds to weare,
   And all the fruitfull spawne of fishes hew
   In endlesse rancks along enraunged were,
That seem'd the *Ocean* could not containe them there.   (III.6.33)

The tale of Er and the Garden of Adonis combine descriptions of metaphysical and natural processes, involving the progression of souls from form to form. The process in each case is ordered, complying with a divine design and a cosmic purpose. In *Jekyll and Hyde*, however, Jekyll's selfish, unscrupulous indifference to any moral system violates this order. He forces (in the horticultural sense) something un-natural, simply because he is irked and thwarted by the human condition. In effect, when he changes into Hyde he is reincarnating himself; and he is aware that this is what he has done. He refers to the transformation as a 'dissolution' (85), during which he experiences 'a horror of the spirit that cannot be exceeded at the

---

13   Edmund Spenser, *Works: A Variorum Edition*, ed. by Edwin Greenlaw and others, 11 vols (Baltimore: Johns Hopkins Press, 1932; 3rd repr. 1961). *The Faerie Queene* occupies vols I–VI. All *Faerie Queene* quotations are taken from this edition. The Garden of Adonis will play an important part in *The Water-Babies*.

hour of birth or death' (83); and then he specifically refers to the process as
'these agonies of death and birth' (85). The drug has the power to disturb
and dissociate the elements (earth, air, fire and water) that make up the
body of Jekyll. During this brief period of dissolution the lower qualities
in his soul reconfigure the elements to fashion a more appropriate hous-
ing. When the process is complete, Jekyll has 'died' and Hyde has been
'born'. Jekyll writes:

> I came to myself as if out of a great sickness. There was something strange in my sen-
> sations, something indescribably new and, from its very novelty, incredibly sweet. I
> felt younger, lighter, happier in body (83).

There are two Platonic influences bearing on this process. The first
(the ugly soul), has already been described. The second has to do with
Jekyll's unfulfilled sinful desires, which are not unlike those of the souls
in the story of Er:

> Most curious, he said, was the spectacle—sad and laughable and strange; for the
> choice of the souls was in most cases based on their experience of a previous life
> (*Republic*, X. 619e).

Er goes on to describe how souls choose lives either to avoid unwanted
associations from their former lives, or to fulfil unrealized desires and
ambitions from their former lives.

It is the same with Jekyll. He writes:

> I had learned to dwell with pleasure, as a beloved day-dream, on the thought of the
> separation of [my two natures]. If each, I told myself, could but be housed in separate
> identities, life would be relieved of all that was unbearable; the unjust might go his
> way, delivered from the aspirations and remorse of his more upright twin; and the
> just could walk steadfastly and securely on his upward path (82).

But his real desire is to be unjust, as he admits later:

> Had I approached my discovery in a more noble spirit, had I risked the experiment
> while under the empire of generous or pious aspirations, all must have been other-

wise, and from these agonies of death and birth I had come forth an angel instead of a fiend (85).[14]

The fiend has come forth; and the fiend is ape-like. His fury is ape-like (47); his spite is ape-like (97); his tricks are ape-like (96); Jekyll's butler Poole describes him as 'like a monkey' (68); and he walks through the streets 'chattering' (94), a behaviour traditionally associated with apes and monkeys.

In a way Hyde is like one of the rabble in Milton's *Comus* (1634). They are described as 'a rout of Monsters headed like sundry sorts of wilde Beasts, but otherwise like Men and Women'.[15] They become like this after drinking a potion brewed by Comus, the son of Bacchus and Circe, both famed for their ability to turn men into beasts:[16]

> Within the navil of this hideous Wood,
> Immur'd in cypress shades a Sorcerer dwels
> Of *Bacchus*, and of *Circe* born, great *Comus*,
> Deep skill'd in all his mothers witcheries,
> And here to every thirsty wanderer,
> By sly enticement gives his banefull cup,
> With many murmurs mixt, whose pleasing poison
> The visage quite transforms of him that drinks,
> And the inglorious likenes of a beast
> Fixes instead, unmoulding reasons mintage
> Character'd in the face.   (520–30)

14   'Come forth' is a term associated with birth, e.g., 'he that shall come forth out of thine own bowels' (Genesis 15.4).

15   *The Poetical Works of John Milton*, ed. by Helen Darbishire (London: Oxford University Press, 1958; repr. 1960), stage directions following line 92. All Milton quotations are taken from this edition.

16   Cf. *The Odyssey*, Bk X, in which Circe turns Odysseus's men into swine. Cf. also *The Faerie Queene*, in which the wild beasts in Acrasia's Bower of Bliss are revealed to be
> Whylome her louers, which her lusts did feed,
> Now turned into figures hideous,
> According to their mindes like monstruous.   (II.12.85–87)

This could just as well be a description of the Fall – in fact it nearly is. As described by Milton in *Paradise Lost*, Adam and Eve, after eating the forbidden fruit, fall prey to lust, then fall asleep. When they awake,

> they in mutual accusation spent
> The fruitless hours, but neither self-condemning,
> And of thir vain contest appeerd no end.   (IX.1187–89)

The Lord in the person of the Son comes to the garden and calls for Adam:

> He came, and with him *Eve*, more loth, though first
> To offend, discount'nanc't both, and discompos'd;
> Love was not in thir looks, either to God
> Or to each other, but apparent guilt,
> And shame, and perturbation, and despaire,
> Anger, and obstinacie, and hate, and guile.   (X.109–14)

Their debased condition is now written on their countenances. Like Hyde, 'Satan's signature' (40) is on their faces. Likewise the types of animals on the heads of the rabble in *Comus* reflect the inner nature of the victims, one of whom is a proverbially lascivious 'bearded Goat' (line 71) – a suitable follower for Comus, whose energies are directed against the heroine's chastity. All of these transformations reflect the emergence of vices which were already present in the rabble. One could say as much about Hyde and leave it at that; but Adam and Eve, and Comus's rabble were all enticed into falling – Jekyll alone chooses deliberately to debase himself. And so begins his Platonic descent into apishness.

One of the earliest recorded cases of this phenomenon is that of a Greek named Thersites who fought in the Trojan war. He was an impudent, rascally, nasty troublemaker who finally went too far, and received such a blow from Achilles that he died.[17] Pope describes him:

---

17   Robert Graves, *The Greek Myths*, 2 vols (Harmondsworth: Penguin, 1966–67), II, 313.

Thersites only clamoured in the throng,
Loquacious, loud, and turbulent of tongue:
Awed by no shame, by no respect controlled,
In scandal busy, in reproaches bold;
With witty malice studious to defame,
Scorn all his joy, and laughter all his aim.
But chief he gloried with licentious style
To lash the great, and monarchs to revile.
His figure such as might his soul proclaim:
One eye was blinking, and one leg was lame:
His mountain-shoulders half his breast o'erspread;
Thin hairs bestrewed his long misshapen head.
Spleen to mankind his envious heart possessed,
And much he hated all, but most the best.[18]　[my emphasis]

The soul of this strange creature sinks down into the underworld, and joins the throng of souls described by Er in *The Republic*, who are waiting to be reincarnated. As has already been mentioned, their choice of future life depends upon the character of their former life. Er watches as one by one the souls make their choice, some changing sex, some changing into animals or birds:

and far away among the last who chose, the soul of the jester Thersites was putting on the form of a monkey (*Republic*, X.620c).

Thersites's soul, which has scarcely managed a human existence before – and then behaved grossly – elects to inhabit the body of a beast, yet still to retain the travesty of a human form. But this has not been arbitrary – it is part of God's design as outlined by Plato in the *Timaeus*. Timaeus explains that the maker of the universe created individual souls which are composed of the same ingredients that make up the soul of the universe.

18　*Pope's Iliad of Homer*, ed. and intro. by A.J. Church, illust. by Wal Paget (London: Cassell, 1910), II.255–68. Note Pope's Platonic introduction (line 263) to the description of Thersites's body. Shakespeare includes him among the Greeks in *Troilus and Cressida*. In the *Dramatis Personae* he is given as, 'a deformed and scurrilous Grecian.' In his very first scene he is beaten by Ajax (II.1). He survives the events of the play by running away when he is challenged on the field of battle (V.7).

These are equal in number to all of the stars, and each soul has been assigned its own star. The maker then

> showed them the nature of the universe, and told them of their future birth and human lot. They were to be sown in the planets, and out of them was to come forth the most religious of animals, which would hereafter be called man. The souls were to be implanted in bodies, which were in a perpetual flux, whence, he said, would arise, first, sensation; secondly, love, which is a mixture of pleasure and pain; thirdly, fear and anger, and the opposite affections: and if they conquered these, they would live righteously, but if they were conquered by them, unrighteously. He who lived well would return to his native star, and would there have a blessed existence;[19] but if he lived ill, he would pass into the nature of a woman, and if he did not then alter his evil ways, into the likeness of some animal, until the reason which was in him reasserted her sway over the elements of fire, air, earth, water, which had engrossed her, and he regained his first and better nature (*Timaeus*, 41–42).[20]

In this passage and the story of Thersites one should keep two points in mind: there is a divine plan operating; and within that plan souls make choices. These choices either advance or retard the souls' progress.

Jekyll, of course, makes the wrong choice, and, as he says, 'The movement was thus wholly toward the worse' (85). He then compounds the offence by wilfully and persistently making the wrong choice until he forfeits the power to choose, and turns himself permanently into a beast.

---

19   Cf. also *Paradise Lost*:
         Witness this new-made World, another Heav'n
         From Heaven Gate not farr, founded in view
         On the cleer *Hyaline*, the Glassie Sea;
         Of amplitude almost immense, with Starrs
         Numerous, and every starr perhaps a World
         Of destind habitation.   (VII.617–22)
20   Aaron Perkus quotes from this passage while arguing that Jekyll passes from man
         (Jekyll), to woman (Hyde as Jekyll's feminine aspect), to beast (entirely Hyde)
         (p. 37).

Henry More

Edmund Spenser and his 'greatest descendant'[21] John Milton are known as poets whose writings are informed by Platonism.[22] However, it would be fair to say of Henry More (1614–87) that he is known as a Platonist and theologian, some of whose philosophical writings are in verse. More belongs to a group of scholars collectively referred to as the Cambridge Platonists.[23] He entered Cambridge in 1631 (Milton left in 1632), and lived there for the rest of his life, taking holy orders in 1641.

More had three great passions: Spenser, Christianity, and Platonism.[24] He manages to include them all in the preface to his poem *Psychozoia, or The life of the Soul* (1647),[25] which he describes on the title page as *A Christiano-Platonicall display of LIFE*:

---

21 Thomas P. Roche, Jr, *The Kindly Flame: A Study of the Third and Fourth Books of Spenser's Faerie Queene* (Princeton: Princeton University Press, 1964), p. 118.

22 See, e.g., Josephine Waters Bennett, 'Milton's Use of The Vision of Er', *Modern Philology*, 36 (1939), 351–58.

23 Benjamin Whichcote (1609–83); John Smith (1616–52); Ralph Cudworth (1617–85); Nathaniel Culverwell (1618?–51); Peter Sterry (d. 1672); Henry More.

24 As with Spenser, 'More's approach to Platonism, like that of most Renaissance scholars, was quite unhistorical. He saw none of the differences between Platonism, Neo-Platonism, Alexandrian mysticism, theurgy, Cabbalism, and modern Italian commentary' (*Philosophical Poems of Henry More: Comprising Psychozoia and Minor Poems*, ed., intro. and notes by Geoffrey Bullough (Manchester: Manchester University Press, 1931), p. xxii).

25 *Psychozoia* was originally published in 1642. More soon had to admit that it was too esoteric. He made revisions, and for the benefit of his readers appended *The Interpretation Generall*, being a comprehensive dictionary of terms used in *Psychozoia* and its sequels, together with a section of explanatory notes, and it was republished in 1647 with the other poems dealing with the soul, under the general title *Psychodia Platonica: or A Platonicall Song of the Soul. The Interpretation Generall* and the full Notes can be found in *Henry More: The Complete Poems*, ed. by Alexander B. Grosart (Edinburgh University Press, 1878; repr. Hildesheim: Olms, 1969). Bullough includes excerpts from the *Interpretation* and the *Notes* in his book. Bullough's introduction and textual notes are very useful; one would do well to consult both works. Bullough

Now this Eternall life I sing of, even in the middest of Platonisme: for I cannot conceal from whence I am, *viz.* of Christ: but yet acknowledging, that God hath not left the Heathen, *Plato* especially, without witnesse of himself. Whose doctrine might strike our adulterate Christian Professors with shame and astonishment; their lives falling so exceeding short of the better Heathen. How far short are they then of that admirable and transcendent high mystery of true Christianisme? To which *Plato* is a very good subservient Minister; whose Philosophy I singing here in a full heat; why may it not be free for me to break out into a higher strain, and under it to touch upon some points of Christianity; as well as all-approved *Spencer* [*sic*], sings of Christ under the name of *Pan*?[26]

This passage gives an indication of the interweaving of Platonic and Christian thought from the earliest days of Christianity;[27] and More saw links going back even further than that. He was a Cabbalist – one who believed that Greek philosophy derived from Moses. Platonism there-fore became for him simply another part of the ancient Judæo-Christian tradition.[28]

In *Psychozoia* More describes *Psyche*, the World Soul or Universal Soul, from whom the individual souls in the natural world come forth. *Psyche* is the third in the Plotinian Triad, the first two being: *T'Agathon* (the Good,

---

writes of More: 'Almost the last of the Spenserian succession in form, he is also an extreme exemplar of the Neo-Platonic tradition. [...] Henry More, having the most intimate of themes, the story of his own soul, [...] produced in *Psychodia Platonica* a series of hybrid poems [...] explicitly extolling the Neo-Platonic theory of soul' (lxxvi). Bullough notes More's debt to Spenser's poetry, especially *The Faerie Queene*, *The Fowre Hymnes*, and *Mother Hubberd's Tale* (xlii). More's Notes in the text are taken from Grosart.

26   Grosart, p. 10.

27   Charles Kingsley refers to St Paul as, 'Saint Paul the Platonist, and yet the Apostle.' See *Alexandria and Her Schools* (Cambridge: Macmillan, 1854), p. 93. (Hereafter *Alexandria*.) He also observes the influence on St John of the Alexandrian Jewish Platonist Philo (b. 20 BC), p. 81.

28   For more detail see Frances A. Yates, *Giordano Bruno and the Hermetic Tradition* (London: Routledge & Kegan Paul, 1964), pp. 84–85; 424. Kingsley, while pointing out the weaknesses in Philo's thought, is still able to write, 'I cannot think that he had to treat his own sacred books unfairly, to make them agree with the root-idea of Socrates and Plato' (*Alexandria*, 86).

or the One), and *Æon* (the intellectual world, or eternal life). In a passage reminiscent of Spenser's Garden of Adonis, More represents Psyche clothed in a mantle of layers, or films, reaching down to the earth:

> The first of these fair films, we *Physis* [Nature] name.
> Nothing in Nature did you ever spy,
> But there's pourtraid: all beasts both wild and tame,
> [...].

> Snakes, Adders, Hydraes, Dragons, Toads, and Frogs,
> Th'own-litter-loving Ape, the Worm, and Snail,
> Th'undaunted Lion, Horses, Men, and Dogs,
> Their number's infinite.   (cant. I, st. 41–42)

>   *Physis* is the great womb
> From whence all things in th'University
> Yclad in divers forms do gaily bloom,
> And after fade away, as *Psyche* gives the doom.   (II.13)

From this great womb the souls pass into the land of *Psychania*, or the Land of Souls (II.24), which is divided into two kingdoms: *Autœsthesia*, or Self-Sensedness; and *Theoprepia* (II.25).[29] Each kingdom is peopled by one of two kinds of soul. More writes in his note to this stanza:

> Let *Psychanie* be as big or little as it will, *Autœsthesia*, and *Theoprepia*, be the main parts of it, and exhaust the whole. Let souls be in the body or out of the body, or where they will, if they be but alive, they are alive to God, or themselves, and so are either *Theoprepians*, or *Autœsthesians*.[30]

Theoprepia becomes the goal of a pilgrim's progress for More's own soul, named Mnemon, borrowed from the *Faerie Queene* (III.9); but first he passes through Autœsthesia, which More divides further into two:

29 '*Theoprepia*, is a condition of the soul, whereby she doth that which would become God himself to do in the like cases, whether in the body, or out of the body' (More, note to *Psychozoia*, II.26, Grosart, p. 143). More may have in mind St Paul: 'whether in the body, or out of the body, I cannot tell: God knoweth' (II Corinthians 12.3).
30 Grosart, p. 143.

One province cleped is great *Adamah*
Which also hight *Beirah* of brutish fashion;
The other Providence is *Dizoia*;
There you may see much mungrill transformation,
Such monstrous shapes proceed from Niles foul inundation.   (II.25)

More's note explains the Dizoians:

> [T]heir condition is as this present Stanza declares, mungrill, betwixt Man and Beast, Light and Darknesse, God and the Devill, *Jacob* and *Esau* struggle in them.[31]

Stevenson employs the same imagery. Jekyll writes that:

> man is not truly one, but truly two. [...] It was the curse of mankind that these incongruous faggots were thus bound together—that in the agonised womb of consciousness these polar twins should be continuously struggling (82).

Here then is the essence of the human condition, the war in the members, outlined by both More and Stevenson: the divine soul, a spark of the One, hampered by brute nature in its attempts to reunite with its source. Those who are immersed in God, More calls Israelites; those who are immersed in themselves, he calls Edomites.[32]

More introduces Dizoia in order to make the point with which he concludes *Psychozoia* – that God is indivisible goodness, while evil takes many forms. He writes of:

the biformity
Of the *Dizoians*; What mongrill sort
Of living wights; how monstrous shap'd they be,
And how that man and beast in one consort;
Goat's britch, mans tongue, goose head, with monki's mouth distort.   (III.70)

And ends with:

Suffice it then we have taught that ruling Right,
The Good is uniform, the Evil infinite.   (III.71)

---

31   Grosart, p. 143.
32   Jacob became known as Israel. Esau became known as Edom.

The second province in Autœsthesia is called Adamah, otherwise known as Beirah (Hebrew for 'brute'). More's hero Mnemon asks his travelling companion Psittaco (parrot) what the name *Beirah* means. The reply is, 'The brutish nature, or brutallitie' (II.49). More writes, in his note to II.25:

> [T]hey that are wholly alive to themselves, their abode is named *Adamah*, which signifieth the corrupt naturall life, the old *Adam*, or *Beirah* because this *Adam* is but a brute, compared to that which *Plotinus* calleth the true Man, whose form, and shape, and life, is wisdome, and righteousnesse: [...] But that low life in the body is but [...] a mixture of all brutish lives together, and is the seat or sink of wickednesse. [...] For vice is congenit or connaturall to beasts.[33]

More provides a catalogue of Beironites (II.136), whose natures, behaviour, and even appearance reveal their animal selves. Among them are the 'All-imitating Ape' and 'crafty Fox famous for subtilty'. Mnemon even encounters a foolish youth called Pithecus (Ape), who is on his way home to his country of Pithecuse (Land of Apes).[34] In More's scheme the ape is a figure of insincerity, ignorance and folly, who gets by in the world by imitating proper behaviour, or whatever he takes to be wiser or better – in this case Pithecus is impressed and persuaded by the nonsense prattled by Psittaco.

Pithecus is thus not unlike the Ape in Spenser's *Mother Hubberd's Tale* (1591), in which a fox and an ape,[35] down on their luck, undertake a succession of bold and increasingly improbable impersonations until they usurp the sleeping Lion's throne. Although 'both were craftie and unhappie witted' (line 49)[36] – that is, mischievous – Spenser makes it clear that the Fox is the smart one, and the Ape merely his willing accomplice.

---

33 Grosart, p. 143.

34 Horst Janson mentions a tale from Ovid in which 'the Cercopes, tailed, dwarf-like creatures', are turned into apes. Janson adds: '[T]he Pithecusae islands were supposedly named after them' (H.W. Janson, *Apes and Ape Lore in the Middle Ages and the Renaissance* (London: Warburg, 1952; repr. Nendeln/Liechtenstein: Kraus, 1976), p. 96). For more detail on this story, see Graves, II, 162–67.

35 A traditional pairing dating back to the Classical period. See Janson, pp. 37–40.

36 Quotations from *Yale Spenser*.

In fact they are complementary to each other: like Jekyll does with Hyde, the Fox dreams up the escapades but relies on the Ape for their execution. Conversely the Ape is dependent on the Fox for direction.

The discontented Fox declares his sad plight to the Ape, who then realizes that his own circumstances are the same, and asks how they should be remedied. The Fox advises that they should beg in the guise of old soldiers, but, he tells the Ape:

> Be you the Souldier, for you likest are
> For manly semblance, and small skill in warre:
> I will but wayte on you, and as occasion
> Falls out, my selfe fit for the same will fashion.   (199–202)

Spenser describes the Ape's disguise, and includes an ape's traditional item of equipment – a stick, or club:

> But neither sword nor dagger did he beare,
> Seemes that no foes revengement he did feare;
> In stead of them a handsome bat he held,
> On which he leaned, as one farre in elde.   (215–18)

A yeoman offers the Ape a labouring position, which he declines on account of his health, but instead offers himself and his dog (the Fox) as shepherds for the yeoman's flock. The Fox of course begins to eat the sheep, and the Ape soon follows. They flee to escape punishment. After some more adventures they come upon the Lion sleeping in the forest, and the Fox persuades the Ape to steal the Lion's crown, sceptre and royal pelt. It is at this point that Spenser draws the distinction between these two villains. They begin to argue about which of them should wear the crown:

> I am most worthie (said the Ape) sith I
> For it did put my life in jeopardie:
> Thereto I am in person, and in stature
> Most like a man, the Lord of everie creature;
> So that it seemeth I was made to raigne,
> And borne to be a Kingly soveraigne.
> Nay (said the Foxe) Sir Ape you are astray:
> For though to steale the Diademe away

Were the worke of your nimble hand, yet I
Did first devise the plot by policie;
So that it wholly springeth from my wit:
For which also I claime my selfe more fit
Than you, to rule: for gouvernment of state
Will without wisdome soone be ruinate.
And where ye claime your selfe for outward shape
Most like a man, Man is not like an Ape
In his chiefe parts, that is, in wit and spirite;
But I therein most like to him doo merite
For my slie wyles and subtill craftinesse,
The title of the Kingdome to possesse.   (1027–46)

In keeping with their characters, the Fox and the Ape arrange to share the spoils: the Ape wears the royal trappings, while the Fox wields the power behind the throne. The Ape begins to believe that he actually is the king, while the Fox brings the kingdom low with his corruption. At last Jove, driven to wrath, sends Mercury to wake the Lion, who, enraged, enters the palace. The Fox rushes to the Lion and blames the Ape. The Lion strips the Fox of his spoils and lets him go; but he cuts off the Ape's tail and trims his ears,

Since which, all Apes but halfe their eares have left,
And of their tailes are utterlie bereft.   (1383–84)[37]

---

37   Janson writes: 'The ape's lack of tail had, of course, been noted in classical times, but it was not until the advent of Christianity that this member – or the absence of it – achieved metaphysical significance. Had not the Lord himself, according to Leviticus XXII.23, declared the tail to be a necessary part of every animal by pronouncing those that lacked one unfit for sacrifice? [...] Clearly, then, possession of a tail meant that the "end" of its owner had been properly determined by the Lord, so that it was "against nature" for any animal to be without one; only man, free to choose between good and evil and thereby to decide his own end (within the limits set him by Original Sin) was legitimately ecaudate' (18–19). From the time of the Early Christian writers until the mediaeval period the ape was associated with the devil because, among other reasons, neither had a tail. See Janson, pp. 19–22.

This is a curious ending. The Fox is acknowledged as the 'first Author of that treacherie' (line 1379), yet his only punishment is public humiliation and the confiscation of his plunder – he ends up no worse off than he was at the beginning, and free to carry on his criminal activities. It is as if the rule of law has no power over slie wyles and subtill craftinesse, those characteristics that are at once both fox-like and yet essentially human; humanity can govern itself only so far.

The fate of the Ape seems appropriately harsh and humiliating. But ultimately it is self-defeating, as William Oram observes:

> Commentators have often noted that the Fox escapes unpunished in this final episode, but it is equally important that the punishment of the Ape has a cosmetic value. Without his tail and with his ears cropped he will be harder to unmask because he will resemble all the more closely the human beings he imitates.[38]

This is true; but surely more telling is the fact that, if it is harder to tell an ape from a human, then it is also harder to tell a human from an ape.

More makes this point in *Psychozoia*. The Beironites seek to distinguish themselves from beasts by the fact that they walk upright; therefore their own name for their country is *Anthropion* ('uprightnesse of body or looking up').[39] But Mnemon refutes this distinction:

> Baboons, and Apes, as well as th'Anthropi
> Do go upright, and beasts grown mad do view the sky.

> Then marken well what great affinitie
> There is twixt Ape, mad Beast, and Satyrs wild,
> And the Inhabitants of *Anthropie*,
> When they are destitute of manners mild,
> And th'inward man with brutishnesse defil'd

---

38 *Yale Spenser*, p. 332.
39 *Interpretation Generall*, Grosart, p. 159. Janson (81) quotes the thirteenth-century encyclopaedist Thomas of Cantimpré: 'Man alone is capable of raising his face towards the heavens, so that he may clearly perceive the source of his salvation' (*De Naturis Rerum*, lib.IV, cap. 96). Janson writes: 'This concept is derived from the Early Christian etymology of ανθρωπος [anthropos] as 'he who looks upward (to God)' (103, n31).

> Hath life and love and lust and cogitation
> Fixt in foul sense, or moving in false guile.   (II.47–48)

In the two provinces of Dizoia and Beirah More presents two grades of sinful humanity. The Dizoians, being a hybrid of man and beast, have yet the capacity to turn away from their lower selves and attain an awareness of God, but are constantly being led astray by their innate sinful tendencies. The Beironites, being unalloyed brute, are lost in their lower selves, and have no other pursuit than their own desires.

Where does this sin and evil come from? It begins with Dæmon, the King of Autœsthesia, 'the fount of foul duality' (II.26). More describes him:

> Or for that he himself is quite divided
> Down to the belly; there's some unity:
> But head, and tongue, and heart be quite discided;
> Two heads, two tongues, and eke two hearts there be.
> This head doth mischief plot, that head doth see
> Wrong fairly to o'reguild. One tongue doth pray,
> The other curse. The hearts do ne're agree.   (II.27)

More writes in his explanatory note to II.28:

> *Dæmon*, that is, the authour of division of man from God, born of self-sensednesse. [Plotinus says that] the first cause of evil to the soul was [...] that they would be their own or of themselves. So delighted with this liberty, they were more and more estranged, till at last like children taken away young from their parents, they in pro‑ cesse of time grew ignorant both of themselves and of their parents.[40]

Dæmon has two sons: Autophilus – 'a lover of himself' – who rules in Dizoia; and Philosomatus – 'a lover of his body' – who rules in Beirah.[41]

More's types have such universal application that one can readily read Jekyll as a Dizoian, and Hyde as a Beironite. Jekyll, the Dizoian mungrill, writes in his Statement, 'all human beings, as we meet them, are commingled

---

40   Grosart, p. 143.
41   *Interpretation Generall*, Grosart, pp. 160; 163.

out of good and evil' (85). And he acknowledges his own condition almost
immediately:

> It was on the moral side, and in my own person, that I learned to recognise the thor-
> ough and primitive duality in man; I saw that, of the two natures that contended in
> the field of my consciousness, even if I could rightly be said to be either, it was only
> because I was radically both (82).

Later he writes:

> Hence, although I had now two characters as well as two appearances, one was wholly
> evil, and the other was still the old Henry Jekyll, that incongruous compound of
> whose reformation and improvement I had already learned to despair (85).

And he calls himself 'a composite' (89), with 'two natures' (89).

Jekyll takes after Autophilus, the lover of himself. He begins his Statement by telling us that he has been born to a large fortune, endowed with
excellent parts, inclined by nature to industry, and so on. All of his problems
arise because he wishes to appear more noble and virtuous in the public
eye than he really is. 'And indeed,' he writes,

> the worst of my faults was a certain impatient gaiety of disposition, such as has made
> the happiness of many, but such as I found it hard to reconcile with my imperious
> desire to carry my head high, and wear a more than commonly grave countenance
> before the public (81).

His self-image prevents him from indulging his passions. But he is also
not without a religious impulse. After the murder of Sir Danvers Carew,
Jekyll resolves to have no more to do with Hyde, and to atone for his
sins.

> He came out of his seclusion, renewed relations with his friends, became once more
> their familiar guest and entertainer; and whilst he had always been known for chari-
> ties, he was now no less distinguished for religion (56).

But, as he writes:

> I was still cursed with my duality of purpose; [...] and it was as an ordinary secret
> sinner that I at last fell before the assaults of temptation.

[...] And this brief condescension to my evil finally destroyed the balance of my soul (92).

By now he is more Hyde than Jekyll; and doomed to enact the scene on the bench in Regent's Park.

Jekyll is sitting there, recognizing only in retrospect that he is poised not only between his two Dizoian selves – the animal and the spiritual – but between his two Autœsthesian selves – the Dizoian and the Beironite, the mungrill and the brute:

> I sat in the sun on a bench; the animal within me licking the chops of memory; the spiritual side a little drowsed, promising subsequent penitence, but not yet moved to begin. After all, I reflected, I was like my neighbours (92).

At this point he has had enough reasons to reform. One would hope that he has learned his lesson, has begun to move away from sin towards charity, good works and prayer; and has accepted that, being of a dual nature, he will have occasional lapses – although from now on as himself – but that his energies now will be mainly directed towards the good side of his nature. His realization at this moment is that he is no better than anyone else. He should have been humbled by his experience:

> and then I smiled, comparing myself with other men, comparing my active goodwill with the lazy cruelty of their neglect. And at the very moment of that vainglorious thought, a qualm came over me (92).

This moment of Pharisaic hubris plunges the Dizoian Jekyll into the Beironite Hyde.

Why? What is Stevenson up to? The moment would be just as dramatic – and more poignant – if Jekyll were severed from humanity while he was feeling closest to it. But this moment of undeserved pride is in keeping for a thrall of Autophilus, who is 'the souls more subtill and close embracements of her self in spirituall arrogancy'.[42]

---

42   More, note to *Psychozoia*, II.28. Grosart, p. 143.

If Jekyll is a typical hybrid Dizoian autophile, Hyde is a typical unalloyed Beironite somatophile. Jekyll recognizes the difference as soon as he sees Hyde in the mirror:

> In my eyes [the ugly idol] bore a livelier image of the spirit, it seemed more express and single, than the imperfect and divided countenance I had been hitherto accustomed to call mine (84–85).

Hyde is the beast who walks upright, declaring himself a man. He is in reality 'a Beast clad in mans cloths',[43] which he becomes literally after the transformation in Regent's Park, and he is forced to spend the day in Jekyll's clothes. Hasty Lanyon describes the effect:

> This person (who had thus, from the first moment of his entrance, struck in me what I can only describe as a disgustful curiosity) was dressed in a fashion that would have made an ordinary person laughable [...]. Strange to relate, this ludicrous accoutrement was far from moving me to laughter. Rather, as there was something abnormal and misbegotten in the very essence of the creature that now faced me – something seizing, surprising and revolting – this fresh disparity seemed but to fit in with and to reinforce it (77–78).

Hyde's ape-like qualities have been noted. Jekyll refers to him as a 'brute' (94), and an 'animal' (92), who has 'nothing human' (94). Just as the Ape is the agent with which the Fox commits his crimes, so Hyde is the body with which Jekyll acts out his base fantasies. Jekyll writes:

> Men have before hired bravos to transact their crimes, while their own person and reputation sat under shelter. I was the first that ever did so for his pleasures. I was the first that could thus plod in the public eye with a load of genial respectability, and in a moment, like a schoolboy, strip off these lendings and spring headlong into the sea of liberty (86).

Jekyll's pleasures are, as he writes, 'undignified; I would scarce use a harder term' (86). He presents the image of himself as a reckless schoolboy indulging in naughty pranks. But he is worse than that. He has deliberately

---

43   More, note to *Psychozoia*, II.137. Grosart, p. 144.

– calculatedly – removed the human restraints from his bestial surrogate so that he might freely indulge all of his forbidden appetites, the dark appetites of his Beironite mind that his Dizoian mind could not even admit to itself.

Did Stevenson have *Psychozoia* in mind when he was writing *Jekyll and Hyde*? Or was he merely dealing with universal themes and imagery which make comparisons inevitable? The latter, most probably. More, as he himself declared, was not being original. A possible source for his compound creatures occurs in Plato's *Republic* (in which Plato himself is drawing on even more ancient sources). Socrates says:

> Let us make an image of the soul [...].
> [...]
> An image like the composite creations of ancient mythology, such as the Chimera or Scylla or Cerberus, and there are many others in which two or more different natures are said to grow into one.
> [...]
> Then do you now model the form of a multitudinous, many-headed monster, having a ring of heads of all manner of beasts, tame and wild, which he is able to put forth and metamorphose at will.
> [...]
> Suppose now that you make a second form as of a lion, and a third of a man; but let the first be far the largest, and the second next in size.
> [...]
> And now join them into one, and let the three somehow grow together.
> [...]
> Next fashion the outside of them into a single image, as of a man, so that he who is not able to look within, and sees only the outer case, may believe the beast to be a single human creature (*Republic*, IX. 588b–e).

This description surely applies to Henry Jekyll, who describes himself as an 'incongruous compound' (85), with an 'animal within' (93); who believes that 'man will be ultimately known for a mere polity of multifarious, incongruous and independent denizens' (82). Indeed, Stevenson's language is reminiscent of Jowett's translation.

Two points remain concerning More's understanding of the soul. More, drawing on Plotinus, and following on from Spenser, also held that soul is form and doth the body make. In *Psychathanasia, or The Immortality of the Soul*, the second poem in *Psychodia Platonica*, he devotes much of Book III, Canto 1 to describing how the soul goes about this process:

> the soule doth frame
> This bodies shape, imploy'd in one long thought
> So wholly taken up, that she the same
> Observeth not, till she it quite hath wrought.   (III.1.15)

He also claims that the soul is present in every living thing – plant, animal and human:

> Thus have I trac'd the soul in all her works,
> And severall conditions have displaid,
> And show'd all places where so e'r she lurks,
> Even her own lurking's of her self bewray'd,
> In plants, in beasts, in men, while here she staid:
> And freed from earth how then she spreads on high
> Her heavenly rayes, that also hath been said.
> Look now, my Muse, and cast thy piercing eye
> On every kind, and tell wherein all souls agree.   (I.2.23)

John Donne

It may seem curious to find a clergyman intruding heathen philosophy into theories of the soul; yet More was not alone, and had a notable precedent in John Donne's 'most ambitious and most disappointing poem',[44] 'The Progresse of the Soule' (or 'Metempsychosis', written 1601, published posthumously 1633). Helen Gardner argues that around the time of the poem's composition (which was never completed), Donne's reading was 'highly

---

44   R.C. Bald, *John Donne: A Life* (Oxford: Clarendon Press, 1970), p. 123.

speculative and unorthodox: cabbalistic, neo-Pythagorean, rabbinical, and Neoplatonic'.[45] And Murray Roston makes the by now familiar point about the transmission of Platonic thought:

> Of [Donne's] familiarity with such tenets of Neoplatonism and his indebtedness to the Renaissance form of it, there can be no doubt. [...] By the time of Donne, Platonism had been sufficiently assimilated by Christianity for him to have no need to turn directly to Plotinus, and the similarities discernible in his own outlook show how much he had in common with the philosophical school as a whole, as well as with its contemporary revival.[46]

Donne introduces his poem in an 'Epistle':

> [T]he Pithagorian doctrine doth not onely carry one soule from man to man, nor man to beast, but indifferently to plants also: and therefore you must not grudge to finde the same soule in an Emperour, in a Post-horse, and in a Mucheron, since no unreadinesse in the soule, but an indisposition in the organs workes this. And therefore though this soule could not move when it was a Melon, yet it may remember, and now tell mee, at what lascivious banquet it was serv'd. And though it could not speake, when it was a spider, yet it can remember, and now tell me, who used it for poyson to attaine dignitie. However the bodies have dull'd her other faculties, her memory hath ever been her owne.[47]

One would not expect to find other clergymen among the admirers of this 'disgusting burlesque on the Pythagorean doctrine of metempsychosis',[48] – or, indeed, to find people who regarded it as a religious work – and yet

---

45 John Donne, *The Elegies, and the Songs and Sonnets*, ed., with intro. and commentary by Helen Gardner (Oxford: Clarendon Press, 1965), p. lix, n1.

46 *The Soul of Wit: A Study of John Donne* (Oxford: Clarendon Press, 1974), p. 131. Roston goes on to argue, however, that Donne should not be regarded as a neo-Platonist: he was temperamentally unsuited to accept the Platonic harmonious equation between the Ideal and the sensible world. See pp. 130–41. 'The Progresse of the Soule' and its 'Epistle' are taken from this edition.

47 Roston, p. 26.

48 Adolphus William Ward (1858), quoted in *John Donne: The Critical Heritage*, ed. by A.J. Smith (London and Boston: Routledge & Kegan Paul, 1975), pp. 430–31 (p. 431). (Hereafter A.J. Smith, *Donne Heritage*.)

in 1836 Richard Cattermole and Henry Stebbing, two 'clergyman authors', included a stanza from it in an anthology of seventeenth-century religious poetry;[49] and in 1847 Edward Farr, who 'wrote on religious topics and compiled books for children', also included a stanza from the poem in an anthology of Jacobean religious verse.[50]

Having established the Pythagorean principle of metempsychosis, Donne then audaciously incorporates it into the story of Adam and Eve (the numbers are the stanza numbers). The soul begins her first life in the apple on the Tree of Knowledge (9). After the apple is plucked and eaten by Eve its soul passes into a mandrake, a vegetable whose root is shaped like a human (13–17).[51] The soul then passes into a sparrow, which exhausts itself and dies through its traditionally promiscuous behaviour (18–22), and passes into a fish:

> a female fishes sandie Roe
> With the males jelly, newly lev'ned was,
> For they had intertouch'd as they did passe,
> And one of those small bodies, fitted so,
> This soule inform'd, and abled it to rowe
> It selfe with finnie oares, which she did fit.   (23)

Here Donne is restating Spenser's 'soule is forme, and doth the bodie make'. Thus it is clear that not only does this soul move freely from body to body, but she moulds each body according to her requirements for that life.

Having been eaten by a swan (24–25), the soul passes into another fish (25–30); then into a whale (31–36); then into a mouse (38–40); then into a wolf, which mates with Abel's sheepdog (41–43); then into the resulting pup embryo (44–45):

> and now just time it was
> That a quick soule should give life to that masse
> Of blood in Abel's bitch, and thither this did passe.

49   A.J. Smith, *Donne Heritage*, pp. 357–58.
50   A.J. Smith, *Donne Heritage*, p. 412.
51   In Classical literature it was thought that mankind originally sprang fully formed from the ground. See, e.g., Plato, *Protagoras*, 321c.

> Some have their wives, their sisters some begot,
> But in the lives of Emperours you shall not
> Reade of a lust the which may equall this;
> This wolfe begot himselfe, and finished
> What he began alive, when hee was dead;
> Sonne to himselfe, and father too.   (43–44)

One may ask how this could be, since a soul cannot reside in two bodies at once. True, but in Donne's day the soul was thought to enter the body only after the limbs were formed.[52]

Having progressed through the vegetable world and successive lives in the airborne and aquatic worlds, the soul now passes into her final incarnation in the animal world, in a body which is still fully animal yet approximates to the ultimate goal of a human form:

> It quickened next to a toyful ape, and so
> Gamesome it was, that it might freely go
> From tent to tent, and with the children play,
> His organs now so like theirs he doth find,
> That why he cannot laugh, and speak his mind,
> He wonders.   (46)

Here Donne is stressing the defining difference between humans and beasts – only humans can talk. The ape may resemble man in many ways; but he will always lack the power of speech.

Our gamesome ape now falls in love with one of Adam's daughters. Donne has fun with him by making him not only the type of the fashionable lover, but the 'wisest of that kinde' (46). This is doubly satirical, given that apes are notorious for imitating humans: the fashionable lovers are actually imitating an ape. Unhappily for our ape, he is killed while attempting

---

52   See *John Donne: The Satires, Epigrams and Verse Letters*, ed., intro. and commentary by W. Milgate (Oxford: Oxford University Press, 1967), p. 186, notes to lines 428–30, 429–30; p. 189, note to lines 504–05. Milgate points out that in this instance Donne 'telescopes the process' (186) by having the soul pass from the wolf into the pup's body while it is yet a 'masse/ Of blood'. Donne's description of the soul's eventual progression into a human body (st.50–51), is 'orthodox' (Milgate, 189).

to show his romantic feelings in a very direct way (46–49). 'The poem', writes R.C. Bald,

> is thus a rapid succession of brief episodes, and the life of each creature provides an opportunity, not, as in a medieval bestiary, for moralizing of a naively serious kind, but for terse and savage satire directed at court and public life through parallels with the activities of the beasts (124).

Nevertheless, Donne's beasts are selected for and exhibit their traditionally associated behaviour.

At last the soul gets a human birth, passing into another one of Adam's daughters. Unfortunately the soul's first human birth is not very auspicious:

> keeping some quality
> Of every past shape, she knew treachery,
> Rapine, deceit, and lust, and ills enow
> To be a woman. *Themech* she is now,
> Sister and wife to *Caine*, *Caine* that first did plow.   (51)

Here Donne claims that the soul carries with her from life to life the negative or evil characteristics of each previous life, gradually accumulating sin upon sin, until by the time she gains a human birth she is more beast than human; or, as Bald puts it, 'when the soul achieves its human habitation, it brings with it its full heritage of bestiality' (125).[53] In *Jekyll and Hyde* Stevenson applies a variant of this theme to explain the presence of Hyde within Jekyll: instead of an individual soul accumulating

---

53   Not all readers interpret the poem in this way. 'G.O.' – probably Giles Oldisworth (1619–78) – a 'royalist divine and poet', annotated, in verse, his copy of Donne's poems. Alongside 'The Progresse of the Soule' he adds a note which may help to explain in part how clergymen have been able to regard it as a religious poem:
      The sum of *this booke* you shall find to bee
      More sin, then [*sic*] Soule keeping some qualitye
      Of every vile beast.
   Quoted in A.J. Smith, *Donne Heritage*, pp. 127–29 (pp. 127; 129).

sins from life to life, each generation carries over and accumulates the sins of its ancestors.[54]

With the first human birth Donne's poem ends. The fragment, being incomplete, describes only the progress of the soul from lower forms upwards through the Great Chain of Being, that system posited, refined, and expanded upon in the writings of Plato, Aristotle, and Plotinus, which states that there is an unbroken series of living forms stretching from the Creator to the lowest form of life down to the inanimate. The highest form of a particular class approximates closely to the lowest form of the next higher class, so there is naturally some overlapping. Thus some marine organisms may appear to be animals, yet pass their lives attached to rocks, in the manner of plants. Likewise seals are animals, yet live partly in water; and bats are animals, yet fly like birds. And the ape is an animal, yet looks and behaves somewhat like man, who is the sole representative of his class. Therefore something of each link in the Chain is shared with the succeeding link, until man contains within him a vestige of all the inferior links.[55] Although in the poem the soul moves in only one direction, Donne's 'Epistle' makes it clear that the soul can move in any direction, as is also the case in the writings of Spenser and More. Moreover the Platonic soul moves freely and easily within a Judæo-Christian universe, which is itself partly defined by Platonic cosmology. Life after life the soul retains the dominant (sinful) characteristic of each form that it inhabits – the lechery of the sparrow; the tyranny of the whale; the rapacity of the wolf; the lust and folly of the ape – until a human such as Henry Jekyll feels himself to be no more than 'a mere polity of multifarious, incongruous and independent denizens' (82); or finds himself, like the man described above by Socrates, inhabited by 'a multitudinous, many-headed monster' (*Republic*, IX.588c). 'Man', writes Donne,

---

54   Stevenson describes the process more clearly in 'Olalla'.
55   I am indebted to Arthur O. Lovejoy's *The Great Chain of Being* (Cambridge, Massachusetts: Harvard University Press, 1936; repr. 1961). See, in particular, chap. 2, pp. 24–66.

is a lumpe, where all beasts kneaded bee,
Wisdome makes him an Arke where all agree;
The foole, in whom these beasts do live at jarre,
Is sport to others, and a Theater;
Nor scapes hee so, but is himselfe their prey:
All which was man in him, is eate away,
And now his beasts on one another feed,
Yet couple'in anger, and new monsters breed.[56]

Milgate lists the several influences acting upon this passage. The 'lumpe'
derives from St Paul's reference to man as a lump of clay in Romans 9.21.[57]
Milgate writes:

> The biblical idea is combined with the legend that Prometheus moulded man out
> of clay, giving him the qualities of different animals (Horace, *Odes*, I.xvi.13ff.; cf.
> Plato, *Protagoras*, 320d, etc.).[58] This was further linked with the theory that, just as
> the rational [human] soul absorbs the inferior souls of sense [animal] and growth
> [plant] and retains their qualities, so in the Chain of Being each stage possesses the
> qualities of beings at a lower stage. [...]
>   These theories account for the *fact* of man's animal qualities. The allegory of the
> beasts in man (his animal passions, etc.) begins with Plato's *Republic*, ix.588–90, and
> becomes a commonplace in the [Church] Fathers (239).

---

56   'To Sir Edward Herbert, at Julyers' (1610), lines 1–8.
57   'Hath not the potter power over the clay, of the same lump to make one vessel unto
      honour and another unto dishonour?'
58   It is said that Prometheus to man's primal matter
            Was compelled to add something from each living creature
                And thus from the wild lion he took
                    Rabid virus to place in our gall.
      Horace, *Odes*, trans. by Edward Bulwer Lytton (London and New York: Routledge,
      1872), p. 41.
      Plato's version is somewhat different. In *Protagoras* 'the gods fashioned [mortal crea-
      tures, including man] out of earth' (320d). Epimetheus distributed the 'proper quali-
      ties' to all the animals (320d), but had exhausted the supply by the time he arrived
      at man (321b–c). Prometheus therefore, to compensate the naked and vulnerable
      man, 'stole the mechanical arts of Hephaestus and Athene, and fire with them [...]
      and gave them to man' (321d).

Ever since the time of the Fathers this commonplace has served as a potent image in the writings of those who concern themselves with the nature of humanity. In the Great Chain of Being the highest members of a species begin to share features in common with the lowest members of the species above them. Conversely the lowest members of a species begin to take on characteristics of the highest members of the species below them. Man stands midway in the Chain between the Creator at the summit and inanimate matter at the bottom. Man therefore shares qualities with both the angels and the apes. If he aspires to God he will take on angelic qualities. If he turns away from God he will take on the qualities of apes, and, if he continues to degrade himself, he will take on the qualities of the quadrupeds. It is interesting to observe that in pre-Darwinian literature man degrades himself, and becomes apish as he descends the Great Chain of Being; after Darwin (in, for example, Charles Kingsley's *The Water Babies*) man degrades himself, and literally reverts to the ape from which he has risen. In both cases the progression is the same, but the mechanism is quite different. Here, then, is an unbroken literary tradition continuing on through a momentous scientific and philosophical upheaval.

Donne addresses man's degradation in his sermons, one of which he bases on Psalm 32.9: 'Do not as the horse, or the mule, who have no under-standing; whose mouth must be held in with bit and bridle, lest they come near unto thee.' Donne stresses the unique and privileged position which man occupies in the Creation; and his consequent responsibility to both himself and his Maker:

> This whole world is one Booke; And is it not a barbarous thing, when all the whole booke besides remains intire, to deface that leafe in which the Authors picture, the Image of God is expressed, as it is in man?[59]

---

59 *The Sermons of John Donne*, ed., with intro. and critical apparatus by Evelyn M. Simpson and George R. Potter, 10 vols (Berkeley and Los Angeles: University of California Press, 1958; repr. 1962), IX, Sermon 17, pp. 371–90 (p. 373). Further references are given after quotations in the text.

In a brilliant passage Donne likens man's position in the Creation to that of a king who debases himself from his natural rank, and thereby throws his whole kingdom into confusion:

> God brought man into the world, as the King goes in state, Lords, and Earles, and persons of other ranks before him. So God sent out Light, and Firmament, and Earth, and Sea, and Sunne, and Moone, to give a dignity to mans procession; and onely Man himselfe disorders all, and that by displacing himselfe, by losing his place (373).

Donne goes on to explain that the rest of Creation keeps its place; and the beasts and plants maintain their several natures – whether it be for good or for ill to their fellows. Man, however, by falling from his original nature, so corrupts the natural order (and his place in it) as to threaten the very fabric of the Great Chain of Being. And he wonders:

> whether if it were possible for Man to doe so, it were lawful for him to destroy any one species of Gods Creatures, though it were but the species of Toads and Spiders, (because this were a taking away one linke of Gods chaine, one Note of his harmony) we have taken away that which is the Jewel at the chaine, that which is the burden of the Song, Man himselfe (373–74).[60]

Donne identifies our dual nature with our loamy origins, invoking both Classical and Christian imagery:[61]

---

60   Cf. Pope's *Essay on Man*:
>   Vast chain of Being! which from God began,
>   Natures ethereal, human, angel, Man,
>   Beast, bird, fish, insect, what no eye can see,
>   No glass can reach; from infinite to thee,
>   From thee to nothing. On superior powers
>   Were we to press, inferior might on ours:
>   Or in the full creation leave a void,
>   Where, one step broken, the great scale's destroyed:
>   From Nature's chain whatever link you strike,
>   Tenth, or ten thousandth, breaks the chain alike.   (I.237–46)
>   *Pope's Essay on Man*, intro. and notes by F. Ryland (London: Bell, 1898).
61   The Roman poet Lucretius (of whom more in the following chapter) wrote that, because we are sprung from the earth, she is our mother. Cf. again Pope's *Essay on Man*:

[W]e all follow our Mother, we grovell upon the earth, whose children we are, and being made like our Father, in his Image, we neglect him. [...] We are not onely inferior to the Beasts, and under their annoyance, but we are our selves become Beasts (374).

As we turn away from our Father we depart further from his image in which we are made; and as we depart further from his image we become comparatively more ugly and deformed. Our deformity is spiritual and moral, but it is reflected in our physiognomy. This is an important point to bear in mind when considering the deformity of Edward Hyde. Donne, in 'Good Friday, 1613. Riding Westward', applies this image of spiritual and physical deformity to himself. He is riding towards the west, but his 'soul's form bends towards the east' (line 10) – the direction of Jerusalem and the scene of the Crucifixion, at which moment Christ paid the ransom for our sins. Donne cries out:

O Saviour, as thou hang'st upon the tree;
I turn my back to thee, but to receive
Corrections, till thy mercies bid thee leave.
O think me worth thine anger, punish me,
Burn off my rusts, and my deformity,
Restore thine image, so much, by thy grace,
That thou mayst know me, and I'll turn my face.　　(36–42)[62]

In his sermon Donne explains that first the angels fell, then man. 'It seemes this fall', he writes,

---

Presumptuous Man! the reason wouldst thou find,
Why formed so weak, so little, and so blind?
[...]
Ask of thy mother earth.　(I.35–39)
Donne refers to 'the earth our mother' in 'To Mr Tilman after he had taken orders', line 52. Stevenson also writes: 'Children we are, children we shall be, till our mother the earth hath fed upon our bones' (*Prayers written at Vailima*, 'For self-Forgetfulness', *Works*, XXVI, 156).
62　John Donne, *The Complete English Poems*, ed. by A.J. Smith (London: Lane, 1974).

hath broake the neck of Mans ambition, and now we dare not be so like God, as we should be. Ever since this fall, man is so far from affecting higher places, then his nature is capable of, that he is still groveling upon the ground, and participates, and imitates, and expresses more of the nature of the Beast then of his owne (372).

And he makes the telling point:

There is no creature but man that degenerates willingly from his naturall Dignity (372).

Do not degenerate from your natural dignity, warns Donne; be not as the horse, or the mule, who have no understanding. If you degenerate willingly from your natural dignity you will cease to reflect God's image and you will grovel in your deformity like a beast upon the ground.

This is precisely what Jekyll does. He deliberately sets about providing himself with a fleshly vehicle in which to indulge his lusts. And he openly confesses:

I had voluntarily stripped myself of all those balancing instincts by which even the worst of us continues to walk with some degree of steadiness among temptations (90).

In the end the balance is permanently destroyed. The deformed beastly Hyde takes over. Finally even words fail him. As Poole and Utterson break down Jekyll's cabinet door, all they hear from within is a 'dismal screech, as of mere animal terror' (69).

The writings of Spenser, More, and Donne present a soul that is a vital agent, actively moving from life to life, and deliberately choosing, then moulding, then inhabiting an appropriate body in a species suitable for its drives and inclinations. In its travels the soul retains the dominant characteristic of each previous life, so that a human being is 'a lumpe, where all beasts kneaded bee'. Likewise, on the Great Chain of Being, there is a mingling of characteristics between the highest members of a species and the lowest members of the species immediately above it; so that an ape and a human have more in common than the human would like to admit. As we pollute and degrade ourselves we fall from our human state towards that of the ape, who, generally, is not a symbol of evil so much as a symbol of mischief and folly; a symbol of humanity stripped of wisdom, discretion, understanding, morality, and restraint. However, when these virtues have been lost, what remains to a human but the vices? What remains but Edward Hyde?

In his sermon Donne describes a Creation under threat from humanity's constant and unrelenting debasement; a Creation in which the Great Chain of Being could be broken at any time by humanity's abdication from its rightful place. The animals, such as the horse and the mule, have no understanding, yet they serve to maintain order by remaining faithful to their natures. Imagine then the confusion and horror that a traveller would experience upon encountering a land where the entire natural order had been disrupted – a country in which not only had the humans degenerated from their natural dignity and become deformed, but the horses had also deviated from their natural place and had apparently gained understanding. In the following chapter Lemuel Gulliver will enter such a land: the land of the Yahoos and the Houyhnhnms.

CHAPTER THREE

Quo Vadis, Maiah Yahoo?

From the day of their first public appearance in 1726, the Yahoos of *Gulliver's Travels* have continued to worry and disturb their readers. In each of his four voyages Gulliver encounters – and reflects upon – degeneration of one kind or another. The Yahoos are by far the most extreme example. How did Swift come by them?

Swift's concerns in the first two voyages are not so much with humanity *per se* as with the kinds of societies which humans produce; hence the size differences between the Lilliputians and the Brobdingnagians, who are both extreme examples of the principle of 'soul is form and doth the body make'. The Lilliputians are tiny because their bodies reflect their moral stature. The Brobdingnagians are big because they, as 'the least corrupted' nation,[1] reflect an ideal (if still necessarily flawed) social and political stability which mankind could attain. As Gulliver notes, 'there is a strict universal Resemblance between the natural and the political Body' (160). But in the Fourth Voyage to Houyhnhnmland the focus changes. Here Gulliver encounters talking horses endowed with reason, whose society greatly resembles Plato's Republic.[2] These horses are handsome, dignified, athletic, and free from the diseases which afflict mankind. They have

---

1   Jonathan Swift, *Gulliver's Travels*, ed. by Robert A. Greenberg (New York: Norton, 1961), p. 256. Further references are given after quotations in the text. This edition is 'substantially that of Volume III of the Dublin edition of Swift's works, published in 1735 by George Faulkner' (p. viii).

2   For commentators who deal with this aspect, see, e.g., Allan Bloom, 'An Outline of *Gulliver's Travels*', in *Ancients and Moderns: Essays on the Tradition of Political Philosophy in Honour of Leo Strauss*, ed. by Joseph Cropsey (New York: Basic Books, 1964), pp. 238–57. See also John F. Reichert, 'Plato, Swift, and the Houyhnhnms', *Philological Quarterly*, 47 (1968), 179–92.

healthy minds in healthy bodies which are fit vehicles for their noble souls. So much for the dominant species and its polity.

Gulliver also finds another animal sharing the country with the Houyhnhnms, whose bodies very much represent the condition of their souls.

> At last I beheld several Animals in a Field, and one or two of the same Kind sitting in Trees. Their Shape was very singular, and deformed, which a little discomposed me, so that I lay down behind a Thicket to observe them better (193).

They are hairy and repulsive. They smell. Their habits are filthy. Gulliver writes:

> Upon the whole, I never beheld in all my Travels so disagreeable an Animal, or one against which I naturally conceived so strong an Antipathy (193).

But when the Houyhnhnms bring Gulliver to their house and stand him next to one of these animals which has been domesticated, Gulliver receives a nasty shock:

> My Horror and Astonishment are not to be described, when I observed, in this abominable Animal, a perfect human Figure; [...] [We were] the same in every Part of our Bodies, except as to Hairiness and Colour (199).

And although he cannot admit it at the time, in retrospect he reveals that, from the beginning, he has been uncomfortably aware of his kinship with these brutes:

> For as to these filthy *Yahoos*, although there were few greater Lovers of *Mankind* [my emphasis], at that time, than myself; yet I confess I never saw any sensitive Being so detestable on all Accounts; and the more I came near them, the more hateful they grew, while I stayed in that Country (199).

But Gulliver's language suggests that the Yahoos are in the process of drifting beyond the realm of the human to that of the ape. As has been noted already, they sit in trees (193). Gulliver writes that, when he went among the herds of Yahoos,

They would approach as near as they durst, and imitate my Actions after the Manner of Monkeys (231).

Traditional descriptions of monkey behaviour – examples of which will shortly be given – involve grinning and chattering.[3] In Brobdingnag a monkey discovers Gulliver when no one else is about. It skips into the room, then comes and looks into the tiny house in which Gulliver is living. Gulliver writes:

After some time spent in peeping, grinning, and chattering, he at last espyed me; [...] and dragged me out (98).[4]

Likewise, when the Yahoos become intoxicated by sucking a particular root,

It would make them sometimes hug, and sometimes tear one another; they would howl and grin, and chatter, and reel, and tumble, and then fall asleep in the Mud (228).

Of the female Yahoos Gulliver writes:

At other Times, if a Female Stranger came among them, three or four of her own Sex would get about her, and stare and chatter, and grin, and smell her all over; and then turn off with Gestures that seemed to express Contempt and Disdain (230).

It is interesting to compare this episode with a letter written to Swift by Esther Vanhomrigh (Vanessa) in June 1722, after she had read in manuscript the sequence with the Brobdingnagian monkey:

[O]ne day this week I was to visit a great lady that has been a travelling for some time passed where I found a very great Assembly of Ladys and Beaus (dressed as I suppose to a nicety) I hope you'l pardon me now I tell you that I heartily wished you

---

3   This tradition survived until at least 1920. In 'This Simian World' the American humourist Clarence Day writes: 'We simians naturally admire a profession [the law] full of wrangle and chatter' (*The Best of Clarence Day* (New York: Knopf, 1948; repr. 1956), pp. 375–428 (p. 386)).

4   The monkey carries Gulliver up to the roof of a building, and, taking him for a baby monkey, begins feeding him with food from its cheek pouches.

a Spectator for I very much question if in your life you ever saw the like scene or one more Extraordinary the Lady's behaviour was blended with so many different character's I can not possibly describe it without tiring your patience but the Audience seemed to me a creation of her owne they were so very Obsequious their form's and gestures were very like those of Babboons and monky's they all grin'd and chatter'd at the same time and that of things I did not understand the room being hung with arras in which were trees very well described just as I was considering their beauty and wishing my self in the countrey with – – – one of these animals snatched my fan and was so pleased with me that it seased me with such a panick that I apprehended nothing less than being carried up to the top of the House and served as a friend of yours was but in this one of their owne species came in upon which they all began to make their grimace's which opportunity I took and made my escape.[5]

Vanessa quite casually represents her fellow guests as some kind of anthropoid animal more akin to the ape than the human. She does this in order to place a comic distance between herself and them. Swift on the other hand has Gulliver (although not immediately) identify himself with the Yahoos for satiric effect.

Swift subtly reveals the similarity between Gulliver and the Yahoos even before Gulliver or the reader becomes aware of it. During his first contact with the Yahoos, Gulliver is approached by one of the males, who 'lift[s] up his fore Paw' (193). Shortly after, Gulliver meets his first Houyhnhnm, who is startled, and stares at him. Gulliver writes:

> We stood gazing at each other for some time; at last I took the Boldness, to reach my Hand towards his Neck, with a Design to stroak it (194).

5   *The Correspondence of Jonathan Swift*, ed. by Harold Williams, 5 vols (Oxford: Clarendon Press, 1963–65), II, 428–29. Williams adds a note: 'Vanessa's description of the company she met at the house of the "great lady" suggests, though not decisively, that some part of the voyage to the country of the Houyhnhnms had been seen by her. On the other hand, the allusion to Gulliver's misadventure with the monkey is evidence beyond question that in some form she had seen chapter five of the voyage to Brobdingnag' (428, n6). Maybe so, but the Voyage to the Houyhnhnms was not completed until the following year. Perhaps Vanessa's letter suggested the female Yahoo behaviour to Swift while he was writing that Voyage.

Ironically Gulliver, who will later report how the Yahoos would 'imitate [his] Actions after the Manner of Monkeys' (231), finds himself unconsciously imitating the action of the Yahoo. But, tellingly, whereas the Houyhnhnm 'softly' removes Gulliver's hand, Gulliver responds violently to the Yahoo by striking him with the flat of his hanger.

The Houyhnhnms, having no other frame of reference, assume that Gulliver is a Yahoo – but a special one. His clothes confuse them; but upon viewing him naked, his master declares that:

> it was plain I must be a perfect *Yahoo*; but that I differed very much from the rest of my Species, in the Whiteness, and Smoothness of my Skin, my want of Hair in several Parts of my Body, the Shape and Shortness of my Claws behind and before, and my Affectation of walking continually on my hinder Feet (205).

Quite a few differences, to be sure. However, the Houyhnhnm elects to ignore them,

> because he was more astonished at my Capacity for Speech and Reason, than at the Figure of my Body, whether it were covered or no (205–06).

The Houyhnhnm acknowledges other differences, Gulliver

> being much more cleanly, and not altogether so deformed; but in point of real Advantage, he thought I differed for the worse (209).

Gulliver lacks the physical attributes which make for a successful Yahoo. But his shortcomings echo the deficiencies which the Brobdingnagian scholars find in him:

> They all agreed that I could not be produced according to the regular Laws of Nature; because I was not framed with a Capacity of preserving my Life, either by Swiftness, or climbing of Trees, or digging Holes in the Earth (82).[6]

---

6   Elsewhere the Houyhnhnm observes, as Gulliver writes: 'That I could neither run with Speed, nor climb Trees like my *Brethren* (as he called them) the *Yahoos* in this Country' (225). Also, 'Nature hath taught them to dig deep Holes with their Nails on the Side of a rising Ground' (232).

The Houyhnhnm's assessment of Gulliver is comprehensive and quite unfair. He begins by listing Gulliver's failings as a Yahoo – his nails are too short; his fore-feet (hands) are too soft to walk on – then moves seamlessly into his shortcomings when compared with a horse – the flatness of his face; the position of his eyes – and finally moves on to his failings when compared with both Houyhnhnm and Yahoo – his body is lacking a hairy coat.

These superficial resemblances and differences are, however, not where the ultimate similarity lies. Gulliver learns that the Houyhnhnm has been comparing him with the Yahoos, 'to observe what Parity there was in our Natures' (228); and he has discovered 'a Resemblance in the Disposition of our Minds' (226). Europeans, according to the Houyhnhnm, are merely physically degenerate Yahoos:

> A Sort of Animals to whose Share, by what Accident he could not conjecture, some small Pittance of *Reason* had fallen, whereof we made no other Use than by its Assistance to aggravate our *natural* Corruptions, and to acquire new ones which Nature had not given us (225).

This is even more damning than the Brobdingnagian King's assessment of Gulliver's countrymen:

> I cannot but conclude the Bulk of your Natives to be the most pernicious Race of little odious Vermin that Nature ever suffered to crawl upon the Surface of the Earth (108).

The King, although a giant, is still a human, and is condemning fellow humans of another race. The Houyhnhnm is condemning the entire human *species*.

Gulliver feels shock and horror at both witnessing the behaviour of the Yahoos and admitting his kinship with them. This shock and horror had been experienced on many occasions by explorers and travellers in other countries, such as Africa and parts of the New World, when encountering the natives and their habits; but the travellers, like Vanessa in her letter, instead of identifying with the natives, distance themselves from these strange peoples by identifying them with monkeys and apes.[7] R.W. Frantz in his analysis of travel accounts which may have provided material for the Fourth Voyage – such as William Dampier's *A New Voyage round the World* (1697), mentioned by Gulliver in his letter to his cousin Richard Sympson – quotes from the travellers' journals as they struggle to come to terms with peoples who, despite having a human body, to the European mind have little else to recommend them for membership to that species.[8] The Hottentots of Southern Africa were of particular concern. Frantz writes:

> In truth, every characteristic, physical and mental, of the Hottentots seemed to discover them as beings who ought hardly to be looked on as rational. Many a voyager considered them as 'the next to Beasts of any People on the Face of the Earth',[9] and as scarcely deserving 'to be reckon'd of the Human Kind'.[10] Daniel Beeckman explicitly said that they could hardly be accepted as rational beings. [Quotation from Beeckman] [...] John Ovington [...] more than any other voyager, stressed the Hottentots' low mentality, and he took the important step of assigning to them a place in the chain of being midway between men and the more highly developed of brute creatures. Giving over an entire section of his *A Voyage to Surat* (1696)[11] to a description of the Cape of Good Hope and its inhabitants, he pointed out that the latter are 'Bestial and sordid',[12] and 'mean and degenerate in their Understandings',[13] and that they 'are the very Reverse of Human kind [...] so that if there's any medium between a Rational Animal and a Beast, the *Hotantot* lays the fairest Claim to that Species'.[14]

---

7   This attitude did not begin with the voyagers of the sixteenth century. The thirteenth-century encyclopaedist Albertus Magnus, in his *De Animalibus*, equates pygmies with apes. Horst Janson writes: 'In the anthropological scale of Albertus, man forms a category by himself, since he is the only animal perfect in mind and body, while all the others, the "brutes", are imperfect in various degrees. These fall into two groups: the man-like creatures (*similtudines hominis*) represented by the pygmy and the ape, and the mass of "ordinary" animals' (*Apes and Ape Lore*, p. 85).

8   R.W. Frantz, 'Swift's Yahoos and the Voyagers', *Modern Philology*, 29 (1931), 49–57.

9   William Funnell, *A Voyage round the World* (1710), in *A Collection of Voyages* (London, 1729), IV, 198–99.

10 Woodes Rogers, *A Cruising Voyage round the World* (1712; 2nd edn, corrected, London, 1726), p. 420.

11 Gulliver's Second Voyage was bound for Surat (63).

12 John Ovington, *A Voyage to Surat* (1696), repr., ed. by H.G. Rawlinson (London, 1929), p. 284.

13 Ovington, p. 286.

14 Ovington, p. 284.

It is no wonder that these savages came to be associated in the minds of the voyagers with apes and monkeys. Sir Thomas Herbert, for example, tells us that their language is 'apishly sounded'.[15] He is not speaking loosely, for he is thoroughly convinced that not least among the amazing attributes of the Hottentots is their remarkable similarity to the Troglodytes. [...] And he even suggests that they 'mixe unnaturally' with the great Apes.[16] Daniel Beeckman tells us that in appearance, too, the Hottentots are like apes. After giving a most vivid portrayal of them, he says with some emphasis: 'They are not really unlike monkeys or baboons in their gestures and postures, especially when they sit sunning themselves, as they often do in great numbers.'[17]

This extended quotation has not been given simply to persuade the reader that the Yahoos sprang from a series of ripping yarns. The point here is that while the mood of the times, and the culture, was to distance the European from the savages by representing them as beasts, Swift goes entirely against the tide by bringing Gulliver into contact with beasts, and having him not only accept them as human, but admit, strangely embrace, and steadfastly cling to his kinship with them – not only for himself, but for all his fellow humans. In fact his fellow humans in one regard are even worse than Yahoos. Gulliver writes:

> When I thought of my Family, my Friends, my Countrymen, or Human Race in general, I considered them as they really were, *Yahoos* in Shape and Disposition, perhaps a little more civilized, and qualified with the Gift of Speech; but making no other Use of Reason, than to improve and multiply those Vices, whereof their Brethren in this Country had only the Share that Nature allotted them (243).

In another place Gulliver is more specific:

15 Sir Thomas Herbert, *Some Years Travels into Divers Parts of Asia and Afrique* (London, 1638), p. 18.
16 Herbert, p. 18.
17 Frantz, pp. 55–56. The final quotation is from Daniel Beeckman, *A Voyage to and from the Island of Borneo, in the East Indies* (1718), in *A General Collection of the Best and Most Interesting Voyages and Travels in All Parts of the World*, ed. by John Pinkerton, 17 vols (1808–14) (London: Longman and others, 1812), XI, 96–158 (pp. 152–53). Beeckman's turn of phrase is reminiscent of Vanessa's, 'their form's and gestures were very like those of Babboons and monky's.'

> I expected every Moment, that my Master would accuse the *Yahoos* of those unnatural Appetites in both Sexes, so common among us. But Nature it seems hath not been so expert a Schoolmistress; and these politer Pleasures are entirely the Productions of Art and Reason, on our Side of the Globe (230).

Of this passage C.M. Webster comments, 'Here Swift makes the Yahoo, for a moment only it is true, partake of the qualities of the Noble Savage.'[18] This moment may be brief, but it introduces, conveniently, the question of origins – are the Yahoos degenerate, or are they natural?

The origins of mankind were a subject of as much debate in Swift's day as in any other. In Shaftesbury's 'The Moralists' Theocles summarizes the argument:

> For either man must have been from eternity or not. If from eternity, there could be no primitive or original state, no state of nature other than we see at present before our eyes. If not from eternity, he arose either all at once (and consequently he was at the very first as he is now) or by degrees, through several stages and conditions, to that in which he is at length settled, and has continued for so many generations.[19]

Swift, of course, held definite views on this subject. He writes:

> The Scripture-system of man's creation, is what all Christians are bound to believe, and seems most agreeable of all others to probability and reason.[20]

The meaning of 'reason' seems to depend very much upon the users and the contexts in which they use it. For example, according to Basil Willey:

---

18 C.M. Webster, 'Notes on the Yahoos', *Modern Language Notes*, 47 (1932), 451–54. The history of the Noble Savage will be dealt with in the next chapter.

19 Anthony, Earl of Shaftesbury, *Characteristics of Men, Manners, Opinions, Times, etc.*, ed., intro. and notes by John M. Robertson, 2 vols (Gloucester, Mass.: Smith, 1900; repr. 1963), II, 80.

20 'Further Thoughts on Religion', *Prose Works of Jonathan Swift*, ed. by Herbert Davis, 14 vols (Oxford: Blackwell, 1957–68), IX, 264.

Milton, like the Cambridge Platonists, exalts 'Reason' as the godlike principle in man, meaning by this term, again like them, the principle of moral control rather than of intellectual enlightenment.[21]

Swift nuanced the term as the argument demanded. Kathleen Williams writes:

> The reason here [i.e., in the quotation above from Swift] invoked is a limited faculty enough and is commonly appealed to in the sermons of [...] other Anglican divines; the elaboration of Swift's opening statement shows that the probability and reasonableness of the scriptural account of man's creation and fall lie in its truth to experience. It is convincing because it accounts for the degenerate nature of man, an observed and experienced fact, and it is not considered as an event probable or improbable in itself. It is reasonable to accept the account not only because it is revealed by an infallible God but because it is true to life: the nature of animals is constant, 'But men degenerate every day, merely by the folly, the perverseness, the avarice, the tyranny, the pride, the treachery, or inhumanity of their own kind.'[22]

21   Basil Willey, *The Seventeenth Century Background: Studies in the Thought of the Age in Relation to Poetry and Religion* (London: Chatto and Windus, 1967), p. 242.

22   Kathleen Williams, *Jonathan Swift and the Age of Compromise* (Lawrence: University of Kansas Press, 1959), pp. 36–37. The quotations from Swift are from 'Further Thoughts on Religion', *Prose Works*, IX, 264. Cf. Donne's sermon: 'There is no creature but man that degenerates willingly from his natural Dignity' (*Sermons*, IX, 372). Of interest also is Swift's statement, paraphrased by Williams as, 'the nature of animals is constant.' Some animals, writes Swift, 'are strong or valiant, and their species never degenerates in their native soil, except they happen to be enslaved or destroyed by human fraud.' Here (with a qualification) he is echoing Donne's, 'They [beasts] are not departed from their native and natural dignity, by any thing that they have done' (*Sermons*, IX, 373). The Houyhnhnms, therefore, by acquiring reason and speech, have departed from their original nature as much as the Yahoos have from theirs. This surely must be a significant factor in any assessment of the Houyhnhnms. Moreover, their reasoning powers are seriously flawed, so they have not managed their elevation with much success. Here I should declare myself on the 'soft' side of the debate about the Fourth Voyage. Put at its simplest, the 'hard' school see the Houyhnhnms as an ideal against which mankind is judged and found wanting. The 'soft' school regard the Houyhnhnms as targets for Swift's satire. For an overview of this debate, see James L. Clifford, 'The Eighteenth Century', *Modern Language Quarterly*, 26 (1965), 111–34. Clifford coined the terms 'hard' and 'soft' for the two opposing approaches.

The question of the origin of the Yahoos has exercised the Houyhn-hnms for many years; and they have developed some theories to explain their unwanted neighbours. General opinion has it,

> That those creatures could not be *Ylnhniamshy* (or *Aborigines* of the Land) because of the violent Hatred the *Houyhnhnms* as well as all other Animals, bore them; which although their evil Disposition sufficiently deserved, could never have arrived at so high a Degree, if they had been *Aborigines*, or else they would have long since been rooted out (237).

This leaves two alternative traditions; of which the first is:

> That many Ages ago, two of these Brutes appeared together upon a Mountain; whether produced by the Heat of the Sun upon corrupted Mud and Slime, or from the Ooze and Froth of the Sea, was never known. That these *Yahoos* engendered, and their Brood in a short time grew so numerous as to over-run and infest the whole Nation (236–37).

Some of the Houyhnhnms feel that there is 'much Truth in this Tradition' (237). Nor are they alone in this supposition. Andrew D. White, in his survey of Western evolutionary thought, discusses the Christian belief – based on Genesis – that:

> While man was directly moulded and fashioned separately by the Creator's hand, the animals generally were evoked in numbers from the earth and sea by the Creator's voice.[23]

And where did this belief come from? White continues:

> The vast majority of theologians agreed in representing all animals as created 'in the beginning', and named by Adam, preserved in the ark, and continued ever afterward under exactly the same species. This belief ripened into a dogma. Like so many other dogmas in the Church, Catholic and Protestant, its real origins are to be found rather in pagan philosophy than in the Christian Scriptures; it came far more from Plato and Aristotle than from Moses and St Paul.[24]

23   Andrew D. White, *A History of the Warfare of Science with Religion in Christendom*, 2 vols (New York: Dover, 1896; repr. 1960), I, 30.
24   White, I, 30–31.

Milton describes the process of creation:

> And God said, let the Waters generate
> Reptil with Spawn abundant, living Soule:
> And let the fowle flie above the Earth, with wings
> Displayd on the op'n Firmament of Heav'n.
> [...]
>   [...] The Waters thus
> With Fish replenisht, and the Aire with Fowle,
> Ev'ning and Morn solemnized the Fift Day.
> The Sixt, and of Creation last arose
> With Eevning Harps and Mattin, when God said,
> Let th' Earth bring forth Soule living in her kinde,
> Cattel and Creeping things, and Beast of the Earth,
> Each in their kinde. The Earth obeyd, and strait
> Op'ning her fertil woomb teemd at a Birth
> Innumerous living Creatures, perfet formes,
> Limbd and full grown: out of the ground up rose
> As from his Laire the wilde Beast.   (*PL*, VII.387–457)[25]

On each day God speaks, then the creative process occurs. Fish appear swimming in the sea; fowl appear flying in the air; beasts emerge from the earth fully formed and in their familiar shape. This is the creation of everything that existed before the Fall.

The alert reader of Milton's Creation will notice that nowhere does Milton mention Yahoos. This is because, as the Houyhnhnm tradition suggests, they were not there. Their creation was of a different order. White explains:

> Thoughtful men of the early civilizations which were developed along the great rivers in the warmer regions of the earth noted how the sun-god as he rose in his

---

25   Milton has been forced to make a choice here for dramatic reasons. According to
      White (I, 51): 'It is true that these sacred accounts of ours contradict each other. In
      that part of the first or Elohistic account given in the first chapter of Genesis the
      waters bring forth fishes, marine animals, and birds (Genesis,i,20); but in that part
      of the second or Jehovistic account given in the second chapter of Genesis both the
      land animals and birds are declared to have been created not out of the water, but
      out of the ground (Genesis,ii,19).'

fullest might caused the water and the rich soil to teem with the lesser forms of life. In Egypt, especially, men saw how under this divine power the Nile slime brought forth 'creeping things innumerable'. Hence mainly this ancient belief that the animals and man were produced by lifeless matter at the divine command, 'in the beginning', was supplemented by the idea that some of the lesser animals, especially the insects, were produced by a later evolution, being evoked after the original creation from various sources, but chiefly from matter in a state of decay.[26]

Among the early Greek philosophers who pondered the origins of life, Thales (624–548) held that life began in the ocean. Anaximander (611–547) proposed also that life began in the ocean, but that humans were the first life form, although they began as fish, and, at a suitable stage of development, came onto land where, like a butterfly emerging from a cocoon, they emerged as humans; and thereafter the species continued a terrestrial existence. Anaximenes (588–524) conceived the theory that all life was produced by the heat of the sun on primordial slime. Thus H.F. Osborn, in his analysis of the history of evolutionary thought, observes:

> This idea of the aquatic or marine origin of life, which is now a fundamental principle of Evolution, is therefore an extremely ancient one.[27]

White and Osborn both go on to trace the survival and development of the ocean-slime idea through Christian thinkers such as St Augustine and St Thomas Aquinas.

Among the literary Christian thinkers, Spenser held this idea:

> For, all that from her [the Earth] springs, and is ybredde,
>> How-euer fayre it flourish for a time,
>> Yet see we soone decay; and, being dead,
>> To turne again vnto their earthly slime:
>> Yet, out of their decay and mortall crime [corruption],
>> We daily see new creatures to arize;

26 White, I, 52.
27 Henry Fairfield Osborn, *From the Greeks to Darwin: an Outline of the Development of the Evolution Idea* (New York: Macmillan, 1894), p. 33. I am indebted to Professor Osborn for the information on the Greek philosophers. Socrates refers to heat producing life from putrefaction in *Phaedo*, 96b.

> And of their Winter spring another Prime,
> Vnlike in forme, and chang'd by strange disguise:
> So turne they still about, and change in restlesse wise.[28]

So did Donne:

> See, Sir, how as the sun's hot masculine flame
> Begets strange creatures on Nile's dirty slime.[29]

So did Henry More:

> Two mighty Kingdomes hath this *Psychany*,
> The one self-feeling *Autæsthesia;*
> The other hight god-like *Theoprepy*,
> *Autæsthesia's* divided into tway:
> One province cleped is great *Adamah*
> Which also hight *Beirah* of brutish fashion;
> The other Providence is *Dizoia;*
> There you may see much mungrill transformation,
> Such monstrous shapes proceed from Niles foul inundation.[30]

---

28   *Mutabilitie Cantos, FQ,* VII.7.18.
29   'To E. of D. with Six Holy Sonnetts', lines 1–2.
30   *Psychozoia*, II.25. More explains the Dizoians in his Notes: 'Their condition is as this present Stanza declares, mungrill, betwixt Man and Beast, Light and Darknesse, God and the Devill, *Jacob* and *Esau* struggle in them' (Grosart, p. 143). The Yahoos are not even at the level of the Dizoians. *Psychozoia* shows that, although he may be a stranger in a strange land, Gulliver is treading familiar ground. More's hero, old Memnon, recounting the story of his travels, comes to the land called Behiron (or Behirah, or Beirah), and is told: 'This same word *Behiron* doth signifie/ The brutish nature, or brutalitie' (II.49). Here he finds the 'swelling hatefull Toad', the 'Lascivious Goat', the 'All-imitating Ape', the 'crafty Fox', and the 'Majestick Horse' (II.136). The frog-like, goat-like, ape-like, fox-like Yahoos would be the natural inhabitants of such a place. Commentators have mentioned the influence of More's other writings on Swift. See, e.g., Phillip Harth, *Swift and Anglican Rationalism: The Religious Background of A Tale of a Tub* (Chicago and London: University of Chicago Press, 1969). Swift mentions More in *A Tale of a Tub*. Ernest Tuveson examines the Voyage to the Houyhnhnms in the light of More's *Divine Dialogues* (1668). Tuveson writes: 'I do not claim More as a "source", although Swift was interested in More's ideas, and had his works in his library. Rather, More serves as a valuable indication of what was in the air' ('Swift:

And so did Milton, who describes how, after seducing Eve and bringing about the Fall, Satan returns to Hell, where he and his followers find themselves changing into serpents:

> dreadful was the din
> Of hissing through the Hall, thick swarming now
> With complicated monsters, [...]
> [...]
> [...] but still greatest hee the midst,
> Now Dragon grown, larger then whom the Sun
> Ingenderd in the *Pythian* Vale on slime,
> Huge Python.   (*PL*, X.521–31)

Here the authors employ increasingly dark uses of the one idea. Spenser employs the conceit neutrally, merely to outline the natural process of birth, growth, death, decay, and new birth. Donne regards the slime as 'dirty' and begetting creatures which, although they may be part of the natural order, are yet 'strange'. More suggests that the process brings forth monsters and corruption out of corruption. Milton, drawing on Greek mythology, associates the slime-engendered serpent Python with the doubly-fallen serpent Satan – the embodiment of sin. Thus Swift's use of this traditional conceit would seem to imply the corrupt, monstrous and sinful nature of the Yahoos.

More than that, Swift shows that the contemptuous attitude of the Houyhnhnms towards the Yahoos is reflected in the belief which the Houyhnhnms hold about their own origins. Gulliver explains that the Houyhnhnms have no fear of death; and relates the incident of a Houyhnhnm matron whose visit to Gulliver's master is delayed by the death of her husband,

> Who, as she said, happened that very Morning to *Lhnuwnh*. The Word is strongly expressive in their Language, but not easily rendered into English; it signifies, *to retire to his first Mother* (240).

The Dean as Satirist', in *Swift: A Collection of Critical Essays*, ed. by Ernest Tuveson (Englewood Cliffs, N.J.: Prentice-Hall, 1964), pp. 101–10 (p. 103, n3)).

This is in keeping with the philosophy of the Roman poet Lucretius (c.98–c.55), who writes:

> It follows that with good reason the earth has gotten the name of mother, since all things have been produced out of the earth.[31]

And he goes on to be more specific and exclusive:

> Wherefore again and again I say the earth with good title has gotten and keeps the name of mother, since she of herself gave birth to mankind and at a time nearly fixed shed forth every beast that ranges wildly over the great mountains, and at the same time the fowls of the air with all their varied shapes.[32]

Creatures generated from slime and ooze are of a lower order in creation than creatures generated from the earth (and are usually unpleasant nuisances like flies and mosquitoes). Therefore if the slime tradition is correct, the gulf between the earth-born Houyhnhnms and the slime-born Yahoos is even deeper than their circumstances suggest. Which leads to the Houyhnhnms' second tradition:

> That the two *Yahoos* said to be first seen among them, had been driven thither over the Sea; that coming to Land, and being forsaken by their Companions, they retired to the Mountains, and degenerating by Degrees, became in Process of Time, much more savage than those of their own Species in the Country from whence these two Originals came (237).[33]

This tradition, in keeping with Swift's theme of degeneration, can also be seen as a short and miniature history of mankind since the Fall – Adam and Eve, cast out of Eden, begetting generation upon generation of children born in sin.

---

31   Lucretius, *On the Nature of Things*, trans. by H.A.J. Munro [1860] (London: Routledge; New York: Dutton [1907]), Bk V, lines 795–96 (p. 175).
32   Lucretius, Bk V, lines 821–25 (Munro, p. 176).
33   Not a nice reminder for Gulliver. Like the original Yahoos in this tradition, he has been driven thither over the sea and forsaken by his companions.

The Houyhnhnms have therefore narrowed the debate over the origins of the Yahoos down to two theories: one of which corresponds with the pagan theory of aquatic or marine origin; and one which corresponds with the Christian belief in ongoing degeneration as a result of the Fall.[34] At the time of Gulliver's arrival, the Houyhnhnms have no way of determining which is correct, because the latter explanation depends on knowledge acquired through revelation, which, of course, is not given to horses. But the debate is about to take a new turn.

In each of his former voyages Gulliver has encountered degenerate humans. In Lilliput 'the degenerate Nature of Man' (41) has produced the current political system; in Brobdingnag he reads a book whose theme is 'that Nature was degenerated in these latter declining Ages of the World' (112); and in Luggnagg he ponders 'that continual Degeneracy of human Nature, so justly complained of in all Ages' (180).[35]

And so it is in Houyhnhnmland. Gulliver's arrival, so similar to that of the two original Yahoos in the second tradition; his uncanny physical resemblance to the Yahoos, which he at first disguises by keeping his clothes on; his success in persuading his master that foreign Yahoos rule in their lands as the Houyhnhnms do in theirs; all this has convinced his master that the Yahoos are degenerate humans.[36] (But of course without the authority of revelation his conviction must remain provisional.)

The Yahoos therefore are not a separate anthropoid species, but a race of degenerate humans. But their degeneration is of a particular kind. In the first three voyages Swift deals with corruption and degeneration within the

---

34 Tuveson's essay examines the question of Original Sin.

35 For political and societal degeneration see Jeffrey Hart, 'The Ideologue as Artist: Some Notes on *Gulliver's Travels*', *Criticism*, 2 (1960), 125–33. For the corruption of human nature see Douglas J. Canfield, 'Corruption and Degeneration in *Gulliver's Travels*', *Notre Dame English Journal*, 9 (1973), 15–22. For gradual physical diminution see Dirk F. Passman, 'Degeneration in *Gulliver's Travels*: Excavations from Brobdingnag', *Swift Studies: The Annual of the Ehrenpreis Centre*, 1 (1986), 46–50.

36 Gulliver also leans towards this theory. In the first edition of the *Travels* he surmises that the two original Yahoos may have been English. This was deleted in the Faulkner edition.

convention of size – humanity is degenerating, therefore it is becoming smaller, less robust, less healthy, and so forth;[37] but, despite this constant falling off, the humans remain human. Soul is form and doth the body make, but the souls remain human, with all of their human vices and virtues, and continue to make for themselves recognizably human vehicles.

But the Yahoos are not immediately recognizable as humans. They have degenerated to the point where all the virtues have gone, and all that remain are the vices.[38] Reason and speech – the two defining human capacities – have also gone, and all that remains is the flesh, which has an inherent drive towards evil.[39] According to Roland Frye:

> The human body was traditionally understood to represent man's natural depravity; it is a logical representation of this tradition, therefore, that the Yahoo has 'a perfect *human* figure'. [Frye's italics] According to this view, the Yahoo would then represent those elements in his nature which man must distrust, and which, in Christian terms, he must seek to subdue. The Yahoo is that fleshly element in human nature which cannot be disavowed, which may in fact degrade man to the level of the brute beasts.[40]

Frye argues that not only do the Yahoos represent fallen man and the flesh, but that this particular flesh exists in a more degraded and polluted condition. Citing Leviticus, he shows that not only is the Yahoos' diet of carrion, asses, dogs, cats, weasels and rats unclean, but they themselves are unclean:

37   One can see the beginnings of this convention in the Old Testament: 'There were giants in the earth in those days; and also after that, when the sons of God came in unto the daughters of men, and they bare children to them, the same became mighty men which were of old, men of renown' (Genesis 6.4).

38   This is debatable: the females obviously care for their young; and when Gulliver picks up the infant Yahoo, others come running when it begins squalling (231–32).

39   'So then with the mind I myself serve the law of God; but with the flesh the law of sin' (Romans 7.25).

40   'Swift's Yahoo and the Christian Symbols for Sin', *Journal of the History of Ideas*, 15 (1954), 201–17 (p. 208).

Leviticus 11.27 declares unclean 'whatsoever goeth upon his paws, among all manner of beasts that go on all four, these are unclean to you [...]'. The connection is made much clearer by Bishop Simon Patrick's 1698 commentary on this text: '*Leviticus 11.27. [And whatsoever goeth upon his paws, etc.]* Hath feet with fingers like unto a hand; for so it is in the Hebrew, *Whatsoever goeth upon his hands:* Such as the Ape [...] etc. whose forefeet resemble hands.'[41]

But the Yahoos are more than simply apelike. Gulliver writes that, 'Their Shape was very singular, and deformed' (193). Frye notes:

The Yahoo may not only be related to Christian symbolism of the flesh, but may also be seen as embodying many of those elements of filth and deformity which are emblematic of sin throughout the Scriptures, beginning with the Levitical pollutions and carrying on far into the New Testament (210).

He follows this with several pages of persuasive examples, adding that:

The tradition here illustrated, a tradition which employed filth and deformity as symbolic of sin, was part of the intellectual climate in and before Swift's time (215).

And he concludes with:

What Swift has done is to appropriate ready-made symbols and a Christian rhetoric apt for his purposes (217).[42]

One would think, then, that Swift's readers would have taken the point. But many of them did not, to the extent that in 1784 Thomas Sheridan felt the need to provide a summary of Swift's intentions:

In your merely animal capacity, says [Swift] to man, without reason to guide you, and actuated only by blind instinct, I will show you that you would be degraded below the beasts of the field. That very form, that very body, you are now so proud of, as giving you such a superiority over all other animals, I will show you owe all their beauty, and all their greatest powers, to their being actuated by a rational soul. Let

---

41   Roland Frye, p. 216. The italics are Frye's. Whilst in Houyhnhnmland Gulliver occasionally eats rabbit – another unclean animal.

42   Not only was this Christian rhetoric apt for Swift's literary purposes, it was in harmony with his own obsessive interest in filth and excrement.

that be withdrawn, let the body be inhabited by the mind of a brute, let it be prone as theirs are, and suffered like theirs to take its natural course, without any assistance from art, you would in that case be the most deformed, as to your external appearance, the most detestable of all creatures.[43]

How does this deformity come about? Platonically it comes about because the body is the physical representation of the soul. An ugly, sinful soul produces an ugly, deformed body. Theologically it comes about because man is made in the image of God. Therefore, as man departs further from God in thought, word, and deed, so he also departs further from the image of God. Gulliver himself, being a fallen creature born in sin, is also prey to this latter malady.[44] After his Houyhnhnm master has seen him naked, he does not regard Gulliver as the norm from which the Yahoos have degenerated, but merely finds him 'not altogether so deformed' (209) as the Yahoos.

Although commentators have concentrated on the religious significance of the Yahoos, they have neglected their Platonic implications. As the Yahoos have departed further from the image of God, their souls have become more brutish, and consequently they have also begun to assume the characteristics of certain animals whose qualities they share. When Gulliver first sees them he observes that:

Their Heads and Breasts were covered with a thick Hair, some frizzled and others lank; they had Beards like Goats, and a long Ridge of Hair down their Backs, and the Fore Parts of their Legs and Feet; but the rest of their Bodies were bare, so that I might see their Skins, which were of a brown Buff Colour. They had no Tails, nor any Hair at all on their Buttocks, except about the *Anus;* which, I presume Nature had placed there to defend them as they sat on the Ground; for this Posture they used, as well as lying down, and often stood on their hind Feet. They climbed high

---

43   *The Works of the Rev. Dr Jonathan Swift, Dean of St Patrick's, Dublin*, ed. by Thomas
       Sheridan, 17 vols (London: Bathurst, Strahan, and others, 1784), I, *The Life of the
       Rev. Dr Jonathan Swift, Dean of St Patrick's, Dublin*, p. 508. See also *Swift: The
       Critical Heritage*, ed. by Kathleen Williams (London: Routledge & Kegan Paul,
       1970), p. 236. Thomas Sheridan (1719–88) was the son of Swift's friend Dr Thomas
       Sheridan (1687–1738).

44   Cf. Donne's deformity in 'Good Friday, 1613. Riding Westward'. See above, chap. 2,
       n64.

Trees, as nimbly as a Squirrel, for they had strong extended Claws before and behind, terminating in sharp Points, and hooked. They would often spring, and bound, and leap with prodigious Agility. The Females were not so large as the Males; they had long lank Hair on their Heads, and only a sort of Down on the rest of their Bodies, except about the *Anus*, and *Pudenda*. Their Dugs hung between their fore Feet, and often reached almost to the Ground as they walked.[45] The Hair of both Sexes was of several Colours, brown, red, black and yellow (193).

The Yahoos have grown hair like animals; they walk alternately on their legs or on all fours, in the manner of apes or monkeys. Ashley Montagu argues that Swift may have invoked Edward Tyson's description of the chimpanzee for such physical details as the colour of the Yahoos' skin, the lack of a tail, and the face. Tyson, a physician and anatomist, arrived at an important scientific conclusion. Montagu writes:

> In his *Orang-Outang* [1699] Tyson gave a detailed description of the anatomy of a juvenile chimpanzee together with an account of its habits. [...] While not regarding the creature as human [...] Tyson pointed out that a detailed study of its structure and habits showed it to be an animal, nay *the* animal which in the whole kingdom of animate Nature stood nearest to man, that in the Great Chain of Being it constituted a link between man and the lower animals.[46]

Swift, aware of Tyson's work, is thus incorporating the latest scientific discoveries in his description of the Yahoos. He is in fact describing a process of devolution, which places the Yahoos in the twilight zone between man and beast; but all that is left of the humanity is the vices.

Gulliver takes a close look at a Yahoo:

> My Horror and Astonishment are not to be described, when I observed, in this abominable Animal, a perfect human Figure; the Face of it indeed was flat and broad, the Nose depressed, the Lips large, and the Mouth wide: But these Differences are common to all savage Nations, where the Lineaments of the Countenance are distorted by the Natives suffering their Infants to lie grovelling on the Earth, or by carrying them on their Backs, nuzzling with their Face against the Mother's Shoulders (199).

45   Observed among Hottentot women when weeding. See Frantz, p. 54.
46   Ashley Montagu, 'Tyson's *Orang-Outang Sive Homo Sylvestris* and Swift's *Gulliver's Travels*', *PMLA*, 59 (1944), 84–89 (p. 85).

So successful is Swift in blurring the distinction between animal and human when describing the Yahoos, that, while Montagu likens them to apes:

> In fact the external characters of the Yahoos would seem to have been derived from the engraving of the Pygmie [i.e., chimpanzee] which appeared in Tyson's book;[47]

Frantz likens them to primitive humans:

> Nauseating descriptions of the depraved Hottentots, whose faces, like those of the Yahoos, were 'flat and broad, the Nose depressed, the Lips large, and the Mouth wide', appeared in print with striking frequency throughout the seventeenth and early eighteenth centuries.[48]

The Yahoos in some ways occupy the same position as that of the early men described by Lucretius. These early men were more robust, but lived as the other animals, without language, without tools, without arts, without clothing or shelter, without any kind of society, digging in the ground for food, hunting the other animals with stones and clubs, and living in fear of predators. Lucretius observes:

> And they were unable to look to the general weal and knew not how to make a common use of any customs or laws. Whatever prize fortune threw in his way, each man would bear off, trained at his own discretion to think of himself and live for himself alone.[49]

Shaftesbury – who refers to Lucretius in his *Characteristics* – in 'The Moralists' has Theocles refer to this stage of human development as,

> that which we suppose of man ere yet he entered into society, and became in truth a human creature. 'Twas the rough draught of man, the essay or first effort of Nature, a species in the birth, a kind as yet unformed; not in its natural state, but under violence, and still restless, till it attained its natural perfection (II, 79).

The Yahoos, however, have degenerated below this stage.

47   Montagu, p. 89.
48   Frantz, p. 53.
49   *On the Nature of Things*, Bk V, lines 958–61 (Munro, p. 180).

Not only are Yahoos physically ape-like, but their dominating character is ape-like. Swift drives this point home through his use of language. In one of his poems he writes:

> Thus think on Kings, ye Name denotes
> Hogs, Asses, Wolves, Baboons & Goats,
> To represent in figure just
> Sloth, Folly, Rapine, Mischief, Lust.[50]

In his poem Swift equates baboons with mischief. Likewise, one of the dominant characteristics of the Yahoos is mischief. Gulliver describes how a Yahoo approaches him and lifts up its paw, 'whether out of Curiosity or Mischief, I could not tell' (193). In each herd of Yahoos there is a dominant male who is 'always more *deformed* in Body, and *mischievous* in *Disposition*,

---

50 'On Poetry: A Rhapsody', *The Poems of Jonathan Swift*, ed. by Harold Williams, 2nd edn, 3 vols (Oxford: Clarendon Press, 1958), II, 659. It is worth placing these lines in their context, in which Swift is describing the true nature of kings:

> For in those [former] Ages Kings we find,
> Were Animals of human kind,
> [...]
> Thus all are destin'd to obey
> Some Beast of Burthen or of Prey
> Tis sung Prometheus forming Man
> Thro' all the brutal Species ran,
> Each proper Quality to find
> Adapted to a human Mind,
> A mingled Mass of Good & Bad,
> The worst & best that could be had
> Then from a Clay of Mixture base
> He shap'd a King to rule ye Race
> Endow'd with Gifts from every Brute
> That best ye regal Nature suit,
> Thus think on Kings, ye Name denotes
> Hogs, Asses, Wolves, Baboons, & Goats
> To represent in figure just
> Sloth, Folly, Rapine, Mischief, Lust.

Perhaps Prometheus had some clay left over, and made a Yahoo.

than any of the rest' (228). (Note how the deformity of the body worsens with the deformity of the character, even among the Yahoos themselves.) Gulliver's Houyhnhnm master declares that Yahoos have 'the strongest Disposition to Mischief' (203). And, 'It is observed,' writes Gulliver, 'that the *Red-haired* of both Sexes are more libidinous and mischievous than the rest' (232).

The Yahoos however are not merely ape-like in their tendency to mischief; they are the products of the Platonic 'mungrill transformation' described by Henry More, and exhibit characteristics of other animals mentioned by Swift in the passage quoted, as well as those of other unclean animals. In Swift's poem above, goats represent lust; and one of the first things Gulliver notices about the Yahoos is that they have 'Beards like Goats'. They climb trees 'as nimbly as a squirrel'. This commonplace is no mere figure of speech in this instance; the reason they can do so is because they have 'strong extended Claws before and behind, terminating in sharp Points, and hooked'. And the squirrel, according to Leviticus, is an unclean animal.

On another occasion when Gulliver is holding a Yahoo child – which he refers to as an 'odious Vermin' – he observes 'the young Animal's Flesh to smell very rank, and the stink [to be] somewhat between a *Weasel* and a *Fox*' (232). Both these animals are unclean. If the yahoos have come to smell like weasels, it is because their minds and bodies have taken on aspects of weasels and foxes; and indeed another of their major characteristics is their 'cunning' (232). Henry More writes of 'The Crafty Fox famous for subtilty'.[51] The Yahoos' delight in 'Rapine' (227) – associated by Swift with wolves – suggests that the long ridge of hair down their backs might be lupine in origin.

Gulliver also records a very significant talent of the Yahoos: 'They swim from their infancy like Frogs, and are able to continue long under Water, where they often take Fish, which the Females carry home to their young' (232). Again, Gulliver is recording not their swimming ability but the manner in which they swim. These strange crepuscular creatures, having

51   *Psychozoia*, II.136.5.

degenerated into a kind of ape with the characteristics of goats, wolves, and various vermin, are now in the process of moving back into the water. As has been mentioned, Swift subscribed to the story of Creation as it appears in the Bible; even so, one could feel justified in thinking that here Swift is hinting at the next phase in the inexorable decline of unregenerate man back into the primordial sea of the ancient Greek philosophers. Tragically, even as the Yahoos move back into the water, they remain unclean; according to Leviticus:

> And all that have not fins and scales in the seas, and in the rivers, of all that move in the waters, and of any living thing which is in the waters, they shall be an abomination unto you (11.10).

And of course the frog is another unclean animal.

Having established that Yahoos like to frolic in the water, Gulliver, adding a deliberately linking 'And upon this occasion', passes on immediately to relate the incident in which a Yahoo maiden, inflamed with desire for the body of a naked Englishman (surely Swift's most ironic moment), jumps on Gulliver as he is bathing in a river. Gulliver writes:

> This was a Matter of Diversion to my Master and his Family, as well as of Mortification to my self. For now I could no longer deny, that I was a real *Yahoo*, in every Limb and Feature, since the Females had a natural Propensity to me as one of their own Species; Neither was the Hair of this Brute of a Red Colour, (which might have been some Excuse for an Appetite a little irregular) but black as a Sloe, and her Countenance did not make an Appearance altogether so hideous as the rest of the Kind; for, I think, she could not have been above Eleven Years old (233).

The first item to deal with in this Nabokovian moment is the Yahoo's age; she is not as hideous as the rest of the herd because she is young. From this we learn that, in keeping with Platonic principles, not only are the Yahoos born deformed in keeping with their brutish souls, but the depraved lives that they lead render them increasingly ugly as they age and their load of sin accumulates.

The second item is Gulliver's final acceptance that he is a Yahoo, because the females (how many have there been?) desire him as one of their own species. This argument simply will not do. In the episode with the Brobdingnagian monkey, he reports that it holds him 'as a Nurse doth a Child she is going to suckle; [...] like a Baby in one of his Fore-Paws, and feeding me with the other, [...] and patting me when I would not eat' (98–99). And he writes, 'I have good Reason to believe that he took me for a young one of his own Species' (98).[52]

Where is the difference? The maternal monkey and the libidinous Yahoo maiden both take him for one of their own species; yet at no stage does it occur to him to think of himself as a monkey. The reason which Gulliver gives is therefore not the real reason for his mental surrender. The real reason demands an admission which he is unable to make: deep down, some part of him is attracted to her. He writes: 'her Countenance did not make an Appearance altogether so hideous as the rest of the Kind', which is a back-hand way of saying that he finds her somewhat good looking. And there is one curious omission from his narrative. He writes: 'She embraced me after a most fulsome Manner' (233). But he does not mention that she smelt. He reports that the maids of honour in Brobdingnag give off 'a very offensive Smell' (95); that the infant Yahoo smells 'very rank' (232); and he relates his master's observation,

> that a Female-*Yahoo* would often stand behind a Bank or a Bush, to gaze on the young Males passing by, [...] at which time it was observed, that she had a most *offensive Smell* (230).

Likewise Gulliver's paramour is introduced 'standing behind a Bank', from where she watches while, as Gulliver writes, as though describing a scene from a pastoral romance, 'I [...] stripped myself stark naked, and went down softly into the Stream' (232). The circumstances are virtually identical; yet she has no smell. Gulliver's own family, however, smell so bad when he returns to England that he cannot bear them to be near him.

52   The ape was traditionally fond of babies, and was represented pictorially abducting them from their cradles. See Janson, pp. 173–74.

Gulliver describes the attack by the Brobdingnagian monkey as, 'the greatest Danger I ever underwent in that Kingdom' (97). He is carried to the top of a roof, 'five Hundred Yards from the Ground, expecting every Moment to be blown down by the Wind' (99). In Glubbdubdrib he is surrounded by ghosts who make his 'Flesh creep with a Horror [he] cannot express' (166). He has been pursued by giants, shipwrecked, attacked by pirates, abandoned at sea; and yet, when he finds himself in the amorous embrace of a juvenile female Yahoo who intends him no harm, he reports that, 'I was never in my Life so terribly frighted' (233).

This is not Gulliver's first close encounter with the fair sex in the course of his travels. In Lilliput he and the Treasurer's wife, Mrs Flimnap, become the subject of court gossip. Gulliver is at great pains in his memoirs to deny any impropriety in their relationship; and explains in minute detail that never on any occasion were they alone together. What he does *not* address is the rumour that 'her Grace had taken a violent Affection for [his] Person' (45). How, then, one may ask, does Mrs Flimnap differ from the Yahoo maiden? And why, then, does Gulliver not assume that he is a Lilliputian?

In Brobdingnag the encounter is much closer. The Queen's maids of honour

> Would often strip me naked from Top to Toe, and lay me at full Length in their Bosoms [...].
> [...] They would strip themselves to the Skin, and put on their Smocks in my Presence, while I was placed on their Toylet directly before their naked Bodies [...]. The handsomest among these Maids of Honour, a pleasant frolicksome Girl of sixteen, would sometimes set me astride upon one of her Nipples (95–96).

Of the bodies of these maids of honour, Gulliver writes that he 'was much disgusted; because, to say the Truth, a very offensive Smell came from their Skins' (95); and that the scene was, 'very far from being a tempting Sight, or from giving me any other Motions than those of Horror and Disgust' (95). Meanwhile, of the female Yahoo, all he can say is that her hair is as black as a sloe, and by Yahoo standards she is a beauty. Of the antics of the frolicksome maids of honour, Gulliver righteously declares: 'I was so much displeased, that I entreated *Glumdalclitch* to contrive some Excuse for not seeing that young Lady any more' (96). However, this righteousness develops a hollow ring when we look more closely at this sequence. Gulliver writes:

> The Maids of Honour *often* [my emphasis] invited *Glumdalclitch* to their Apartments, and desired she would bring me along with her, *on Purpose to have the Pleasure of seeing and touching me* [my emphasis]. They would *often* [my emphasis] strip me naked from Top to Toe [...].
>
> [...] The handsomest among these Maids of Honour, a pleasant frolicksome Girl of sixteen, would *sometimes* [my emphasis] set me astride one of her Nipples (95–96).

He seems to have borne this particular cross for quite a length of time.

Commentators are greatly amused by Gulliver's lengthy chivalric defence of Mrs Flimnap's honour, given that the size difference renders any sort of physical liaison between them impossible. But does it? Gulliver adds an intriguing detail about the frolicksome maid of honour: she would

> sometimes set me astride one of her Nipples; *with many other Tricks, wherein the Reader will excuse me for not being over particular* (96). [my emphasis]

Gulliver may well be able to return home to his wife, the patient Mrs Mary Burton, and solemnly declare, 'I did not have sex with that woman'; but one cannot help thinking that the distinction could well be uncomfortably nice.

Be that as it may, the embrace of the sloe-haired nymph provides the first opportunity – or threat – for Gulliver to have a sexual encounter which could be consummated. *This* is why he is 'so terribly frighted' (233). And of course he declines the offer. Had he succumbed, he would have been sinning; but which sin would he have committed? Would he have offended against Exodus 20.14 – 'Thou shalt not commit adultery' – or against Leviticus 18.25 – 'Neither shalt thou lie with any beast to defile thyself therewith'? In Gulliver's mind it is surely the latter. And the thought haunts him. He writes that, upon his eventual return home:

> My Wife and Family received me with great Surprise and Joy, because they concluded
> me certainly dead;[53] but I must freely confess, the Sight of them filled me only with
> Hatred, Disgust and Contempt; and the more, by reflecting on the near Alliance I
> had to them. [...] And when I began to consider, that by copulating with one of the
> *Yahoo*-Species, I had become a Parent of more; it struck me with the utmost Shame,
> Confusion and Horror (253–54).

Past and present, human and Yahoo merge, as Gulliver's hapless wife re-
enacts the scene in the river in Houyhnhnmland:

> As soon as I entered the House, my Wife took me in her Arms, and kissed me; at
> which, not being used to the Touch of that odious Animal for so many Years, I fell
> in a Swoon for almost an Hour (254).

Gulliver's callous reminiscence (recollected five years after the event)
becomes more callous by the use of the term 'odious animal', which he
has used formerly to describe the Yahoos. It becomes even more callous,
and equally ironic, when we consider the context:

> I expressed my Uneasiness at [my master's] giving me so often the Appellation of
> *Yahoo*, an odious Animal, for which I had so utter an Hatred and Contempt (205).

Gulliver prepares to live out the remainder of his life by purchasing a
couple of horses, with whom he sits in his stable. 'My horses understand
me tolerably well', he writes; 'I converse with them at least four Hours
every Day' (254).[54] But the members of his family do not fare so well. He
will not let any of them take him by the hand; and five years elapse before
he will allow his wife to sit at the dinner table with him – at the far end.
What has brought a once normal man to this pass?

---

53   Which, in a way, he is.
54   Gulliver here is not simply deluding himself, but has also forgotten his Bible (and
     possibly Donne's sermon as well). The Psalmist writes: 'Be ye not as the horse, or as
     the mule, which have no understanding' (Psalm 32.9). James Wilson lists this among
     several biblical passages which may have been on Swift's mind during the writing
     of the Fourth Voyage. See 'Swift, the Psalmist, and the Horse', *Tennessee Studies in
     Literature*, 3 (1958), 17–23. Wilson makes no mention of Donne's sermon.

In Brobdingnag Gulliver's self-image collapses under the onslaught of the giants' contemptuous attitude towards him because of his size. In Houyhnhnmland the pressure is more pernicious – here the pressure is aimed at his character. After giving his master an account of European civilization, Gulliver writes:

> The Reader may be disposed to wonder how I could prevail on my self to give so free a Representation of my own Species, among a Race of Mortals who were already too apt to conceive the vilest Opinion of Human Kind, from that entire congruity betwixt me and their *Yahoos*. But I must freely confess, that the many Virtues of those excellent *Quadrupeds* placed in opposite View to human Corruptions, had so far opened my Eyes, and enlarged my Understanding, that I began to view the Actions and Passions of Man in a very different Light; and to think the Honour of my own Kind not worth managing; which, besides, it was impossible for me to do before a Person[55] of so acute a Judgment as my Master, *who daily convinced me of a thousand Faults in my self, whereof I had not the least Perception before* [my emphasis], and which with us would never be numbered even among human Infirmities (224).

Just as in Brobdingnag Gulliver had become unable to endure the sight of himself in a mirror, now:

> When I happened to behold the Reflection of my own Form in a Lake or Fountain, I turned away my Face in Horror and detestation of my self; and could better endure the Sight of a common *Yahoo*, than of my own Person (243).

Why should the sight of a common Yahoo be preferable? It is because Gulliver is in the process of redefining himself to his own advantage. In Brobdingnag he had felt respect for the Brobdingnagians. In Houyhnhnmland he feels much more:

> I admired the Strength, Comeliness and Speed of the Inhabitants; and such a Constellation of Virtues in such amiable Persons produced in me the highest Veneration (243).

---

55   Gulliver is beginning to regard the Houyhnhnms as the true humans. Later he refers to them as 'people' (240), and 'persons' (243).

In Brobdingnag he could not wait to return home to his family, because finally he was fed up with the Brobdingnagians' attitude towards him, and what he came to regard as their insularity and parochialism. But in Houyhnhnmland he has grown to worship the Houyhnhnms. Therefore:

> When I thought of my Family, my Friends, my Countrymen, or human Race in general, I considered them as they *really* [my emphasis] were, Yahoos in Shape and Disposition, perhaps a little more civilized, and qualified with the Gift of Speech; but making no other use of Reason, than to improve and multiply those Vices, whereof their Brethren in this Country had only the Share that Nature allotted them (243).

In this passage Gulliver is parroting, almost verbatim, the words of his equine master. And that is not all:

> By conversing with the *Houyhnhnms*, and looking upon them with Delight, I fell to imitate their Gait and Gesture, which is now grown into a Habit; and my Friends often tell me in a blunt Way, that *I trot like a Horse*;[56] which, however, I take for a great Compliment: Neither shall I disown, that in speaking I am apt to fall into the Voice and manner of the *Houyhnhnms*, and hear myself ridiculed on that Account without the least Mortification (243–44).

Gulliver has decided to define himself as a species with a representative of one. He has determined to divorce himself as much as possible from the human race. The Yahoos are anthropoids without reason; the Europeans are anthropoids with a tincture of reason which debases them even further. Gulliver cannot help being an anthropoid with a tincture of reason, but he will be one who walks and talks like a Houyhnhnm; and one whose reason is properly directed:

> I had not been a Year in this Country, before I contracted such a Love and Veneration for the Inhabitants, that I entered on a firm Resolution never to return to human Kind, but to pass the rest of my Life among these admirable Houyhnhnms in the Contemplation and Practice of every Virtue; where I could have no Example or Incitement to Vice (224–25).

56   A slip on Swift's part. At the time of writing, Gulliver is too misanthropic to have any friends.

This sounds a worthy ambition; but the reason for Gulliver's resolution is less worthy:

> At first, indeed, I did not feel that natural Awe which the *Yahoos* and all other Animals bear towards them; but it grew upon me by Degrees, much sooner than I imagined, and was mingled with a respectful Love and Gratitude, *that they would condescend to distinguish me from the rest of my Species* (243). [my emphasis]

Gulliver's master refers to him as 'a certain wonderful *Yahoo*' (237); and describes how:

> He observed in me all the Qualities of a *Yahoo*, only a little more civilized by some Tincture of Reason; which however was in a Degree as far inferior to the *Houyhnhnm* Race, as the *Yahoos* of their Country were to me (238).

Gulliver therefore finds himself in a unique position in Houyhnhnmland – he is on the side of the angels. As long as he stays there he is above all the other Yahoos (his fellow Europeans would debase his newly minted coinage).

Gulliver reveres the Houyhnhnms, but their reason cannot comprehend his true nature, and, fearful lest he may turn feral and employ his reason to incite a Yahoo uprising, they expel him. A party of them come down to the shore to see him off, 'out of Curiosity, and perhaps [...] partly out of Kindness' (247). They watch the beginning of 'this desperate Voyage' (247) with equanimity, all except Gulliver's companion the Sorrel Nag who, being of the servant caste and therefore with a less perfectly developed faculty of reason, continues to call after him, '*Hnuy illa nyha maiah Yahoo*, Take Care of thy self, gentle *Yahoo*' (248).

When Gulliver is forced to leave Houyhnhnmland his world falls apart; he has invested too much in his new identity, and his mind is now set on that course. In the land of the Houyhnhnms, humans had merely been a potential threat to his uniqueness. Now they become a reality. His only method of coping is to stop regarding himself as a Yahoo (albeit an ennobled one), and instead to begin regarding himself as an honorary Houyhnhnm. He turns all of his disappointment and frustration on those whose existence unwittingly reminds him constantly of both the standing which he has lost and his own appalling origins. But in the end he remains unique – walking and talking like a horse, and sitting for hours on end happily chattering on to his two uncomprehending stallions. And in the end he is not only unique, but maintains his superiority over all the English Yahoos:

> I write for the noblest End, to inform and instruct Mankind, over whom I may, without Breach of Modesty, pretend to some Superiority, from the Advantages I received by conversing so long among the most accomplished *Houyhnhnms* (257).

Gulliver feels that he has risen above his condition by his long and fruitful association with the noble Houyhnhnms. But a couple of lines from Donne's sermon may help to put Gulliver's boast in perspective. Donne writes, 'Descend not to the qualities of the Horse and the Mule.'[57] And what is the quality of the horse which Donne singles out for condemnation? Donne writes:

> Here we may contract it best, if we understand Pride by the Horse, and Lust by the Mule; [...] Though both sins, pride and lust, might be taxed in the horse, yet pride is proper to him.[58]

And he goes on to make a point that is applicable to both Gulliver and Henry Jekyll:

> It is not much controverted in the Schooles, but that the first sin of the Angels was Pride. But because (as we said before) the danger of man is more in sinking down, then in climbing up, in dejecting, then in raising himselfe, we must therefore remember, that it is not pride, to desire to be better. [...] The Angels sin was pride; but their pride consisted not in aspiring to the best degrees that their nature was capable of: but in this, that they would come to that state, by other meanes then were ordained for it.[59]

Gulliver, then, foolishly thinking that he has been acquiring reason from the Houyhnhnms, reveals in the end that he has simply acquired their pride.

---

57   *Sermons*, IX, 375.
58   *Sermons*, IX, 377.
59   *Sermons*, IX, 377–78.

In some ways Gulliver's predicament in Houyhnhnmland is not unlike that faced by Jekyll. Gulliver and Jekyll both partake in mankind's dual nature; whereas the Yahoos are pure beast and Hyde is pure evil. Gulliver is confronted by living examples of two conditions – the life of brute sensation, and the life of detached reason. He distances himself from the former, and attempts – without success – to embrace the latter. But of course, while sharing aspects of both, he conforms absolutely to neither. Likewise Jekyll attempts to 'dissociate' the 'unjust' from the 'upright' (82), naively expecting that he will be left with an uncontaminated higher self. Both are deluded. In the end Gulliver walks like a Houyhnhnm and talks like a Houyhnhnm, but he knows that with his clothes off he still looks like a Yahoo. And in the end Jekyll not only fails to separate himself from Hyde, but becomes him.

Were the Yahoos an influence on Stevenson's conception of Hyde? Even if (as seems unlikely) Stevenson had not read *Gulliver's Travels*, and even if (as seems even more unlikely) he had never heard of the Yahoos, he was influenced by the religious, philosophical, and literary conventions from which they sprang. They are hairy; Hyde is hairy. They are ape-like; Hyde is ape-like. They chatter; Hyde chatters. They are deformed in an unspecified way; Hyde is deformed in an unspecified way. They are creatures entirely given over to the lower passions; so is Hyde. Gulliver detests them on sight; people detest Hyde on sight. The vices which produce the Yahoos over many generations break forth all at once in the same degraded form, as Hyde. Swift's conceit, derived from the Greeks, absorbed by the Church, broadcast from the pulpit in his day, justified and enlarged upon by his supporters and generations of interpreters, finds re-affirmation in the words of one of Stevenson's literary heroes, Sir Walter Scott – words which could equally epitomize the thesis of *Jekyll and Hyde*:

> The picture of the Yahoos, utterly odious and hateful as it is, presents to the reader a moral use. It was never designed as a representation of mankind in the state to which religion, and even the lights of nature, encourage men to aspire, but of that to which our species is degraded by the wilful subservience of mental qualities to animal instincts, of man, such as he may be found in the degraded ranks of every society, when brutalized by ignorance and gross vice. In this view, the more coarse and disgusting the picture, the more impressive is the moral to be derived from it,

since, in proportion as an individual indulges in sensuality, cruelty, or avarice, he approaches in resemblance to the detested Yahoo.[60]

What, then, are the Yahoos? Their ugliness and deformity is an outward expression of their foul souls, within both Platonic philosophy and Christian doctrine. But where do they stand in the scheme of things? On the Great Chain of Being they could stand between man and the apes; or just below the apes and just above the quadrupeds; or somewhere between land animals and water creatures. But how did they arrive at any of these points? Did they evolve according to heathen natural philosophy, or did they fall according to the word of God in the Bible? After debating the issue Swift of course makes it clear that they are in fact degenerate humans, and that they are incapable of improvement. With the Yahoos Swift shows that being ape-like and deformed is the outward expression of moral and spiritual delinquency, that it occurs within a traditional religious framework, and in itself implies nothing about mankind's origins. The existence of such a notion clearly has implications for the proposed reading of *Jekyll and Hyde*.

60   Walter Scott, *The Works of Jonathan Swift, D.D.*, 19 vols (Edinburgh: Constable, 1814), I, 337–38.

PART TWO

The Wild Man Tradition

CHAPTER FOUR

The Wild Man, the Noble Savage, and the Child of Nature

The Wild Man

The discussion of the Yahoos in the previous chapter could well have mentioned an important tradition to which they belong – the tradition of the Wild Man; but this rich and long-lasting tradition is so large and complicated that it requires a chapter of its own. The present chapter therefore serves as both an elaboration on the previous chapter, and an introduction to the following chapter on the evolutionary theories of Lord Monboddo and their employment in Thomas Love Peacock's *Melincourt*. And of course it introduces another important element for an understanding of both Edward Hyde – who is, among other things, a Wild Man – and Olalla, who is a Child of Nature.

Just as the present chapter provides an elaboration on the previous one, likewise the previous chapter anticipates this. Maximillian Novak writes:

> Probably the most important work connected with the various transmutations of the Wild Man is *Gulliver's Travels*. Even before we come upon the Yahoos, we find, in the materials associated with the Wild Man, numerous works from which Swift might have taken hints, from the men so small that they could be carried about in cages to the tales of wild men and their encounters with giants. But it is particularly when we meet the Yahoos in the fourth part that we encounter a version of the Wild Man myth.[1]

---

1   'The Wild Man Comes to Tea', in *The Wild Man Within: An Image in Western Thought from the Renaissance to Romanticism*, ed. by Edward Dudley and Maximillian E. Novak ([Pittsburgh]: University of Pittsburgh Press, 1972), pp. 183–221 (pp. 211–12).

Swift does not refer to the Yahoos as Wild Men, but they obviously fit within the Wild Man tradition. Take, for example, the following quotation from Richard Bernheimer about the Wild Man, and judge whether it does not apply equally to the Yahoo:

> The wild man holds thus a curiously ambiguous and ill-defined position in God's creation, being neither quite man enough to command universal agreement as to his human identity, nor animal enough to be universally classified as such.[2]

While Bernheimer makes no mention of Yahoos, Novak outlines the correspondences between the Yahoos and Wild Men; and he draws on some very familiar material with which to do so:

> In so many ways they represent what was reported of orangutans and sometimes of the Hottentot. Like Tyson's orangutan, they are capable of going on their hind legs, though they generally travel on all fours; like the traditional Wild Man, they are hairy. The female Yahoo who attacks Gulliver resembles those lascivious male anthropoids who were so fond of women, and the long dugs of the females that hang down to the ground recall the Hottentot women who would throw their breasts over their shoulders to feed their children. As was sometimes reported of the Hottentots, the Yahoos are incapable of language and merely howl, grin, or chatter (212).

This passage contains the same bewildering confusion of comparisons which were examined in the previous chapter: the Yahoos are likened with equal justification to both apes and Hottentots – and now, again with equal justification, to Wild Men as well. To add to the confusion, Bernheimer notes that pendulous breasts are also typical of Wild Women (33); and although Novak says that Hottentots grin and chatter (212), grinning and chattering – as was pointed out in the previous chapter – are traditional descriptions of monkey- and ape-behaviour; so in employing these terms travellers are likening Hottentots to apes and monkeys, in the same way that Swift likens the Yahoos to apes and monkeys.

---

2   *Wild Men in the Middle Ages: A Study in Art, Sentiment, and Demonology* (New York: Octagon, 1970), p. 6. I am indebted to this work for the following information on Wild Men. Further references are given after quotations in the text.

The gradual devolution of the Yahoos into their present brutish appearance was not without precedents, even, apparently, in real life. The sixteenth-century Peruvian writer Garcilaso de la Vega told of one Pedro Serrano who, shipwrecked on an island for seven years, grew hair all over his body, which he exhibited upon his return to civilization.[3]

As Bernheimer writes, the Yahoos conform to the mediaeval attitude that:

> God had not created the wild man in his present lowly estate. Instead, the creature had been brought to its condition by loss of mind, by upbringing among beasts, or by outrageous hardships, all conditions which tended to depress man to something less than human. The status of the wild man was thus reached not by a gradual ascent from the brute, but by a descent (8).

The Yahoos resemble the Wild Man physically, and have arrived at their condition through a descent from a former state; but there the similarity ends. Bernheimer continues:

> We find therefore that instead of explaining the existence of the wild man on theological grounds, medieval writers preferred to think of him psychologically and sociologically.
> [...] Wildness in human beings was thus due to degeneration caused by extraneous circumstances and therefore was morally irrelevant and without theological implications (8).

This is not the case with the Yahoos. By their own actions they brought corruption upon themselves over the course of generations. Swift therefore presents his readers with the paradox that the Yahoos sink to the level of beasts as a result not of a developing tendency towards beastliness, but of the continuing and constant expression of their human qualities. Their physical condition reflects their moral condition, not only in their brutishness, but also in the illnesses which plague them chronically, and which are unknown to the robust Wild Man.

---

3   This story is mentioned in Bernheimer, p. 93; and given in greater detail by Stanley L. Robe, 'Wild Men and Spain's Brave New World', in Dudley and Novak, *The Wild Man Within*, pp. 39–53 (pp. 51–52).

What is a Wild Man? They come in all shapes and sizes, from solitary mossy half-wooden giants rampaging through forests, to communities of dwarfs bathing, cleaning, and throwing banquets in caverns under
mountains. But through the entire range between these extremes we find
a consistency of attributes. Bernheimer gives us a few pointers on what to
look for in the breed:

> [I]t is a hairy man curiously compounded of human and animal traits, without,
> however, sinking to the level of an ape. It exhibits upon its naked human anatomy a
> growth of fur, leaving bare only its face, feet, and hands, at times its knees and elbows,
> or the breasts of the female of the species. Frequently the creature is shown wield-
> ing a heavy club or mace, or the trunk of a tree; and, since its body is usually naked
> except for a shaggy covering, it may hide its nudity under a strand of twisted foli-
> age worn around the loins. Where any characteristics other than these appear, there
> is a possibility that instead of a wild man we may be beholding another imaginary
> figure such as a devil, faun, or satyr. The creature itself may appear without its fur,
> its club, or its loin ornament. Any one of its characteristics may be said to designate
> the species (1–2).

In many instances he also lacks the power of speech.[4]
    Arthur Dickson offers more detail:

> [H]is prototype in the main is the wood-spirit of popular belief. This creature, as
> modern folklore knows him, lives in the forest depths; has a hairy body, or green
> clothing; is frequently of great physical strength; sometimes carries an uprooted
> tree as a club; is sometimes reputed to attack the unwary passer, particularly the
> women and children; but sometimes, too, is captured, tamed, and taught to render
> useful service.
>   [...]
>   To sum up: the Wild Man of medieval romance is a composite of many elements,
> chief of which are the wood-spirit of popular belief and custom, of art and pageantry;
> the eccentric recluse of actual life; and the märchen hero who owes his extraordi-
> nary strength to his animal birth or upbringing. In medieval story, he makes travel
> dangerous in the forest, or (rarely) shows himself helpful; is frequently sought and
> captured; and occasionally becomes a member of human society.[5]

4   Bernheimer, pp. 9; 11.
5   *Valentine and Orson: A Study in Late Medieval Romance* (New York: Columbia
     University Press, 1929; repr. AMS Press, 1975), pp. 114; 124. (Hereafter, Dickson.)

The Wild Man tradition is extremely ancient – dating back to at least the third millennium BC. In the Sumerian epic of Gilgamesh we find the Wild Man Enkidu, formed from clay by the goddess of creation Aruru:

> His body was rough, he had long hair like a woman's; it waved like the hair of Nisaba, the goddess of corn. His body was covered with matted hair like Samuqan's, the god of cattle. He was innocent of mankind; he knew nothing of the cultivated land.
>
> Enkidu ate grass in the hills with the gazelle and lurked with wild beasts at the water-holes; he had joy of the water with the herds of wild game. [A trapper tells his father,] 'He fills in the pits which I dig and tears up my traps set for the game; he helps the beasts to escape and now they slip through my fingers.'[6]

Enkidu is a natural Wild Man, that is, he has lived all his life in the wild, and away from civilization.

During the Classical Greek period travellers brought back stories of encounters with barbarous tribes who had long hair, dressed in the skins of animals, and whose speech seemed to be no more than a series of howls and grunts. Herodotus reports such peoples in Libya;[7] but an even more fruitful territory was India. Alexander the Great's adventure into that land brought back tales of giants, cannibals, and men with ears big enough to curl up and sleep in – of whom more later. Equally bizarre, but probably accurate, were descriptions of extremely hairy wild men, who, although they were hairy and wild, were definitely not men. Bernheimer writes:

> According to Pliny there existed in India a race of so-called Choromandi named *silvestres*, that is wild, creatures possessed of hairy bodies, yellow eyes, and canine teeth, who were incapable of speech and could let out only horrible shrieks. These creatures may not have been altogether fabulous, since their description fits a large monkey such as the eastern gibbon. It seems to be generally true that whatever little was known in antiquity about the large anthropoid apes did not suffice to identify them as animals, so that they were usually described as hairy, speechless humans and thus, by implication, as wild men (87).

---

6   *The Epic of Gilgamesh*, English version and intro. by N.K. Sandars (Harmondsworth: Penguin, 1972; repr. 1975), p. 63.

7   Bernheimer, p. 86.

This centuries-old confusion and uncertainty doubtless led to the tradition – which continued well into the later nineteenth century – of the ape carrying the Wild Man's club. Thus, by association, one of the defining characteristics of the Wild Man became incorporated into the stock image of the ape. This traditional weapon appears as the stick, bat or club wielded by the Ape in *Mother Hubberd*, the 'orang-outang' of Tyson and the seventeenth-century travellers, and the natural man or 'orang-outang' of Lord Monboddo and Thomas Love Peacock's *Melincourt*, as well as other nineteenth-century representations of apes.

Moving along several centuries we come to the fifteenth-century romance *Valentine and Orson*. This work has a rich ancestry, and has left an almost equally rich posterity. Arthur Dickson writes that this French romance (in which King Arthur of Britain is beheaded),

> was composed between 1475 and 1489, and based upon a lost fourteenth-century French poem, of which there are several versions in other languages [...]; and that the stories of both the older poem and the later prose, based originally (I believe) on a folk tale, are amplified by additions from the most widely various sources—*chansons de geste*, romances, saints' lives, chronicles, popular traditions, and contemporary events—so that the whole forms a sort of compendium of many of the most popular elements of chivalric fiction, and the study of its sources throws light on the history of many common romance and folk-lore motifs.[8]

Valentine and Orson are the twin sons of the Emperor Alexander of Greece, born in a forest to the Emperor's falsely accused and wrongfully exiled wife, Bellisant. Orson is immediately taken by a bear and carried away in its jaws. Bellisant, leaving Valentine, crawls after the bear, but falls in a swoon. Meanwhile her brother, King Peppin of France, on his way to Constantinople to see her, comes across Valentine lying alone, and, assuming him to be abandoned, instructs one of his squires to raise him in Paris, where he grows up to be a handsome and valiant knight. Orson

---

8   *Valentine and Orson*, trans. by Henry Watson [1503–05?], ed. and intro. by Arthur Dickson (London: Oxford University Press, 1937; repr., New York: Kraus, 1971), pp. ix–x. (Hereafter, *V and O*.) Further references to this edition are given after quotations in the text.

in his own way fares just as well. The bear's cubs, instead of eating him, play with him, whereupon the bear's maternal instincts take over, and she suckles him for a year. Orson grows up exhibiting the characteristics of a fierce Wild Man:

> The chylde was all roughe because of the neutrifaction of the beer, as a wilde beest. So he began to go in the woode, and became great *with*in a while and began for to smyte the other beastes of the forest, in suche wyse that they all douted hym, and fledde before him. For he fered nothyng in the worlde. In suche estate was the chylde ledyng a beastes lyfe *the* space of .xv. yeare. He became so great and strong, that none durste passe through the forest for hym, for bothe men and beastes he put vnto death, and eate their flesh al raw as the other beastes did, and liued a beastual life and not humayne. He was called Orson because of the beere that had nouryshed hym, and he was also rough as a beere. He dyd so muche harme in the forest, and was so sore redoubted, that there was none, were he neuer so valiau*n*t and hardy, but that he had great fere to encountre the wylde man. The renowne sprange so of hym, that all they of the countrey aboute chaced and hunted him with force of strength, but nothyng auaylled all their deade, for he fered neyther gynnes nor weapons, but brake al in peces. Now he is in the forest ledang [*sic*] the life of a wilde beast, without wering of any cloth, or any worde speaking (*V and O*, p. 38).[9]

Apart from all this, he is able to outrun a horse (86), and he also indulges in the traditional Wild Man behaviour of abduction and rape (64);[10] although – as both history and *Melincourt* demonstrate – this behaviour could equally well derive from his noble blood.

Valentine comes into the wood to fight with and capture Orson. During the encounter Orson displays typical Wild Man behaviour, and employs his traditional weapon:

> [Valentine] went towarde Orson with his sworde for to haue smyten him, but Orson lepte a back and went to a lyttel tree, the which tree he bowed and bracke it, and made thereof an horryble staffe, and after came vnto Valentyne and gaue him suche a strooke *that* he made hym for to fall vpon one knee (69).

9   The italics are Dickson's.
10   See Bernheimer, chap. 5.

Bernheimer writes:

> The tree torn out by its roots [...] appears in artistic representations such as [...]
> some of the tapestries of the fifteenth century from the area of the upper Rhine. In
> carnival disguises such as those of Nuremberg and Basel the mummers were often
> required to carry a little tree; and even where the artist made the wild man carry
> a club or mace, instead of the tree out of which it was fashioned, the weapon was
> given a buckled and twisted shape to make sure that its origin from wood uprooted
> and coarsely hewn be well understood (26).

Later, when Orson has been partly tamed by Valentine but not yet
civilized, he is called upon to joust with the Green Knight (by virtue of his
green armour, another Wild Man) for the honour of the Lady Fezonne,
daughter of the Duke of Aquitaine. His choice of weapon is a 'grete clubbe
of wodde' (112). Valentine persuades him to arm himself and fight like a
knight; but these weapons are of no use against the Green Knight, and
Orson finally overcomes him with brute strength.

Fezonne's reaction to the sight of Orson reveals that, although by his
upbringing he has become a Wild Man, his blood is noble and his soul is
pure. When Valentine presents him to Fezonne, she asks:

> But tell me I praye you wherefore you clothe not this valyaunt man no better than
> you haue brought to me. For he is marueylusly well made of his membres, and well
> formed, streight and hardy of countenaunce, & I beleue that & he were bayned in a
> hoote house, his flesshe woulde be whyte and softe (101).

And immediately she is 'stryken at the harte more ardauntly then euer she
was before of any other' (101).

Orson quickly adapts to the knightly life, becomes – following a minor
operation to his tongue – able to speak, and in time succeeds to the throne
of his father the Emperor of Greece; but following the death of his wife
he retreats to a forest again, living the life of a hermit and, in an almost
ironic blending of lifestyles, exists on a diet which belongs to both hermit
and Wild Man:

> Orson made great sorow[.] And after the deeth of her he ete but brede and rotes, and
> small froytes that he founde in the wodde where as he dyd remayne (326).

Orson remained a popular figure in literature, theatre and pageantry until the early part of the twentieth century. This work influenced Spenser, Shakespeare, Cervantes and Bunyan; and was an influence – both directly, and indirectly via Spenser – on Thomas Love Peacock. Dickson writes:

> Sir Philip Sidney referred to it [the story of Valentine and Orson] as to something well known; it was the subject of at least one lost Elizabethan play; 'Orson', to the seventeenth century, was almost synonymous with 'wild man'; Uncle Toby, no less than Old Scrooge, delighted in the story as a schoolboy; the pantomimic art of Grimaldi made it familiar to the generation of Byron and Hazlitt; Godwin, Southey, De Quincey, Dickens, Browning and Meredith, are among the writers who make allusion to it. For four centuries, edition has followed edition, to a total of at least seventy-four, the latest in 1919.[11]

As has been mentioned, *Valentine and Orson* was an influence on Spenser. But Orson was not the only Wild Man available for inspiration; and when Spenser wrote *The Faerie Queene* he provided his readers with a host of Wild Men, only one of whom bore a resemblance to Orson. Spenser obviously knew his Wild Man lore, because he describes representatives of the several and distinct Wild types.

The first is old Sylvanus, the god of the fauns and satyrs, who is discovered leaning 'on Cypresse stadle stout,/ And with an yuie twyne his wast [...] girt about' (I.6.14). Sylvanus displays both the traditional tree trunk used as a staff or club, and the traditional girdle. He lives in a wood, surrounded by a host of dancing and piping creatures including fauns (who are benign and protective), satyrs (who are lustful), hamadryads (wood nymphs), and naiads (river nymphs).

Sir Satyrane, as his name suggests, is satyr-like, but not, like most satyrs, lustful. His father – a satyr – abducts a woman and keeps her for his sexual pleasure (I.6.22). She becomes pregnant. He lets her go eventually, but keeps the child, whom he raises in the woods, teaching him to be fearless. Satyrane's status as a Wild Man thus rests on both his lineage and his upbringing. As Bernheimer notes, from the time of the ancient Greeks

---

11 Dickson, p. 1. Dickson provides a list of English versions and allusions. See Dickson, pp. 284–98.

and Romans, Wild Men were associated with 'the demons of lower mythology, the centaurs, satyrs, and Pan, the fauns and sylvans and Silenus' (93).[12]
On the other hand, an upbringing in the woods tends to promote physical, psychological and moral health far beyond that achieved by the city
dweller exposed to the corrupting and debilitating effects of civilization.
This leads to the Wild Man type known as the 'Unsophisticated Youth',[13]
represented in *The Faerie Queene* by the young Tristram:

> A goodly youth of amiable grace,
> Yet but a tender slip, that scarse did see
> Yet seuenteene yeares, but tall and faire of face
> That sure he [Calidore] deem'd him borne of noble race.
> All in a woodmans iacket he was clad
> Of Lincolne greene.   (VI.2.5)

Tristram – heir to his dead father's crown – has grown up in the woods,
away from the perils threatened by his usurping uncle; and his noble blood,
no less than his innate goodness, has seen him grow into a naturally chivalrous person.

Sir Artegall also grows up away from mankind, but comes to maturity
not as an Unsophisticated Youth, but as the feared champion of justice.
Spenser likens him to Hercules,

> Who all the West with equall conquest wonne,
> And monstrous tyrants with his club subdewed;
> The club of Iustice dread, with kingly powre endewed.   (V.1.2)

Hercules is also a Wild Man. Bernheimer points out that 'in Greek and
Roman art Hercules is shown carrying a club and clad in the skin of the slain
lion of Nemea' (101). Artegall is therefore a Wild Man both by upbringing
and by association. Fittingly he makes his first appearance at a tourney in
the guise of a Salvage Knight:

---

12   For a gist of this association, from the Greeks to Satyrane, see Bernheimer,
     pp. 93–100.
13   Dickson, p. 124. See also ibid., pp. 128–29.

> In quyent disguise, full hard to be descride.
> For all his armour was like saluage weed,
> With woody mosse bedight, and all his steed
> With oaken leaues attrapt, that seemed fit
> For saluage wight, and thereto well agreed
> His word, which on his ragged shield was writ,
> *Saluagesse sans finesse*, shewing secret wit. (IV.4.39)[14]

He puts to flight all his opponents, until he is unhorsed by the virgin warrior Britomart.

Artegall has a companion, an iron man:

> His name was *Talus*, made of yron mould,
> Immoueable, resistlesse, without end.
> Who in his hand an yron flale did hould,
> With which he thresht out falshood, and did truth vnfould. (V.1.12)

Talus, apart from one brief moment (V.6.9), lacks any feeling except righteous indignation, and in the execution of his wrath is ruthless to the extent that Artegall has to restrain him. Talus will return later.

Thus far Spenser's Wild Men have been virtuous. His villains, however, are truly hideous. One such is the giant Orgoglio (Pride):

> his stature did exceed
> The hight of three the tallest sonnes of mortall seed.

> The greatest Earth his vncouth mother was,
> And blustring *Æolus* his boasted sire,
> Who with his breath, which through the world doth pas,
> Her hollow womb did secretly inspire,
> And fild her hidden caues with stormie yre,
> That she conceiu'd; and trebling the dew time,
> In which the wombes of women do expire,

---

14 Note the traditional association of the Wild Man with the oak tree, for which I am indebted to Roger Bartra, *The Artificial Savage: Modern Myths of the Wild Man*, trans. by Christopher Follett (Ann Arbor: University of Michigan Press, 1997), p. 214. For two Salvage Knights jousting, see Bernheimer, plate 11.

> Brought forth this monstrous masse of earthly slime,
> Puft vp with emptie wind, and fild with sinfull crime.
> [...]
>   his stalking steps are stayde
> Vpon a snaggy Oke, which he had torne
> Out of his mothers bowelles, and it made
> His mortall mace, wherewith his foemen he dismayde.   (I.7.8–10)

This giant harks back to the archaic forerunners of humanity, emerging like Lucretian man from the earth itself. His club is the traditional uprooted oak. Nor is he alone. Orgoglio has an equally hideous and baneful brother – Disdain:

> His lookes were dreadfull, and his fiery eies
>   Like two great Beacons, glared bright and wyde,
>   Glauncing askew, as if his enemies
>   He scorned in his ouerweening pryde;
>   And stalking stately like a Crane, did stryde
>   At euery step vppon the tiptoes hie,
>   And all the way he went, on euery syde
>   He gaz'd about, and stared horriblie,
> As if he with his lookes would all men terrifie.
>
> He wore no armour, ne for none did care,
>   As no whit dreading any liuing wight.   (VI.7.42–43)

Whereas Orgoglio carries the oaken club, Disdain has apparently upgraded, and uses one of iron (VI.7.43).

By far the most horrible example of the Wild type is the savage personification of Lust in Book IV:

> It was to weet a wilde and saluage man,
>   Yet was no man, but onely like in shape,
>   And eke in stature higher by a span,
>   All ouergrowne with haire, that could awhape
>   An hardy hart, and his wide mouth did gape
>   With huge great teeth, like to a tusked Bore:
>   For he liu'd all on rauin and on rape
>   Of men and beasts; and fed on fleshly gore,
> The signe whereof yet stain'd his bloudy lips afore.

His neather lip was not like man nor beast,
   But like a wide deepe poke, downe hanging low,
   In which he wont the relickes of his feast,
   And cruell spoyle, which he had spard, to stow:
   And ouer it his huge great nose did grow,
   Full dreadfully empurpled all with bloud;
   And downe both sides two wide long eares did glow,
   And raught downe to his waste, when vp he stood,
More great then th' eares of Elephants by *Indus* flood.

His wast was with a wreath of yuie greene
   Engirt about, ne other garment wore:
   For all his haire was like a garment seene;
   And in his hand a tall young oake he bore,
   Whose knottie snags were sharpned all afore,
   And beath'd in fire for steele to be in sted.
   But whence he was, or of what wombe ybore,
   Of beasts, or of the earth, I have not red:
But certes was with milke of Wolues and Tygres fed.   (IV.7.5–7)

Spenser has left nothing out in the description of this Wild Man. He is naked, hairy, wears a green ivy wreath about his waist, carries an oak tree as a club, docs not speak, preys on men and beasts, and abducts women whom he uses to satisfy both his lust and his stomach (IV.7.12). He may have been born of some unspecified beast, or have sprung straight from the earth; he was nourished with the milk of wolves and tigers – both noted for their fierceness; and he lives in a cave in a forest.

As Spenser says, this is no man, but simply a deformed parody of one. He is in fact another Platonic embodiment of evil low passions, which Spenser suggests by associating his sinful soul with his misshapen body. The huntress Belphoebe kills him with an arrow through the throat:

Whom when on ground she groueling saw to rowle,
   She ran in hast his life to haue bereft:
   But ere she could him reach, the sinfull sowle
   Hauing his carrion corse quite sencelesse left,
   Was fled to hell, surcharg'd with spoile and theft.
   Yet ouer him she there long gazing stood,
   And oft admir'd his monstrous shape.   (IV.7.32)

Spenser's final Wild Man – the Salvage Man of Book VI[15] – is a mixture of the noble and the savage, and returns us firmly to the tale of Valentine and Orson. In his first appearance he comes to the rescue of Sir Calepine and his Lady Serena, who are being set upon by the vile Sir Turpine. Drawn by Serena's cries, the Salvage comes running from the woods, and finds Turpine on horseback pursuing the wounded Calepine.

> The saluage man, that neuer till this houre
>   Did taste of pittie, neither gentlesse knew,
>   Seeing his sharpe assault and cruell stoure
>   Was much enmoued at his perils vew,
>   That euen his ruder hart began to rew,
>   And feele compassion of his euill plight,
>   Against his foe that did him so pursew:
>   From whom he meant to free him, if he might,
> And him auenge of that so villenous despight.   (VI.4.3)

He runs at Turpine, who thrusts his spear at his breast. The Salvage, protected by magic, is unharmed, but the predominating aspect of his character is aroused:

> With that the wyld man more enraged grew,
>   Like to a Tygre that hath mist his pray,
>   And with mad mood againe vpon him flew,
>   Regarding neither speare, that mote him slay,
>   Nor his fierce steed, that mote him much dismay,
> The saluage nation doth all dread despize.   (VI.4.6)

Turpine, confounded by the Salvage's strength, gallops away. The Salvage chases him, and almost succeeds in catching him, so great are his strength and speed. At last the Salvage returns to Calepine, and Serena who, having witnessed his ferocity, fears for her life as he approaches. But now his noble blood begins to find gentle and courteous expression.

---

15   His story is given in some detail, as he will be compared in the next chapter with Peacock's hero Sir Oran Haut-ton.

> But the wyld man, contrarie to her feare,
>   Came to her creeping like a fawning hound,
>   And by rude tokens made to her appeare
>   His deepe compassion of her dolefull stound,
>   Kissing his hands, and crouching to the ground;
>   For other language had he none nor speach,
>   But a soft murmure, and confused sound
>   Of senselesse words, which nature did him teach,
> T'expresse his passions, which his reason did empeach.   (VI.4.11)

Nature has also taught him herb-lore. He applies the juice of a herb to Calepine's wound, then leads his charges to his den in the forest. Bernheimer writes of the Greco-Roman tradition of the idealized natural man – of whom Spenser's Salvage is a type:

> Negatively speaking, primitive man abstains from the luxuries of sophisticated life and thus finds it easy to do without the arts that make it possible: the arts of war, of mining and metallurgy, and of navigation. In a positive way this abstention from all that enriches life materially shields primitive man from the vices of avarice and trickery and bellicosity. Since even agriculture and cattle breeding are unknown to him, he finds himself leading a life without possessions but also without toil and burden. As a means of livelihood Virgil and Juvenal allow him the hunt, while most other writers make him a vegetarian, following Empedocles' assertion that in the Golden Age man was on affectionate terms with the animals and birds and thus could not commit the disloyalty of slaughtering them. Acorns and fruits are thus all he can afford, and it is assumed that they suffice for his needs. Indeed, this diet favours his health and he may expect to live to a ripe old age (103).

The Salvage's den exhibits the traditional requirements of the Wild Man's lair; and, through a combination of innate sensibility and a lack of agricultural skill, he, like the idealized natural man, is a vegetarian:

> Farre in the forrest by a hollow glade,
>   Couered with mossie shrubs, which spredding brode
>   Did vnderneath them make a gloomy shade;
>   Where foot of liuing creature neuer trode,
> Ne scarse wyld beasts durst come, there was this wights abode.

Thether he brought these vnacquainted guests;
　　To whom faire semblance, as he could, he shewed
　　By signes, by lookes, and all his other gests.
　　But the bare ground, with hoarie mosse bestrowed,
　　Must be their bed, their pillow was vnsowed,
　　And the frutes of the forrest was their feast:
　　For their bad Stuard neither plough'd nor sowed,
　　Ne fed on flesh, ne euer of wyld beast
Did taste the bloud, obaying natures first beheast.　　(VI.4.13–14)

The Salvage's way of life is not that of a brute; on the contrary, it belongs to that of the natural man from the Golden Age, as can be seen from Milton's description in *Paradise Lost* of Adam and Eve's bower in Eden:

　　　　　　　　it was a place
Chos'n by the sovran Planter, when he fram'd
All things to Mans delightful use; the roofe
Of thickest covert was inwoven shade
Laurel and Mirtle, and what higher grew
Of firm and fragrant leaf; on either side
Acanthus, and each odorous bushie shrub
Fenc'd up the verdant wall; each beauteous flour,
Iris all hues, Roses, and Gessamin
Reard high thir flourisht heads between, and wrought
Mosaic; underfoot the Violet,
Crocus, and Hyacinth with rich inlay
Broiderd the ground, more coulord then with stone
Of costliest Emblem: other Creature here
Beast, Bird, Insect, or Worm durst enter none;
Such was thir awe of Man. In shadier Bower
More sacred and sequesterd, though but feignd,
Pan or *Silvanus* never slept, nor Nymph,
Nor *Faunus* haunted. Here in close recess
With Flowers, Garlands, and sweet-smelling Herbs
Espoused *Eve* deckd first her Nuptial Bed.　　(IV.690–710)

And their vegetarian diet:

　　　　to thir Supper Fruits they fell,
Nectarin Fruits which the compliant boughes
Yeilded them, side-long as they sat recline [*sic*]

> On the soft downie Bank damaskt with flours:
> The savourie pulp they chew, and in the rinde
> Still as they thirsted scoop the brimming stream;
> [...]
> [...] About them frisking playd
> All Beasts of th' Earth.   (IV.331–41)

Milton, following Genesis, willy nilly finds himself associating Adam and Eve with the idealized Wild Man and Woman.

The Salvage tends his guests' wounds with herbs from the forest, and nurses Calepine back to health; but Serena's wounds are beyond his skill. After Calepine becomes separated from them, the Salvage continues to comfort and protect Serena; and when she determines to venture abroad on Calepine's horse he clumsily dons some of Calepine's gear and accompanies her on foot, showing her all due courtesy as if he were a true knight.

> So forth they traueld an vneuen payre,
>   That mote to all men seeme an vncouth sight;
>   A saluage man matcht with a Ladie fayre,
>   That rather seem'd the conquest of his might,
>   Gotten by spoyle, then purchaced aright.
>   But he did her attend most carefully,
>   And faithfully did serue both day and night,
>   Withouten thought of shame or villeny,
> Ne euer shewed signe of foule disloyalty.   (VI.5.9)

This stanza grows out of a fundamental shift in the Wild Man tradition; a shift evolving from a deepening disenchantment with the realities of the chivalric way of life. Traditionally the Wild Man had been a threat to the Lady – as in the episode with Lust (*FQ*, IV.7) – and would be defeated by her knight; but, in what Bernheimer calls 'a major turning point in the history of European civilization' (122), during the fourteenth century the Wild Man began to win. Spenser's Salvage man has developed into not only a protector of the Lady, but a protector of the Lady against decadent knighthood.

Serena and the Salvage happen upon Prince Arthur and his squire Timias, who is also carrying a wound. Timias, thinking the worst, attempts to apprehend the Salvage, who unceremoniously knocks him to the ground.

Serena intercedes, and tells her sad story and the part played by the vile
Turpine. Arthur leaves Serena and Timias in the care of a hermit, and sets
out to take revenge on Turpine. The Salvage meanwhile, seeing Arthur's
'royall vsage and array,/ [Has] greatly growne in loue of that braue pere'
(VI.5.41), and, despite Arthur's attempts to bid him stay, goes with him.

By the time they arrive at Turpine's castle, the Salvage has become
a *de facto* squire to Arthur, stabling his horse after Arthur alights. Yet, in
contrast with his mild demeanour towards his friends, he still behaves like
a wild beast towards their enemies. As he returns from the stable he sees
Turpine's groom laying hands on Arthur to throw him out. His response
is by now predictable: he becomes enraged and tears the groom to pieces
(VI.6.22).

A mighty battle ensues, in which the Salvage slays many of Turpine's
men, and has to be prevented by Arthur from killing even more. Arthur overcomes Turpine, but chivalrously spares his life at the pleading of Turpine's
lady (VI.6.31). However, when the Salvage comes upon Turpine, it is a different matter. The ferocity of the Salvage is awakened not by present danger
to himself or others, but by an almost conditioned response of hostility to
a foe regardless of the foe's demeanour. The Prince, having originally felt
the same way but having yoked his impulse beneath the laws of chivalry,
is now obliged to restrain the Salvage again (VI.6.40).

In a later scene the Salvage is described holding 'his weapon [...],/ That
was an oaken plant, which lately hee/ Rent by the root' (VI.7.24). A.C.
Hamilton tells us in a gloss that 'plant' means 'young tree'.[16] In his final
appearance the Salvage is again inflamed by the sight of violence directed
towards the innocent and helpless. During Arthur's fight with the villains
Scorn and Disdain, the Salvage, again enraged, falls upon Scorn and, having
rent him with his nails and teeth, proceeds to deal with him in his customary manner until the customary conclusion:

> And from him taking his owne whip, therewith
> So sore him scourgeth, that the bloud downe followeth.

16 Edmund Spenser, *The Faerie Queene*, ed. by A.C. Hamilton (London and New York:
    Longman, 1977), p. 669.

And sure I weene, had not the Ladies cry
   Procur'd the Prince his cruell hand to stay,
   He would with whipping, him haue done to dye:
   But being chekt, he did abstaine streight way,
   And let him rise.   (VI.8.28–29)

For all his strength and ferocity, there is nothing ape-like about this Wild Man. Like Orson, he is fully human, in fact, again like Orson, he is of noble blood, apparently abandoned in the woods as a baby, and, apart from the charm protecting him, left to fend for himself without the society of other human beings. One would assume that, like Orson and other Wild Men, he was suckled by some kind of beast; although, unlike Orson and other Wild Men, he has not grown a coat of hair. He is a man of action, driven by his passions, be they rage, pity, or devotion. He lacks both the restraint which society develops, and the capacity to articulate emotions and concepts, which language provides. But, physically and morally unspoiled, he is a truer example of ideal man than many of those around him. He is, in fact, the natural man.

The Noble Savage

Spenser's noble Wild Man serves as a convenient introduction to a figure who was to become a potent image for writers and philosophers in the following two centuries: the Noble Savage. Hoxie Fairchild notes that this figure grew, much like his Wild cousin, from

> the fusion of three elements: the observation of explorers; various classical and medieval conventions; the deductions of philosophers and men of letters.[17]

---

17   Hoxie Neale Fairchild, *The Noble Savage: A Study in Romantic Naturalism* (New York: Russell & Russell, 1928 ; repr. 1961), p. 2. Further references are given after quotations in the text.

Whereas, as was noted in the chapter on *Gulliver*, the natives of Africa were regarded as little better than beasts, the natives of the New World came to embody all the virtues of the Golden Age. The Noble Savage thus stood in stark contrast to the morally and physically degenerate Europeans who discovered them. Fairchild finds a remarkable instance of this contrast in

> A unique treatment of the Noble Savage idea. [...] The Land of the Houyhnhnms is an ideal realm, set up for our admiration and shame, in contrast to the sordid and vicious life of man. This part of *Gulliver* is a Utopian Voyage, a form which applies to old visions of an ideal state the technic of the explorers' narratives. [...] Frequently, though by no means invariably, the Utopias discovered in these explorations of the fancy are peopled by Noble Savages.
>
> Such, beneath their equine disguise, are the Houyhnhnms. The source of their virtues is the lack of everything prized in civilized society. They have no war, no weapons, no laws or lawyers, no diseases or doctors, no politicians, no ministers of state, no nobility (45–46).[18]

Thus Gulliver inhabits a society temporarily peopled by Wild Men (Yahoos), Noble Savages (Houyhnhnms), and one degenerate European (himself) who gradually assumes the characteristics of both Wild Man and Noble Savage: he dresses in the skins of animals; and he comes to enjoy perfect health, and to despise the civilization which bred him and to which he must return. This provides a philosophical explanation for why he would rather stay with the savages who wound him on his return journey, than with the Europeans who eventually rescue him.

Despite their moral elevation, Noble Savages were still associated in many ways with Wild Man lore: being either naked or clothed in the skins of animals; lacking agriculture; and living in a wild natural environment. Is it any wonder, then, that literary descriptions of the Noble Savage sometimes employed Wild Man imagery? Indeed, some *are* Wild Men. According to Roger Bartra:

---

18   Fairchild appears to have fallen into Swift's trap and based her judgment of the Houyhnhnms on Gulliver's report. This does not, however, invalidate her point about them being Noble Savages.

> In a famous narrative contained in the *Dial of Princes* [by Fray Antonio de Guevara] appears a character, the villein of the Danube, who is one of the oldest incarnations of the noble savage. The text [was] written around 1520 and published in 1529 [...]. This character, whose name is Mileno, is represented as a wild man, with his traditional attributes: hairy and bearded and holding a tree in one hand and more resembling a beast than a human being.[19]

The condition of Noble Savagery is not racially dependent – one may be European, and have grown up in a natural environment. In Voltaire's *L'Ingénu* (1767)[20] a Canadian Huron Indian arrives on the coast of Brittany, unaware that he is actually the nephew of the people who encounter him on the shore. He is a creature of physical perfection and naturalness:

> His figure and his dress attracted the notice of the brother and sister. His head was uncovered, and his legs bare; his feet were shod in small sandals; from his head his long hair flowed in tresses; a small close doublet displayed the beauty of his shape. He had a sweet and martial air [... and] an air of [...] natural simplicity.[21]

He is also tall (213).

Then begins his association with Wild Man imagery. A suggestive but not conclusive parallel is the fact that he was suckled by a Huron (218), in the same way that a Wild Man like Orson was suckled by a bear. He runs fifty leagues to strike a malefactor with his club (215). After his beloved has been devoured by a bear he kills it and wears its skin (215). Apart from his long tresses, his chin is 'somewhat hairy' (218). And when his uncle and aunt have him baptized, he is given the name of Hercules (226).

The Huron may conform to the Wild Man type on the outside, but intellectually he performs the role of the Noble Savage, which is to display the superior wisdom which comes from the contemplation of nature. He is thrown into prison and shares his cell with an old scholar named

19   *Artificial Savage*, p. 50.

20   The title in English is *Master Simple*.

21   Jean François Marie Arouet de Voltaire, *Candide: And Other Tales*, intro. by H.N. Brailsford, Everyman's Library, no. 936 (London: Dent [1937]; repr. 1967), p. 212. Further references are given after quotations in the text.

Gordon. They pass their time philosophizing. After one exchange Gordon remarks:

> I [have] consumed fifty years in instruction, and I fear I have not attained to the natural good sense of this child, who is almost a savage! I tremble to think I have so arduously strengthened prejudices, and he listens to simple Nature alone (247).

Robert Bage's *Hermsprong* (1796) features another European raised in the American wilderness.[22] Whereas Voltaire's Huron never knew his parents, young Hermsprong lives with his parents within a native American community. He grows up to be tall (156), and muscular (196). His eventual wife, Miss Campinet, thinks him 'possessed of the finest face she ever beheld' (73). His generosity and benevolence go hand in hand with an inflexible moral code. He prefers to go everywhere on foot, with his man-servant following on horseback with the luggage. Although he has grown up among savages and the wilderness, his father has given him a sound education, which, he admits, may have hampered his development:

> [T]he active part of my life was spent like that of other young Indians, whose very sports are athletic, and calculated to render man robust, and inure him to labour and fatigue. Here I always found my superiors. I could not acquire the speed of many of my companions; my sense of smelling was less acute—my sagacity inferior. I owe this probably to the sedentary portion of my life spent with my father in learning languages, in mathematics, in I know not what. [...]
> Such was the life I led amongst the aborigines of America; I am fond of the remembrance of it.—I never there knew sickness, I never there felt ennui (169–70).

Despite these periods of imposed inactivity, he is still capable of prodigious feats worthy of a Wild Man:

> I could almost run up a tree like a squirrel; almost catch an antelope; almost, like another Leander, have swum over a sea to a mistress, had I had one (170).

22   Robert Bage, *Hermsprong: or, Man as he is not*, ed. and intro. by Vaughan Wilkins (London: Turnstile Press, 1951). Further references are given after quotations in the text. Bage was at one time the business partner of Charles Darwin's grandfather Erasmus. The business – an ironworks – failed.

Hermsprong is thus an individual who combines the natural virtues of a Noble Savage with the acquired benefits of a classical education.

Hermsprong comes in conflict with many examples of civilized man, most of whom are stupid, or craven, or corrupt, or morally bankrupt. But in Sir Philip Chestrum – who conspires with Miss Campinet's father to marry her – Bage plumbs the depths to which civilized man can sink. Whereas the splendid world of nature has not only developed Hermsprong's body to a state of beauteous perfection; the unsullied environment has also enlarged his mind and soul. The inner and the outer man, both nourished alike, dwell in harmony, the one appropriately reflecting the other. Sir Philip – an embodiment of all the ills that civilized flesh is heir to – appears to have had the sins of many degenerate fathers visited upon him:

> [T]he child was feeble, small, and half animated. He grew, indeed, to the height of five English feet, but not equally. His legs bore too large a proportion to his body. In short, he might resemble that important personage, who, Sir John Falstaff said, looked like a man made after supper of a cheese paring (125).

But Sir Philip has not simply suffered from being at the bottom of a stagnant gene pool; his closeted upbringing teaches him nothing, and his deformed body is a fitting vehicle for an equally deformed soul which, both from its own inclination and from a lack of moral nourishment, is contemptible:

> In this young gentleman's case, there was no occasion to consider the arguments for public and private education; his constitution and his mother both determined for the latter; but the office of preceptor was almost a sinecure, for dear Sir Philip was too weak for study, and never stood in the least need of correction. When, therefore, he arrived at the age of freedom, he found himself possessed of great wealth, without the least inclination to spend it; of unbounded pride, without necessary judgment to correct it; of literature, not quite none; and of the smallest possible quantity of human kindness (125–26).

The Child of Nature

As the Noble Savage tradition declined under the weight of increasing familiarity with native peoples who were themselves declining under the European onslaught, writers switched their focus from the Savage, to the environment which produced him. The result was the Child of Nature. This creature need not have been bred in some exotic region among naked copper savages; it was enough simply to have avoided the polluting influence of civilization. Fairchild writes:

> Every reader of romantic literature is familiar with the child of nature—generally, though not always, a girl—who is born and grows to maturity in the heart of some wild region untouched by civilization, and who imbibes beauty, innocence and an unerring moral sense from the scenery which surrounds her (366).
>
> These children usually derive from nature great physical beauty; love of the scenes amid which they live; a sense of kinship with all living creatures; exquisite sensibilities; and a moral instinct independent of, and often hostile to, analytical reason (374).

In William Godwin's *Fleetwood* (1805) the eponymous hero provides a perfect illustration of the transition from Noble Savage to Child of Nature. Fairchild deals with him in two separate chapters, describing him initially as 'something of a Noble Savage' (156); and later as 'the best example of the male child of nature' (375). Fleetwood's father, a widower, goes to live in northern Wales, and takes his young son with him. Fleetwood says:

> I had few companions. The very situation which gave us a full enjoyment of the beauties of nature, inevitably narrowed both the extent and variety of our intercourse with our own species. My earliest years were spent among mountains and precipices, amidst the roaring of the ocean and the dashing of waterfalls. A constant familiarity with these objects gave a wildness to my ideas, and an uncommon seriousness to my temper.[23]

---

23   *Fleetwood: or, The New Man of Feeling. Collected Novels and Memoirs of William Godwin*, ed. by Mark Philp and others, 8 vols (London: Pickering and Chatto, 1992), V, p. 17. Further references are given after quotations in the text.

While the father admires nature from his window, or from the end of his garden, or during a leisurely ramble on horseback, the son becomes a vital and vigorous part of the majestic landscape. Fleetwood recalls:

> My limbs [...] were full of the springiness which characterises the morning of life. I bounded along the plains, and climbed the highest eminences; I descended the most frightful declivities, and often penetrated into recesses which had perhaps never before felt the presence of a human creature. I rivalled the goat, the native of the mountains, in agility and daring (18).

He goes about accompanied by a faithful dog. He does not hunt or fish, declaring, 'I could not with patience regard torture, anguish, and death, as sources of amusement' (26). When, later, he goes to Paris, the ladies refer to him as '*the handsome Englishman*' (53).

While he is growing up his separation from mankind is not merely physical. He climbs to mountain tops,

> anxious to see what mountains, valleys, rivers, and cities were placed beyond. I gazed upon the populous haunts of men as objects that pleasingly diversified my landscape; but without the desire to behold them in nearer view. I had a presentiment that the crowded streets and the noisy mart contained larger materials for constituting my pain than pleasure. The jarring passions of men, their loud contentions, their gross pursuits, their crafty delusions, their boisterous mirth, were objects which, even in idea, my mind shrunk from with horror (18).

Just as Hermsprong says that he 'was born a savage' (73), so Fleetwood says that growing up he 'had been a solitary savage' (29). Fairchild notes that when Fleetwood goes to Oxford, 'for the first few weeks of his university life he behaves precisely like the typical Noble Savage in contact with civilization' (152). He is superior and aloof, disdaining the shallow, malicious wit of his fellows. But there is a flaw in his clay. At Oxford he lacks the strength to resist becoming morally compromised; and in Paris he debauches himself with decadent married women.

Fleetwood's upbringing too, although in one sense ideal, has not fitted him for any kind of society. Having grown up with an indulgent father and a benevolent but ineffectual tutor, he cannot bear any kind of contradiction or defiance. He relies on the opinions and examples of others;

and he cannot reason things clearly for himself. Each mistake leads him to retreat further.

In the middle of this increasingly fevered tale of misanthropy, misogyny, intrigue, jealousy, betrayal and madness, Godwin finds time to insert a very fine passage on child labour. In *Hermsprong* the physical and mental shortcomings of Sir Philip Chestrum spring from decadent blood, and are, one might say, inflicted from within a degenerate social class, upon itself. Sir Philip has, like a mould, sprung organically from his environment. In *Fleetwood* Godwin describes the debilitating effect of social forces upon the poor, and what happens to potentially happy and healthy children who do not grow up as Noble Savages. After his disastrous affairs in Paris, Fleetwood flees to the Swiss alps, where he is taken up by his father's lifelong friend M. Ruffigny, who tells him the story of his life. Born into a wealthy Swiss family; orphaned at a young age; he is betrayed by his guardian uncle and left, at the age of eight, with a mill owner in Lyons who puts him to work in his silk mill. Ruffigny says:

> I was most attentive to the employment of the children, who were a pretty equal number of both sexes. There were about twenty on each floor, sixty in all. [...]
>
> Not one of the persons before me exhibited any signs of vigour and robust health. They were all sallow; their muscles flaccid, and their form emaciated. Several of the children appeared to me, judging from their size, to be under four years of age – I never saw such children (88–89).

Ruffigny – who in old age has retired to the Swiss mountains, grows his own food, appears to be vegetarian (68), and reads every day but finds more enjoyment in exercise[24] – understands that humans are creatures of nature and must be allowed to develop naturally. Deprived of a healthy natural environment, they wither like a plant deprived of light; and this deprivation acts on both body and mind:

---

24   Fairchild calls him 'the old Houyhnhnm' (154). According to Bartra: 'In the eighteenth century the idea began to spread that the Alps were a dwelling place of rustic felicity representing a privileged/ideal space for the adoration of nature, in which context the mountains and the purity of the air acquired a sort of symbolic value' (205).

Liberty is the parent of strength. Nature teaches the child, by the play of the muscles, and pushing out his limbs in every direction, to give them scope to develope themselves. Hence it is that he is so fond of sports and tricks in the open air, and that these sports and tricks are so beneficial to him. He runs, he vaults, he climbs, he practises exactness of eye and sureness of aim. His limbs grow straight and taper, and his joints well knit and flexible. The mind of a child is no less vagrant than his steps; it pursues the gossamer, and flies from object to object, lawless and unconfined: and it is equally necessary to the developement of his frame, that his thoughts and his body should be free from fetters. But then he cannot earn twelve sous a week. These children were uncouth and ill-grown in every limb, and were stiff and decrepit in their carriage, so as to seem like old men. At four years of age they could earn salt to their bread; but at forty, if it were possible that they should live so long, they could not earn bread to their salt. They were made sacrifices, while yet tender; and, like the kid, spoken of by Moses, were seethed and prepared for the destroyer in their mother's milk. This is the case in no state of society, but in manufacturing towns. The children of gipsies and savages have ruddy cheeks and a sturdy form, can run like lapwings, and climb trees with the squirrel (90).[25]

Ruffigny escapes and finds his way to Paris, where he is saved by Fleetwood's grandfather, who takes him to live in England, and brings him up as a brother to his own son, who is happy to share his inheritance with the foundling.

By the time that Fleetwood has reached the age of forty-five his retiring habits and his self-absorbed isolation have done him no good. The noble examples of his father, his grandfather and Ruffigny cast a shadow over the rest of mankind, and he falls into what he refers to as 'the most incorrigible species of misanthropy, which, as Swift expresses it, loves John, and Matthew, and Alexander, but hates mankind' (138).[26]

25 Pamela Clemit in her introductory note to *Fleetwood* writes: 'In preparation for writing the scenes of child factory labour in the first volume, Godwin visited a silk mill at Spitalfields in July 1804 and wrote to the British Museum to get exact information about the "Silk Throwing Machine" used in the south of France; he may also have drawn on his earlier visit to the Wedgwoods' potteries at Etruria in 1797' (p. vi). The Mosaic reference is to Exodus 23.19: 'Thou shalt not seethe a kid in his mother's milk.' The brutalizing effects of child labour will play a prominent role in *The Water-Babies*.

26 Fleetwood is referring to Swift's letter to Pope of 29 September 1725, after he had completed *Gulliver's Travels*: 'I have ever hated all nations, professions, and communities,

While travelling in Westmoreland he hears of an interesting family who live apart from society. The father, Macneil, has been a friend of Jean-Jacques Rousseau. The mother has disgraced herself in her youth by eloping with her music teacher to Italy, where her seducer, disappointed in his financial expectations, locks her up in an old castle. Macneil, who has met her before her elopement, rescues her and returns her to her father. Eventually they marry and have three daughters; but polite society will have nothing to do with Mrs Macneil or her daughters. They retire from the world, and educate the girls themselves. The eldest, Amelia, is an artist. The second, Barbara, is a musician. The youngest, Mary, is a true Child of Nature.

Fairchild writes: 'Romantic literature is full of [Children of Nature], and many of them are compared to flowers' (368). The association of purity, beauty, and flowers did not of course begin with Romantic literature. Milton, for example, having previously associated Adam and Eve with the idealized Wild Man and Woman (*PL*, IV.690), specifically associates Eve with flowers, and her fall with their decay:

> Here in close recess
> With Flowers, Garlands, and sweet-smelling Herbs
> Espoused *Eve* deckd first her Nuptial Bed.   (IV.708–10)

While she is eating the forbidden fruit,

> *Adam* the while
> Waiting desirous her return, had wove
> Of choicest Flours a Garland to adorne
> Her Tresses, and her rural labours crown,
> As Reapers oft are wont thir Harvest Queen.   (IX.838–42)

Eve approaches, and tells him how she has eaten the fruit:

> *Adam*, soon as he heard
> The fatal Trespass don by *Eve*, amaz'd,
> Astonied stood and Blank, while horror chill

---

and all my love is toward individuals: [...]. But principally I hate and detest that animal called man, although I hartily [*sic*] love John, Peter, Thomas, and so forth.' *Correspondence*, III, 103.

Ran through his veins, and all his joints relaxd;
From his slack hand the Garland wreath'd for *Eve*
Down dropd, and all the faded Roses shed.   (IX.888–93)

Just as the floral Child of Nature is not confined to Romantic literature; in like wise floral imagery is not confined to the Child of Nature: it
applies as well to the Noble Savage. Voltaire's Master Simple the Huron
'has a complexion of lilies and roses' (213). And thus it is with Godwin's
Noble Savage/Child of Nature: Fleetwood says that he 'felt like a tender
flower of the garden, which the blast of the east wind nips, and impresses
with the tokens of a sure decay' (18). Mary Macneil virtually is a flower.
She lives among flowers:

> The youngest was a gardener and botanist. She had laid out her father's grounds, and
> the style in which they were disposed did the highest credit to her imagination. One
> side of the family sitting-parlour was skirted with a greenhouse, of the same length as
> the room, and which seemed to make a part of it. This apartment was furnished with
> nearly every variety which Flora had ever produced in our island, or which curiosity
> has imparted, and were entirely cultivated by her hand (160).

She has taken on the qualities of a flower:

> Her delight was in flowers; and she seemed like one of the beauties of her own par-
> terre, soft, and smooth, and brilliant, and fragrant, and unsullied (171).

And, as a true Child of Nature, she is the most beautiful of the three
daughters, her beauteous soul having fashioned for itself a Platonically
suitable body:

> Mary had a complexion which, in point of fairness and transparency, could not be
> excelled: her blood absolutely spoke in her cheeks; the soft white of her hands and
> neck looked as if they would have melted away beneath your touch; her eyes were
> so animated, and her whole physiognomy so sensitive, that it was scarcely possible
> to believe that a thought could pass in her heart, which might not be read in her
> face (161).

After the loss of Mary's family at sea, Fleetwood marries her and takes
her to his estate in Wales, where he is delighted to find that she has the
strength, agility and endurance of a Noble Savage:

It was with pleasure that I perceived I could take her a walk of ten or twelve miles in extent, or invite her to climb the highest precipices, without her sustaining the smallest injury. When a woman is so unfortunately delicate, or has been so injudiciously brought up, as to be unable to walk more than a mile at a time, this effects a sort of divorce, deciding at once that, in many of the pleasures most gratifying to her husband's feelings and taste, she can be no partaker (198).

Mary is so much at home in the wilderness that Fleetwood comes to regard her not only as belonging to the landscape, but as a creature of vegetation herself. One afternoon she sets off to collect some rare wild flowers. Fleetwood remains at home in a bad mood, but reasons with himself and determines to follow after her. He teases himself with the pleasure which he will enjoy on seeing her again in her proper environment:

How beautiful will the carnation of her cheeks, and the lilies of her soft fingers, the fairest blossoms creation ever saw, appear amidst the parterre of wild flowers that skirts the ridge of Mount Idris! I think I see her now, as she stoops to cull them (201).

In this brief history the Wild Man has gradually emerged from the forest and the wilderness, wrenched from the bowels of the earth, or detached from the heart of a tree; savage, violent, hairy, indistinguishable from – and sometimes actually – a beast. This Wild Man, untamed, ferocious, lustful, is a foe of, and threat to, the orderly and civilized folk of the villages, towns and cities who have removed and isolated themselves from the mysterious, unpredictable and dangerous primitive natural world. In so doing they have cut themselves off from the physical, psychological, and moral nourishment which it also affords; and have begun to degenerate accordingly. Meanwhile the natural world comes to be regarded as the cradle and nurse of the Wild Man's descendant, the Noble Savage, and the Noble Savage's more domestic offspring, the Child of Nature. Hand in hand with this progression the Wild Woman, a monstrous, moss-encrusted, leafy hag, has also evolved into a flower. Throughout the manifold incarnations of the Wild Man, the same images persist, until the tradition reaches its dazzling apotheosis in *Melincourt*. The aspect which one needs to bear in mind in all of this long, evolving tradition is the gradual movement away from ugliness, sin, lust, untamed beastliness, and violence in the Wild

Man; and the corresponding movement towards beauty, goodness, and purity of body, mind and soul in the Child of Nature. In *Jekyll and Hyde* and 'Olalla' Stevenson embodies both of these extremes – Hyde is a Wild Man, and Olalla is a Child of Nature. But whereas other Children of Nature are essentially pure, Olalla is all too aware of the Hyde which lurks within and constantly threatens to overwhelm her; and it is she who will provide a crucial insight into the origins of Hyde.

This chapter has introduced the Child of Nature, with her beauty, her purity, and her goodness. *Melincourt* will show these virtues in action, and establish a standard of purity against which to set the beautiful and pious Olalla.

CHAPTER FIVE

Of Apes and Peacocks

Melincourt might seem an odd choice for inclusion in this work: the ape is the hero, while the humans provide the degenerates. The book does, however, continue the examination of mankind's origins; the relationship between man and beast; evolution; degeneration; and the association between soul and body. Peacock presents the same light-hearted view of our early ancestors that Stevenson does in his essays concerning Probably Arboreal.[1] Moreover Peacock provides a particular frame of reference with which to approach 'Olalla', one of the keys to an understanding of *Jekyll and Hyde*. Most importantly, whereas our previous writers deal with the human condition by looking back to the Classical authors, in *Melincourt* Peacock blends the Ancients with modern scientific scholars of evolutionary theory, thereby moving one step closer to the amalgam of thought in *Jekyll and Hyde*.

Lord Monboddo

In *Melincourt* Peacock utilizes the writings of one of the natural man's more notorious champions, the Scottish judge, laird, and philosopher James Burnett, Lord Monboddo (1714–99). Whereas Swift had presented a fiction of mankind degenerating into an ape-like creature, Monboddo firmly believed that mankind had risen from a more primitive condition, but that in so doing, had lost in size, physical strength, health, vitality,

[1]   'The Manse' and 'Pastoral', *Works*, XII. See above, p. 26.

and moral fibre. In this he follows the progression outlined by Lucretius. William Knight writes:

> Perhaps the most remarkable thing about Monboddo was his anticipative wisdom, his prevision of future theories as to the origin of man, and his descent or ascent from lower types. As an anatomist, he unconsciously followed Epicurus and Leucippus; while, as a virtual evolutionist, he holds an honoured place between Lucretius and Darwin.[2]

Yet despite this honoured place, Knight finds fault with Monboddo's system, which he laid out in two monumental works, *Of the Origin and Progress of Language* (6 volumes, 1773–92), and *Ancient Metaphysics* (6 volumes, 1779–99). Knight writes:

> Monboddo's assertion that the race had degenerated—mentally, morally, and physically—was however curiously illogical, when taken in connection with his admission of the animal ancestry of man. The ascent, and not the descent, of man was the natural corollary of the conclusion he had reached in his anthropological studies. If our race has emerged from lower forms its continual progress, after the human stage was reached—and not its subsequent degeneracy—was the logical sequence to which his position led up (29).

Knight here is viewing Monboddo's system through the prism of his own logic, not Monboddo's. Monboddo's system consisted of two tightly interwoven strands of thought. The first is the Lucretian theme, in which mankind rises from a state of bestiality to arrive at language, civilization, and high culture. The second is the deteriorationist theme, in which mankind has degenerated physically and morally from a former Golden Age – in Monboddo's opinion, the Classical period. Thus Monboddo saw no contradiction in mankind's rise, perfection, and subsequent decline. In this he anticipated the views of Huxley,[3] Kingsley, and H.G. Wells in *The Time Machine*.

---

2   William Knight, *Lord Monboddo and Some of His Contemporaries* (London: Murray, 1900), p. 1. For a discussion of the validity of this claim, see Emily Cloyd, *James Burnet* [*sic*]: *Lord Monboddo* (Oxford: Clarendon Press, 1972), pp. 160–68.

3   Huxley writes: '[I]t is an error to imagine that evolution signifies a constant tendency to increased perfection. That process undoubtedly involves a constant remodelling of the organism in adaptation to new conditions: but it depends on the nature of those

As a thinker, he was regarded with mixed feelings. Henry Cockburn writes:

> Classical learning, good conversation, excellent suppers, and ingenious though unsound metaphysics were the peculiarities of Monboddo. He was reputed a considerable lawyer in his own time; and his reports show that the reputation was well founded. [...] He went very often to London, almost always on horseback, and was better qualified than most of his countrymen to shine in its literary society. But he was insufficiently appreciated; and he partly justified and indeed provoked this, by taking his love of paradox and metaphysics with him, and dealing them out in a style of academical formality; and this even after he ought to have seen, that all that people cared about his dogmas was to laugh at their author. It is more common to hear anecdotes about his maintaining that men once had tails, and similar follies, than about his agreeable conversation and undoubted learning.[4]

But Monboddo – albeit posthumously – found an ally in Charles Darwin:

> The early progenitors of man must have been once covered with hair, both sexes having beards; their ears were probably pointed, and capable of movement; and their bodies were provided with a tail, having the proper muscles.[5]

---

conditions whether the direction of the modifications effected shall be upward or downward. Retrogressive is as practicable as progressive metamorphosis.' Huxley is of course not addressing the question of concomitant moral and physical decline; but Monboddo – along with Godwin, Peacock, and Kingsley – presents cities and industrial towns as physical environments calculated to warp and destroy bodies as well as souls. Huxley continues, using a simile which Monboddo would have applauded: 'If our globe is proceeding from a condition in which it was too hot to support any but the lowest living thing to a condition in which it will be too cold to permit of the existence of any others, the course of life upon its surface must describe a trajectory like that of a ball fired from a mortar; and the sinking half of that course is as much a part of the general process of evolution as the rising' ('The Struggle for Existence in Human Society', *Evolution and Ethics, Collected Essays*, IX, 195–236 (p. 199)).

4   Henry Cockburn, *Lord Cockburn's Works: Vol. 2, Memorials of His Time* (Edinburgh: Black, 1872), pp. 97–98. Cockburn was a Judge of the Court of Session in Scotland; and wrote his memoirs between 1821 and 1830. The Preface is dated 1856, three years before *The Origin of Species*.

5   *Descent of Man*, p. 524. Emily Cloyd writes: 'Erasmus Darwin, the grandfather of Charles Darwin, knew Monboddo's works and mentioned him in *The Temple of Nature* (1801), but Charles Darwin does not mention him' (168). In the light of

History has proven Monboddo's mockers wrong; but even at the time they were judging him too harshly. He was neither naive nor credulous, as he is at pains to demonstrate. He recounts a story told by a traveller:

> His name is *Keoping*, a Swede by birth, who, in the year 1647, went to the East Indies, and there served aboard a Dutch ship of force, belonging to the Dutch East-India company, in quality of lieutenant. In sailing through those seas they had occasion to come upon the coast of an island in the gulf of Bengal called *Nicobar*, where they saw men with tails like those of cats, and which they moved in the same manner.[6]

Some of the seamen go ashore, and the natives eat them.

Monboddo did not blindly accept this yarn because it suited his argument – even though he had come across it in a work by an acknowledged authority. He writes:

> The story is told in the 6th volume of Linnæus's *Amœnitates academicæ*, in an academical oration of one *Hoppius*, a scholar, as I suppose, of Linnæus, who relates the story upon the credit of this Keoping, with several more circumstances than I have mentioned. As I knew nothing then of any other author who had spoken of men with tails, I thought the fact extraordinary, and was not disposed to believe it without knowing who this Keoping was, and what credit he deserved. I therefore wrote to Linnæus, inquiring about him, and desiring to know where his book was to be found.[7]

Linnæus wrote back (Monboddo quotes part of the letter), giving publishing details, approving the author's veracity, and citing other accounts of encounters with men who were nocturnal, without speech, and caudate. Finally Monboddo was persuaded to accept the story. He gives two reasons why. The first seems to be based primarily on his experience as a judge. He finds that the Swedish lieutenant

---

Darwin's claim, it is interesting to note Gulliver's observation of the Yahoos, that 'Their Heads and Breasts were covered with a thick Hair, some frizzled and others lank; they had Beards like Goats' (193).

6   *Of the Origin and Progress of Language*, 6 vols (London: Cadell; Edinburgh: Balfour, 1773–92; facsimile repr. Menston: Scolar Press, 1967), I, 234–35. (Hereafter *O & P*.)

7   *O & P*, I, 236, footnote.

writes in a simple plain manner, not like a man who intended to impose a lie upon the world, merely for the silly pleasure of making people stare; and if it be a lie (for it cannot be a mistake), it is the only lie in his book; for everything else that he has related of animals and vegetables has been found to be true.[8]

The second is based partly on an acceptance of the first, partly on the state of knowledge of the day, and partly on the testament of authority stretching back to the Ancients:

I am convinced, that we have not yet discovered all the variety of nature, not even in our own species [...]. I am therefore disposed to believe, upon credible evidence, that there are still greater varieties in our species than what is mentioned by this traveller: for that there are men with tails, such as the antients gave to their satyrs, is a fact so well attested that I think it cannot be doubted. [Footnote: See *Linnæi Systema Naturae*, vol.1. p. 33, and *Buffon's Natural History*.][9]

Like Swift, Monboddo was an admirer of the Ancients; but in his case it amounted to adulation.[10] He absorbed Classical thought, and lived a life that was both benignly patrician, and Spartan. Knight writes:

His personal habits were frugal, if somewhat eccentric. Very fond of exercise in the open air, he rose early—six o'clock—and always took a cold bath, summer and winter (even during frost), in a house erected for the purpose at some distance from the mansion, near a running stream which supplied it with water. He took a light dinner early during the day, supper being his chief meal. Before going to rest he had an air-bath, and then anointed himself with oil, in imitation of the Ancients, his lotion being composed of 'rose-water, olive oil, saline, aromatic-spirit, and Venetian soap' (12).[11]

Following his morning bath, writes Knight,

He read his Plato usually at breakfast, and, therefore, required an edition which he could conveniently hold in his hand at that time (26).

8   *O & P*, I, 236–38.
9   *O & P*, I, 238.
10   According to Emily Cloyd this probably derived from his early education which 'had the effect of narrowing James's mind so much that it could not ever again admit any learning without a Greek or Roman foundation' (5).
11   No reference given for the quotation.

Among the Moderns he approved of Henry More's fellow Cambridge Platonist, Ralph Cudworth, 'for he was thoroughly learned in the Ancient Philosophy.'[12] He thought Lord Shaftesbury's 'The Moralists' 'the best philosophical Drama that has been composed, since the days of Plato.'[13] His antipathy to Dr Johnson was inflamed by Johnson's dismissal of Milton,[14] whom he regarded as not only 'the greatest writer both in verse and prose that we have in our language';[15] but also, 'the only poet in English that can be compared with Homer.'[16]

He divided writing into 'three general characters of style: The simple, the highly ornamented, and the middle between these two'.[17] At the one extreme he finds that Shaftesbury 'has the richest and most copious style of any writer in English; [...] in this he has imitated Plato'.[18] At the other extreme,

> The author, in English, that has excelled the most in [the simple] style is Dr Swift, in his *Gulliver's Travels* [...]. I think I do not go too far when I pronounce it the most perfect work of the kind, ancient or modern, that is to be found.[19]

He advised one correspondent that, in metaphysical matters, the Church of England might benefit from a thorough study of 'the pious Philosophy of the ancients, and particularly the Philosophy of Plato, which has ever been acknowledged to be more agreeable to the doctrines of Christianity than any other'.[20]

Monboddo looked back fondly on a complicated history of advancement and decline – as in fact did Lucretius: on the one hand, mankind is evolving from a state of brutishness to a state of culture, civilization, and

---

12   Knight, p. 125. Letter to Richard Price, 15 September 1780.
13   Knight, p. 141. Letter to Samuel Horsley, 11 December 1780. Monboddo devotes an entire chapter to 'The Moralists' in *O & P*, IV, 341–94.
14   Knight, p. 264. Letter to John Young, 17 February 1784.
15   *O & P*, V, 253.
16   Knight, p. 214. Letter to Sir George Baker, 2 October 1782.
17   *O & P*, III, 181.
18   *O & P*, III, 282.
19   *O & P*, III, 195–96.
20   Knight, p. 118. Letter to Samuel Horsley, 24 July 1780.

philosophy. On the other hand, mankind is degenerating both in stature and physical prowess. In Monboddo's mind this dual process achieved an ideal mating in the golden age of Classical Greece. After that, the physical decline continued, but now went hand in hand with a mental and moral decline as well, brought on, ironically, by the very civilization which had been so hardly won. Monboddo did not simply dream this up: he was working within a long tradition, also operating in *Gulliver's Travels*, a work which was first published in Monboddo's twelfth year. During Gulliver's voyage to Laputa he visits Glubbdubdrib, where the Governor is able to summon the ghosts of the dead. Gulliver requests him to summon the ghosts of such famous leaders as Alexander the Great and Julius Caesar, and philosophers such as Socrates and Aristotle. Gulliver then requests to see the ghosts of those who lived between two- and three hundred years before, and finally those who lived only one hundred years before. He reflects:

> As every Person called up made exactly the same Appearance he had done in the World, it gave me melancholy Reflections to observe how much the Race of human Kind was degenerate among us, within these Hundred Years past (173).

Imagine, then, how much we must have diminished since the days of the Ancients. Monboddo reckoned up the dimensions of the Greek heroes from the Homeric texts:

> Homer has said nothing positively, of the size of any of his heroes, but only comparatively [...]. But [...] he has given us a very accurate description of the persons of several of the Greek heroes; which I am persuaded he had from very good information. In this he tells us, that Ulysses was shorter than Agamemnon by the head, shorter than Menelaus by the head and shoulders, and that Ajax was taller than any of the Greeks by the head and shoulders; consequently, Ulysses was shorter than Ajax by two heads and shoulders, which we cannot reckon less than four feet. Now, if we suppose these heroes to have been no bigger than we, then Ajax must have been a man about six feet and a half, or at most seven feet; and if so, Ulysses must have been most contemptibly short, not more than three feet, which is certainly not the truth, but a most absurd and ridiculous fiction, such as we cannot suppose in Homer: whereas, if we allow Ajax to have been twelve or thirteen feet high, and, much more, if we suppose him to have been eleven cubits,[21] as Philostratus makes him, Ulysses, though four feet

21   Between sixteen and a half feet, and twenty feet.

short of him, would have been of a good size, and, with the extraordinary breadth which Homer observes he had, may have been as strong a man as Ajax.[22]

By Monboddo's most conservative estimate, Ulysses would have been eight feet tall. We certainly have declined. Monboddo, alas, had declined along with the rest: he was not quite five feet tall.[23]

Hand in hand with this physical diminution went our degeneration in every other way. In Peacock's *Headlong Hall* (1816) Mr Escot the Monboddan deteriorationist gives a graphic description of this slow fall:

> The first inhabitants of the world knew not the use either of wine or animal food; it is, therefore, by no means incredible that they lived to the age of several centuries, free from war, and commerce, and arbitrary government, and every other species of desolating wickedness. But man was then a very different animal to what he now is: he had not the faculty of speech; he was not encumbered with clothes; he lived in the open air; his first step out of which, as Hamlet truly observes, is *into his grave.* [Footnote: See Lord Monboddo's *Ancient Metaphysics.*][24] His first dwellings, of course, were the hollows of trees and rocks. In process of time he began to build: thence grew villages; thence grew cities. Luxury, oppression, poverty, misery, and disease kept pace with the progress of his pretended improvements, till, from a free, strong, healthy, peaceful animal, he has become a weak, distempered, cruel, carnivorous slave.[25]

The wild – or natural – man of Lucretius existed alongside the other beasts, inferior to some, superior to a few. The natural man of Monboddo, however, existed in an almost pre-lapsarian state of gentle innocence, lacking speech and arts, but innately noble and capable of realizing the full human potential which his civilized modern brothers have forfeited.

22   *Antient Metaphysics: or, The Science of Universals. With an Appendix, containing an Examination of the Principles of Sir Isaac Newton's Philosophy*, 6 vols (London: Cadell; Edinburgh: Balfour, 1779–99), III, 146. Quoted in *Melincourt* (New York: AMS Press, 1967), p. 207–08. Further references to *Melincourt* will be given after quotations in the text.

23   Emily Cloyd, raising more questions than she answers, adds: 'and, for much of his life, proportionately small' (57).

24   See also *O & P*, I, 205.

25   Peacock, *Headlong Hall* (New York: AMS Press, 1967), p. 39.

From the safe distance of two centuries it is easy to smile on Monboddo's quirks and eccentricities. He was difficult; he was opinionated; and towards the end of his life he may have been drifting towards dementia. But his beliefs went beyond mere philosophical propositions: they determined the kind of life he led, and he maintained them heroically although they brought him little comfort, as this moving passage from Emily Cloyd demonstrates:

> On 16 June 1774, Monboddo and Boswell walked together in the Meadows, near Parliament House. Monboddo's son Arthur had died on 27 April, at the age of eleven, and the loss was naturally still very much on the father's mind. It was a personal loss of great importance, but it meant other things to him, too—it meant the dwindling end of a family line which had been great, strong, and vigorous, and it symbolized as well the history of man, declining from the physical greatness and intellectual stature of the Greeks to the physical and intellectual meanness of modern man. One need only compare a Plato and a Hume to see what was happening. Family legend told Monboddo of giants in his line, and there were stories of great strength, of curling stones used as hay weights; but in him the family had dwindled to less than five feet in height and to a constitution which maintained its vigour only by strenuous exercise, air baths, and careful diet; in his son, there was not enough strength to maintain twelve years of life. Boswell remarked on Monboddo's manly composure in discussing his loss, and the talk soon turned to matters of language (59–60).

Melincourt

And so to *Melincourt* (1817), whose hero Sir Oran Haut-ton, Baronet, M.P., musician, gardener, boozer and orang-outang, became so popular that, when the novel was published again in 1856, it appeared under the title: *Melincourt, or, Sir Oran Haut-ton.*[26]

---

26 Although Sir Oran was popular, the book itself was not a great success; hence the delay before the second edition.

The first thing to note about this work is that Peacock has included a Wild Man (Sir Oran), a Noble Savage (Sir Oran's patron Sylvan Forester), and a Child of Nature (the heroine Anthelia Melincourt) – although, as will become apparent, these categories tend to overlap each other.

Anthelia's name (Greek: *Antheilion* = *little flower*) is enough to suggest that she is a Child of Nature.[27] She grows up in Westmoreland (the district of Mary Macneil, the Child of Nature in *Fleetwood*), and the magical power of nature works its spell on both her mind and body. Peacock writes:

> The majestic forms and wild energies of Nature that surrounded her from her infancy, impressed their character on her mind, communicating to it all their own wildness, and more than their own beauty. Far removed from the pageantry of courts and cities, her infant attention was awakened to spectacles more interesting and more impressive: [...]. The murmur of the woods, the rush of the winds, and the tumultuous dashing of the torrents, were the first music of her childhood. A fearless wanderer among these romantic solitudes, the spirit of mountain liberty diffused itself through the whole tenour of her feelings, modelled the symmetry of her form, and illumined the expressive but feminine brilliancy of her features (9).

Her studies are appropriate to her environment:

> [A]nd when she had attained the age at which the mind expands itself to the fascinations of poetry, the muses of Italy became the chosen companions of her wanderings, and nourished a naturally susceptible imagination by conjuring up the splendid visions of chivalry and enchantment in scenes so congenial to their development (10).

Of course, by the time she is twenty-one and an orphan, and the inevitable suitors are beginning to swarm, she is completely uninterested; and Peacock is beginning his attack on the present degenerate age:

> Her knowledge of love was altogether theoretical; and her theory, being formed by the study of Italian poetry in the bosom of mountain solitude, naturally and necessarily pointed to a visionary model of excellence which it was very little likely the modern world could realize (12).

27   Her surname may in part derive from *meli* = *honey*.

Sylvan Forester is a Noble Savage by temperament and philosophical persuasion, rather than upbringing. He has had a university education, and has retired to an ancient abbey in Westmoreland, Rednose Abbey, which he has partially restored and renamed Redrose Abbey, 'as being more analogous to [his] notions of beauty' (34). It is also analogous to his notions of ideal love. This Noble Savage has not simply fled to the countryside, but has come 'with a view of carrying on in peace and seclusion some peculiar experiments on the nature and progress of man' (34). His tautological name, however, also places him immediately among the Wild Men: *Sylvan=forest dweller; Forester=forest dweller*, and is also another name for a Wild Man.[28] Furthermore, as we shall see, Peacock is fond of combining words to create names; if we combine SYLVan and forESTER, we arrive at SYLVESTER, which identifies him strongly with Sir Oran, whose scientific name is *Homo Sylvestris*. His dwelling is covered in ivy, the Wild Man's girdle; and he has left the woods around the abbey in 'a fine state of wildness' (36; 37). His temperament of course shines on his countenance, making him a 'very bright-eyed wild-looking young man' (170). He keeps no horses, regarding them as 'a selfish and criminal species of luxury' (271). His estate has been laid out specifically to prevent the entry of carriages, to preserve the tenants 'from the contagious exhibitions and examples of luxury' (275). To protest the slave trade he denies himself and his guests sugar (chapter 5). And he is 'always fond of railing at civilized life, and holding forth in praise of savages and what [he calls] original men' (34). He is, in fact, an ideal mate for Anthelia.

Peacock's introduction of Sir Oran is both subtle and extended. Sir Telegraph Paxarett has been summoned by his aunt Mrs Pinmoney to try his luck with Anthelia's affections. Driving towards Melincourt in his barouche he happens on Forester and recognizes him as an old college

---

28 Bernheimer, p. 128. See also *The Faerie Queene*, III.1, where Florimell is pursued by a 'foster'. We should not confuse Spenser's use of *foster*, meaning Wild Man, with Peacock's Mr Foster in *Headlong Hall*. Peacock gives his derivation: 'Foster, quasi φωστηρ,—from φαος and τηρεω, lucem servo, conservo, observo, custodio,—one who watches over and guards the light; a sense in which the word is often used amongst us, when we speak of *fostering* a flame' (8).

chum. Forester invites him to stay the night and shows him around the abbey grounds. Sir Telegraph asks:

> 'But who is that gentleman, sitting under the great oak yonder, in the green coat and nankins?[29] He seems very thoughtful.'
>
>   'He is of a contemplative disposition,' said Mr Forester: 'you must not be surprised if he should not speak a word during the whole time you are here. The politeness of his manner makes amends for his habitual taciturnity' (37–38).

Forester introduces them. It then takes fourteen pages, dinner – at which Sir Oran shows 'great proficiency in the dissection of game' (39) – and a discussion about sugar before Forester reveals that Sir Oran is an orang-outang. But Peacock has in another sense announced from the first that Sir Oran is a Wild Man. He is dressed in the traditional green garment, and seated beneath an oak – the tree under which is traditionally found not only the Wild Man, but the original man of Lucretius.[30] He shares his contemplative disposition with Godwin's Noble Savage/Child of Nature Fleetwood, and with the noble Wild Man of the Golden Age.[31] His hairiness, hidden beneath his garments, is represented by 'a pair of enormous whiskers' (38). Both he and the Wild Man lack the gift of speech.

Sir Oran is a multi-faceted creation. He spends his infancy in the woods of Angola, in the typical environment of a Wild Man. But then he is caught by a native couple who bring him home, where he grows up in the typical environment of a Noble Savage. Forester explains:

> [T]hey brought him up in their cottage as the play-fellow of their little boys and girls, where, with the exception of speech, he acquired the practice of such of the simpler arts of life as the degree of civilization in that part of Africa admits (54–55).

Note here the inversion of the Wild Man tradition in which a human child is raised among beasts.

29   Trousers made from yellow cotton.
30   Lucretius, *On the Nature of Things*, V, lines 939–40 (Munro, p. 179).
31   In *Headlong Hall* Mr Escot the deteriorationist says: 'The wild and original man is a calm and contemplative animal' (120).

Forester's old friend Captain Hawltaught buys Oran from his owners, and after a few years spent at sea, they retire to a little village in the west of England to take care of their garden. Captain Hawltaught plants cabbages, and Oran becomes 'a very expert practical gardener' (57). He also becomes proficient on the flute and French horn; and in the evenings, both of them drunk, he accompanies the Captain as he sings his shanties. In his acquired taste for drink Oran is again conforming to the Wild Man type, who may be captured by being made drunk, or, like Orson, encounters alcohol when he comes in from the wild. His occupation in the garden identifies him with the type of Wild Man who protects and husbands his wild environment.

Following the death of the Captain, Forester, who has always regarded this natural man as a project, takes Oran to live with him in order to give him a philosophical education and, hopefully, teach him to speak. To protect Oran from impolite behaviour towards him, Forester purchases him a baronetcy and one half of the elective franchise of a rotten borough, and makes over to him an estate.

Upon hearing this t(ale Sir Telegraph remarks:

> By the by, you put me very much in mind of Valentine and Orson. This wild man of yours will turn out some day to be the son of a king, lost in the woods, and suckled by a lioness (63).

Forester and Sir Oran share a fraternal relationship like that of Valentine and Orson, and one may easily discern parallels in the two stories;[32] but the exploits of Forester and Sir Oran, as the plot unfolds, seem to be modelled more on those of Prince Arthur and the Salvage Man in *The Faerie Queene*.

Hand in hand with this insistence on Sir Oran's pedigree as a Wild Man, Peacock adds another layer of observations and suppositions by

---

32 Marilyn Butler writes: 'Peacock lightly finds equivalents in *Melincourt* for many essentials of [Valentine and Orson]' (*Peacock Displayed: A Satirist in his Context* (London: Routledge & Kegan Paul, 1979), p. 322, n18).

modern natural philosophers – in particular, Lord Monboddo.[33] Having
first introduced Sir Oran with Wild Man imagery – clad in green, sitting
under an oak – Peacock shifts the focus to the orang-outang's relationship
to man; and presents him in a more scientific light. He then proceeds to
fashion a tale in which Sir Oran performs many Wild Man actions, which
receive corroboration not from Wild Man lore, but from the assertions of
natural philosophers, and the testimony of travellers who have witnessed
the behaviour of orang-outangs. The result is a fascinating story in which
we find ourselves drawn into a world which seems to have been constructed
jointly by Spenser and Monboddo; a world which is greater and more
bewilderingly joyous than the sum of its parts.

Every last detail about Sir Oran's appearance and behaviour (apart
from his dress sense and his horticultural pursuits) is corroborated by an
extensive footnote from one or more of Peacock's sources, the most fre-
quent being Monboddo. Forester, who on several occasions recites large
slabs of Monboddo verbatim, says of his protégé:

> He is a specimen of the natural and original man—the wild man of the woods; called,
> in the language of the more civilized and sophisticated natives of Angola, *Pongo*, and
> in that of the Indians of South America, *Oran Outang*.[34]

33   Also quoted are Buffon's *Histoire Naturelle* (44 vols, 1749–1804), Linnæus's *Systema
      Naturæ* (1735), and Rousseau's *Discours sur l'origine et les fondements de l'inégalité
      parmi les Hommes* (1755).

34   Since he comes from Angola, Sir Oran is obviously not what we know as an orang-
      outang, which is a native of Borneo and Sumatra, from where it derives its name.
      In Chapter I of *Man's Place in Nature* Huxley devotes several pages to a history of
      researches into chimpanzees and gorillas, both of whom were known indifferently
      as 'pongo', an apparent corruption of an African place name. The confusion between
      'pongo' and 'orang-outang' may be seen in a passage in Buffon's *Histoire Naturelle*,
      vol. XIV (1766). He entitles a chapter 'Les Orang-outangs ou le Pongo et le Jocko'.
      Huxley quotes from a note appended to Buffon's title: 'Orang-outang, nom de cet
      animal aux Indes orientales: Pongo, nom de cet animal à Lowando, Province de
      Congo' (*Man's Place in Nature*, intro. by Ashley Montagu (Ann Arbor: University
      of Michigan Press, 1971), p. 24). It is possible that some further confusion resulted in
      Buffon's 'Indes orientales' eventually becoming Forester's 'Indians of South America'.
      One should therefore regard Sir Oran as the ideal, hairy, natural 'orang-outang' or
      'Wild Man of the woods'.

[...]

   Some presumptuous naturalists have refused his species the honours of humanity; but the most enlightened and illustrious philosophers agree in considering him in his true light as the natural and original man. One French philosopher, indeed, has been guilty of an inaccuracy, in considering him as a degenerated man: degenerated he cannot be; as his prodigious physical strength, his uninterrupted health, and his amiable simplicity of manners demonstrate. He is, as I have said, a specimen of the natural and original man—a genuine fac simile of the philosophical Adam (52–54).

Peacock appends to this speech the following footnote from Monboddo, which encapsulates the latter's entire argument:

   His body, which is of the same shape as ours, is bigger and stronger than ours [...] according to that general law of nature above observed (*that all animals thrive best in their natural state*). His mind is such as that of a man must be, uncultivated by arts and sciences, and living wild in the woods. [...] If ever men were in that state which I call natural, it must have been in such a country and climate as Africa, where they could live without art upon the natural fruits of the earth. [...] If this be so, then, the short history of man is, that the race having begun in those fine climates, and having, as is natural, multiplied there so that the spontaneous productions of the earth could not support them, they migrated into other countries, where they were obliged to invent arts for their subsistence; and with such arts, language, in process of time, would necessarily come (*Melincourt*, 53).

Having stated his case with a philosophical detachment, Monboddo cannot resist a splenetic outburst against his opponents:

   That my facts and arguments are so convincing as to leave no doubt of the humanity of the oran outang, I will not take upon me to say; but this much I will venture to affirm, that I have said enough to make the philosopher consider it as problematical, and a subject deserving to be inquired into. *For, as to the vulgar, I can never expect that they should acknowledge any relation to those inhabitants of the woods of Angola*; but that they should continue, through a false pride, to think highly derogatory from human nature what the philosopher, on the contrary, will think the greatest praise of man, that from the savage state in which the oran outang is, he should, by his own sagacity and industry, have arrived at the state in which we now see him. *Origin and Progress of Language*, bk ii. chap. 5 (*Melincourt*, 53–54).

   Peacock draws the reader's attention to the principle underpinning his book, by putting part of a passage from Rousseau into Forester's mouth:

It is still more curious to think that modern travellers should have made beasts, under the names of Pongos, Mandrills, and Oran Outangs, of the very same beings whom the ancients worshipped as divinities under the names of Fauns and Satyrs, Silenus and Pan (63–64).

Peacock then goes on to show the seamless blending of myth, lore, and poetic imagination which provided the language for the expression of contemporary philosophical and scientific thought. Forester refers to 'a learned mythologist' – based on Peacock's friend Thomas Taylor 'the Platonist' (1758–1835), who always addressed the classicist Peacock as 'Greeky-Peaky'.[35] Forester says:

I introduced him to Sir Oran, for whom he immediately conceived a high veneration, and would never call him by any name but Pan. His usual salutation to him was in the following words:

[...]

King of the world! enthusiast free,
Who dwell'st in caves of liberty!
And on thy wild pipe's notes of glee
Respondest Nature's harmony!
Leading beneath the spreading tree
The Bacchanalian revelry!

'This,' said he, 'is part of the Orphic invocation of Pan. It alludes to the happy existence of the dancing Pans, Fauns, Orans, *et id genus omne*, whose dwellings are the caves of rocks and the hollows of trees, such as undoubtedly was, or would have been, the natural mode of life of our friend Pan among the woods of Angola. It alludes, too, to their musical powers, which in our friend Pan it gives me indescribable pleasure to find so happily exemplified. The epithet *Bacchic*, our friend Pan's attachment to the bottle demonstrates to be very appropriate; and the epithet Κοσμοκράτωρ, king of the world, points out a striking similarity between the Orphic Pan and the Troglodyte of Linnæus, *who believes that the earth was made for him, and that he will again be its sovereign*' (65–67).[36]

35   *Headlong Hall*, Introduction, p. xcviii.
36   Forester states earlier: 'Linnæus has given him the curious denominations of *Troglodytes*, *Homo nocturnus*, and *Homo silvestris*: but he evidently thought him a man: he describes him as having a hissing speech, thinking, reasoning, believing that the earth was made for him, and that he will one day be its sovereign' (62–63). Linnæus is quoted in the Latin in a footnote.

In this passage we can see an unbroken line of thought, from ancient Greece to Peacock's day, in which Pans, Wild Men, and Orans have become virtually indistinguishable: the mythological wood gods, the Wild Man, and the natural man of Monboddo all dwell in the hollows of trees or in caves in the rocks; Sir Oran's ability on the flute, 'a fact attested, not by a common traveller, but by a man of science, Mr Peiresc, and who relates it, not as a hearsay, but as a fact consisting with his own knowledge' (57),[37] is attributed to Pan's inherent skills; his taste for alcohol, which is a failing of Wild Men, is also noted by Buffon as a sign of orang sophistication when dining at table (*Melincourt*, p. 58, footnote), and by the learned mythologer as the appropriate behaviour of a Bacchant faun.[38]

Although the focus so far has been on Sir Oran's relationship to the Wild Man, it is worth noting also his qualities as a Noble Savage. He is taller than everyone else;[39] he is enormously strong; he enjoys excellent health. Put simply, his temperament and innate benevolence are those of a Noble Savage; while his actions when roused are those of a Wild Man. His contemplative disposition has been noted above. Morally he is superior to the bulk of his human fellows. Captain Hawltaught 'used to observe, he could always say he had an honest man in his house, which was more than could be said of many honourable houses where there was much vapouring about honour' (57). Forester reiterates this sentiment by quoting directly from Monboddo: '*With regard to his moral character, he is undoubtedly a man, and a much better man than many that are to be found in civilized*

---

37   This is a footnote quoting Monboddo, *O & P*, book ii, chap. 5.

38   Charles Darwin in *The Descent of Man* also notes the vices of our simian cousins: 'Many kinds of monkeys have a strong taste for tea, coffee, and spiritous liquors: they will also, as I have myself seen, smoke tobacco with pleasure.' He goes on to describe the effect of strong beer on African baboons, and their consequent hangovers. He concludes with an appropriate moral observation: 'An American monkey, an Ateles, after getting drunk on brandy, would never touch it again, and thus was wiser than many men' (396–97). The habit of associating primates with mythological figures persisted even after Darwin's revelations. In 1894 an Abyssinian baboon was named *Cynocephalus Hamadryas* = *dog-headed tree-dwelling wood-nymph*. See *OED*, *cynocephalus* and *hamadryad*.

39   In a footnote Peacock quotes Monboddo describing a 'young [orang-outang] but six and a half feet tall' (56).

countries' (*Melincourt*, p. 71). It is therefore Sir Oran who embodies the ideal man, while those around him are degenerated from this state, and only a few are striving to recapture it. Peacock employs this heretical conceit for some Swiftian attacks on his own species. Forester relates how he took Sir Oran to London, a place in Forester's philosophy equivalent to Babylon with pollution, within whose confines are found 'the sordid and sickly victims of commerce, and the effeminate and enervated slaves of luxury' (289):

> The theatres delighted him, particularly the opera, which not only accorded admirably with his taste for music; but where, as he looked round on the ornaments of the fashionable world, he seemed to be particularly comfortable, and to feel himself completely at home (60).

The joke of course is not that Sir Oran has risen to the noble condition where he is at ease with the fashionable world, but that the denizens of the fashionable world of London resemble those lesser simiae of his home in Angola.

The one point to keep in mind about Sir Oran Haut-ton and Sylvan Forester, is the same point that G.K. Chesterton made about Henry Jekyll and Edward Hyde:

> The real stab of the story is not in the discovery that the one man is two men; but in the discovery that the two men are one man (72).

Sir Oran and Forester are obviously not one physical person, as Jekyll and Hyde are, but they do form a complementary pair, as Jekyll and Hyde do not. Sir Oran lacks the gift of speech; Forester lacks the gift of silence. He talks, at length, with and to anyone who comes near him. Sir Oran is the natural man being exposed to civilization; Forester is the philosopher satiated and disgusted with the modern world, in retreat to a nobler, more simplified life. Forester is the thinker; Sir Oran is the man of action. Forester possesses 'so much intellectual superiority to the generality of mankind' (205); Sir Oran 'is prodigiously strong' (106n). Both halves of the pair fall in love with Anthelia, and both halves end up with her; but significantly it is Sir Oran who strikes up the first acquaintance, in the natural setting of the wood beyond Melincourt Castle, when Anthelia (who spends most of her time in her library reading Italian poetry) is out communing with nature, whilst avoiding her suitors, most of whom are degenerate specimens of humanity, and none of whom measure up to her ideals:

> She was roused from her reverie by sounds of music, issuing from the grove of pines, through which she had just passed, and which skirted the hollow. The notes were wild and irregular, but their effect was singular and pleasing. They ceased. Anthelia looked to the spot from which they had proceeded, and saw, or thought she saw, a face peeping at her through the trees; but the glimpse was momentary. There was in the expression of the countenance, something so extraordinary, that she almost felt convinced her imagination had created it; yet her imagination was not in the habit of creating such physiognomies. She could not, however, apprehend that this remarkable vision portended any evil to her; for, if so, alone and defenceless as she was, why should it be deferred? (102).

There are several things at work here. Anthelia the Child of Nature shares with the natural man the habit of contemplation. Sir Oran is first introduced to her as a Pan figure playing wild music on his flute, unseen in the woods. She is the only person who encounters him first in a wild environment. When she sees him she is not afraid.

She walks on, is caught in a downpour, and marooned on a rock in the middle of a rising torrent.

> She looked towards the pine grove, through which she had descended in the morning; she thought of the wild music she had heard, and of the strange face that had appeared among the trees. Suddenly it appeared again: and shortly after, a stranger issuing from the wood, ran with surprising speed to the edge of the chasm.
>
> Anthelia had never seen so singular a physiognomy; but there was nothing in it to cause alarm. The stranger seemed interested for her situation, and made gestures expressive of a design to assist her. He paused a moment, as if measuring with his eyes the breadth of the chasm, and then returning to the grove, proceeded very deliberately to pull up a pine. [Footnote: 'I have heard the natives say, he can throw down a palm-tree, by his amazing strength, to come at the wine.'—*Letter of a Bristol Merchant, in a note to the Origin and Progress of Language*, book ii. c.4.] (106).

Sir Oran runs with the speed of a Wild Man, and emerges from the woods in the same way that the Salvage Man emerges to aid Serena. Sir Oran makes friendly gestures in the same manner as the Salvage. He then performs the defining Wild Man act of pulling up a tree; but by Peacock's time this act has entered the scientific literature as an accomplishment of the orang-outang, thus coming, as it were, full circle, and enabling Peacock to paint a seemingly straightforward scene of great richness and complexity.

After the spectacular rescue, Peacock tells us that:

> Sir Oran Haut-ton, as we conjecture, had taken a very long ramble [...] and had sat down in the pine-grove to solace himself with his flute, when Anthelia, bursting upon him like a beautiful vision, rivetted him in silent admiration to the spot whence she departed, about which he lingered in hopes of her reappearance, till the accident which occurred on her return enabled him to exert his extraordinary physical strength, in a manner so remarkably advantageous to her (110).

Why should an orang-outang be smitten with a human? One could invoke Beauty and the Beast, and leave it at that; but that still leaves the question unanswered. It is important to remember what Sir Oran and Anthelia represent; and that these representations are essentially fluid. Anthelia is a Child of Nature, and as such is loved by wild creatures. The reason for this is simple; Fairchild writes: 'It is evident that humanitarian feeling toward animals, based not so much on reflective pity as on a genuine kinship with all instinctive and irreflective beings, is often associated with the [Child of Nature]' (371). This 'genuine kinship' exists between Forester, Anthelia, and Sir Oran; and it is that which eventually unites the Wild Man, the Noble Savage, and the Child of Nature.

Forester has already found his Wild aspect in the person of Sir Oran, and is in search of the perfect woman. He describes her to his friend Mr Fax, in a way that leaves little doubt that what he is looking for is a flowery Child of Nature:

> She should have no taste for what are called public pleasures. Her pleasures should be bounded in the circle of her family, and a few, a very few congenial friends, her books, her music, her flowers—she should delight in flowers—the uninterrupted cheerfulness of domestic concord, the delightful effusions of unlimited confidence. The rocks, and woods, and mountains, boundaries of the valley of her dwelling, she should be content to look on as the boundaries of the world (117).

'You say nothing of beauty,' replies Fax, giving Forester the opportunity to reveal that he is a true Platonist:

> As to what is usually called beauty, mere symmetry of form and features, it would be an object with me in purchasing a statue, but none whatever in choosing a wife. Let her countenance be a mirror of such qualities as I have described, and she cannot be otherwise than beautiful. I think with the Athenians, that beauty and goodness are inseparable (118–19).[40]

Anthelia, meanwhile, is looking for a Noble Savage in the guise of a knight-errant. In a conversation with Mrs Pinmoney she lists the qualities of her ideal man, in which the reader may see that some apply as well to Sir Oran as to Forester:

> I would require him to be free in all his thoughts, true in all his words, generous in all his actions—ardent in friendship, enthusiastic in love, disinterested in both—prompt in the conception, and constant in the execution, of benevolent enterprise—the friend of the friendless, the champion of the feeble, the firm opponent of the powerful oppressor—not to be enervated by luxury, nor corrupted by avarice, nor intimidated by tyranny, nor enthralled by superstition—more desirous to distribute wealth than to possess it, to disseminate liberty than to appropriate power, to cheer the heart of sorrow than to dazzle the eyes of folly.
>
> THE HONOURABLE MRS PINMONEY
> And do you really expect to find such a knight-errant? The age of chivalry is gone.
>
> ANTHELIA
> It is, but its spirit survives. Disinterested benevolence, the mainspring of all that is really admirable in the days of chivalry, will never perish for want of some minds calculated to feel its influence, still less for want of a proper field of exertion. [...] And I believe it possible to find as true a knight-errant in a brown coat in the nineteenth century, as in a suit of golden armour in the days of Charlemagne (23–24).[41]

40 What, then, of Sir Oran, who, like Socrates, and, indeed, Gabriel Utterson, is good but far from beautiful? I shall address this paradox later in this chapter, and in Chapter Ten.

41 Marilyn Butler, in her chapter on *Melincourt* (58–101), discusses Peacock's use of chivalry 'as a positive ideal about which he is serious, and as a satiric tool which undercuts his enemies' (82).

The reference to the brown coat is ambiguous enough to include both Forester and Sir Oran. By the end of the story, Forester and Sir Oran have jointly either performed all of the actions, or come to embody all of the qualities recited above by Anthelia. Nor should one forget that she embodies all of the qualities as well: she refuses sugar and all other products of slavery, and she has saved a family from destitution and placed them in a cottage and farm on her estate. Desmond, the recipient of Anthelia's largesse, asks Forester,

> '[W]hat can repay her benevolence?'
> 'I will answer for her,' said Mr Forester, 'though she is as yet personally unknown to me, that she loves benevolence for its own sake, and is satisfied with its consummation' (159).

Forester, who has never met a woman who lives up to his ideals, visits Anthelia with Sir Oran on business arising from the rescue. She receives them in her library. Forester begins:

> You have an admirable library, Miss Melincourt: and I judge from the great number of Italian books, you are justly partial to the poets of that exquisite language. The apartment itself seems singularly adapted to the genius of their poetry, which combines the magnificent simplicity of ancient Greece with the mysterious grandeur of the feudal ages. Those windows of stained glass would recall to an enthusiastic mind the attendant spirit of Tasso; and the waving of the cedars beyond, when the wind makes music in their boughs, with the birds singing in their shades and the softened dash of the torrent from the dingle below, might, with little aid from fancy, be modulated into that exquisite combination of melody which flowed from the enchanted wood at the entrance of Renaldo, and which Tasso has painted with a degree of harmony not less magical than the music he describes (164).[42]

42   Butler points out that Anthelia resembles a heroine from Tasso; and that 'Forester, Sir Oran and Anthelia are not characters in a novel, but figures from romance. There is no attempt to give them the surface detail of novel characters; instead, they have the elusive depth of allegory. Equally, the adventure in which all three are involved, of quest and rescue, has the dream-like inconsequence of romance' (68). Butler considers *Melincourt* in relation to Tasso, Spenser, and other works of romance (66–69). Peacock abandoned 'Ahrimanes', a poem based on *The Faerie Queene*, shortly before beginning *Melincourt*.

Note here that Forester is standing in the library, gazing through the window, and painting an Arcadian picture of the natural scene which, only a few days before, had been so wild and threatening, and in which Sir Oran had been so much at home and so necessary. In his present environment Sir Oran is at a disadvantage, being able neither to speak nor read. However, his manners remain impeccable.

After a rarefied Classical discussion, Forester and Anthelia each find that the other fulfils all of the requirements for the ideal mate; and when dinner is announced, Forester offers his hand to Anthelia. Sir Oran is left to escort the match-making matron Mrs Pinmoney. This is a significant moment. After Sir Oran saved Anthelia from the torrent, she 'requested the favour of his company to dinner at Melincourt' (109). Sir Oran had been obliged politely to refuse, as he was due home. In the end, it is the civilized Forester who accepts Anthelia's invitation, and walks into the dining room with her on his arm, in which all three sit down to dinner. Their first communal moment cannot happen without all three of them.

The fly in this wild ointment is one of the suitors for Anthelia's hand, 'Lord Anophel Achthar [Footnote: ΑΝΩΦΕΛον ΑΧΘος ΑΡουρας. Terræ pondus inutile.],[43] son and heir of the Marquis of Agaric [Footnote: AGARICUS, in Botany, a genus of plants of the class Cryptogamia, comprehending the mushroom, and a copious variety of toadstools.]' (80), who, following the self-serving advice of his parasite the Reverend Mr Grovelgrub lays plans to abduct Anthelia and keep her prisoner until she agrees to marry him. Grovelgrub meanwhile has his own plans to undermine Lord Anophel and ingratiate himself with Anthelia.

In *Hermsprong* the moral difference between Hermsprong and Sir Philip Chestrum is accentuated by their physical differences; in *Melincourt* there is no description of Lord Anophel, but we draw our own conclusions. Sir Oran the Wild Man has come from the fruitful forests of Africa, and has

---

43   ANOPHELon ACHTHos ARouras. David Garnett politely translates it as 'A useless cumber of the ground' (*The Novels of Thomas Love Peacock*, ed., intro. and notes by David Garnett (London: Hart-Davis, 1948), p. 144, n1). Peacock probably had in mind something closer to his description of the property owned by another of Anthelia's suitors, Mr Harum O'Scarum: 'a vast tract of undrained bog' (83).

learned the art of horticulture; he toils happily in his garden, and nurtures
the yeoman cabbage. Forester the Noble Savage lives in an establishment
which he has named after a potent image of courtly love – Redrose. Living
on his estate he has a maiden aunt called Miss Evergreen, which implies
that his mother was an Evergreen, and therefore a Child of Nature. His
estate – modelled on Monboddo's – is described thus:

> The valley expanded into a spacious amphitheatre, with a beautiful stream winding
> among pastoral meadows, which, as well as the surrounding hills, were studded with
> cottages, each with its own trees, its little garden, and its farm. Sir Telegraph was
> astonished to find so many human dwellings in a space that, on the modern tactics
> of rural œconomy, appeared only sufficient for three or four *moderate* farms […].
> Anthelia, as their path wound among the cottages, was more and more delighted
> with the neatness and comfort of the dwellings, the exquisite order of the gardens,
> the ingenuous air of happiness and liberty that characterized the simple inhabit-
> ants, and the health and beauty of the little rosy children that were sporting in the
> fields (284–85).

Anthelia the Child of Nature is a wild flower blooming in a land that is
both wildly beautiful and agriculturally productive. Lord Anophel is a
useless piece of dirt engendered by a toxic fungus.

The first abduction attempt moves our heroes into Spenser territory.
Like the Salvage Man, Sir Oran is characteristically unrestrained in defence
of his beloved, while Forester's efforts are divided between comforting the
distressed heroine and preventing Sir Oran from going too far. Anthelia
goes for one of her rambles in the woods. Suddenly,

> a mantle was thrown over her. She was wrapped in darkness, and felt that she was
> forcibly seized by several persons, who carried her rapidly along. She screamed, but
> the mantle was immediately pressed on her mouth, and she was hurried onward.
> After a time the party stopped: a tumult ensued: she found herself at liberty, and
> threw the mantle from her head. […] Two men were running away in the distance:
> two others, muffled and masked, were rolling on the ground, and roaring for mercy,
> while Sir Oran Haut-ton was standing over them with a stick [Footnote: 'They use
> an artificial weapon for attack and defence, viz. a stick, which no animal merely brute
> is known to do.'—*Origin and Progress of Language*, book ii. chap. 4.], and treating
> them as if he were a thresher, and they were sheaves of corn. By her side was Mr
> Forester, who, taking her hand, assured her that she was in safety, while at the same
> time he endeavoured to assuage Sir Oran's wrath, that he might raise and unmask
> the fallen foes (202–03).

Here begins the merging of our two heroes into one.[44] Sir Oran's apparently Monboddon application of a stick in fact derives (as a later scene will confirm) from Talus, Artegall's Iron Man in *The Faerie Queene*. Peacock describes Sir Oran beating the villains 'as if he were a thresher, and they were sheaves of corn'. Spenser writes of Talus, 'Who in his hand an yron flale did hould,/ With which he thresht out falshood, and did truth vnfould' (V.1.12). Hamilton writes that this iron flail is

> a military weapon in the Renaissance, adapted from the wooden flail or thresher. [...] It is an instrument of punishment [...] but its end is to unfold truth. [...] Apparently Talus is not to be regarded as separate from the exercise of Artegall's virtue (532).

Artegall is the embodiment of justice, and Talus is his instrument. They are not independent of each other. The comparison between these two and Forester and Sir Oran does not withstand close scrutiny beyond a certain point. Forester is not the embodiment of justice: he is the embodiment of noble virtues. Sir Oran is not the instrument of Forester's justice: when he acts, it is upon his own wild impulse. Nevertheless, Hamilton's felicitous statement that 'Talus is not to be regarded as separate from the exercise of Artegall's virtue' (532) applies equally to Forester and Sir Oran; Forester simply could not achieve his ends without his irascible companion. However, despite Peacock's verbal allusion to Talus (and an explicit allusion later), Sir Oran's behaviour here is not unlike that of Spenser's Salvage in the fight with Scorn and Disdain. The Salvage overcomes Scorn and then begins to scourge him with his own whip; and were it not for Arthur's restraining hand,

> He would with whipping, him haue done to dye:
> But being chekt, he did abstaine streight way,
> And let him rise.   (VI.8.29)

44   Clare Simmons writes: 'Peacock's choice of name for his (human) hero, which itself suggests a "man of the woods" (Sylvan or Sylvanus, a traditional name for a wild man found in such works as the *Faerie Queene*, is also the name for the orang-outang in *Count Robert of Paris*) may hint that there is little difference between man and orang-outang. Sir Oran is, in many respects, Sylvan Forester's alter-ego' ('A Man of few Words: The Romantic Orang-Outang and Scott's *Count Robert of Paris*', *Scottish Literary Journal*, 17.1 (May 1990), 21–34, (p. 24)).

This conflation of Talus and the Salvage recurs later, during Sir Oran's election to Parliament in the Borough of Onevote. The electors, having been plied with ale and divers foodstuffs, offer to chair Sir Oran through the crowd. He politely declines the offer. They politely insist. He politely declines again. They attempt 'with gentle force to overcome his scruples' (249). He grabs a stick from a farmer and begins to lay about him 'like Artegall's Iron Man, or like Ajax among the Trojans, or like Rhodomont in Paris, or like Orlando among the soldiers of Agramant' (249). He fights his way through the mob and leaps onto the box of Sir Telegraph's barouche 'from whence he shook his sapling at the foe, with looks of mortal defiance' (250). Peacock probably had in mind the sequence in *The Faerie Queene* of the giant with the scales, and Talus's attack on the mob who followed him (V.2.51–54). But the mention of Sir Oran shaking his sapling at the foe is a reminder that he is above all a Wild Man – like the Salvage, as the following scene from *The Faerie Queene* illustrates.

After Arthur and the Salvage leave the villain Turpine's castle, Turpine follows them at a distance, intent on more mischief. Arthur lies down to sleep while the Salvage forages for fruit in the wood. He returns to find Turpine about to attack the sleeping Arthur, whereupon:

> Himselfe vnto his weapon he betooke,
> That was an oaken plant, which lately hee
> Rent by the root; which he so sternely shooke,
> That like an hazell wand, it quiuered and quooke.   (VI.7.24)

After the abduction of Anthelia has been foiled, Forester reveals that he has felt a need to involve himself emotionally with the connection between Anthelia and Sir Oran:

> Anthelia, as she walked homeward, leaning on Mr Forester's arm, inquired to what happy accident she was indebted for the timely intervention of himself and Sir Oran Haut-ton. Mr Forester informed her, that having a great wish to visit the scene which had been the means of introducing him to her acquaintance, he had made Sir Oran understand his desire, and they had accordingly set out together (204).

In fact, all three become psychically connected with that scene in the moments before the attack. Anthelia also has 'wandered alone to the ruined bridge, to contemplate the scene of her former misadventure' (201). She hears the sounds of the villains in the woods, and becomes scared, but, 'She paused again to listen: the soft tones of a flute sounded from a distance: these gave her confidence, and she again proceeded' (202). The first rescue – by Sir Oran from the forces of nature – is about to be repeated, this time by Sir Oran and Forester together, from the designs of degenerate men.

Although, as Marilyn Butler points out, Sir Oran, Forester and Anthelia are figures from romance (68), it appears that Peacock is not content to leave it at that. As with his blending of Spenserian and Monboddon themes, he cleverly arranges things so that Forester and Sir Oran are both in love with Anthelia, but within separate genres, as it were. Forester is a normal, if somewhat eccentric, gentleman, who begins as a reclusive philosopher-landlord, falls in love, marries, settles down and raises a family. He begins and ends unremarkably, as if he were a stock character in a conventional novel. Peacock writes:

> The course of mutual love between Anthelia and Mr Forester was as smooth as the gliding of a skiff down a stream, through the flowery meadows of June: and [...] there was a very apparent probability that their intercourse would terminate in that grand climax and finale of all romantic adventure—marriage (311–12).

Again Peacock employs the image of the flower, this time associated with true love and its natural union; which is the theme of a song sung previously by Anthelia – an expression of her yearning for true love and her as yet unacknowledged anticipation of union with the owner of Redrose Abbey:

THE FLOWER OF LOVE
'Tis said the rose is Love's own flower,
Its blush so bright, its thorns so many;
And winter on its bloom has power,
But has not on its sweetness any.
For though young Love's ethereal rose
Will droop on Age's wintry bosom,
Yet still its faded leaves disclose
The fragrance of their earliest blossom.
[...]
Why did not Love the amaranth choose,
That bears no thorns, and cannot perish?
Alas! no sweets its flowers diffuse,

And only sweets Love's life can cherish.
But be the rose and amaranth twined,
And Love, their mingled powers assuming,
Shall round his brows a chaplet bind,
For ever sweet, for ever blooming (191–92).[45]

Sir Oran's fortunes are less certain. Anthelia, who has been constantly in the company of Forester and Sir Oran for some time, returns to Melincourt Castle, leaving Forester content and happy in the conventional anticipation of matrimony. However:

> Mr Forester observed with concern, that his friend Sir Oran's natural melancholy was visibly increased, and Mr Fax was of opinion that he was smitten with the tender passion: [...]. But Sir Oran grew more and more fond of solitude, and passed the greater part of the day in the woods, though it was now the reign of the gloomy November, which, however, accorded with the moody temper of his spirit; and he often went without his breakfast, though he always came home to dinner. His perpetual companion was his flute, with which he made sad response to the wintry wind (312).

Note here that Peacock is again emphasizing Sir Oran's mythical associations by reprising, now in a minor key, his lines from the learned mythologer's Orphic invocation to Pan: 'And on thy wild pipe's notes of glee/ Respondest Nature's Harmony' (66).

Having earlier given examples from Monboddo on the orang-outang's capacity for forming deep attachments (56n.), Peacock presents the familiar image of a devoted pet pining for its owner, but then refocuses the image with the introduction of the flute, and the heightened language of the 'sad response to the wintry wind' (312), to present the equally familiar image of the courtly lover pining for his Lady. Thus in one single passage

---

45   Amaranth is a real flower, but in this context is a fabled flower that never fades. Cf.
      Milton's description of
          Immortal Amarant, a Flour which once
          In Paradise, fast by the Tree of Life
          Began to bloom, but soon for Mans offence
          To Heav'n remov'd where first it grew, there grows,
          And flours aloft shading the Fount of Life.   (*PL*, III.353–57)

Sir Oran represents an orang-outang, a mythological wood god, and a courtly lover.

But our courtly lover, lacking speech, is hopelessly disadvantaged. Forester and Anthelia, being less instinctive, have to talk their way into each other's heart; and in a charming scene on the sea shore Anthelia not only displays a sympathy of feeling with Forester, but displays her floral origins in a speech absolutely teeming with blossoms and other images of nature:

> The morning is the infancy of the day, and, like the infancy of life, has health and bloom, and cheerfulness and purity, in a degree unknown to the busy noon, which is the season of care, or the languid evening, which is the harbinger of repose. Perhaps the song of the nightingale is not in itself less cheerful than that of the lark: it is the season of her song that invests it with the character of melancholy. It is the same with the associations of infancy: it is all cheerfulness, all hope: its path is on the flowers of an untried world. The daisy has more beauty in the eye of childhood than the rose in that of maturer life. The spring is the infancy of the year: its flowers are the flowers of promise and the darlings of poetry. The autumn too has its flowers; but they are little loved, and little praised: for the associations of autumn are not with ideas of cheerfulness, but with yellow leaves and hollow winds, heralds of winter, and emblems of dissolution (218–19).

Forester delivers a speech beginning, 'Fresh air and liberty are all that is necessary to the happiness of children' (220), which could have come directly from Ruffigny in *Fleetwood*. It ends as a soliloquy on the enduring power of first love. This exchange is a recognition not only of sensibilities, but of natures – the Noble Savage and the Child of Nature.

Poor Sir Oran finds himself socially included but emotionally excluded, as he attempts to maintain contact with Anthelia through his only medium of communication – his music. On the excursion to Forester's estate:

> They followed a narrow winding path, through rocky and sylvan hills. They walked in straggling parties of ones, twos, and threes. Mr Forester and Anthelia went first. Sir Oran Haut-ton followed alone, playing a pensive tune on his flute (278).

The second abduction attempt is successful; Lord Anophel locks Anthelia away in the wonderfully named Alga castle, situated on the sea shore. Here Peacock extends his botanical joke at Lord Anophel's expense.

As has been mentioned, Lord Anophel is the son of the Marquis of Agaric, and Agaricus is a species of mushroom, which is of the class Cryptogamia. Alga is also of the class Cryptogamia. The *OED* defines *cryptogamia* thus: 'A large division of the vegetable kingdom, being the last class in the Linnæan system, comprising those plants which have no stamens and pistils, and therefore no proper flowers; including Ferns, Mosses, Algæ, Lichens, and Fungi.' Anthelia is a flower; Lord Anophel is not. His attempt to breed with her is botanically doomed. One may also infer from the name of his castle and its position on the sea shore that the Marquis's line is deteriorating from generation to generation. The Marquis is a mushroom or toadstool, but he would seem to be located safely on land. Lord Anophel, his son and heir, is identified with seaweed, and dwelling in the littoral zone between land and sea. The line, representing the most primitive specimens in the plant kingdom, seems to be heading back into the foamy scum from which mankind emerged.

As the news of Anthelia's disappearance spreads, search parties fan out across the country, but without success. Forester, who has initially gone about in a carriage, elects to do a more thorough search on foot. He, Fax, and Sir Oran – who at this stage is unaware of Anthelia's disappearance – set out on their quest.[46]

As the quest continues, Sir Oran's role is to perform the feats which Forester undertakes, but lacks the physical strength, and the savage nature, to carry through. He becomes the Salvage to Forester's Arthur.

When they are staying at Cimmerian Lodge, the home of Moley Mystic (a satirical attack on Coleridge), a fire breaks out in Mystic's room.

> Mr Forester and Sir Oran Haut-ton ran for water: Mr Fax rang the nearest bell: Mr Mystic vociferated 'Fire!' with singular energy: the servants ran about half-undressed: pails, buckets, and pitchers, were in active requisition; till Sir Oran Haut-ton ascending the stairs with the great rain-water tub, containing one hundred and eight gallons of water [Footnote: 'Some travellers speak of his strength as wonderful; greater, they

---

46 Marilyn Butler writes: 'Sir Oran goes on his travels to investigate the current state of England, as did other fictional Noble Savages – Voltaire's Huron, [...] and Bage's Hermsprong' (78). She analyses Forester's quest in relation to Renaissance allegory (86–87).

say, than that of ten men such as we.'—*Ancient Metaphysics*, vol.iii. p. 105.], threw the whole contents on the flames with one sweep of his powerful arm (341).

One evening they stop in an inn, and are sitting down to dinner in 'an apartment separated from another only by a moveable partition, which allowed the two rooms to be occasionally laid into one' (389). An argument begins in the adjoining apartment between a pair of runaway lovers and the girl's heavy father, 'Sir Gregory Greenmould, and the old valetudinarian he had chosen for his daughter, Sir Bonus Mac Scrip' (392). Sir Gregory calls for his varlets and rascals.

> A violent trampling of feet and various sounds of tumult ensued, as if the old gentleman and his party were tearing the lovers asunder by main force; and at length an agonizing scream from the young lady seemed to announce that their purpose was accomplished. Mr Forester started up with a view to doing all in his power to assist the injured damsel; and Sir Oran Haut-ton, who, as the reader has seen, had very strong feelings of natural justice, and a most chivalrous sympathy with females in distress, rushed with a desperate impulse against the partition, and hurled a great portion of it, with a violent crash, into the adjoining apartment (391–92).

Again Sir Oran hurls himself, like the Salvage, into the fray, while Forester merely leaps up 'with a view' to doing something (probably delivering a speech on the evils of arranged marriages). Peacock contrasts the civilized, socially responsible – therefore constrained – gentleman, with the unrestrained natural man of action; but shows that, working in concert, they achieve their chivalrous purpose:

> As Sir Oran was not habituated to allow any very long process of syllogistic reasoning to interfere between his conception and execution of the dictates of natural justice, he commenced operations by throwing the assailants one by one down stairs [...]. Sir Bonus Mac Scrip retreated through the breach, and concealed himself under the dining-table in Mr Forester's apartment. Mr Forester succeeded in preventing Sir Gregory from being thrown after his myrmidons: but Sir Oran kept the fat Baronet a close prisoner in the corner of the room, while the lovers slipped away into the inn-yard, where the chaise they had ordered was in readiness (392–93).

Peacock is at pains to emphasize the symbolically consanguineous relationship between Forester and Sir Oran, who experience a profound mutuality of sentiment during their quest when they return to Melincourt Castle in the hope of hearing news of Anthelia. The servant old Peter Gray receives them, and leads them into the library.

> The moment the door was thrown open, Mr Forester started, and threw himself forward into the apartment towards Anthelia's chair; but before he reached it, he stopped, placed his hand before his eyes, and turning round, leaned for support on the arm of Mr Fax. He recovered himself in a few minutes, and sate down by the table. [...]
> Mr Forester observed, from the appearance of the drawing materials, that they had been hastily left, and he saw that the last subject on which Anthelia had been employed was a sketch of Redrose Abbey. He sate with his head leaning on his hand, and his eyes fixed on the drawing in perfect silence. [...]
> Sir Oran Haut-ton kept his eyes fixed on the door with looks of anxious impatience, and showed manifest and increasing disappointment at every re-entrance of old Peter, who at length summoned them to dinner (352–53).

The philosopher is distraught because he knows that his beloved is missing, but the natural man is fretful simply because his beloved is absent.

> Mr Fax was not surprised that Mr Forester had no appetite, but that Sir Oran had lost his, appeared to him extremely curious. The latter grew more and more uneasy, rose from table, took a candle in his hand, and wandered from room to room, searching every closet and corner in the Castle [...]. Sir Oran at length having left no corner of the habitable part of the Castle unexamined, returned to the dining-room, and throwing himself into a chair began to shed tears in great abundance.
> Footnote: 'He is capable of the greatest affection, not only to his brother oran outangs, but to such among us as use him kindly. And it is a fact well attested to me by a gentleman who was an eye-witness of it, that an oran outang aboard his ship conceived such an affection for the cook, that when upon some occasion he left the ship to go ashore, the gentleman saw the oran outang shed tears in great abundance.' —*Origin and Progress of Language*, book ii. chap. 4 (353–54).[47]

At this point there is nothing to distinguish between the philosopher and the natural man.

By the end of the quest, the other characters have begun to feel this merging of identities of our heroes. Lord Anophel visits Anthelia in her

---

47   This footnote is originally given by Peacock on p. 56. On p. 354 the reader is simply referred to the note on p. 56.

room in Alga Castle where she sits playing her harp and gazing out at the sea. He tells her that all her friends 'have now gone home in despair'.

ANTHELIA

That, my Lord, I cannot believe; for there is one, at least, who I am confident will never be weary of seeking me, and who, I am equally confident, will not always seek in vain.

LORD ANOPHEL ACHTHAR

If you mean the young lunatic of Redrose Abbey, or his friend the dumb Baronet,

Lord Anophel's confusion is appropriate: Anthelia's assertion applies equally to either. But it also applies equally to both. Lord Anophel continues with another lie, but one which reveals an unconscious acknowledgment of their Wild and Noble status:

they are both gone to London to attend the opening of the Honourable House; and if you doubt my word, I will show you their names in the Morning Post, among the Fashionable Arrivals at Wildman's Hotel (446–47).

At last the searchers come to the shore near Alga Castle, where the keen sighted Sir Oran spies in the distance Grovelgrub taking a constitutional. He recognizes the cleric at once as one of the foiled abductors from the original attempt, and overtaking him, threatens him, in true Wild Man style, with his stick. Forester restrains 'the rage of Sir Oran' (451) while Grovelgrub confesses, then they storm the castle. Again, as Arthur has to restrain the Salvage at the sight of Turpine in his castle, it is the civilized Forester who acts as a socializing influence on the behaviour of Sir Oran, as it threatens to go beyond acceptable bounds. But, on this final occasion, Forester is beginning to neglect the social niceties, and focus only on Anthelia.

[T]he door was burst open, and Sir Oran Haut-ton appeared in the aperture, with the Reverend Mr Grovelgrub in custody, whom he dragged into the apartment, followed by Mr Forester and Mr Fax.[48] Mr Forester flew to Anthelia, who threw herself

---

48 Note how the natural wild impulse of this symbiotic pairing always runs ahead of the civilized restraining intellect.

into his arms, hid her face in his bosom, and burst into tears: which when Sir Oran saw, his wrath grew boundless, and quitting his hold of the Reverend Mr Grovelgrub (who immediately ran down stairs, and out of the castle, as fast as a pair of short thick legs would carry him), seized on Lord Anophel Achthar, and was preparing to administer natural justice by throwing him out at the window; but Mr Fax interposed, and calling Mr Forester's attention, which was totally engaged with Anthelia, they succeeded in rescuing the terrified sprig of nobility (449–50).[49]

Anthelia thanks her deliverer with a speech that is touchingly appropriate to her character, yet laughingly inappropriate to an age in which chivalry (despite the activities of the heroes) is dead:

'O Forester!' said Anthelia, 'you have realized all my wishes. I have found you the friend of the poor, the enthusiast of truth, the disinterested cultivator of the rural virtues, the active promoter of the cause of human liberty. It only remained that you should emancipate a captive damsel, who, however, will but change the mode of her durance, and become your captive for life' (452).

Anthelia progresses from being rescued by Sir Oran alone in a wild natural setting; to being rescued by Sir Oran and Forester in a natural setting, but where nature is neutral; to being rescued by Sir Oran and Forester in a civilized but degenerate setting. The next move is into an ideal, rural, permanently secure setting. She and Forester marry; or, as Carl Dawson puts it: 'Sir Oran having finally rescued the beleagured heroine, Forester wins his lady.'[50]

Peacock then does something very interesting. Apart from the mention of 'little Foresters' (455) sitting on Anthelia's uncle's knee, he makes no further reference to the relationship between Forester and Anthelia. As a well-off gentleman and his wife, they simply settle down conventionally, and get on with raising a family. However,

---

49   Sir Oran represents the warlike, vengeful aspect of chivalry, while Forester represents the protective. At this point the two halves of the centaur dissociate, and have to be reunited by Fax.

50   *His Fine Wit: A Study of Thomas Love Peacock* (London: Routledge & Kegan Paul, 1970), p. 206.

Sir Oran Haut-ton continued to reside with Mr Forester and Anthelia. They discovered in the progress of time, that he had formed for the latter the same kind of reverential attachment, as the Satyr in Fletcher forms for the Holy Shepherdess [there follows a long footnote containing extracts from Fletcher's *The Faithful Shepherdess* (1609)]: and Anthelia might have said to him in the words of Clorin:

'—They wrong thee that do call thee rude:
Though thou be'st outward rough and tawny-hued,
Thy manners are as gentle and as fair,
As his who boasts himself born only heir
To all humanity.'[51]

His greatest happiness was in listening to the music of her harp and voice: in the absence of which he solaced himself, as usual, with his flute and French horn. He became likewise a proficient in drawing; but what progress he made in the art of speech, we have not been able to ascertain (453–54).

Anthelia has 'married' both halves of this composite creature: the Forester half provides her with children and domestic tranquillity – the commonplaces of marriage – and in him she finds a true meeting of minds. Sir Oran remains forever the devoted Wild courtly lover, and it is in this devotion that Peacock presents a true meeting of souls. Sir Oran and Anthelia may not be able to converse in words, but they commune at a deeper level with their music. Peacock's final image is of a family of forest creatures playing happily together under the watchful gaze and benign protection of the Wild Man.[52]

51 Butler points out that Fletcher adapted his Satyr from Spenser. She goes on: 'Spenser's Sir Satyrane, in Book I of the *Faerie Queene*, and Fletcher's Satyr, in the pastoral play *The Faithful Shepherdess*, are two rough but loyal creatures, who prove their native nobility by championing a woman and saving her from rape by a so-called civilised man. It is, of course, highly ironic that they should do this, since the satyr's partly bestial nature traditionally connoted lust' (69).
52 This is in keeping with the Renaissance pictorial tradition of the satyr marrying a woman or nymph and raising a family in the forest. Cf. also Dürer's 1498 engraving *Hercules*, in which a Wild Man protects a satyr and his family from attack. See Bartra, fig.16, opp. p. 54.

In this marriage of bodies, minds and souls between the Wild Man, the Noble Savage and the Child of Nature, they become, as it were, one single organism. None can exist without the other two; indeed, as a married couple, Forester and Anthelia have become one flesh. Anthelia makes the home; Forester provides for his extended family; Sir Oran protects them all.

Of particular interest to the student of *Jekyll and Hyde* is the outward appearance of Sir Oran, and the response of people upon first meeting him. Both Hyde and Sir Oran are described as ugly. Hyde's appearance is grotesque, deformed, threatening, baffling, and disgusting. This is because his body is the outer expression of his foul and evil soul. Sir Oran's body, however, is upright, tall, strong, and athletic, as befits the natural man. Moreover his soul is pure, his mind is gentle, and he is of a loving disposition. His face is ugly, but his benign and noble character shines through and overcomes the initial misgivings of those with whom he comes in contact. The running joke in the story revolves around the fact that none of the human characters realize that they are meeting an orang-outang:

> Sir Telegraph looked earnestly at the stranger, but was too polite to laugh, though he could not help thinking there was something very ludicrous in Sir Oran's physiognomy, notwithstanding the air of high fashion which characterized his whole deportment, and which was heightened by a pair of enormous whiskers, and the folds of a vast cravat. He therefore bowed to Sir Oran with becoming gravity, and Sir Oran returned the bow with very striking politeness.
>
> 'Possibly,' thought Sir Telegraph, 'possibly I may have seen an uglier fellow' (38).

Sir Oran saves Anthelia from the torrent, giving Peacock the opportunity to ridicule the effete upper class:

> The remarkable physiognomy and unparallelled strength of the stranger caused much of surprise, and something of apprehension, to mingle with Anthelia's gratitude: but the air of high fashion, which characterized his whole deportment, diminished her apprehension, while it increased her surprise at the exploit he had performed (107).

After the rescue, a search party arrives, among whom is Anthelia's ancient hypochondriac uncle, Mr Hippy.[53]

> Anthelia communicated to him the particulars of the signal service she had received from the stranger, whom Mr Hippy stared at heartily, and shook hands with cordially.
> [...]
> 'I wonder who he is,' said Mr Hippy, as they walked rapidly homewards: 'manifestly dumb, poor fellow! a man of consequence, no doubt: no great beauty, by the by' (107–09).

Forester is not unaware of Sir Oran's social predicament; and has taken pains to remedy it. He tells Sir Telegraph:

> There is to a stranger something ludicrous in a first view of his countenance, which led me to introduce him only to the best society, where politeness would act as a preventive to the propensity to laugh; for he has so nice a sense of honour (which I shall observe, by the way, is peculiar to man), that if he were to be treated with any kind of contumely, he would infallibly die of a broken heart, as has been seen in some of his species [Footnote: *Origin and Progress of Language*, book ii. chap. 4.]. With a view of ensuring him the respect of society, which always attends on rank and fortune, I have purchased him a baronetcy, and made over to him an estate (61).

And it works. During Sir Oran and Forester's first visit to Melincourt Castle, Mrs Pinmoney, seeing Forester and Sir Oran standing together, takes Sir Telegraph aside:

THE HONOURABLE MRS PINMONEY
Who is that very bright-eyed wild-looking young man?

SIR TELEGRAPH PAXARETT
That is my old acquaintance [...] Sylvan Forester [...].

[...]

THE HONOURABLE MRS PINMONEY
And who is that *very* tall and remarkably ugly gentleman?

---

53   He is in fact 'an old relation, a medium, as it were, between cousin and great uncle' (26).

SIR TELEGRAPH PAXARETT

That is Sir Oran Haut-ton, Baronet; to which designation you may shortly add M.P. for the ancient and honourable borough of Onevote.

THE HONOURABLE MRS PINMONEY

A Baronet! and M.P.! Well, now I look at him again, I certainly do not think him so very plain: he has a very fashionable air. Haut-ton! French extraction, no doubt. And now I think of it, there is something very French in his physiognomy (170–71).

In *Melincourt*, with its orang-outangs, Lucretian men, Pans, fauns, satyrs, sylvans, troglodytes, Wild Men, Noble Savages, Children of Nature, flowers, trees, cabbages, creepers, toadstools, algae, Homer, Spenser, Virgil, Shakespeare, Milton, Tasso, Wordsworth, Coleridge, Buffon, Linnæus, Rousseau, Monboddo, and a galaxy of others too numerous to mention, Peacock has given us a brief history of man, from his natural beginnings to his present degenerate condition. But he has not done it from within a religious framework; he has done it from within an eccentric evolutionary framework; and he has done this through the enduring, constantly evolving figure of the Wild Man: a figure which will emerge from the shadows some decades later in the form of Edward Hyde.

Melincourt provides a striking example of an ape who, although ugly, is neither deformed nor evil. He is violent when roused, and has fallen victim to the human scourge of alcohol; but he is tall, polite, honourable, considerate, gentle, protective and loving; and all of these qualities are not simply derived from Peacock's imagination, but attested to by eye-witnesses and natural philosophers. It would be incautious, therefore, to conclude that Hyde's apishness is a defining sign of his evil nature. His apishness no doubt reveals his archaic origins, but the primitive is not necessarily the evil. Hyde's evil is expressed not in his apishness, but in his deformity, and that requires a Platonic or Christian explanation.

In the next chapter we shall examine a text which overtly deals with the three great themes underpinning *Jekyll and Hyde*: Platonism, Darwinism, and the Bible.

PART THREE

Reconciling Plato, Darwin, and the Bible

CHAPTER SIX

Charles Kingsley: The Missing Link

The ongoing fusion of Christian and Platonic thought is evident in the writings of Spenser, More, Milton, and Donne. In *Gulliver's Travels* Swift informs his predominantly Christian writing with Platonic political theory and a Platonic view of the relationship between mind and body. Moreover he addresses the subject of evolution (within the Lucretian system) and degeneration (within the Platonic system). *Melincourt* blends myth and Wild Man lore with evolutionary theory of the most romantic and speculative kind, based on serious scholarship. With the arrival of Charles Kingsley (1819–75) all of these themes come together. Kingsley was not only a disciple of Plato and Jesus, but of Charles Darwin as well. His ability to absorb and, in his own opinion, to reconcile all three masters did not reside in the virtue of consistent thought. He was able quite unblushingly to discard the Platonic doctrine of the fixity of species, and embrace the Darwinian theory of evolution by natural selection, while at the same time turning the Darwinian process into a Platonically operated part of God's Creation. Likewise his hold on theological doctrine was equally idiosyncratic. Guy Kendall comments on Kingsley's

> extraordinarily uncritical treatment of Scripture, taking isolated texts apart from their context and treating them as of equal value and authority, in Old and New Testaments alike, with a rather literal application.[1]

Yet at the same time it was the authority of Scripture which helped Kingsley assimilate Darwin's theory. In the preface (1871) to his *Westminster Sermons* he discusses Natural Theology and the questions which it must address: one of them being the problem of Race. Kingsley declares –

---

1   Guy Kendall, *Charles Kingsley and His Ideas* (London: Hutchinson, 1947), p. 133.

using a term associated with Darwin – that all of the races in the world 'had one common ancestor'.[2] However, he continues, 'this is not matter of natural Theology. What is matter thereof, is this.'[3] And he raises a theme which lies at the heart of *Jekyll and Hyde* – heredity:

> Physical science is proving more and more the immense importance of Race; the importance of hereditary powers, hereditary organs, hereditary habits, in all organized beings, from the lowest plant to the highest animal.[4]

He goes on to discuss competition between individuals and competition between races, leading to oppression and extermination; and then shows how Darwin is simply following in the footsteps of Scripture:

> The Natural Theology of the future must take count of these tremendous and even painful facts. She may take count of them. For Scripture has taken count of them already. It talks continually—it has been blamed for talking so much—of races; of families; of their wars, their struggles, their exterminations; of races favoured, of races rejected; of remnants being saved, to continue the race; of hereditary tendencies, hereditary excellencies, hereditary guilt. Its sense of the reality and importance of descent is so intense, that it speaks of a whole tribe or a whole family by the name of its common ancestor; and the whole nation of the Jews is Israel, to the end.[5]

It is this biblical Darwinism – mankind, risen from a common prehistoric ancestor and burdened with hereditary guilt – which will provide another aid to understanding the mystery of Edward Hyde.

Kingsley of course was not alone in these feats of mental gymnastics. Georg Roppen, in his survey of the works of some Victorian 'evolutionary' writers, observes:

> The idea of evolution does not [...] impose upon the writer a rigid formula: it is for the poets to make their choice, to impose upon the specific theory their own visionary

---

2   *Westminster Sermons* (London: Macmillan, [1874]; repr. 1894), p. xvi.
3   *Westminster Sermons*, p. xvi.
4   *Westminster Sermons*, p. xvi.
5   *Westminster Sermons*, p. xvii.

pattern. Thus the scientific data remain to them merely framework concepts, a bridge towards significance, value, duty, and the ultimate mysteries of existence.[6]

In a chapter entitled 'Evolution in the Platonic Tradition' Roppen discusses the poetry of Tennyson and Browning, with whom 'the idea of evolution becomes a seminal theme in English poetry of the nineteenth century' (163).[7] However, as the title of the chapter indicates, evolution does not manage to displace Platonism, nor, for that matter, its bedfellow Christianity. In *The Water-Babies* Kingsley brings these three great themes together in an obvious and accessible way; and in so doing provides a text which thematically serves as a precursor to *Jekyll and Hyde*. But how did Kingsley, a minister of the Church, come to write such a book?

Charles Kingsley

This son of a clergyman imbibed his father's vocation from his infancy, and from the age of four would deliver sermons from a make-believe pulpit in his nursery.[8] However, his enthusiasm waned, and during his time at Cambridge he turned from Christianity. Susan Chitty comments:

> In adolescence his faith had not been strong. The only mention of religion in his letters to his mother was a dutiful promise, too often repeated, to read his Bible. It was in Nature, not in God, that he found inspiration.[9]

6   *Evolution and Poetic Belief: A Study in Some Victorian and Modern Writers* (Oslo: Oslo University Press, 1956), p. 458. Roppen mentions Kingsley only in passing, and not in connection with the above quotation.

7   Roppen, p. 163.

8   *Charles Kingsley, His Letters and Memories of His Life*, ed. by his wife (Frances E. (Fanny) Kingsley), 2 vols (London: King, 1877), I, 8. (Hereafter *CKL*.) Fanny includes the infant prodigy's first sermon.

9   Susan Chitty, *The Beast and the Monk: A Life of Charles Kingsley* (London: Hodder & Stoughton, 1975), p. 53.

If Kingsley found inspiration in Nature, he found comfort and wisdom in Plato. When in 1839 he won an academic prize at Cambridge, he chose an edition of Plato in eleven volumes.[10] However, Nature and Plato could not prevent him from falling into bad habits while he was studying there. By day he indulged the gentleman's pursuits of hunting, fishing and shooting; by night he indulged the rake's pursuits of smoking, drinking and gambling at cards; and – on at least one occasion which he afterwards bitterly repented – he had a sexual encounter.[11] Fortunately salvation was at hand.

In July 1839 Kingsley met his future wife Frances (Fanny) Grenfell, and immediately felt, as a good Platonist and metempsychosist, that their newly begun relationship 'yet seemed old—from the first more of a rec-ognition than an acquaintance'.[12] At the time he was not in a good way, as Fanny recounts:

> He was then full of religious doubts; and his face, with its unsatisfied hungering look, bore witness to the state of his mind. It had a sad longing expression, too, as if he had all his life been looking for a sympathy he had never found—a rest which he would never attain in this world. His peculiar character had not been understood hitherto, and his heart had been half asleep. It woke up now, and never slept again.[13]

Neither, it would seem, did Fanny's. She fell in love with Kingsley and, being deeply religious, took it upon herself to redeem this lost sheep. She writes to him:

> How I remember your wild troubled look that first day, as if you lived such a *lone* life, and I felt, from our first conversation, that I alone could understand you, that I alone had the key to your spiritual being and could raise you to your proper height.[14]

---

10   *CKL*, I, 43. Kingsley was also thoroughly familiar with the Cambridge Platonists, especially Henry More (*Alexandria*, p. 127; *CKL*, II, 96), and he was a lover of Milton's poetry (*CKL*, II, 456).

11   Chitty, p. 57. Chitty quotes from a collection of unpublished letters to Fanny, in the possession of Kingsley's literary executrix, Mrs Angela Covey-Crump. Letter 45, 1843. (Hereafter ULF.)

12   *CKL*, I, 44.

13   *CKL*, I, 44.

14   Unpublished letter from Fanny to Charles, 14 March 1854. Quoted in Chitty, p. 55.

After an initial kick against the pricks, Kingsley took to redemption with gusto, and underwent a mediaeval mortification of his flesh, which included fasting, scourging, sleeping on the floor, a specially made undergarment of canvas to mimic a hair shirt, and, on one occasion, lying naked on thorns.[15]

He was a person of enormous energy (he once walked the fifty-two miles from Cambridge to London in one day),[16] and gloried in 'the excitement of animal exercise'.[17] But it was the animal side of his nature that had led him into his 'wild beast life',[18] and it had to be curbed. He writes to Fanny that his 'superfluous excitement has to be broken in like that of a dog or a horse—for it is utterly animal'.[19] And, in 1850, the year of Stevenson's birth, he writes in *Alton Locke*:

> That there is a duality in us—a lifelong battle between flesh and spirit—we all, alas! know well enough.[20]

He decided to fight this war in the members with the help of a strong ally:

> I feel more and more daily that a clergyman's life is the one for which both my *physique* and *morale* were intended—that the profession will check and guide the faulty parts of my mind, while it gives full room for my energy—that energy which had so nearly ruined me; but will now be devoted utterly, I hope, to the service of God.[21]

Kingsley was ordained in July 1842, and at once took up his duties as a curate at Eversley. But he was also intending to marry Fanny; and, as some of his unpublished letters show, his snake had been scotched, not killed.

---

15 The full horrors of Kingsley's penance, and his bizarre courtship of Fanny, may be found in Chitty.
16 *CKL*, I, 52.
17 *CKL*, I, 51.
18 Quoted in Chitty, p. 57. No details.
19 *CKL*, I, 52.
20 *Alton Locke, Tailor and Poet* (London: Macmillan, 1889), p. 4. Further references are given after quotations in the text.
21 *CKL*, I, 53.

His carnal impulses and divine aspirations found a curious accommodation, as Chitty relates:

> 'Matter is holy,' he told Fanny, 'awful glorious matter. Let us never use those words *animal* and *brutal* in a degrading sense. Our animal enjoyments must be religious ceremonies.' He carried the analogy to almost unbelievable lengths. 'When you go to bed tonight, forget that you ever wore a garment, and open your lips for my kisses and spread out each limb that I may lie between your breasts all night (Canticles 1,13)' [ULF no.22, 2 October 1843]. 'At a quarter past eleven lie down, clasp your arms and every limb around me, and with me repeat the *Te Deum* aloud.'[22]

The complexity of Kingsley's emotions at this time may be seen in a letter to Fanny in which he moves seamlessly from the Christian penitent – 'Darling, one resolution I made in my sorrow, that I would ask a boon of you and I wish to show you and my God that I have gained purity and self-control' – to the Platonist – 'that intense though my love is for your body, I do not love it but as an expression of your soul' – to the Hindu tantric yogi – 'And therefore, when we are married, will you consent to remain for the first month in my arms a virgin bride, a sister only?'[23]

By the day of their wedding in January 1844, they were both worn out and ill. But Kingsley had been saved; and later that year became Rector at Eversley. The suffering which he had endured during his reformation (not to mention his life-shortening addiction to tobacco which, despite the pleadings of his wife and mother he could never master) should have left him with an understanding of how hard it can be for people to overcome their failings; but oddly enough he had neither patience nor sympathy for those vessels of weaker clay, 'the idle and drunken, the reckless and improvident, who always must and always ought to suffer.'[24]

For someone who had returned to his faith with such travail, and abode in it with such vigorous determination, Kingsley 'became a convert to Darwin's views'[25] with apparent ease, but as the following letter shows,

---

22   Chitty, p. 80.
23   Chitty, p. 81. ULF no.53, 1843.
24   *CKL*, II, 111. Sermon, 'Why should we pray for fair weather?' (1860).
25   *CKL*, II, 175.

he was not just a man of God, he was also a man of science, who was as deeply committed to the one as the other:

> Those who fancy me a 'sentimentalist' and a 'fanatic' little know how thoroughly my own bent is for physical science; how I have been trained in it from earliest boyhood; how I am happier now in classifying a new polype, or solving a geognostic problem of strata, or any other bit of hard Baconian induction, than in writing all the novels in the world; or how, again, my theological creed has grown slowly and naturally out of my physical one, till I have seen, and do believe more and more utterly, that the peculiar doctrines of Christianity (as they are in the Bible, not as some preachers represent them from the pulpit) coincide with the loftiest and severest science. This blessed belief did not come to me at once, and therefore I complain of no man who arrives at it slowly, either from the scientific or religious side; nor have I yet spoken out all that is in me, much less all that I see coming; but I feel that I am on a right path, and please God, I will hold it to the end.[26]

Even so, it still would have needed an enormous effort of will to accept that mankind had risen from an ape; and before the *Origin* persuaded him, Kingsley was hostile to the idea. But being Kingsley, it was not enough to disagree; he needed a counter-argument. He writes in *Westward Ho!* (1855):

> Humboldt has somewhere a curious passage, in which, looking on some wretched group of Indians, squatting stupidly round their fires, besmeared with grease and paint, and devouring ants and clay, he somewhat naïvely remarks, that were it not for science, which teaches us that such is the crude material of humanity, and thus the state from which we all have risen, he should have been tempted rather to look upon these hapless beings as the last degraded remnants of some fallen and dying race. One wishes that the great traveller had been bold enough to yield to that temptation, which his own reason and common sense presented to him as the real explanation of the sad sight, instead of following the dogmas of a so-called science, which has not a fact whereon to base its wild notion, and must ignore a thousand facts in asserting it. His own good sense, it seems, coincided instinctively with the Bible doctrine, that man in a state of nature is a fallen being, doomed to death—a view which may be a sad one, but still one more honourable to poor humanity than the theory that we all began as some sort of two-handed apes. It is surely more hopeful to believe that

26   *CKL*, I, 380. Letter to Thomas Cooper, 1854.

those poor Ottomacs or Guahibas were not what they ought to be, than to believe that they were. It is certainly more complimentary to them, to think that they had been somewhat nobler and more prudent in centuries gone by, than that they were such blockheads as to have dragged on, the son after the father, for all the thousands of years which have elapsed since man was made, without having had wit enough to discover any better food than ants and clay.[27]

Darwin, however, expressed the exact opposite opinion, although in *The Descent of Man* he couches it in much the same language:

> To believe that man was aboriginally civilised and then suffered utter degradation in so many regions, is to take a pitiably low view of human nature. It is apparently a truer and more cheerful view that progress has been much more general than retrogression; that man has risen, though by slow and interrupted steps, from a lowly condition to the highest standard as yet attained by him in knowledge, morals and religion (511).

Although as a man of science the pre-Darwin Kingsley rejected evolution theory, as a writer he allowed it to play on his imagination. In *Alton Locke*, in a chapter entitled 'Dreamland', Alton lies delirious in a fever, and watches himself as he sinks into darkness:

> And I was at the lowest point of created life; a madrepore rooted to the rock, fathoms below the tide-mark; and worst of all, my individuality was gone (265).

At this point Kingsley introduces the kind of evolution that appeals to him – not evolution of the species, but evolution of the individual through successive Platonic incarnations:

> He who falls from the golden ladder must climb through ages to its top. He who tears himself in pieces by his lusts, ages only can make him one again. The madrepore shall become a shell, and the shell a fish, and the fish a bird, and the bird a beast; and then he shall become a man again, and see the glory of the latter days (265).

Alton then becomes successively a shell, a fish, a bird, a beast, and a human. But Kingsley departs from this scheme in one significant detail.

---

27   *Westward Ho!* (London: Dent, 1906; repr. 1960), pp. 445–46. Kingsley also refers to another group of Indians as 'low-browed, dirty Orsons' (444).

From a bird, Alton becomes an extinct prehistoric mylodon; but when he dies he reincarnates not as a human, but as yet another beast – an ape. This beast is not only physically closest to mankind, but feels 'germs of a new and higher consciousness' (269). The ape thus occupies for Kingsley an intermediate state on the golden ladder of the Great Chain of Being between pure brute and pure human.

What enabled Kingsley to arrive subsequently at the point where he could claim to accept Darwin's theory? For one thing, his ability to use it to suit himself. He writes to Darwin:

> Ah, that I could begin to study nature anew, now that you have made it to me a live thing, not a dead collection of names. But my work lies elsewhere now. Your work, nevertheless, helps mine at every turn. It is better that the division of labour should be complete, and that each man should do only one thing, while he looks on, as he finds time, at what others are doing, and so gets laws from other sciences which he can apply, as I do, to my own.[28]

And this is how he applies Darwin:

> We were taught—some of us at least—by Holy Scripture, to believe that the whole history of the universe was made up of Special Providences. If, then, that should be true which Mr Darwin writes: 'It may be metaphorically said that natural selection is daily and hourly scrutinising throughout the world, every variation, even the slightest; rejecting that which is bad, preserving and adding up that which is good, silently and incessantly whenever and wherever opportunity offers at the improvement of every organic being'—if that, I say, were proven to be true, ought God's care and God's providence to seem less or more magnificent in our eyes? Of old it was said by Him without whom nothing is made: 'My Father worketh hitherto, and I work.' Shall we quarrel with Science if she should show how those words are true? What, in one word, should we have to say but this?—We knew of old that God was so wise that He could make all things; but behold, He is so much wiser than even that, that He can make all things make themselves.[29]

28 *CKL*, II, 173. Letter of 14 June 1863.
29 'The Natural Theology of the Future', *Scientific Lectures and Essays* (London: Macmillan, 1890), p. 332. This lecture was delivered in 1871.

But Kingsley already had a lifelong and more cherished companion to share his belief 'that the God of Nature and the God of Grace are one',[30] and that was his favourite author, Edmund Spenser.[31] Fanny Kingsley writes:

> [F]rom first to last Sir Thomas Malory's 'Morte d'Arthur', and Spenser's 'Faerie Queen' [*sic*], were among his most beloved books. Spenser was more dear to him than even Shakespeare; and in later life, when his brain was weary, especially on Sunday evenings, he would turn instinctively for rest and refreshment to the 'Faerie Queen'.[32]

It is in Spenser that he finds the kindred sentiment which informs *The Water-Babies:*

> I cannot but believe it to have been a mighty gain to such men as Sidney, Raleigh, and Spenser, that they had drunk, however slightly, of the wells of Proclus and Plotinus. One cannot read Spenser's Fairy Queen, above all his Garden of Adonis, and his cantos on Mutability, without feeling that his Neoplatonism must have kept him safe from many a dark eschatological superstition, many a narrow and bitter dogmatism, which was even then tormenting the English mind and must have helped to give him altogether a freer and more loving conception, if not a consistent or accurate one, of the wondrous harmony of that mysterious analogy between the physical and the spiritual, which alone makes poetry (and I had almost said philosophy also) possible, and have taught him to behold alike in suns and planets, in flowers and insects, in man and in beings higher than man, one glorious order of love and wisdom, linking them all to Him from whom they all proceed, rays from His cloudless sunlight, mirrors of His eternal glory.[33]

Kingsley's love of Spenser led him to include the poet in *Westward Ho!* In 1580 Spenser was secretary to Lord Grey of Wilton, Deputy of Ireland. Kingsley describes a scene during a military campaign in Ireland, in which young Amyas Leigh interrupts a debate between Spenser and Raleigh about poetry. Raleigh asks Spenser:

---

30 Ibid., p. 314.
31 *CKL*, II, 399.
32 *Charles Kingsley: His Letters and Memories of His Life*, ed. by his wife (Frances E. Kingsley) (London and New York: Macmillan, 1883; repr. 1904), p. 10.
33 *Alexandria*, pp. 126–27.

Wilt put the lad into the 'Fairy Queen', then, by my side? He deserves as good a place there, believe me, as ever a Guyon, or even as Lord Grey your Arthegall (200).

Several swashbuckling years later, when Amyas and his brother Frank are visiting their mother in London, they are surprised to see her enter the room with Spenser, who, she tells them, 'Has been vowing to me to give your adventure a whole canto to itself in his "Fairy Queen"' (335). After a discussion in which Spenser offers to include Mrs Leigh as well, Kingsley breaks off the scene with an author's aside to the reader:

How that conversation ended I know not, nor whether Spenser fulfilled his purpose of introducing the two brothers and their mother into his 'Fairy Queen'. If so, the manuscripts must have been lost among those which perished (along with Spenser's baby) in the sack of Kilcolman by the Irish in 1598. But we need hardly regret the loss of them; for the temper of the Leighs and their mother is the same which inspires every canto of that noblest of poems (337).

Kingsley's Spenser may or may not have put Amyas in *The Faerie Queene*, but there can be little doubt that, just as Kingsley wove Spenser into *Westward Ho!* so he also wove elements of *The Faerie Queene* into *The Water-Babies*.

The Water-Babies

In 1862, while Kingsley was Professor of Modern History at Cambridge and tutor by appointment to the Prince of Wales, he wrote *The Water-Babies* for his youngest son Grenville. It was serialized in *Macmillan's Magazine*, and in 1863 reincarnated as a book.

The Water-Babies tells the story of Tom, a Yorkshire chimney-sweep in the employ of the loutish and drunken Mr Grimes. When we first meet Tom, the animal is dominant in him; and he is more beast than human. He can neither read nor write, and has no interest in learning to do so. He does not wash. He has a taste for beer – although it would probably be

safer than the water. He does not say his prayers, and has never heard of
God. His ambition in life is to follow in his master's footsteps and become
a lazy drunken brute who bullies his apprentices. Knowing little but the
low mores of his surroundings and the skills of survival, Tom goes one day
with his master to clean the chimneys of the grand Harthover House. On
the way they meet an Irishwoman who seems to know all about Grimes's
misdeeds. She talks with Tom as they walk; he hears for the first time of a
place beyond his own experience, and it awakens in him a desire for something which he has never seen:

> Then he asked her where she lived; and she said far away by the sea. And Tom asked
> her about the sea; and she told him how it rolled and roared over the rocks in winter
> nights, and lay still in the bright summer days, for the children to bathe and play
> in it; and many a story more, till Tom longed to go and see the sea, and bathe in it
> likewise. [34]

Here the Fairy has sown the seed which will lead to Tom's salvation.

Grimes, hungover and oppressed by the heat of the day, dips his head
in a cooling spring, but makes the point:

> 'Twasn't for cleanliness I did it, but for coolness. I'd be ashamed to want washing
> every week or so, like any smutty collier-lad (10).

When Tom begins to wash his face, Grimes beats him, but is prevented by
the Irishwoman, who utters a prophetic pronouncement:

> Those that wish to be clean, clean they will be; and those that wish to be foul, foul
> they will be (12).

Tom and Grimes arrive at Harthover, and Tom is sent up the chimney.
He becomes lost in the pitch dark, but is 'as much at home in a chimney
as a mole is underground' (17). He comes down into a room unlike any
that he has seen before. It is all white. There are two pictures of Jesus: one

---

34   Charles Kingsley, *The Water-Babies: A Fairy-Tale For A Land Baby*, illust. by Rosalie
     K. Fry (London: Dent, 1973), p. 9. Further references are given after quotations in
     the text.

with him surrounded by children; the other, of the crucifixion. Here we see the two aspects of God's love: the care of the innocents; and sacrifice for others. Next Tom sees all the apparatus for purification, including 'a large bath, full of clean water' (18). Finally he sees Ellie, the embodiment of worldly purity, asleep in bed:

> Under the snow-white coverlet, upon the snow-white pillow, lay the most beautiful little girl that Tom had ever seen. Her cheeks were almost as white as the pillow, and her hair was like threads of gold spread all about over the bed (18–19).

Ellie's appearance conforms with traditional figures of purity, as one can see by comparing her with any of several heroines from *The Faerie Queene*. For example, Una's complexion is whiter than snow (I.1.4), and in her final appearance she is clad in garments 'All lilly white, withouten spot, or pride' (I.12.22). Furthermore she accompanies and supports Redcross in his quest. The beautiful warrior-virgin Britomart wears a 'snow-white smocke' (III.1.63) under her armour, and has long golden hair which reaches to her heels (IV.1.13). The even more beautiful Florimell has golden hair which streams behind her as she rides (III.1.16). Fidelia in the House of Holiness appears 'araied all in lilly white' (I.10.13), and one can find a verbal association with Ellie in part of her name – FidELIa.

Tom gazes in awe:

> And then he thought, 'And are all people like that when they are washed?' And he looked at his own wrist, and tried to rub the soot off, and wondered whether it ever would come off. 'Certainly I should look much prettier then, if I grew at all like her' (19).

At Tom's moment of self-realization Kingsley does not simply describe Tom, but for the first time mentions his inner condition:

> And looking round, he suddenly saw, standing close to him, a little ugly, black, ragged figure, with bleared eyes and grinning white teeth. He turned on it angrily. What did such a little black ape want in that sweet young lady's room? And behold, it was himself reflected in a great mirror, the like of which Tom had never seen before.
>
> And Tom, for the first time in his life, found out that he was dirty; and burst into tears with shame and anger; and turned to sneak up the chimney again and hide (19).

But God has other plans for Tom, and will not let him return to the darkness and dirt of his former life. Tom trips over the fire-irons, which wakes Ellie who screams at the sight of him. Ellie's Nurse rushes in and attempts to catch him; so he is forced to jump out of the window and climb down a tree, 'like a cat' (21), says Kingsley, keeping the focus on Tom's animal self. The entire staff of the great house pursue Tom who runs 'up the park with his little bare feet, like a small black gorilla fleeing to the forest' (23). When he comes to the estate's boundary wall he climbs over it 'like a squirrel' (24); and finds himself out on the moors and entering into the natural world of spiders, lizards, birds, and foxes. He comes, to the top of Lewthwaite Crag; and a thousand feet below, a stream running through the valley. He begins to climb down, 'as if he had been born a jolly little black ape, with four hands instead of two' (36).[35]

By the time he arrives at the bottom, Tom is almost literally dying of thirst; he needs water that he might live. But when he stumbles into the school run by the old dame (who, it is eventually revealed, is Grimes's mother), she gives him, not water, but milk. Nor, when she offers him bread, can he eat it. He needs water both to revive and purify him.

Lying in the hay in an outhouse where the old dame has put him to rest, he is tormented by his unclean state:

> and then he fell half asleep, and dreamt that he heard the little white lady crying to him, 'Oh, you're so dirty; go and be washed'; and then that he heard the Irishwoman saying, 'Those that wish to be clean, clean they will be' (40).

During his flight Tom has begun to hear church bells ringing – at first a long way off. He consistently heads towards them, knowing that there will be people near them who will give him something to eat and drink. By the time he is lying in the hay the church bells have become louder and more insistent. He wants to go to church, but worries that he will not be let in because he is so dirty.

---

35   Harking back to Swift and Gulliver, all of the animals to which Tom is likened – mole, cat, squirrel and ape – are unclean according to the Levitican proscriptions.

He must go to the river and wash first. And he said out aloud again and again, though being half asleep he did not know it, 'I must be clean, I must be clean.'

And all of a sudden he found himself, not in the outhouse on the hay, but in the middle of a meadow, over the road, with a stream just before him, saying continually, 'I must be clean, I must be clean.' [... He] went on to the bank of the brook, and lay down on the grass, and looked into the clear, clear limestone water, [...] while the little silver trout dashed about in fright at the sight of his black face; and he dipped his hand in and found it so cool, cool, cool; and he said, 'I will be a fish; I will swim in the water; I must be clean, I must be clean.'

So he pulled off all his clothes in such haste that he tore some of them, which was easy enough with such ragged old things. And he put his poor hot sore feet into the water; and then his legs; and the further he went in the more the church bells rang in his head.

'Ah,' said Tom, 'I must be quick and wash myself; the bells are ringing quite loud now; and they will stop soon, and then the doors will be shut, and I shall never be able to get in at all.'

Tom was mistaken: for in England the church doors are left open all service time, for everybody who likes to come in [... to] God's house, which belongs to all alike (41–42).

Tom sinks into the water and falls asleep.

There is quite a lot happening in this passage, which is an elegant blending of Platonism and Christianity. From the Christian perspective Tom is the soiled heathen, or the prodigal son, seeking redemption; and entering through baptism into the church of Christ which is open to all who repent of their sins. From the Platonist perspective Tom is ensuring himself a superior birth in his next life by focusing obsessively, in his last moments, on the words of the Irishwoman, before his soul passes into the other realm and chooses a new body. This new body will be chosen based on a reaction against the former life, and a new-found desire for a better life.

But there is still much to be done before Tom is purged of his animal life, as the Irishwoman realizes. She has followed Tom all the way from Harthover, and has slipped unseen into the water before him:

and her shawl and her petticoat floated off her, and the green water-weeds floated round her sides, and the white water-lilies floated round her head, and the fairies of the stream came up from the bottom, and bore her away and down upon their arms; for she was the Queen of them all; and perhaps of more besides (42).

She tells the fairies that she has brought them a little brother, who has turned into a water-baby, leaving his husk behind him:

> But mind, maidens, he must not see you, or know that you are here. He is but a savage now, and like the beasts which perish; and from the beasts which perish he must learn (42–43).[36]

Thus Kingsley reveals that the Irishwoman is the Queen of the fairies, or the Fairy Queen. She is the first of the fairies whom we shall encounter in this tale; and, as Kingsley shows towards the end, they are all facets and embodiments of the great force represented in Spenser's *Mutabilitie Cantos* as Dame Nature. Spenser gives a detailed picture of Dame Nature, citing Chaucer as an authority.[37] Chaucer describes her thus:

> Tho was I war wher that ther sat a queene
> That, as of lyght the somer sonne shene
> Passeth the sterre, right so over mesure
> She fayrer was than any creature.
> And in a launde, upon an hil of floures,
> Was set this noble goddesse Nature.   (298–303)[38]

In the *Mutabilitie Cantos* the heathen gods assemble for a parliament on Arlo Hill in Ireland (a place which Spenser loved). The Titaness Mutabilitie claims herself to be mightier than the gods, and therefore fitter to

---

36   'Nevertheless man being in honour abideth not: he is like the beasts that perish' (Psalm 49.12).
37   So hard it is for any liuing wight,
         All her array and vestiments to tell,
         That old *Dan Geffrey* (in whose gentle spright
         The pure well head of Poesie did dwell)
         In his *Foules parley* durst not with it mel.   (VII.7.9)
     The Goddess Nature tradition of course pre-dated Chaucer. See the notes to the *Mutabilitie Cantos* in the *Faerie Queene* Variorum edn, vol. VI, and see also Appendix I to Book VII.
38   *The Parlement of Foules*, in *The Works of Geoffrey Chaucer*, ed. by F.N. Robinson, 2nd edn (London: Oxford University Press, 1966; repr. 1974).

be sovereign of heaven and earth, which are obviously under her sway; and appeals to the God of Nature to arbitrate.

> Then forth issewed (great goddesse) great dame *Nature*,
>   With goodly port and gracious Maiesty;
>   Being far greater and more tall of stature
>   Then any of the gods or Powers on hie:
>   Yet certes by her face and physnomy,
>   Whether she man or woman inly were,
>   That could not any creature well descry:
>   For, with a veile that wimpled euery where,
> Her head and face was hid, that mote to none appeare.
>
> That some doe say was so by skill deuized,
>   To hide the terrour of her vncouth hew,
>   From mortall eyes that should be sore agrized;
>   For that her face did like a Lion shew,
>   That eye of wight could not endure to view:
>   But others tell that it so beautious was,
>   And round about such beames of splendor threw,
>   That it the Sunne a thousand times did pass,
> Ne could be seene, but like an image in a glass.   (VII.7.5–6)

The earth brings forth a pavilion of dainty trees which bow themselves into a throne. Nymphs sprinkle Dame Nature's footstool with sweet flowers. This, then, is the goddess whom Chaucer calls, 'Nature, the vicaire of the almyghty Lord' (line 379). This, too, as we shall see, is Kingsley's Fairy Queen.

Kingsley introduces his Dame Nature in the humble and unremarkable form of the Irishwoman,

> trudging along with a bundle at her back. She had a grey shawl over her head, and a crimson madder petticoat; so you may be sure she came from Galway. She had neither shoes nor stockings, and limped along as if she were tired and footsore: but she was a very tall, handsome woman, with bright grey eyes, and heavy black hair hanging about her cheeks (8–9).

Spenser says that Dame Nature is tall; Kingsley says that the Irishwoman is tall. Spenser says that her face is 'beautious'; Kingsley, that she is 'handsome'. Spenser describes her veil 'that wimpled every where'; Kingsley describes the 'grey shawl over her head', and the 'heavy black hair hanging about her cheeks'. Spenser tells how, after delivering her judgment, 'Natur's selfe did vanish, whither no man list' (VII.7.59); Kingsley tells how, after delivering her prophetic judgment on Grimes and Tom, the Irishwoman vanishes, much to their surprise (12).

Kingsley locates most of his action in a natural world reminiscent of Spenser's Garden of Adonis. Spenser says:

> It sited was in fruitfull soyle of old,
>   And girt in with two walles on either side;
>   The one of yron, the other of bright gold.   (III.6.31)

Tom descends Lewthwaite Crag – a limestone cliff one thousand feet high – just before he drowns in the stream and becomes a water-baby. At the far end of the natural world, stands the great ice Shiny Wall surrounding Peacepool, 'where the good whales go when they die' (108). It is from here that Tom travels on to the Other-end-of-Nowhere. Thus the natural world of the water-babies is girt in with two walls.

Of life forms in the Garden of Adonis Spenser says:

> Infinite shapes of creatures there are bred,
>   And vncouth formes, which none yet euer knew.   (III.6.35).

Kingsley paints an aquatic world vibrantly exploding with life in all its variety. Tom's journey – from the stream in which he drowns, to the river, to the seashore and across the vast ocean – includes everything from microscopic pond life to great whales, especially creatures that evolve from one bizarre form to another. And overseeing all is the Queen of the Fairies – or the Fairy Queen, also known as Dame Nature. Spenser says:

> In that same Gardin all the goodly flowres,
>   Wherewith dame Nature doth her beautifie,
>   And decks the girlonds of her paramoures,
>   Are fetcht: there is the first seminarie
>   Of all things, that are born to liue and die,
> According to their kindes.   (III.6.30)

Tom has gone into the water for an education, which involves not only learning to understand and appreciate nature, but to mature intellectually and evolve morally and spiritually through the interaction. He engages with the other creatures in the stream, beginning with insect larvae, then fish, then otters. He teases the other creatures, so they avoid him until he has learnt to behave responsibly. The season changes and the creatures begin moving down to the sea – including the fairies, who have been hiding from Tom. He follows downstream. One night he witnesses Grimes and his cronies poaching salmon. They are attacked by gamekeepers, and during the fight Grimes falls into the water and drowns. Tom arrives at the sea and befriends a lobster.

Ellie, meanwhile, has been taken on holiday to the seaside. One day she is walking along the shore in company with a Professor who scoops up Tom in a little net. Tom gets away, and Ellie, attempting to catch this strange creature, slips and knocks her head on a rock. She lingers in bed for a few days until the fairies come and take her.

Tom, who has spent most of his time in the water being naughty and tormenting the other creatures, saves the life of the lobster; and earns enough merit to meet other water-babies. He travels with them to their underwater home, St Brandan's fairy isle, where he begins to learn the difference between right and wrong.

And what about the water-babies themselves? They are the 'thousand thousand naked babes' from the Garden of Adonis (III.6.32). Kingsley says that there are 'millions' (107) of them. But who are they? They live in St Brandan's underwater isle, which Plato called Atlantis:

> And there were the water-babies in thousands, more than Tom, or you either, could count.—All the little children whom the good fairies take to, because their cruel mothers and fathers will not; all who are untaught and brought up heathens, and all who come to grief by ill-usage or ignorance or neglect; all the little children who are overlaid, or given gin when they are young, or are let to drink out of hot kettles, or to fall into the fire; all the little children in alleys and courts, and tumbledown cottages, who die by fever, and cholera, and measles, and scarlatina, and nasty complaints which no one has any business to have, and which no one will have some day, when folks have common sense; and all the little children who have been killed by cruel masters, and wicked soldiers; they were all there, except, of course, the babes of Bethlehem who were killed by wicked King Herod; for they were taken straight to heaven long ago, as everybody knows, and we call them the Holy Innocents (141).

These are the children whose lives have been blighted, and who have not been able to realize their potential. These are the ones who have to be taught in their underwater nursery by two fairies of opposite appearance. The ugly and severely just Mrs Bedonebyasyoudid – representing the Pauline observation, 'whatsoever a man soweth, that shall he also reap' (Galatians 6.7) – teaches them not to do wrong by punishing them for their actions.[39] The beautiful and loving Mrs Doasyouwouldbedoneby – representing Christ's injunction, 'what so ever ye would that men should do to you, do ye even so to them' (Matthew 7.12; see also Luke 6.31) – teaches them to do right by telling them about God and proper conduct. These two Dames, both embodiments of Dame Nature – and both, like Dame Nature and the Irishwoman, tall – have opposite appearances and opposite functions, although their aim – reformation – is the same.[40]

It would seem that Kingsley has modelled the sweet Mrs Doasyouwouldbedoneby on Charissa in Spenser's House of Holiness in *The Faerie Queene*, where Una has taken Redcross for rest and improvement. Spenser describes Charissa:

> She was a woman in her freshest age,
>   Of wondrous beauty, and of bountie rare,
>   With goodly grace and comely personage,
>   That was on earth not easie to compare;
>   Full of great loue, but *Cupids* wanton snare
>   As hell she hated, chast in worke and will;
>   Her necke and breasts were euer open bare,
>   That ay thereof her babes might sucke their fill;
> The rest was all in yellow robes arayed still.
>
> A multitude of babes about her hong,
>   Playing their sports, that ioyed her to behold,
>   Whom still she fed, whiles they were weake and young,
>   But thrust them forth still, as they wexed old.   (I.10.30–31)

---

39   After Tom puts pebbles into anemones' mouths, she gives him a sweet; but it is in fact a pebble.

40   In an address to the inaugural meeting of the Ladies' Sanitary Association in July 1861, Kingsley says, 'Nature is fierce when she is offended, as she is bounteous and kind when she is obeyed' (*CKL*, II, 85).

Kingsley describes Mrs Doasyouwouldbedoneby:

> [S]he was the most nice, soft, fat, smooth, pussy, cuddly, delicious creature who ever
> nursed a baby; and she understood babies thoroughly, for she had plenty of her own,
> whole rows and regiments of them, and has to this day.[41] And all her delight was,
> whenever she had a spare moment, to play with babies, in which she showed herself
> a woman of sense; for babies are the best company, and the pleasantest playfellows,
> in the world; at least, so all the wise people in the world think. And therefore when
> the children saw her, they naturally all caught hold of her, and pulled her till she sat
> down on a stone, and climbed into her lap, and clung round her neck, and caught
> hold of her hands; and then they all put their thumbs into their mouths, and began
> cuddling and purring like so many kittens, as they ought to have done (150).

She spies Tom. The other babies tell her that he is a new arrival, and never
had a mother.

> 'Then I will be his mother, and he shall have the very best place; so get out all of
> you, this moment.'
> And she took up two great armsful of babies—nine hundred under one arm, and
> thirteen hundred under the other—and threw them away, right and left, into the
> water. But they [...] did not even take their thumbs out of their mouths, but came
> paddling and wriggling back to her like so many tadpoles, till you could see nothing
> of her from head to foot for the swarm of little babies (151).

Kingsley regarded the blighting of these little lives not only as a shame
and disgrace, but anti-Christian; and it was something that touched him
deeply:

> Oh! it is a distressing thing to see children die. God gives the most beautiful and
> precious thing that earth can have, and we just take it and cast it away; we cast our
> pearls upon the dunghill, and leave them. [...] I believe it to have been a priceless

---

41   The end of this sentence may be inspired by Spenser's description of the Garden of
      Adonis:
          Infinite shapes of creatures there are bred,
              And vncouth formes, which none yet euer knew,
              And euery sort is in a sundry bed
              Set by it selfe, andranckt in comely rew.   (III.6.35)
      Mrs Doasyouwouldbedoneby hardly seems the type to keep babies in rows.

boon to the child to have lived for a week, or a day; but oh, what has God given to this thankless earth, and what has the earth thrown away, in nine cases out of ten, from its own neglect and carelessness?[42]

In a sermon he deplores the march of progress which leaves casualties in its wake:

Shall we pass over the waste—the hereditary waste of human souls [...] in every great city in the world?—waste of human souls, human intellect, human character—waste, saddest of all, in the image of God in little children. That cannot be necessary. There must be a fault somewhere. It cannot be the will of God that one little one should perish by commerce or by manufacture, any more than by slavery or by war.[43]

And, as he reprises the image of Tom sinking into the purifying stream, he makes the Platonic observation:

Their souls are like their bodies, not perfect, but beautiful enough, and fresh enough to shame any one who shall dare to look down upon them. Their souls are like their bodies, hidden by the rags, foul with the dirt, of what we miscall civilization. But take them to the pure stream; strip off the ugly shapeless rags; wash the young limbs again, and you shall find them, body and soul, fresh and lithe, graceful and capable— capable of how much, God alone, who made them, knows.[44]

Kingsley says that the souls of the urchins are 'not perfect'. He puts all the water-babies in the same spiritual category, in the passage quoted above, where he distinguishes between the water-babies and the Holy Innocents who 'were taken straight to heaven'. These, then, are children who should be given another chance. But it is too late for those who have perished – some without even the benefit of baptism, who may not enter the kingdom of God. To Kingsley the Christian this is a deplorable loss and a tragedy which cannot be remedied. But to Kingsley the Platonist it is yet another painful step in the soul's upward evolution towards perfection, and the person's upward evolution towards true humanity.

---

42   *CKL*, II, 83–84. Address to the Ladies' Sanitary Association.
43   'On Human Soot', a sermon preached in Liverpool on behalf of the Kirkdale Ragged School, June 1870. *CKL*, II, 324.
44   *CKL*, II, 325.

But every human being who struggles towards salvation labours under the burden of duality – the duality of which Kingsley was only too well aware from his own personality. He saw the negative side of this duality as an expression of the animal part of our nature; but he saw this not as a metaphor, but as an actual fact. In a hair-raising letter he writes:

> I see by-the-bye that you have given out two 'Orations against taking away human life'. I wish you would let me see them. [...] It is a painful and difficult subject. After much thought, I have come to the conclusion that you cannot take away *human* life. That *animal* life is all you take away; and that very often the best thing that you can do for a poor creature is to put him out of this world, saying, 'You are evidently unable to get on here. We render you back into God's hands that He may judge you, and set you to work again somewhere else, giving you a fresh chance as you have spoilt this one.' But I speak really in doubt and awe.[45]

Now begins a crucial phase in Tom's personal development. Just as Kingsley himself had rebelled initially during his reformation, so Tom lapses badly by stealing sweets from Mrs Bedonebyasyoudid's cabinet. When at last he confesses, she forgives him at once; but the damage has been done. Tom's body is now covered in prickles.

> Which was natural; for you must know and believe that people's souls make their bodies, just as a snail makes its shell (I am not joking, my little man; I am in serious, solemn earnest). And, therefore, when Tom's soul grew all prickly with naughty tempers, his body could not help growing prickly too, so that nobody would cuddle him, or play with him, or even like to look at him (161).

Here, as Kingsley says, is the 'doctrine of this wonderful fairy-tale' (64). Unfortunately, Kingsley's example of the prickles does nothing more than further confuse an already confused issue. Tom's prickles grow in response to his actions and moral decisions; in other words, Tom's existing body acquires features which reflect his actions. This is not what Kingsley has in mind when he writes to Professor George Rolleston:

45   *CKL*, II, 380. Letter to Thomas Cooper, 1854. Kingsley's thinking may be based on the words of Jesus: 'And fear not them which kill the body, but are not able to kill the soul' (Matthew 10.28). The '*human* life' is the human soul; and the '*animal* life' is the body.

I am glad to see that you incline to my belief, which I hardly dare state in these days, even to those who call themselves spiritual, viz., that the soul of each living being down to the lowest, secretes the body thereof, as a snail secretes its shell, and that *the body is nothing more than the expression in terms of matter, of the stage of development to which the being has arrived.* [my emphasis][46]

Tom's prickles are a Platonic reaction, but Kingsley's snail doctrine is an attempt to reconcile his theology with Darwinism; and specifically relates to the kind of body which the soul brings with it into the world; as the following letter, written a few months after the last, shows:

I am very busy working out points of Natural Theology, by the strange light of Huxley, Darwin, and Lyell. [...]
   [...]
   A Passage between me and [Huxley ...] may amuse you. He says somewhere, 'the ape's brain is almost exactly like the man's, and so is his throat. See, then, what enormously different results may be produced by the slightest difference in structure!' I tell him, 'not a bit; You are putting the cart before the horse, like the rest of the world. If you won't believe my great new doctrine (which, by the bye, is as old as the Greeks), that souls secrete their bodies, as snails do shells, you will remain in outer darkness. [...] I know an ape's brain and throat are almost exactly like a man's—and what does that prove? That the ape is a fool and a muff, who has tools very nearly as good as a man's, and yet can't use them, while a man can do the most wonderful thing with tools very little better than an ape's.
   'If men had had ape's [*sic*] bodies they would have got on very tolerably with them, because they had men's souls to work the bodies with. While an ape's soul in a man's body would be only a rather more filthy nuisance than he is now. You fancy that the axe uses the workman, I say that the workman uses the axe, and that though he can work rather better with a good tool than a bad one, the great point is, what sort of workman is he—an ape-soul or a human soul?'
   Whereby you may perceive that I am not going astray into materialism as yet.[47]

Kingsley's doctrine is, in short, soul is form and doth the body make. It may seem fanciful that a man who espoused the pursuit of science should

---

46   *CKL*, II, 143–44. Letter to Professor George Rolleston, 12 October 1862. As one can see from the date, the letter was written around the time that Kingsley was writing *The Water-Babies.*
47   *CKL*, II, 171–72. Undated letter to Rev. F.D. Maurice, 1863.

attempt to counter Huxley with an idea which he could have picked up over dinner with Spenser. But, as he says, it is as old as the Greeks, and has exercised an ongoing influence. In Plato's *Timaeus* Timaeus says:

> [T]he gods created in us the desire of sexual intercourse, contriving in man one animated substance, and in woman another (91a).

The 'animated substance' in men is sperm, and in women is the uterus. Each agent of procreation has its own soul independent of the body in which it is contained.

Henry More, in his *Interpretation Generall*, under the heading *Sperm*, explains its function:

> It signifies ordinarily seed. I put it for the *Logos spermaticos*, [...] or the invisible plasticall form that shapes every visible creature.[48]

And the Swedish scientist and mystic Emanuel Swedenborg (1688– 1772) describes the process:

> Every one's soul is from the father, and it is only clothed with a body by the mother. [...] The soul is in the seed, for from the seed impregnation takes place, and the seed is what is clothed with a body by the mother.[49]

> [F]or in man's seed is his soul in perfect human form, covered over with substances from the purest things of nature, from which, in the mother's womb, is formed a body.[50]

48   Grosart, p. 164.
49   *Angelic Wisdom Concerning the Divine Providence* (London: The Swedenborg Society, 1934), par.338. Swedenborg was influenced directly by Plato, and also by the Cambridge Platonists and Milton when he was studying in England. In his philosophy he was a Platonist, with an especial interest in neo-Platonism. See Cyriel Odhner Sigstedt, *The Swedenborg Epic: The Life and Works of Emanuel Swedenborg* (New York: Bookman, 1952), p. 179.
50   *The Delights of Wisdom Concerning Conjugial Love*, [1767; first English edn 1794], trans. by Alfred Acton (London: Swedenborg Society, 1953), par.183. Kingsley found 'many noble and beautiful things' in the Swedish philosopher's writings (*CKL*, II, 94). Anne Bloomfield argues for Swedenborg's influence on *The Water-Babies* in

Kingsley is therefore working within a long Platonic tradition, which has taken on an increasingly scientific explanation. He is, in his mind, countering science with science.

But the focus of Kingsley's attention with his snail doctrine is not to address Darwin's assertion that mankind has evolved from apes, but to demonstrate how mankind could degenerate back into apes. Kingsley was advancing his 'degeneration theory' in 1862. In his letter to Professor Rolleston quoted above, he says:

> I wish you would *envisager* that gorilla brain for once in a way, and the baboon brain also under the fancy of their being *degraded* forms.
>
> I shall torment you and your compeers with my degradation theory, till you give me a plain Yes or No from facts.[51]

Of course, he was not alone in his speculations, as one can see from Huxley:

> It is an error to imagine that evolution signifies a constant tendency to increased perfection. That process undoubtedly involves a constant remodelling of the organism in adaptation to new conditions; but it depends on the nature of those conditions whether the direction of the modifications effected shall be upward or downward. Retrogressive is as practicable as progressive metamorphosis.[52]

From Monboddo:

> The necessary consequence of men living in so unnatural a way with respect to houses, clothes, and diet, and continuing to live so for many generations, each generation adding to the vices, diseases, and weaknesses produced by the unnatural life of the preceding is, that they must gradually decline in strength, health, and longevity, till at length the race dies out.[53]

'Muscular Christian or Mystic? Charles Kingsley Reappraised', *International Journal of the History of Sport*, 11 (1994), 172–90.

51   *CKL*, II, 144.

52   'The Struggle For Existence in Human Society' [1888], *Evolution and Ethics, Collected Essays*, IX, 195–236 (p. 199).

53   *Ancient Metaphysics*, V, 237. Quoted in *Melincourt*, p. 277.

From the explorer Thomas Savage:

> [Chimpanzees] are very filthy in their habits. [...] It is a tradition with the natives generally here, that they were once members of their own tribe: that for their depraved habits they were expelled from all human society, and that through an obstinate indulgence of their vile propensities, they have degenerated into their present state of organization.[54]

And from Kingsley's friend and one-time patron, Thomas Carlyle (1795–1881):

> Perhaps few narratives in History or Mythology are more significant than that Moslem one, of Moses and the dwellers by the Dead Sea. A tribe of men dwelt on the shores of that same Asphaltic Lake; and having forgotten, as we are all too prone to do, the inner facts of Nature, and taken up with the falsities and outer semblances of it, were fallen into sad conditions,—verging indeed towards a certain far deeper Lake. Whereupon it pleased kind Heaven to send them the Prophet Moses, with an instructive word of warning, out of which might have sprung 'remedial measures' not a few. But no: the men of the Dead Sea discovered, as the valet-species always does in heroes or prophets, no comeliness in Moses; listened with real tedium to Moses, with light grinning, or with splenetic sniffs and sneers, affecting even to yawn; and signified, in short, that they found him a humbug, and even a bore. Such was the

54 'Observations on the external characters and habits of the Troglodytes Niger', *Boston Journal of Natural History*, 4 (1843–44), 362–86 (p. 385). Quoted in Huxley, *Man's Place in Nature*, p. 58. Savage adds an aside which makes one wonder how the chimps could be any more vile than their relatives who expelled them: 'They are, however, eaten by them, and when cooked with the oil and pulp of the palm-nut considered a highly palatable morsel.' Kingsley may have known this passage by Savage; he writes of apes that, 'the wild negroes, among whom they live, hold them in abhorrence, and believe that they were once men like themselves, who were gradually changed into brute beasts, by giving way to detestable sins' (*The Gospel of the Pentateuch and David* (London: Macmillan, 1885), sermon VII, 'Joseph', pp. 91–103 (p. 97)). This sermon was preached on 8 March 1863. *Man's Place in Nature* was published in January 1863, but the lectures which comprise it were written in 1861. Kingsley corresponded with Huxley about the gorilla brain while he was writing *The Water-Babies*, so he could have had access to Huxley's lectures before they were published. Then again, he may simply have read Savage's book.

candid theory these men of the Asphalt Lake formed to themselves of Moses. That
probably he was a humbug, that certainly he was a bore.

Moses withdrew; but Nature and her rigorous veracities did not withdraw. The
men of the Dead Sea, when we went next to visit them, were all 'changed into Apes'
[footnote: Sale's Koran (*Introduction.*)]; sitting on the trees there, grinning now in
the most *un*affected manner; gibbering and chattering very genuine nonsense; finding
the whole Universe now a most indisputable Humbug! The Universe has *become* a
Humbug to these Apes who thought it one. There they sit and chatter, to this hour:
only, I believe, every Sabbath there returns to them a bewildered half-consciousness,
half reminiscence; and they sit, with their wizened smoke-dried visages, and such an
air of tragicality as Apes may; looking out through those blinking smoke-bleared eyes
of theirs,[55] into the wonderfullest smoky Twilight and undecipherable disordered
Dusk of Things; wholly an Uncertainty, Unintelligibility, they and it; and for commentary thereon, here and there an unmusical chatter or mew: — truest, tragicallest
Humbug conceivable by the mind of man or ape! They made no use of their souls;
and so have lost them. Their worship on the Sabbath now is to roost there, with
unmusical screeches, and half-remember that they had souls.[56]

Carlyle writes that the tribe have lost their souls. What he means is that
they have lost their rational souls. Having neglected to nourish their human
souls, they have forfeited them, and the human souls have been replaced
with the souls of apes, those shadowy denizens of the land somewhere
between human and beast. Accordingly, their bodies have followed suit.
This is reminiscent of Thomas Sheridan's analysis of the Yahoos:

In your merely animal capacity, says [Swift] to man, without reason to guide you, and
actuated only by blind instinct, I will show you that you would be degraded below
the beasts of the field. That very form, that very body, you are now so proud of, as
giving you such a superiority over all other animals, I will show you owe all their

55 'And looking round, [Tom] suddenly saw, standing close to him, a little ugly, black,
     ragged figure with bleared eyes and grinning white teeth' (19).
56 Thomas Carlyle, *Past and Present* [1843] (London: Oxford University Press, 1960),
     bk 3, chap. 3: 'Gospel of Dilettantism', pp. 157–58. Carlyle became a fierce opponent
     of Darwinism. Also note the traditional apish behaviour of grinning and chattering.
     Carlyle was a strong and ongoing influence on Stevenson, who sent a postcard to
     Charles Baxter in June 1874 in which he mentions an expectation of meeting Carlyle.
     See *RLS Letters*, letter 284, II, 24. McLynn writes that as a young man Stevenson
     planned a biography of Carlyle (41); and that Carlyle declined the meeting (103).

beauty, and all their greatest powers, to their being actuated by a rational soul. Let that be withdrawn, let the body be inhabited by the mind of a brute, let it be prone as theirs are, and suffered like theirs to take its natural course, without any assistance from art, you would in that case be the most deformed, as to your external appearance, the most detestable of all creatures.[57]

So taken was Kingsley with his degradation theory, that it appears not once, but twice in *The Water-Babies*. In its first appearance it seems little more than an abstract of the Carlyle passage in a new setting:[58]

And where is the home of the water-babies? In St Brandan's fairy isle.

Did you never hear of the blessed St Brandan, how he preached to the wild Irish, on the wild Kerry Coast; he and five other hermits, till they were weary, and longed to rest? For the wild Irish would not listen to them, or come to confession and to mass, but liked better to brew potheen, and dance the pater o'pee, [...] and burn each other's houses; till St Brandan and his friends were weary of them, for they would not learn to be peaceable Christians at all.

So St Brandan went out to the point of old Dunmore, and looked over the tide-way roaring round the Blasquets, at the end of the world, and away into the ocean, and sighed—'Ah that I had wings as a dove!' And far away, before the setting sun, he saw a blue fairy sea, and golden fairy islands, and he said, 'Those are the islands of the blest.' Then he and his friends got into a hooker, and sailed away and away to the westward, and were never heard of more. But the people who would not hear him were changed into gorillas, and gorillas they are until this day (137).[59]

Here is the heart of *The Water-Babies*; here is the heart of Kingsley's approach to the human soul – use it or lose it. And this is the engine that powers his degradation theory, as expressed in his sermon on 'The Wages

57 See above, Chapter 3, n44.
58 Kingsley mentions *Past and Present* in a letter shortly before beginning *The Water-Babies*. See *CKL*, II, 136. David Rosen points out that Fanny gave Kingsley a copy of the book and that it 'greatly influenced him' ('The Volcano and the Cathedral: Muscular Christianity and the Origins of Primal Manliness', in *Muscular Christianity: Embodying the Victorian Age*, ed. by Donald E. Hall (Cambridge: Cambridge University Press, 1994), pp. 17–44 (p. 25)). C.N. Manlove writes that the story of the Doasyoulikes is 'derived from' Carlyle's tale. See *Modern Fantasy: Five Studies* (Cambridge: Cambridge University Press, 1975), p. 270, n93.
59 Kingsley regarded the poor Irish as chimpanzees. See below.

of Sin'. He begins by saying that the sinner continues in his sin by comforting himself with the thought that God's punishments are arbitrarily
determined, and that – somehow – God will forgive him and waive the
punishment:

> But, it is a very terrible, heart-rending thought, for a man to find out that what he
> will receive is not punishment, but wages; not punishment, but the end of the very
> road he is travelling on. That the wages of sin, and the end of sin, to which it must
> lead, are death; and that every time he sins he is earning those wages, deserving them,
> meriting them, and therefore receiving them by the just laws of the world of God.[60]
> That does torment him, that does terrify him, if he will look steadfastly at the broad
> plain fact. You need not dream of being let off, respited, reprieved, pardoned in any
> way. The thing cannot be done. It is contrary to the laws of God, and of God's uni-
> verse. [...] Your sins are killing you by inches; all day long they are sowing in you the
> seeds of disease and death. Every sin which you commit with your body shortens
> your bodily life. Every sin you commit with your mind, every act of stupidity, folly,
> wilful ignorance, helps to destroy your mind, and leave you dull, silly, devoid of right
> reason. Every sin you commit with your spirit, every sin of passion and temper, envy
> and malice, pride and vanity, injustice and cruelty, extravagance and self-indulgence,
> helps to destroy your spiritual life, and leave you bad, more and more unable to do
> the right and avoid the wrong, more and more unable to discover right from wrong;
> and that last is spiritual death, the eternal death of your moral being. There are three
> parts in you—body, mind, and spirit; and every sin you commit helps to kill one of
> these three, and, in many cases, to kill all three together.[61]

This is bad enough on an individual level, but when it happens throughout an entire society the consequences are catastrophic. And Kingsley
found examples of decaying humanity before his very eyes. In 1860 he took
a holiday in Ireland, from where he writes to his wife:

> This place is full of glory—very lovely, and well kept up. [...]
>   But I am haunted by the human chimpanzees I saw along that hundred miles of
> horrible country. I don't believe they are our fault. I believe there are not only many

---

60   These laws are embodied in Mrs Bedonebyasyoudid, who tells the emprickled Tom,
      'You put them there yourself, and only you can take them away' (162).
61   *The Water of Life, and other Sermons* (London: Macmillan, 1890), sermon IV,
      pp. 40–55 (pp. 44–45). Also quoted in *CKL*, II, 208–09. The sermon was preached
      at the Chapel Royal, St. James's, in 1864.

more of them than of old, but that they are happier, better, more comfortably fed and lodged under our rule than they ever were. But to see white chimpanzees is dreadful; if they were black, one would not feel it so much, but their skins, except where tanned by exposure, are as white as ours.[62]

As for the 'black chimpanzees':

[T]he niggers say that monkeys are men, only they won't work for fear of being made to talk; no, won't talk for fear of being made to work; that's it (right for once, as I live!) and put their hands over their eyes at night for fear of seeing the old gentleman—and I'm sure that's just like a reasonable creature, I used to when I was a little boy; and you see the niggers have lived among them for thousands of years, and are monstrous like them, too, d'ye see, and so they must know best.[63]

Kingsley also identifies black people with apes in Alton Locke's dream:

I was a baby-ape in Borneon forests, perched among fragrant trailers and fantastic orchis flowers; and as I looked down, beneath the green roof, into the clear waters paved with unknown water-lilies on which the sun had never shone, I saw my face reflected in the pool—a melancholy, thoughtful countenance, with large projecting brow—it might have been a negro child's (268–69).

62   *CKL*, II, 107. Letter of 4 July 1860. Brantlinger and Boyle cite this letter when noting the ape-like Edward Hyde's resemblance to 'the stereotype of the [ape-like] Irish hooligan'. They also suggest that the cane with which he murders Carew 'might easily have been a shillelagh' (*100 Years*, pp. 273; 274).

63   *CKL*, II, 142. 'Speech Of Lord Dundreary In Section D, On Friday Last, On The Great Hippocampus Question'. This gem arose in response to a debate which Kingsley attended in Cambridge in October 1861 between Huxley and Sir Richard Owen (1804–92). 'In this debate over the classification of mammals according to their brains, Owen had elevated man above the rest of nature on account of his brain; Huxley insisted that the mind as well as the body was a product of evolution, and pointed to his discoveries, such as that the *Hippocampus minor* is found in the brains of both man and ape, to substantiate this' (Leo Henkin, *Darwinism in the English Novel 1860–1910: The Impact of Evolution on Victorian Fiction* (New York: Russell and Russell, 1963), p. 83). The *hippocampus minor* appears in *The Water-Babies* as the 'hippopotamus major' (109–10). Huxley gives his side of the argument in *Man's Place in Nature*, pp. 133–38.

Brutishness is the fate of lesser individuals and lesser races. But Kingsley foresaw a great destiny for the English people, which he expresses in almost Messianic language in his 1846 lecture, 'How to Study Natural History':

> And bear in mind, as I said just now, that this study of natural history is the gram-mar of that very physical science which has enabled England thus to replenish the earth and subdue it. Do you not see, then, that by following these studies you are walking in the very path to which England owes her wealth; that you are training in yourselves that habit of mind which God has approved as the one which He has ordained for Englishmen, and are doing what in you lies toward carrying out, in after life, the glorious work which God seems to have laid on the English race, to replenish the earth and subdue it?[64]

This passage reveals a great deal about Kingsley's attitudes. In *Westward Ho!* Kingsley refers to 'the Bible doctrine, that man in a state of nature is a fallen being, doomed to death'.[65] But in his lecture he twice mentions the English ability 'to replenish the earth and subdue it'. The quotation is from Genesis 1.28:

> And God blessed [Adam and Eve], and God said unto them, Be fruitful, and multiply, and replenish the earth, and subdue it: and have dominion over the fish of the sea, and over the fowl of the air, and over every living thing that moveth upon the earth.

God here is addressing Adam and Eve *before* the Fall; and it is likely that Kingsley has not chosen the quotation lightly, but is using it to suggest a return by the educated Christian Englishman to a state of pre-Lapsarian nobility which makes his superiority over other peoples not only a right but a duty. He returns to this theme in his address to the Ladies' Sanitary Association, in which he begins by pointing out that, if their aims are real-ized, there will be a national population explosion as they save the lives of between thirty and forty percent of the children who are being born; and that, from a purely economic viewpoint, it might be better to let them die. But, he continues, if the ladies believe,

64   *Scientific Lectures and Essays*, p. 308.
65   See the full quotation above, n26.

that of all races upon earth now, probably the English race is the finest, and that it gives not the slightest sign whatever of exhaustion; that it seems to be on the whole a young race, and to have very great capabilities in it which have not yet been developed, and above all, the most marvellous capability of adapting itself to every sort of climate, and every form of life that any nation, except the old Roman, ever had in the world: if they consider with me that it is worth the while of political economists and social philosophers to look at the map, and see that about four-fifths of the globe cannot be said as yet to be in anywise inhabited or cultivated, or in the state in which men could make it by any fair supply of population and industry and human intellect:—then, perhaps, they may think with me that it is a duty, one of the noblest duties, to help the increase of the English race as much as possible, and to see that every child that is born into this great nation of England be developed to the highest pitch to which we can develop him, in physical strength and in beauty, as well as in intellect and in virtue.[66]

Meanwhile, Tom – Kingsley's Everyboy – is in his undersea nursery. From Mrs Bedonebyasyoudid he has learned the prudence of not doing wrong; from Mrs Doasyouwouldbedoneby he has learned the virtue of doing right. To speed Tom's education he is given a schoolmistress – Ellie, who has been sent from her beautiful home (which she visits on Sundays) to teach him, although she did not want to. Tom also wants to go there, but is not morally fit. He begs her 'to teach him to be good' (162), which she does – she teaches him (as Kingsley puts it, addressing the young reader) 'what you have been taught ever since you said your first prayers at your mother's knee' (163). But his education is not yet complete, and he longs to know where Ellie goes when she goes home on Sundays; and so comes his greatest challenge, and the final step in his moral evolution. He asks Mrs Bedonebyasyoudid why he cannot go with Ellie on Sundays.

'Little boys who are only fit to play with sea-beasts cannot go there,' she said. 'Those who go there must go first where they do not like, and do what they do not like, and help somebody they do not like' (165).

Ellie has done this in coming to teach Tom; but a comparable effort seems too much for him. After more tears and tantrums Tom finds his situation

---

66   *CKL*, II, 81–82.

unendurable, and determines to undertake a quest to help Grimes, whom
Mrs Bedonebyasyoudid has stuck in a chimney at the Other-end-of-
Nowhere. This is a true rite of passage, which Kingsley returns to more
than once. Mrs Bedonebyasyoudid comforts Tom:

> And then she told him how he had been in the nursery long enough, and must go
> out now and see the world, if he intended ever to be a man; and how he must go all
> alone by himself, as everyone else that was ever born has to go, and see with his own
> eyes, and smell with his own nose, and make his own bed and lie on it, and burn his
> own fingers if he put them into the fire (169).

Tom prepares to set of for the Other-end-of-Nowhere, but worries
that he does not know the way. Mrs Bedonebyasyoudid tells him:

> 'Little boys must take the trouble to find out things for themselves, or they will
> never grow to be men [...].'
> 'Well,' said Tom, 'it will be a long journey, so I had better start at once. Good-bye,
> Miss Ellie; you know I am getting a big boy, and I must go out and see the world'
> (180–81).

Ellie displays the pluck of Victorian womanhood, and like Una farewelling
Redcross, sends him off on his quest:

> 'I know you must,' said Ellie: 'but you will not forget me, Tom. I shall wait here till
> you come' (181).

Tom travels north, acquiring the canine equivalent of a water-baby
on the way, and comes to the pack-ice and Shiny Wall. There is no way
through, so he must dive under the floe.

> So Tom dived under the great white gate which never was opened yet, and went on
> in black darkness, at the bottom of the sea, for seven days and seven nights. And yet
> he was not a bit frightened. Why should he be? He was a brave English lad, whose
> business is to go out and see all the world (197).[67]

---

67   Kingsley's Shiny Wall, the Arctic ice-shelf which closes off the entrance to the North
     West Passage, may owe somewhat to Milton's watery crystal wall in the Creation
     sequence of *Paradise Lost*:

He surfaces in Peacepool, and asks a whale the way to Mother Carey. The whale directs him to what appears to be a large iceberg.

'That's Mother Carey,' said the whale, '[...] There she sits making old beasts into new all the year round' (199).

Tom swims towards the iceberg, and finds:

The grandest old lady he had ever seen—a white marble lady, sitting on a white marble throne. [...]
  [...]
  [...] Her hair was as white as the snow—for she was very very old—in fact, as old as anything you are likely to come across, except the difference between right and wrong (200).

Mother Carey[68] is Kingsley's penultimate expression of Dame Nature; and he has borrowed some of her attributes from Spenser. Spenser describes Dame Nature as she, like Mother Carey, sits upon her throne:

This great Grandmother of all creatures bred
  Great *Nature*, ever young yet full of eld,
  Still moouing, yet vnmoved from her sted;
  Vnseene of any, yet of all beheld. (VII.7.13)

Immediatly the Mountains huge appeer
  Emergent, and thir broad bare backs upheave
  Into the Clouds, thir tops ascend the Skie:
  So high as heav'd the tumid Hills, so low
  Down sunk a hollow bottom broad and deep,
  Capacious bed of Waters: thither they
  Hasted with glad precipitance, uprowld
  As drops on dust conglobing from the drie;
  Part rise in crystal Wall, or ridge direct,
  For haste; such flight the great command impressd
  On the swift flouds. (VII.285–95)
Cf. also Milton's description of the parting of the Red Sea, through which God lets the Israelites pass 'As on drie land between two crystal walls' (XII.197).
68 '*Mater cara* or *madre cara* ("mother dear", with reference to the Virgin Mary)' (Brewer, *Dictionary of Phrase and Fable* (Cassell, 1970), quoted in Manlove, p. 267, n63).

Kingsley describes what Tom sees:

> [F]rom the foot of the throne there swum away, out and out into the sea, millions of new-born creatures, of more shapes and colours than man ever dreamed. And they were Mother Carey's children, whom she makes out of the sea-water all day long (200).

But Mother Carey makes her children within specifically Darwinian principles. In Kingsley's lecture 'The Natural Theology of the Future', already quoted above, he says:

> We knew of old that God was so wise that He could make all things; but behold, He is so much wiser than even that, that He can make all things make themselves.[69]

And so it is with Mother Carey. Tom says to her:

> 'I won't trouble your ladyship any more; I hear you are very busy.'
> 'I am never more busy than I am now,' she said, without stirring a finger.
> 'I heard, ma'am, that you were always making new beasts out of old.'
> 'So people fancy. But I am not going to trouble myself to make things, my little dear. I sit here and make them make themselves' (201).

For Kingsley, Nature is the creative expression of 'a living, immanent, ever-working God'.[70]

After many adventures – including a visit to Gulliver's island of Laputa (222) – Tom arrives at the Other-end-of-Nowhere, and is taken to meet Grimes who is still stuck in the chimney. Tom's task is to forgive Grimes and do what he can to help him; Grimes's task is to repent. When he genuinely does so, hearing of the death of his mother, his tears wash away

---

69   See above, n28. Kingsley is here restating an argument put forward by Erasmus Darwin: 'For if we may compare infinities, it would seem to require a greater infinity of power to cause the causes of effects, than to cause the effects themselves' (*Zoonomia*, 2nd edn, 2 vols (London: Johnson, 2nd edn, 1796), I, 509).

70   *CKL*, II, 171. Letter to Revd F.D. Maurice, 1863.

both the soot which covers him and the mortar from between the bricks which hold him. Beaten, penitent, Grimes is given one last chance, and set to sweep out the crater of Mt Etna.

Tom's quest is complete. Mrs Bedonebyasyoudid (who has appeared suddenly at the Other-end-of-Nowhere) returns him to St Brandan's isle – via her backstairs, Kingsley's equivalent of Spenser's hinder gate[71] – where Ellie has been waiting for 'many a hundred years' (242). They are 'both quite grown up—he into a tall man, and she into a beautiful woman' (242). Mrs Bedonebyasyoudid – now grown beautiful – changes into Mother Carey – now grown young – then into the Irishwoman, then into 'neither of them, and yet all of them at once' (243), and is finally transfigured into she whom we must call Dame Nature. She speaks:

> 'My name is written in my eyes, if you have eyes to see it there.'
> And they looked into her great, deep, soft eyes, and they changed again and again into every hue, as the light changes in a diamond.
> 'Now read my name,' said she, at last.
> And her eyes flashed, for one moment, clear, white, blazing light: but the children could not read her name; for they were dazzled, and hid their faces in their hands (243).[72]

71   He letteth in, he letteth out to wend,
         All that to come into the world desire;
         A thousand thousand naked babes attend
         About him day and night, which doe require,
         That he with fleshly weedes would them attire:
         Such as him list, such as eternall fate
         Ordained hath, he clothes with sinfull mire,
         And sendeth forth to liue in mortall state,
         Till they againe returne backe by the hinder gate.   (III.6.32)
    Manlove (46) draws his readers' attention to a passage in Kingsley's sermon 'The Wages of Sin': 'We cannot escape the consequences of our actions. [...] There are no backstairs up which we may be smuggled into heaven.' See *CKL*, II, 209, where Fanny Kingsley excerpts the sermon. See also *Westward Ho!*, p. 355, where Kingsley again affirms the existence of a backstairs to heaven.
72   Kingsley likens God to the Sun in his lecture from *Alexandria and Her Schools*. See above, n32.

This passage points directly to Spenser's Dame Nature, and her position as God's regent on Earth.[73] Chaucer and Spenser both liken the beauty and radiance of Nature's face to the light of the Sun. Chaucer says that her beauty excels that of other creatures, as the light of the summer Sun excels that of a star; Spenser says that the beams of splendour about her face are a thousand times more dazzling than the Sun. Spenser then specifically identifies Nature (whose gender may be either male or female) with the transfigured Christ. He writes:

> Her garment was so bright and wondrous sheene,
> That my fraile wit cannot deuize to what
> It to compare, nor finde like stuffe to that,
> As those three sacred *Saints*, though else most wise,
> Yet on mount *Thabor* quite their wits forgat,
> When they their glorious Lord in strange disguise
> Transfigur'd sawe; his garments so did daze their eyes.   (VII.7.7)

And here is St. Matthew:

> And after six days Jesus taketh Peter, James, and John his brother, and bringeth them up into an high mountain apart.
> And was transfigured before them: and his face did shine as the sun, and his raiment was white as the light.
> [...]
> [...] A bright cloud overshadowed them: and behold a voice out of the cloud, which said, This is my beloved Son, in whom I am well pleased; hear ye him.
> And when the disciples heard it, they fell on their face, and were sore afraid (17.1–6).

73   Stephen Prickett argues for another source: 'The reference is, of course, to the final Canto of Dante's *Paradiso*, where in the climax of the "high fantasy" the Godhead is described as three interlocking circles of different colours, each reflecting the other, dazzling the poet's vision as it draws up his will into "the Love that moves the sun and other stars"' [endnote 43: Canto XXXIII, lines 142–45.] (*Victorian Fantasy* (Sussex: Harvester Press, 1979), p. 167).

Just as the humble wandering carpenter's son is transfigured and revealed as the Son of God; so the Irishwoman, transformed through the incorporation of her several aspects, is revealed finally as an agent of Divine power.

Tom's adventure has taken him from illiterate 'heathen' (159) sweep to cultivated, educated man of science. When he is a child he understands as a child, and Nature appears to him through the glass of his simple understanding. When he becomes a man, and turns again to gaze upon Nature, he is dazzled by her beauty and miraculous complexity. Nature transfigured is Nature understood. Mrs Bedonebyasyoudid tells Ellie:

> 'You may take him home with you now on Sundays, Ellie. He has won his spurs in the great battle, and become fit to go with you, and be a man; because he has done the thing he did not like.'
>
> So Tom went home with Ellie on Sundays, and sometimes on week-days, too; and he is now a great man of science, and can plan railroads, and steam-engines, and electric telegraphs, and rifled guns, and so forth; and knows everything about everything, [...]. And all this from what he learnt when he was a water-baby, underneath the sea (243–44).

Although it is not clearly expressed, Tom and Ellie have both reincarnated into more evolved people. Kingsley of course has left himself with no way in which to demonstrate Ellie's evolution, but Tom has left his half-beast self behind and evolved into a God-fearing Victorian man of science. He has followed the advice of Tennyson:

> Arise, and fly
> The reeling Faun, the sensual feast;
> Move upward, working out the beast,
> And let the ape and tiger die.[74]

---

74 *In Memoriam* [1850], intro. and notes by Kingsley Hart (London: The Folio Society, 1975), CXVIII.25–28. Charles Kingsley quotes this stanza in the preface to *Westminster Sermons* (p. xviii). Note yet again how mankind is possessed by beasts both real and mythic.

This is not simply within one life, but many:

> I held it truth, with him who sings
>> To one clear harp in divers tones,
>> That men may rise on stepping stones
> Of their dead selves to higher things.[75]

Tom has won his spurs; but he has also had a narrow escape. Just before he sets out on his quest, Mrs Bedonebyasyoudid tells him:

> You were very near being turned into a beast once or twice, little Tom. Indeed, if you had not made up your mind to go on this journey, and see the world, like an Englishman, I am not sure but that you would have ended as an eft in a pond (177).

One can see this Platonic degenerative process at work in Tom's encounter with a flock of mollymocks on his way to Shiny Wall:

> 'Who are you, you jolly birds?' asked Tom.
> 'We are the spirits of the old Greenland skippers (as every sailor knows), who hunted here, right whales and horse-whales, full hundreds of years agone. But, because we were saucy and greedy, we were all turned into mollys, to eat whale's blubber all our days' (196).

In Plato's *Phaedo* Socrates explains that the souls of inferior men wander as ghosts until their desire for a body leads them to incarnate again in bodies which reflect their character:

> And those who have chosen the portion of injustice, and tyranny, and violence, will pass into wolves, or into hawks and kites:–whither else can we suppose them to go? (82a).

This, of course, as Kingsley keeps insisting, is not arbitrary. In Plato's *Laws* the unnamed Athenian says:

> The ruler of the universe has ordered all things with a view to the excellence and preservation of the whole, and each part, as far as may be, has an action and passion appropriate to it. [...] Now, as the soul combining first with one body and then with

75   *In Memoriam*, I.1–4.

another undergoes all sorts of changes, either of herself or through the influence of another soul, all that remains to the player of the game is that he should shift the pieces; sending the better nature to the better place, and the worse to the worse, and so assigning to them their proper portion (X, 903b–e).

This, then, is the Platonic process of coming and going in form after form. It is important to note that this process is one in which an individual soul moves into an appropriate body, which already exists as an identifiable type.

Darwinism, however, says that species evolve slowly through the survival of those individuals most adapted to the changing environment. It is a purely physical, undirected process (which just happens to have culminated in the English gentleman). Fortunately for Kingsley's equanimity he was able to absorb from evolutionary theory whatever he found congenial, and disregard the rest. Darwinism fitted neatly with his theory of degraded races, and he was able to take the theory to its logical Darwinian conclusion in the story of the Doasyoulikes. Kingsley seems to have been quite excited by it, as he writes to Fanny:

> I have got a deal more [of *The Water-Babies*] ready, among others a wonderful waterproof picture-book, in which Tom sees how a race of men, in time, become gorillas by being brutish. I have worked out the theory till I quite believe it.[76]

Mrs Bedonebyasyoudid, who owns the waterproof book, says of the gorillas:

> Folks say now that I can make beasts into men, by circumstance, and selection, and competition, and so forth. Well, perhaps they are right; and perhaps, again, they are wrong. [...] Whatever their ancestors were, men they are; and I advise them to behave as such, and act accordingly. But let them recollect this, that there are two sides to every question, and a downhill as well as an uphill road; and, if I can turn beasts into men, I can, by the same laws of circumstance, and selection, and competition, turn men into beasts (177).

She then goes straight on to say, 'You were very near being turned into a beast once or twice, little Tom', which completely blurs the distinction

76   *CKL*, II, 137.

between Platonic metempsychosis and Darwinian evolution; and by the end of the book one is left with the impression that in Kingsley's mind there probably is not one – at least, not when it comes to de-volution.

When Kingsley introduces the 'great and famous nation of the Doas-youlikes' (171) they are humans living an Arcadian existence where all of their needs are met providentially, 'till there were never such comfortable, easy-going, happy-go-lucky people in the world' (172).

Kingsley begins the story of their sad decline with a catastrophe. The Doasyoulikes are living near a volcano, which blows up some time in the next five hundred years, killing two-thirds of the people. But they are too lazy to move, and assume that the volcano will not erupt again. However, all of their traditional, easy food sources are gone, and they have to dig in the ground for roots and nuts. They have forgotten how to plough, and, anyway, have eaten all their seed-corn. They begin their descent – first into Irishmen:

> So they lived miserably on roots and nuts, and all the weakly little children had great stomachs, and then died.
>   'Why,' said Tom, 'they are growing no better than savages.'
>   'And look how ugly they are all getting,' said Ellie.
>   'Yes [said Mrs Bedonebyasyoudid]; when people live on poor vegetables instead of roast beef and plum pudding, their jaws grow large, and their lips grow coarse, like the poor Paddies who eat potatoes' (174).

Then into uncivilized primitives:

> And she turned over the next five hundred years. And there they were all living up in trees, and making nests to keep off the rain. And underneath the trees lions were prowling about (174).

Now Kingsley introduces the Darwinian mechanisms of competition and selection as the survivors turn into Lucretian Wild Men:

> 'Why,' said Ellie, 'the lions seem to have eaten a good many of them, for there are very few left now.'
>   'Yes,' said the fairy; 'you see it was only the strongest and most active ones who could climb the trees and so escape.'

'But what great, hulking, broad-shouldered chaps they are,' said Tom, 'they are a rough lot as ever I saw.'

'Yes, they are getting very strong now; for the ladies will not marry any but the strongest and fiercest gentlemen, who can help them up the trees out of the lions' way' (174).

Five hundred years later their feet are evolving into hands, by which some have an advantage in the trees, out-compete the others, and pass on their improved limbs while their competitors die out.

Now Kingsley introduces environmental pressure:

'But there is a hairy one among them,' said Ellie.

'Ah!' said the fairy, 'that will be a great man in his time, and chief of all the tribe.'[77]

And, when she turned over the next five hundred years, it was true.

For this hairy chief had had hairy children, and they hairier children still; and everyone wished to marry hairy husbands, and have hairy children too; for the climate was growing so damp that none but the hairy ones could live: all the rest coughed and sneezed, and had sore throats, and went into consumptions, before they could grow up to be men and women (175).

Five hundred years later we find them drifting in the twilight between man and beast:

'Why, there is one on the ground picking up roots,' said Ellie, 'and he cannot walk upright.'

No more he could; for in the same way that the shape of their feet had altered, the shape of their backs had altered also.

'Why,' cried Tom, 'I declare they are all apes' (175).

Kingsley here draws the crucial distinction between humans and animals – humans can talk. The Doasyoulikes, despite outward appearances, are still human; and are to be judged as humans:

'Something fearfully like it, poor foolish creatures,' said the fairy. 'They are grown so stupid now, that they can hardly think: for none of them have used their wits for many hundred years. They have almost forgotten, too, how to talk. For each stupid

---

77   Note that they have also degenerated socially, from a nation to a tribe.

child forgot some of the words it heard from its stupid parents, and had not wits
enough to make fresh words for itself. Beside, they are grown so fierce and suspi-
cious and brutal that they keep out of each other's way, and mope and sulk in the
dark forests, never hearing each other's voice, till they have forgotten almost what
speech is like. I am afraid they will all be apes very soon, and all by doing only what
they liked' (175–76).

And so Kingsley comes to the end of the Doasyoulikes. They have
lost the use of language, and have become true beasts. And he ends this
cautionary tale with a little joke:

> And in the next five hundred years they were all dead and gone, by bad food and wild
> beasts and hunters; all except one tremendous old fellow with jaws like a jack, who
> stood full seven feet high; and M. du Chaillu came up to him, and shot him, as he
> stood roaring and thumping his breast. And he remembered that his ancestors had
> once been men, and tried to say, 'Am I not a man and a brother?' but had forgotten
> how to use his tongue; and then he had tried to call for a doctor, but he had forgot-
> ten the word for one. So all he said was 'Ubboboo!' and died (176).[78]

This 'joke' requires some explanation. Beginning in 1789, the Society
for the Abolition of the Slave Trade mounted its first great campaign to
raise public awareness. One of the Society's weapons in this campaign was
a plaque, reproduced as cameos, showing a black man in chains asking the

---

78   Paul du Chaillu (1830?–1903) was a French-born adventurer who travelled in Africa,
     where he famously encountered live gorillas. The year 1861 saw both the publication of
     his *Explorations and Adventures in Equatorial Africa*, and his appearance at the same
     British Association meeting which hosted the *Hippocampus* debate between Huxley
     and Owen. Most likely Kingsley heard du Chaillu lecture there on his exploits. The
     scene between the Doasyoulike and du Chaillu is reminiscent of that described by
     Sir Walter Scott: 'The last [orang-outang] we have heard of was seen, we believe, in
     the island of Sumatra; it was of great size and strength, and upwards of seven feet
     high. It died defending desperately its innocent life against a party of Europeans,
     who, we cannot help thinking, might have better employed the superiority which
     their knowledge gave them over the poor native of the forest. It was probably this
     creature, seldom seen, but when once seen never forgotten, which occasioned the
     ancient belief in the god Pan, with his sylvans and satyrs' (*Count Robert of Paris* [1832]
     (London and Edinburgh: Black, 1894), pp. 200–01). Note how Scott also links the
     orang-outang with mythic figures.

rhetorical question: 'AM I NOT A MAN AND A BROTHER?' The plaque was designed by Josiah Wedgwood, Charles Darwin's grandfather.

In 1861 *Punch* published a cartoon which relied in part on the reader knowing the connection between the Wedgwoods and Darwin, which had been strengthened by his marriage to his cousin Emma Wedgwood in 1839. The cartoon shows a large ape, wielding the traditional staff, wearing a placard on which is written the very un-rhetorical question: 'AM I A MAN AND A BROTHER?'[79] Kingsley obviously has this recent cartoon in mind for the last Doasyoulike.

But Kingsley is giving one more turn of the screw. By conflating the Wedgwood cameo and the *Punch* cartoon, he is inviting his readers, yet again, to identify black people with apes.[80]

Finally, having told a tale of Darwinian evolution, over a long – if inadequate – time, Kingsley looks past the mechanism to the true reason for the decline. Ellie turns to Mrs Bedonebyasyoudid:

> 'But could you not have saved them from becoming apes?' said little Ellie, at last.
>
> 'At first, my dear; if only they would have behaved like men, and set to work to do what they did not like. But the longer they waited, and behaved like the dumb beasts, who only do what they like, the stupider and clumsier they grew; till at last they were past all cure, for they had thrown their own wits away' (176–77).

Here we have it: the soul secretes the body as the snail secretes its shell. Kingsley need not look to Darwin for the physical degradation of the Doasyoulikes; he already has the principle explained by Timaeus in Plato's *Timaeus*:

> But the race of birds was created out of innocent lightminded men [...]. The race of wild pedestrian animals, again, came from those who had no philosophy in any of their thoughts, and never considered at all about the nature of the heavens, because they had ceased to use the courses of the head, but followed the guidance of those parts of the soul which are in the breast. In consequence of these habits of theirs

79 'Monkeyana', *Punch*, 40 (18 May 1861), 206.
80 In his sermons Kingsley is more circumspect. In the preface to his *Westminster Sermons* he declares that the Negro is 'a man and a brother' (p. xvi).

they had their front legs and their heads resting upon the earth to which they were drawn by natural affinity; and the crowns of their heads were elongated and of all sorts of shapes, into which the courses of the soul were crushed by reason of disuse (91d–e).

Timaeus goes on to describe creatures with even less sense, as they are drawn closer and closer to the earth until they lose the need for legs and go upon their stomachs. The most ignorant take up abode in the sea as fish or oysters. 'These', says Timaeus,

> are the laws by which all animals pass into one another, now, as in the beginning, changing as they lose or gain wisdom and folly (92c).

No doubt Kingsley was exaggerating somewhat when he proclaimed himself a convert to Darwin's views; after all, the story of the Douasyoulikes shows that Kingsley's thinking did not progress beyond the opinion he expressed in 1855 in *Westward Ho!*, that uncivilized races are degraded from a former superior state, rather than risen from something lower. But in the story of the Doasyoulikes – based as it is on an existing tradition which owes nothing to Darwin – he shows that he has accepted and adopted the most contentious aspect of Darwin's theory – the relationship between man and ape. In a book filled with fairies and water-babies; in which the souls of the old Greenland skippers reincarnate as birds; Kingsley takes pains to show that – although individual souls may transmigrate from body to body and species to species – when it comes to changes over generations, the physical mechanisms have to be the Darwinian ones of circumstance, selection, and competition. Furthermore, that when this Darwinian process takes place, the human race has to devolve into the one animal to which scientifically it is known to be related – the ape.

Darwin's *Origin of Species* opened the door to a new kind of scientific evolutionary fiction, while at the same time defining the limits of what it could do: we come from apes, we go back to apes. Although we may eventually return to oysters, we do not degenerate into something with feathers while we are on the way.

Stevenson is similarly inspired and constrained by the new science. Henry Jekyll, learned, disciplined, energetic, driven by societal pressures to conform to the muscular Kingsleyan model, is a secret Doasyoulike. He does not want to do the thing he does not like, preferring instead to indulge his vices; he has an 'aversion to the dryness of a life of study' (85); he cannot keep to his good resolutions; he returns again and again to the evil draught; and finally indulges his lower passions in the vehicle of his own body. Each sin, each lapse, leaves him more beast-like both in body and soul, until he finds himself too far down the path of degeneration – animal in form, yet still human enough to reason and speak.

But although Jekyll is a Doasyoulike, his transformation into Hyde occurs within his own body, and within years, not centuries. Hyde's hairy, ugly body is therefore the equivalent of Tom's prickles,

> for you must know and believe that people's souls make their bodies, just as a snail makes its shell [...]. And, therefore, when Tom's soul grew all prickly with naughty tempers, his body could not help growing prickly too, so that nobody would cuddle him, or play with him, or even like to look at him (161).

Tom finds the strength of character to remove his prickles. Jekyll's tragedy happens because he has no strength of character. He is helpless to avert his downfall, while at the same time – to take the Kingsleyan view – he gets what he deserves.

The first comment one could make about *The Water-Babies* is that it is strongly autobiographical: the half-beast Tom (Kingsley) is saved from his 'beast life' by the pure and virtuous Ellie (Fanny). The second comment is that it is heavily influenced by *The Faerie Queene*. I do not wish to suggest that Kingsley set out to base his work on Spenser's; but, there are many suggestive parallels between the two. The intention of Spenser is 'to fashion a gentleman or noble person in vertuous and gentle discipline',[81] which is also the intention of Kingsley, whose gentleman enjoys the added virtue of scientific knowledge. Spenser's heroes undertake a series of quests; Tom undertakes a quest. Kingsley appears to have adapted characters and locales from Spenser; and the conclusions of both works involve the revelation of

---

81   Letter to Sir Walter Raleigh, 23 January 1589. Quoted in *Edmund Spenser's Poetry*, ed. by Hugh Maclean (New York: Norton, 1968), p. 1.

the refulgent Dame Nature. Spenser and Kingsley were kindred spirits in their Christiano-Platonic view of nature and their belief that God was working unceasingly in the natural world. Is it any wonder, then, that Kingsley, deliberately or not, employed Spenserian material in a work so intimately connected with themes which Spenser had also addressed?

How, then, should one define *The Water-Babies*? Is it Darwinian? Christian? Platonist? Undoubtedly it is all three. But which lies at its heart; and which has been incorporated and adapted to the major theme? This is an important question, because it is one which we must also ask about *Jekyll and Hyde*.

Scholars of Darwin-inspired literature include *The Water-Babies* among their texts. But they also comment on Kingsley's distortion of Darwin's theory. Leo Henkin writes:

> The purpose of the tale seems to have been to adapt Darwin's theory of the natural selection of species to the understanding of children, by giving it a moral and religious as well as a scientific application (199).

Henkin is therefore saying that the Darwinism is the cornerstone of the story, and has been overlaid with religious language and symbolism. Gillian Beer, however, argues that Kingsley adapted Darwinism to his original cosmic view:

> Kingsley, in his images of extinction, of degeneration, and or recapitulation and development, mythologises Darwinian theory with remarkable insight. [...] In its unguarded and unanalytic response to Darwin's ideas and rhetoric, Kingsley's work represents the first phase of assimilation. He grasped much of what was fresh in Darwin's ideas while at the same time retaining a creationist view of experience.[82]

Peter Morton explains how Kingsley was able to do it:

> He found no, or little, difficulty in absorbing the new image of a God who creates a single primeval form capable of endless proliferation and variation. [...] We notice, however, that Kingsley fits evolutionary theory into his theology, not by importing

---

82   *Darwin's Plots: Evolutionary Narrative in Darwin, George Eliot and Nineteenth-Century Fiction* (London: Routledge & Kegan Paul, 1983), p. 138.

the supernatural into biology as [Alfred Russel] Wallace did, but by making natural selection itself an agent of divine power.[83]

How does this work? In *The Water-Babies* natural selection is a mechanism controlled and ordered by Mother Carey, or Dame Nature, who would appear to be a mythical figure. Where, then, is the divine power? For an answer to this – and to gain an insight into Kingsley's ability to accommodate propositions at variance with his theology – we must turn again to Spenser. In the transfiguration of Mrs Bedonebyasyoudid (243), Kingsley presents the revealed Dame Nature as a being of dazzling brilliant light. In the *Mutabilitie Cantos* Spenser's language associates Nature with the dazzling transfigured Christ; but in his 'Hymne of Heavenly Beautie' Spenser employs the same imagery in his description of God Himself. Spenser tries to picture the beauty of God's presence, and the even greater beauty of God's qualities,

> By which he lends us of himselfe a sight.

> Those unto all he daily doth display,
> And shew himselfe in th'image of his grace,
> As in a looking glasse, through which he may
> Be seene, of all his creatures vile and base,
> That are unable else to see his face,
> His glorious face which glistereth else so bright,
> That th'Angels selves can not endure his sight. (112–19)[84]

---

83 *The Vital Science: Biology and the Literary Imagination, 1860–1900* (London: Allen & Unwin, 1984), p. 68.

84 Cf. Milton's description of God in *Paradise Lost*, III.372–82, which could well owe somewhat to Spenser:

> Thee Father first they [angels] sung Omnipotent,
> Immutable, Immortal, Infinite,
> Eternal King; thee Author of all being,
> Fountain of Light, thy self invisible
> Amidst the glorious brightness where thou sit'st
> Thron'd inaccessible, but when thou shad'st
> The full blaze of thy beams, and through a cloud
> Drawn round about thee like a radiant Shrine,

How, then, asks Spenser, if the angels can not look upon God, can puny creatures such as we do so? He gives the answer:

> The meanes therefore which unto us is lent,
> Him to behold, is on his workes to looke,
> Which he hath made in beauty excellent,
> And in the same, as in a brasen booke,
> To reade enregistred in every nooke
> His goodnesse, which his beautie doth declare,
> For all thats good, is beautifull and faire.[85]

This could almost have been written by Kingsley: God may be seen; God may be understood; God may be even, to a degree, worshipped, in His great work – the natural world. In Kingsley's lecture quoted above he writes that the neo-Platonism evident in Spenser's *Faerie Queene*,

> above all his Garden of Adonis, and his cantos on Mutability, [...] must have [...] taught him to behold alike in suns and planets, in flowers and insects, in man and in beings higher than man, one glorious order of love and wisdom, linking them all to Him from whom they all proceed, rays from His cloudless sunlight, mirrors of His eternal glory.[86]

Does God the Creator, then, oversee the minutiae of nature? Yes; but not in person. God has a consort:

> There in his bosom *Sapience* doth sit,
> The soveraine dearling of the *Deity*,
> Clad like a Queene in royall robes, most fit
> For so great powre and peerelesse majesty.[87]

> Dark with excessive bright thy skirts appeer,
> Yet dazle Heav'n, that brightest Seraphim
> Approach not, but with both wings veil thir eyes.

85   'Heavenly Beautie', 127–33.
86   *Alexandria*, pp. 126–27. See above, n32. In a letter to Fanny as early as 1842 Kingsley writes that there are three ways in which she may study God. The third way is: 'From His works. [...] Do not study matter for its own sake, but as the countenance of God! [... Study the beauties of nature] as allegories and examples from whence moral examples may be drawn' (*CKL*, I, 88).
87   'Heavenly Beautie', 183–86.

And of course she partakes in the divine effulgence, which also shines out through the transfigured Christ, through Spenser's Nature, and through Kingsley's Mother Carey:

> And all with gemmes and jewels gorgeously
> Adornd, that brighter then the starres appeare,
> And make her native brightnes seeme more cleare.[88]

She, like Chaucer's Nature, is 'the vicaire of the almyghty Lord':[89] she wears a crown, and carries a sceptre,

> With which she rules the house of God on hy,
> And menageth the ever-moving sky,
> And in the same these lower creatures all,
> Subjected to her powre imperiall.
> Both heaven and earth obey unto her will,
> And all the creatures which they both containe.[90]

One cannot take the argument too far: like Donne's, Spenser's creatures 'do in state remaine,/ As their great Maker did at first ordaine' (199); whereas Kingsley's creatures, including mankind, are in a state of continual flux. The point to bear in mind is that natural selection is a mechanism by which Dame Nature manages her affairs here on Earth; and by studying the works of Nature we come to recognize and appreciate the hand of God. However, the type, or Idea, of Nature is the Judaeo-Christian Sapience, or Wisdom, the vicar of the Lord, whose will prevails in both Heaven and Earth.[91] Therefore Darwin's theory of natural selection, which violates

---

88   'Heavenly Beautie', 187–89.
89   *Parlement of Foules*, 379.
90   'Heavenly Beautie', 193–98.
91   The Spenserian Kingsley could not have been unaware of the relationship between Sapience and Nature. Josephine Waters Bennett writes that Sapience ('the personification of the divine Wisdom, or Mind of God') and Nature ('a Neo-Platonic goddess who emanates from ultimate divinity') are not 'distinct and independent', but manifestations at different levels of one divine power. See 'Spenser's Venus and the Goddess Nature of the *Cantos of Mutabilitie*', *Studies in Philology*, 30 (1933), 160–92 (pp. 163–64). Here is yet another example of the mingling of Platonic and Christian thought in Spenser and his successors.

both Platonic philosophy and Christian theology, in Kingsley's system fits neatly into God's plan because God ordained it through His servants. Thus in *The Water-Babies* Kingsley has not given equal weight to Platonism, Christianity, and Darwinism, but, in order to tell a moral tale about the human condition, he has subsumed Darwinism within his original and formative Platonic and Christian beliefs.

Kingsley was forty years old when Darwin published *The Origin of Species*. He had an intense and focused religious upbringing; he was by inclination a Platonist; he was also, by inclination, an ardent natural philosopher; he read the Bible, Plato, Spenser, Milton, Swift, Carlyle, Darwin, and Huxley. All of these influences, and more, come together in the great intellectual log-jam that is *The Water-Babies*. Consequently an ape, for Kingsley, is not simply an animal: it is a symbol of lower inner impulses in the soul which we must transcend, as we find in Tennyson; it is a symbol of a degraded condition, both inner and, then, outer, as we find in Carlyle; it is an unfinished primitive related stage of human evolution, as we find in Darwin. Most importantly, it can exist as the morally, intellectually, and spiritually fallen aspect within the soul of a normal human being, which may be glimpsed on occasion by those with eyes to see:

> And looking round, he suddenly saw, standing close to him, a little ugly, black, ragged figure, with bleared eyes and grinning white teeth. He turned on it angrily. What did such a little black ape want in that sweet young lady's room? And behold, it was himself reflected in a great mirror, the like of which Tom had never seen before.
>
> And Tom, for the first time in his life, found out that he was dirty; and burst into tears with shame and anger; and turned to sneak up the chimney again and hide (19).

Surely it is asking too much of human nature to expect that hundreds of years of literature, language, and symbolism should relinquish their grip on the creative imagination with the arrival of Darwin's theory. *The Water-Babies* shows that, rather than retreat, this ancient and ever-evolving culture was able to accommodate Darwinism and, while acknowledging it, adapt it and use it to its own purpose, in much the same way (as I shall argue in the following chapters) that Stevenson – who also read the Bible, Spenser, Milton, Carlyle, Tennyson and Darwin – does in *Jekyll and Hyde*.

PART FOUR

Analyzing *Jekyll and Hyde*

We come now to a consideration of *Jekyll and Hyde* as a Darwinian–Christian–Platonic text, in the light of the preceding chapters. It is worth recalling here that at the time of the book's publication various readers identified all three influences operating in it. An anonymous reviewer for a Christian magazine found that it was

> an allegory based on the two-fold nature of man, a truth taught us by the Apostle PAUL in Romans vii., 'I find then a law that, when I would do good, evil is present with me'.[1]

John Addington Symonds focused on the atavistic figure of Hyde and the spectre of biological determinism arising from Darwin's theory:

> Physical and biological Science on a hundred lines is reducing individual freedom to zero, and weakening the sense of responsibility. I doubt whether the artist should lend his genius to this grim argument. It is like the Cave of Despair in the Faery Queen.[2]

James Ashcroft Noble, also invoking Spenser, saw Hyde as a Platonic manifestation of Jekyll's evil soul:

> The fateful drug acts with its strange transforming power upon the body as well as the mind; for when the first dose has been taken the unhappy victim finds that 'soul is form and doth the body make', and that his new nature, of evil all compact, has found for itself a corresponding environment (204).[3]

Each of these readers makes a valid observation, yet at the same time each is providing only a partial explanation for the presence of Hyde within Henry Jekyll. We must not forget that while Stevenson was reading Spencer, Darwin, and Huxley, he was also reading Spenser, Milton, and the Bible. Kingsley accepted Darwinism on one level, and then used it to suit his own higher purpose, which was theological. Nor was he coy about the process. Stevenson, when he became a man, put away childhood belief, but

1   See Maixner, p. 224.
2   *Letters*, III, 121. See also Maixner, pp. 210–11.
3   *Academy*, 29 (23 January 1886), 55. See also Maixner, p. 204.

retained all of the language, all of the myth, and many of the values that went with it. His writing reveals the same blending and interweaving of biblical, Platonic, and scientific language that one can find in Kingsley. In *Jekyll and Hyde* Darwinism provides an adequate frame of reference on the physical level, but it then gives way to Platonism and the Bible as Stevenson engages with his more profound concerns. It is only when we view Hyde through all three lenses, and focus them together on the underlying theme of heredity, that a clear picture begins to emerge.

CHAPTER SEVEN

Hyde the Wild Man

Probably the simplest way of approaching Hyde is to start at the outside and work inwards. His outside presents the reader immediately with a Wild Man.[1] Not only was Stevenson aware of the Wild Man tradition, but at one time he planned to make his own contribution to it with a short story entitled – after, one suspects, not a lot of thought – 'The Wild Man of the Woods'.[2] According to Arthur Dickson's description of the Wild Man, quoted above in Chapter Four, he

> has a hairy body, [...] is frequently of great physical strength; [...] carries [...] a club; is sometimes reputed to attack the unwary passer, particularly the women and children.[3]

And Bernheimer writes:

> The creature itself may appear without its fur, its club, or its loin ornament. Any one of its characteristics may be said to designate the species.[4]

Hyde's most obvious characteristic is his hairiness; although it is mentioned only by Jekyll; and then only twice (88, 92); and then only in reference to Hyde's hands, which are 'lean, corded, knuckly, of a dusky pallor, and thickly shaded with a swart growth of hair' (88). One might argue that

---

1   Edwin Eigner refers to Hyde as 'a wild man who turns particularly evil' (*Robert Louis Stevenson and Romantic Tradition* (Princeton, N.J.: Princeton University Press, 1966), p. 178). 'Wild' is here synonymous with 'savage' or 'uncivilized'; and, since he also applies 'wild' to describe Heathcliff in *Wuthering Heights*, one could safely assume that appearance does not come into it.

2   *RLS Letters*, letter 669 to Sidney Colvin, December 1879, III, 33–35 (p. 35).

3   Dickson, p. 9.

4   *Wild Men in the Middle Ages*, p. 2.

this hardly constitutes a case of hirsutism, but the fact remains that only Hyde's face and hands are open to view, and that most of what is open to view is covered in hair.

Hyde's next Wild Man characteristic is the stick with which he murders Carew, which the maid who witnesses the crime describes as 'a heavy cane' (46), and the narrator describes as 'of some rare and very tough and heavy wood' (47) – thereby investing it with an exotic origin, making it a suitable weapon for a Wild Man. The maid reports, not that Hyde struck Carew with the cane, but that he 'clubbed him to the earth' (47), thereby reinforcing the image of Wildness.

The attack itself is also in keeping with Wild Man behaviour. This is Hyde's second recorded attack on the unwary passer – the first being the trampling of the young girl, who embodies both the feminine and the child in one. Hyde's final attack on an unwary passer occurs on his way to his midnight rendezvous with Lanyon, when a woman offers him a box of lights, and he hits her in the face (94). Attacks on women by Wild Men usually involved rape. At least one reader of *Jekyll and Hyde* found a flavour of this in the trampling scene. Gerard Manley Hopkins writes: 'The trampling scene is perhaps a convention: he [Stevenson] was thinking of something unsuitable for fiction.'[5]

The attack on Carew involves another dominant aspect of the Wild Man character – irascibility. The maid reports that, as Carew was speaking politely to Hyde,

> He answered never a word, and seemed to listen with an ill-contained impatience. And then all of a sudden he broke out in a great flame of anger, stamping with his foot, *brandishing the cane*, [my emphasis] and carrying on [...] like a madman. [...] And next moment, with ape-like fury, he was trampling his victim under foot, and hailing down a storm of blows, under which the bones were audibly shattered and the body jumped upon the roadway (46–47).

5   *The Letters of Gerard Manley Hopkins to Robert Bridges*, ed., notes and intro. by Claude Abbott (London: Oxford University Press, 1935; 2nd edn, rev. 1955), letter 138, 28 October 1886, p. 238. See also Maixner, pp. 228–30 (p. 229). See also Dury for the contemporary association of Hyde with a paedophile known as 'the London Minotaur' (*Jekyll*, p. xxxiii–xxxiv).

As an indication of this Wild Man's 'great physical strength', we learn that the cane

> with which the deed had been done, although it was of some rare and very tough and heavy wood, had broken in the middle under the stress of this insensate cruelty (47).

Hyde's strength is also noted by Lanyon, who is 'struck' with his 'great muscular activity' (77).

But more than strength and irascibility are required for the performance of such a crime. Jekyll's Statement provides the clue to persuade the reader that Hyde is a true Wild Man. Jekyll writes:

> With a transport of glee, I mauled the unresisting body, tasting delight from every blow (90).

Had he taken a bite out of his victim the picture would have been complete.

Again one might argue that all of these comparisons are simply circumstantial – that Stevenson is thinking of Hyde solely as a hairy ape; that Enfield also carries a cane (30); that the trampling is an example of Hyde's callousness, and the murder an example of his growing viciousness. How, then, explain the fact that Jekyll – and, increasingly, the 'troglodytic' (40) Hyde – lives, ultimately takes shelter in, and finally dies in, the former house of one Dr Denman? The word 'former' is used advisedly here, because in some minds the house seems to have remained the property of its late owner. Lanyon, for example, in his letter to Utterson, refers not to entering Jekyll's laboratory, but to entering 'old Dr Denman's surgical theatre' (76). Among Jekyll's household the building is 'indifferently known as the laboratory or the dissecting-room' (51). Utterson refers to the door at the back of Jekyll's house as 'the old dissecting-room door' (41). The narrator explains that Jekyll 'had bought the house from the heirs of a celebrated surgeon; and his own tastes being rather chemical than anatomical, had changed the destination of the block at the bottom of the garden' (51) from that of a dissecting-room, to a laboratory.

Martin Tropp asks:

Why this seemingly unnecessary detail? Stevenson's equation of Jekyll's chemical experiments with dissection and surgery, and especially placing the dissecting rooms in a separate place with a disguised entrance on a back street, would no doubt bring to mind the 'resurrectionist' scandals earlier in the century.[6]

True enough; but the 'seemingly unnecessary detail' of real importance is not the admittedly highly significant association of Jekyll's experiments with his predecessor's dissections, but the mention of his predecessor's name. Stevenson drops this pearl into his narrative with the same sly ease – and with the same intention – as Peacock does in *Melincourt* when Lord Anophel Achthar mentions that Forester and Sir Oran Haut-ton are staying at Wildman's Hotel in London (447). After all, where else would a couple of Wild Men stay? Likewise Jekyll – the aspiring Wild Man – and Hyde – the actual Wild Man – have secured a dwelling whose former inhabit-ant was a Denman; and, as we saw in the chapter on the Wild Man, Wild Men are as often as not Cave Men.

Stevenson specifically has Utterson reflect that Jekyll in his younger days had been 'wild' (41). The youthful exuberant wildness of Jekyll finds its full evil expression in the Wild form of Hyde. Jekyll, 'the professional son of Denman', as Veeder calls him,[7] being a composite character, moves freely between the respectable front of the house and the disreputable back, as did his predecessor. Hyde, being elementally Wild, inhabits only the part which has maintained its association with Denman – the dissect-ing-rooms, and, at their furthest extremity, Jekyll's private cabinet. Not only does he inhabit this part, but he is metaphorically born there. Jekyll describes what happened during his first transformation into Hyde. He drinks the potion:

6   Martin Tropp, 'Dr Jekyll and Mr Hyde, Schopenhauer, and the Power of the Will', *Midwest Quarterly*, 32 (1991), 141–55 (p. 149).
7   *100 Years*, p. 122.

The most racking pangs succeeded: a grinding in the bones,[8] deadly nausea, and a horror of the spirit that cannot be exceeded at the hour of birth or death. Then these agonies began swiftly to subside, and I came to myself (83).

And what of 'old Dr Denman's surgical theatre'? In its day it must, on occasions, have resembled the den of a Wild Man, with the Doctor and his 'eager students' (51) engaged in cutting up and dismembering bodies lying naked on the tables, and even then beginning to exhibit signs of decay. Even worse, some of the bodies had very likely been dug up from their graves or murdered by the traffickers. Thus the door, which in Denman's day opened to admit the victims of an evil and ghoulish trade, now opens for the sole purpose of admitting Hyde to his lair after one of his escapades (33), one of which is the murder of Carew.

One can find the original of Denman's theatre in Stevenson's earlier short story *The Body-Snatcher* (written in 1881, published in 1884).[9] A comparison of *Jekyll and Hyde* and *The Body-Snatcher* may provide an insight into Stevenson's vision of the wild creature lurking in Jekyll's soul. *The Body-Snatcher* revolves around the premises of 'a certain *extra mural* [my emphasis] teacher of anatomy',[10] Mr K—, based on the real Dr Robert Knox who notoriously employed Burke and Hare to provide him with bodies for dissection. Denman, having his theatre at the back of his house, is obviously without the walls of the medical schools as well. K—'s pupils are 'eager' (480); Denman's are also 'eager' (51). K—'s sub-assistant Fettes, who has the charge of the theatre and lecture-room (465–66), is the moral

8   Stevenson here may be recalling a phrase from his childhood: 'Fee, fi, fo, fum, I smell the blood of an Englishman. Be he alive or be he dead, I'll grind his bones to make my bread.' He writes to his cousin Bob Stevenson, 'There are two English epics: *Paradise Lost* and *Jack the Giant Killer*' (*RLS Letters*, letter 63, September 1868, I, 151).

9   Commentators have noted correspondences between *Jekyll and Hyde* and *The Body-Snatcher*, but make no reference to Wild Men. See Douglas S. Mack, 'Dr Jekyll, Mr Hyde, and Count Dracula', in *Beauty and the Beast: Christina Rossetti, Walter Pater, R.L. Stevenson and their Contemporaries*, ed. by Peter Liebregts and Wim Tigges (Amsterdam: Rodopi, 1996), pp. 149–56. See also Mighall, *Jekyll*, pp. xiv–xvii.

10   *The Body-Snatcher, Works*, VII, 457–88 (p. 465). Further references are given after quotations in the text.

prototype of Henry Jekyll. The 'slave of his own desires and low ambitions' (466), he leads a double life:

> Cold, light, and selfish in the last resort, he had that modicum of prudence, miscalled morality, which keeps a man from inconvenient drunkenness or punishable theft. He coveted, besides, a measure of consideration from his masters and his fellow-pupils, and he had no desire to fail conspicuously in the external parts of life. Thus he made it his pleasure to gain some distinction in his studies, and day after day rendered unimpeachable eye-service to his employer, Mr. K—. For his day of work he indemnified himself by nights of roaring, blackguardly enjoyment; and when that balance had been struck, the organ that he called his conscience declared itself content (466–67).

K— lodges Fettes 'in the same wynd, and at last in the same building, with the dissecting rooms' (466). The *OED* defines 'wynd' as, 'A narrow street or passage turning off from a main thoroughfare; a narrow cross-street.' K—'s theatre shares a geographical similarity with Denman's. Fettes, like Jekyll and Hyde, lives on the premises, where at night:

> He would be called out of bed in the black hours before the winter dawn by the unclean and desperate interlopers who supplied the table. He would open the door to these men (466).

For his part, K— attempts to remain apart from any moral taint; but the narrator makes it plain that he is thoroughly implicated:

> 'Ask no questions,' he would tell his assistants, 'for conscience sake.' There was no understanding that the subjects were provided by the crime of murder. Had that idea been broached to him in words, he would have recoiled in horror; but the lightness of his speech upon so grave a matter was, in itself, an offence against good manners, and a temptation to the men with whom he dealt (467–68).

K—'s first assistant is another young doctor, by the name of Wolfe Macfarlane, with whose introduction we see the full complexity of the strange life which these respected professional men are leading. Whereas Fettes appears cravenly debauched, Macfarlane is more of the upper-class man about town, who on the one hand is clubbable, and on the other has a taste for the seamy side of life. He is a high favourite among all the reckless students, clever, dissipated, and unscrupulous to the last degree. He had travelled and studied abroad. His manners were agreeable and a little forward. He was an authority on the stage, skilful on the ice or the links with skate or golf-club; he dressed with nice audacity, and, to put the finishing touch upon his glory, he kept a gig and a strong trotting-horse (470).

Stevenson then immediately undercuts Macfarlane's glory by mentioning the use to which the horse and gig are put during the night, when no one can see this respectable pair:

[W]hen subjects were scarce the pair would drive far into the country in Macfarlane's gig, visit and desecrate some lonely graveyard, and return before dawn with their booty to the door of the dissecting room (470).

These are not nice people. They are, in Stevenson's eye, beasts. Macfarlane's given name – Wolfe, by which the narrator refers to him five times (459; 459; 470; 475; 477) – requires no explanation; and it is he who provides the other animal imagery, which also implicates K—. Macfarlane murders a crony and brings the body late one night to the dissecting room. By force of character he makes the unwilling Fettes an accomplice. He tells Fettes:

There are two squads of us—the lions and the lambs. If you're a lamb, you'll come to lie upon these tables [...]; if you're a lion, you'll live and drive a horse like me, like K—, like all the world with any wit or courage. You're staggered at the first. But look at K—! (478).

Fettes passes an awful week waiting to be caught; but when it is clear that they have got away with it, he tells Macfarlane that he has 'cast in his lot with the lions and foresworn the lambs' (479).

However, Macfarlane's assessment of themselves as lions is challenged by the narrator. Word comes of a burial in a country graveyard. Our two heroes set off to rob the grave:

Somewhat as two vultures may swoop upon a dying lamb, Fettes and Macfarlane were to be let loose upon a grave in that green and quiet resting-place (481).

A comparison of *Jekyll and Hyde* and *The Body-Snatcher* reveals that Stevenson did not choose Denman's name at random. *The Body-Snatcher* shows that the association of beasts with dissecting rooms was already in Stevenson's head before he began *Jekyll and Hyde*. Furthermore the beasts are cruel animals of prey – wolves, lions – or unclean despicable carrion feeders – vultures. The comparison, then, is not between Denman and Jekyll and their respective experiments, but between Denman and K—. Similarly, by extension, one may be justified in viewing Jekyll and Lanyon as standing in the same relationship to Denman as Fettes and Macfarlane stand in relationship to K—. Indeed, Jekyll's purchasing the property, and Lanyon's familiarity with 'old Dr Denman's surgical theatre' (76) (a pleasant euphemism), would suggest as much.

Utterson recalls that Jekyll was 'wild' in his youth (41). If his youth was anything like that of Fettes and Macfarlane, then he was wild indeed. He lives in a house, some of whose apartments still bear their grisly association with Dr Denman. He metaphorically gives birth to Hyde in the most remote den of the complex. Hyde lives part of his life in the den, and finally dies there. He is a hairy, irascible, violent, stick-wielding night stalker; in other words, a typical Wild Man.

CHAPTER EIGHT

The Darwinian Hyde

[A] comical story of an ape touches us quite differently
after the proposition of Mr Darwin's theory.

So wrote Stevenson in his review 'On Lord Lytton's *Fables in Song*'.[1]

There are not many laughs to be had in *Jekyll and Hyde*; but the principle remains. One is therefore bound to ask oneself the question: Is this a Darwinian text? Hyde's apishness suggests to many that it is. Hyde snarls (40); he is 'troglodytic' (40); his fury is 'ape-like' (47); he is 'like a monkey' (68); he gives out a 'screech, as of mere animal terror' (69); he drinks 'pleasure with bestial avidity' (86); he begins 'to growl for licence' (92); he is 'the animal within [Jekyll] licking the chops of memory' (92); he walks about 'chattering to himself' after the manner of an ape or monkey (94); he is a 'brute' (94); his tricks are 'ape-like' (96); as is his spite (97).

Here we find, within the broad category of animal imagery, two independent streams running side by side. Hyde looks and behaves like an ape in his hairiness, his swiftness, his chattering, his rage, his tricks, and his spite. The self which has been trying to get free of Jekyll is the primitive, proto-human brute which Darwinism proclaims as our common ancestor. But that is not all that has been trying to get out. In his Statement Jekyll writes that 'man will be ultimately known for a mere polity of multifarious, incongruous and independent denizens' (82). Ironically, the ape-like creature that we see is not the worst of Hyde. The other stream of imagery involves, not early man, but something more dreadful – predators. Wolves,

1   *The Fortnightly Review*, June 1874. Reprinted in *Works*, XXIV, 49–62 (p. 50).

lions, and tigers all snarl, growl, and lick their chops. Here may be a continuation of *The Body-Snatcher*'s presence; or it may be that Stevenson is contemplating an even more primitive and bestial state of the human condition, one which has continued as an ever-present shadow on the soul of modern man. Indeed, in one of the more celebrated passages in Jekyll's Statement Stevenson appears to cast his mind back to the very origins of life itself, and to imply that sin is a fundamental property of existence. Jekyll writes that he

> thought of Hyde, for all his energy of life, as of something not only hellish but inorganic. This was the shocking thing; that the slime of the pit seemed to utter cries and voices; that the amorphous dust gesticulated and sinned; that what was dead, and had no shape, should usurp the offices of life (95).

Here Stevenson is presenting a straightforward evolutionary concept – life springing from inorganic matter. But, although Huxley gave it the name of Abiogenesis in 1870, it is not necessarily based on modern scientific theory; it began with the ancient Greeks. The Roman poet Lucretius also held that all life grew out of the earth. As for the primaeval slime from which all creatures (including, thanks to Darwin, mankind) have evolved, the Egyptians thought they saw life spontaneously generating in the slime on the banks of the Nile. One of the theories which the Houyhnhnms held to explain the existence of the Yahoos was that they were produced by the Sun's heat on slime.

The two concepts, of life developing from inorganic matter, and living creatures generating from slime, came together in the writings of (among others) the German nature-philosopher Lorenz Oken (1776–1857):

> Every organic thing has arisen out of slime [*Ur-Schleim*], and is nothing but slime in different forms. This primitive slime originated in the sea, from inorganic matter, in the course of planetary evolution. The origin of life (*generatio originaria*) occurred upon the shores, where water, air, and earth were joined.[2]

---

2   *Elements of Physiophilosophy* [1805], trans. by Alfred Tulk (London: Ray Society, 1847). Quoted in Osborn, pp. 125–26. Osborn glosses '*Ur-Schleim*' as '(?protoplasm)'.

Likewise, Huxley:

> In nature, nothing is at rest, nothing is amorphous; the simplest particle of that which men in their blindness are pleased to call 'brute matter' is a vast aggregate of molecular mechanisms performing complicated movements of immense rapidity, and sensitively adjusting themselves to every change in the surrounding world. Living matter differs from other matter in degree and not in kind; the microcosm repeats the macrocosm; and one chain of causation connects the nebulous original of suns and planetary systems with the protoplasmic foundation of life and organisation.[3]

Thus, although Jekyll appears to be echoing contemporary scientific theory, he could have derived it from anywhere; in fact, as will be argued later, Stevenson may have been looking far beyond Darwin when he was writing the passage.

What, then, of the ape, to which Hyde is likened? Stevenson obviously recognized the Darwinian implications of such an association; and, equally obviously, he need not have made it. In his recounting of the tale's genesis, he makes no mention of Hyde's appearance – he is simply another person.

Furthermore, Stevenson seems to have taken some pains to make Hyde as authentically ape-like as possible, drawing a figure who exhibits many of the characteristics of apes – in particular, chimpanzees – described in Huxley's *Man's Place in Nature*.

This little book, a thorough and detailed attempt to demonstrate to the lay reader that mankind is related to the lower animals, began life in 1861, when Huxley 'was invited to give two addresses on "The Relation of Man to the Lower Animals" at the Philosophical Institute of Edinburgh'.[4] These lectures, which Cyril Bibby describes as 'scandalous',[5] were delivered in 1862 'in the belief that "After all, it is as respectable to be modified monkey as

---

3   'The Connection of the Biological Sciences with Medicine', *Science and Education, Collected Essays*, III, 347–73 (p. 371).
4   Cyril Bibby, *Scientist Extraordinary: The Life and Scientific Work of Thomas Henry Huxley* (Oxford: Pergamon Press, 1972), p. 48.
5   Bibby, p. 55.

to be modified dirt".[6] Huxley later 'gathered together the substance of his writings and lectures on this topic, and worked them into *Evidences as to Man's Place in Nature*.[7] Naturally, given its authorship, it was a great success. Ashley Montagu writes:

> [It] was T.H. Huxley's first book, and his most important. It was published in January 1863 in an edition of one thousand copies, an edition which was soon exhausted and immediately reprinted. In July of the same year the American edition appeared. Both in England and America the book was steadily reprinted for the next forty years.[8]

There is no biographical evidence to suggest that Stevenson read *Man's Place in Nature*; indeed, his only mention of reading anything by Huxley comes after the publication of *Jekyll and Hyde*;[9] but a comparison of the two works reveals many curious parallels. Huxley writes: 'It is quite certain that the ape which most nearly approaches man, in the totality of its organization, is either the Chimpanzee or the Gorilla' (86). As turning into a gorilla may have been a bit obtrusive in late-Victorian London, Stevenson would have had no decision to make. Moreover, the chimpanzee appears to have suited his purpose. He begins by employing a fairly general term to describe Hyde.

When, after lying in wait for some time, Utterson finally meets Hyde, he is left 'the picture of disquietude. [...] "God bless me, the man seems hardly human! Something troglodytic, shall we say?"' (40). From the earliest reports of man-like apes, the term *troglodyte* was used indiscriminately. But by the mid-nineteenth century, Huxley is able to write:

6   Bibby, p. 55. Bibby is quoting from a letter by Huxley to Frederic Dyster, catalogued by Warren Dawson (1946), held in the archives of Imperial College of Science and Technology, folio 18, 97.

7   Bibby, p. 49.

8   T.H. Huxley, *Man's Place in Nature*, intro. by Ashley Montagu (Ann Arbor: University of Michigan Press, 1971), p. 1. Further references are given after quotations in the text.

9   *RLS Letters*, V, 353–54.

For the purpose which I have at present in view, it is unnecessary that I should enter into any further minutiæ respecting the distinctive characters of the genera and species into which these man-like Apes are divided by naturalists. Suffice it to say, that the Orangs and the Gibbons constitute the distinct genera, *Simia* and *Hylobates*; while the Chimpanzees and Gorillas are by some regarded simply as distinct species of one genus, *Troglodytes*; by others as distinct genera—*Troglodytes* being reserved for the Chimpanzees, and *Gorilla* for the Engé-ena or Pongo (35–36).

Hyde's face is 'pale' (40), and 'ugly' (84). His hand is 'lean, corded, knuckly, of a dusky pallor, and thickly shaded with a swart growth of hair' (88). Huxley says of chimpanzees that 'their hair is black, while the skin of the face is pale' (35). He also quotes one William Smith, describing a mandrill: 'The face, which is covered by a white skin, is monstrously ugly' (21).[10] Huxley goes on to say that the animal 'was, without doubt, a Chimpanzee' (22).

Hyde is described as speaking 'a little hoarsely' (39). Utterson recalls after the meeting that Hyde 'spoke with a husky, whispering and somewhat broken voice' (40). Huxley, drawing on an article by Dr Thomas Savage, remarks: 'The ordinary voice of the chimpanzee, however, is affirmed to be hoarse, guttural, and not very loud' (59).[11]

Utterson finds Hyde 'dwarfish' (40). Huxley writes that 'the adult Chimpanzees [...] never exceeded, though the males may almost attain, five feet in height' (56). Huxley refers to Tyson's treatise, and his description of a 'Pygmie':

> This 'Pygmie', Tyson tells us, 'was brought from Angola, in Africa; [...] Its hair 'was of a coal-black colour, and strait [*sic*][...]. From the top of the head to the heel of the foot, in a straight line, it measured twenty-six inches.' [Here Huxley includes two figures (Tyson's figures 3 and 4) of a hairy biped carrying a walking stick.]
>
> These characters, even without Tyson's good figures (figs. 3 & 4), would have been sufficient to prove his 'Pygmie' to be a young Chimpanzee. But the opportunity of

10 Huxley is quoting from William Smith, *A New Voyage to Guinea* ([n.p.: n.pub.], 1744), p. 51.

11 Thomas Savage, 'Observations on the External Characters and Habits of the *Troglodytes Niger*', *Boston Journal of Natural History*, vol. 4 (1843–44), 362–86 (p. 365). Savage refers to 'a hoarse guttural sound' (365). Huxley infers that it is 'not very loud'.

examining the skeleton of the very animal Tyson anatomised having most unexpectedly presented itself to me, I am able to bear independent testimony to its being a
veritable *Troglodytes Niger*, though still very young (17–19).

Huxley's figure 6, 'The Anthropomorpha of Linnæus', consists of four
strange-looking creatures, one of whom is seated on a bench holding a staff
of almost Mosaic proportions. This anthropomorph, named *Pygmæus
Edwardi*, is copied, Huxley tells us, 'from the figure of a young "Man of
the Woods", or true Orang-Utan, given in Edwards's *Gleanings of Natural
History* (1758)' (14).[12] This figure presents us with an all too common
problem – is it a source for Stevenson? It and Hyde share five common
factors. They are both hairy. They both own a solid stick. Hyde is 'dwarfish'; the Satier is a 'pygmie'. They are both named Edward. They both sit
on a bench, Hyde's being in Regent's Park (92).

In his Statement Jekyll remembers 'that tempest of impatience with
which I listened to [Carew]' (90). The maid who witnesses the murder
tells how Hyde 'broke out in a great flame of anger, stamping with his foot,
[...] and carrying on [...] like a madman. [... He] broke out of all bounds,
and clubbed [Carew] to the earth. And next moment, with ape-like fury,
he was trampling his victim underfoot' (46–47). Huxley reports that the
Asiatic man-like Ape 'may be capable of great viciousness and violence
when irritated: and this is especially true of adult males' (55).

Hyde has a peculiar walk; the narrator notes that his footsteps 'fell
lightly and oddly, with a certain swing' (69). The Gibbon, notes Huxley,
'walks rather quick in the erect posture [...]. When he walks [...] he turns
the leg and foot outwards, which occasions him to have a waddling gait
and to seem bow-legged' (39–40).[13] Huxley's figures 3 and 4 also show a
bow-legged, waddling gait in the chimpanzee.

12   George Edwards (1694–1773) was an English natural historian, ornithologist, artist
      and etcher. His original figure is titled 'The Satier'.
13   Huxley is quoting from George Bennett, *Wanderings in New South Wales, Batavia,
      Pedir Coast, Singapore, and China: being the journal of a naturalist in those countries,
      during 1832, 1833, and 1834*, 2 vols (London: Bentley, 1834), vol.2, chap. 8.

On the last night, when Utterson and Poole stand listening to the footsteps pacing up and down inside Jekyll's cabinet, Utterson asks, 'Is there never anything else?' The reply comes, 'Once I heard it weeping. [...] Weeping like a woman or a lost soul' (69). Huxley, quoting William Smith, says that they (i.e., mandrills, i.e., chimps) 'cry when vexed or teased, just like children' (21).[14]

Utterson, by now convinced that Jekyll is dead and that his murderer Hyde is lurking within the cabinet, orders Poole to break down the door. 'Poole swung the axe over his shoulder; the blow shook the building, and the red baize door leaped against the lock and hinges. A dismal screech as of mere animal terror rang from the cabinet' (69). Stevenson here could almost have inverted Huxley's observation: 'When shot [chimps] give a sudden screech, not unlike that of a human being in sudden and acute distress' (59).[15]

The 'haunting sense of unexpressed deformity with which [Hyde] impressed his beholders' (50) can also be explained by his likeness to a chimpanzee. When he is forced to visit Lanyon in the middle of the night, Lanyon is 'struck [...] with his remarkable combination of great muscular activity and great apparent debility of constitution' (77). The 'apparent debility of constitution' refers to Hyde's smallness and the pallor of his skin, which are characteristics of chimpanzees. As for the 'great muscular activity', Huxley remarks on 'the ape-like arrangement of certain muscles which is occasionally met with in the white races of mankind' (166–67).

Hyde has access to Jekyll's money and, presumably, to his tailor. Although he is 'very plainly dressed' (39), his clothes would still be carefully cut to cover some of his deficiencies. However, when he enters Lanyon's house he is wearing Jekyll's clothes. Lanyon writes:

> His clothes, that is to say, although they were of rich and sober fabric, were enormously too large for him in every measurement – the trousers hanging on his legs and rolled up to keep them from the ground, the waist of the coat below his haunches, and the collar sprawling wide upon his shoulders (77–78).

14   William Smith, p. 51.
15   Huxley is quoting from Thomas Savage, p. 386.

Lanyon does not mention, in all this detail, whether Hyde's *sleeves* were rolled up. Hyde's hands are unimpeded: he 'laid his hand upon my arm and sought to shake me' (78); he 'paused and put his hand to his throat' (78); he 'laid his hand upon his heart' (79); he 'plucked away the sheet' from the drawer on the floor (79); holding a graduated glass he 'measured out a few minims of the red tincture and added one of the powders' (79). Jekyll in his Statement describes the transformation in Regent's Park: 'I looked down; my clothes hung formlessly on my shrunken limbs; the hand that lay on my knee was corded and hairy' (92).[16] If he can still see his hand, then his arms have not shrunk to the same extent as the rest of him, therefore he is proportioned more like a chimpanzee, which, according to Huxley, 'has arms which reach below the knees' (35).[17]

If Hyde is not only hairy like an ape, pale like an ape, hoarse like an ape, and gaited like an ape, but also proportioned to a degree like an ape, then his deformity would be both noticeable and obscure at the same time, arising as it would from a violation of normal expectations in his beholders.

In a Darwinian landscape, why make a character hairy and ape-like unless you were making a Darwinian point? The answer lies simply in the fact that Stevenson *was* inhabiting a Darwinian world, whose philosophical mood was determined by the new awareness of man's place in nature. This mood was reflected – and influenced – by writers such as Huxley, of whom James Paradis writes:

> The concept of an organic dualism had begun to take shape in Huxley's final essays. [...] Huxley began to think in psychic dimensions, to conceive of man as a divided entity, one foot in a primordial past and the other in his civilized present, unable to possess completely either his primitive or his civilized self. [...] The primitive self remained intact, although it shared the body with a rational entity Huxley associated with the conscious mind. Neither aspect of this divided self could eliminate the other half; rather, both existed in a kind of painful equilibrium, a never-ending war.[18]

16   Note that the Satier's hand is resting on his knee.
17   Huxley notes (34–35) that of all the apes, the chimpanzee has the shortest arms in pro-
       portion to its legs, thereby making it the ape closest to a human in its proportions.
18   *T.H. Huxley: Man's Place in Nature* (Lincoln and London: University of Nebraska
       Press, 1978), pp. 151–52.

Parts of this passage could almost be a paraphrase of the opening pages of Jekyll's Statement.

This organic dualism no longer invoked the Platonic system of souls selecting appropriate vehicles in which to express their impulses, as we saw in the story of Er; it no longer invoked the images of Spenser's Bower of Bliss, or More's Dizoia, or Milton's *Comus*, in which particular bestial tendencies lurking within individuals betray themselves in the outer countenance. Organic dualism – planted firmly in the Adonisian garden of Darwinian natural selection – spoke loudly, not of beast *in* man, but of beast *as* man. But Darwinism defined the beast, and insisted that there was no other. In his bestial actions man did not reflect lions, tigers, wolves, goats, foxes, or any other beast of the field: he reflected the ape.

Stevenson's decision to make Hyde ape-like suggests that his intention was to give the story a surface of reality – if, to paraphrase Henry James, one may speak of reality in such a case. James objected to Jekyll's powders. In a review of *Jekyll and Hyde* he writes:

> The powders constitute the machinery of the transformation, and it will probably have struck many readers that this uncanny process would be more conceivable (so far as one may speak of the conceivable in such a case), if the author had not made it so definite.[19]

Stevenson made much about the story definite. Locations are definite; houses are definite; individuals are definite. *The Body-Snatcher*, although it begins realistically, is a simple horror story with a simple horror ending which relies on an unspecified supernatural agency. *Jekyll and Hyde*, however, determinedly aims for realism throughout, even to the last tragic detail of the unknown impurity in the salt. The powders are definite (if somewhat vaguely described); and the beast which lurks in Jekyll is the beast which contemporary science gave Stevenson's readers to expect. The story thus rises above the level of fable, to the level of a true scientific description of the inner nature of man.

19 *Century Magazine*, xxxv (April 1888), 869–79. Reprinted in 'Robert Louis Stevenson', in James's *Partial Portraits* (London: Macmillan, 1888; repr. 1919), pp. 137–74 (p. 171). Quoted in Maixner, p. 309.

Is *Jekyll and Hyde* then a Darwinian text? Yes. And no. Or, rather, partly. It is a Darwinian text insofar as Stevenson deliberately draws on contemporary scientific thought in order to drive home the point that within each of us there is a dark ungovernable self whose origins reach back to the very birth of life on this planet – in other words, that we have not fallen from a state of grace, but risen from a state of sordid brutality to arrive at a condition far from accomplished perfection. One might say that Jekyll and Hyde are organic dualism personified.

Or are they? They are certainly dualism personified, but is it entirely organic? Is Hyde a truly Darwinian figure? He is troglodytic, and ape-like, which would seem to place him firmly in the Darwinian basket, along with Stevenson's comic Lucretian men from 'The Manse' and 'Pastoral'.[20] However, one cannot overlook the fact that at one point Stevenson appears to state unequivocally that Hyde is *not* a reversion to an earlier primitive form. Jekyll describes the accursed night in which he compounds his elements, watches them boil and smoke together in the glass, then, with a strong glow of courage, drinks off the potion. After the transformation, curious to see his new self, he steals from his cabinet towards his house to view his reflection in his bedroom mirror:

> I crossed the yard, wherein the constellations looked down upon me, I could have thought, with wonder, *the first creature of that sort that their unsleeping vigilance had yet disclosed to them* (84). [my emphasis]

If Hyde were a reversion to a more primitive form from a Darwinian perspective, then surely the constellations would recognize him from the time when his fellows roamed the earth. Moreover Stevenson tells the reader unequivocally what sort of creature Hyde is. Jekyll writes:

> [A]ll human beings [...] are commingled out of good and evil: and Edward Hyde, alone, in the ranks of mankind, was pure evil (85).

---

20   Stevenson knew his Lucretius; in a letter of 8 October 1887 to Edmund Gosse he
     quotes, in Latin, from *De Rerum Natura*. See *RLS Letters*, letter 1899, VI, 24–25.

This is not a biological assessment; it is a moral assessment. We may therefore safely conclude that Hyde is not simply a Darwinian reversion. Stevenson also contradicts Darwin's optimistic forecast for humanity's future. Darwin writes:

> Hence we may look with some confidence to a secure future of great length. And as natural selection works solely by and for the good of each being, all corporeal and mental endowments will tend to progress towards perfection.[21]

Jekyll, however, writes:

> I have been made to learn that the doom and burthen of our life is bound for ever on man's shoulders; and when the attempt is made to cast it off, it but returns upon us with more unfamiliar and more awful pressure (83).

With his allusions to troglodytes and apes, Stevenson has knowingly pointed his readers in the Darwinian direction (or allowed them to infer it), but then appears to contradict himself. But if Hyde is not a Darwinian throwback, what is he? For an answer to that question, we must look to see what Henry Jekyll has to say about him.

21   *Origin of Species*, p. 373.

CHAPTER NINE

Hyde, Milton, and the Bible

Thus far we have seen that Hyde exhibits the characteristics of a Wild Man; and it has been argued that some of his characteristics may be actually derived from real apes. But where does Hyde stand in relation to Jekyll? And what does he 'stand for'? Jekyll begins his Statement by observing that his 'profound duplicity of life' arises from 'man's dual nature' (81); moreover that this duality is 'thorough and primitive' (82), which suggests that it stems from our bestial troglodytic origins. However, as we saw in Chapter One, the reviewer in *The Rock* referred to primitive man as, 'man "made in the image of God" before the fall of our ancestors.'[1] Hyde's origins are therefore ambiguous, but lent a biblical flavour by Jekyll's allusion to St Paul when he writes of 'the perennial war among my members' (82). St Paul writes, in his letter to the Romans:

> But I see another law in my members, warring against the law of my mind, and bringing me into captivity to the law of sin which is in my members (7.23).[2]

On a physical level Stevenson presents Jekyll and Hyde as warring brothers. On the very first page he introduces the theme of Cain and Abel: '"I incline to Cain's heresy," [Utterson] used to say quaintly: "I let my brother go to the devil in his own way"' (29). The thought of Cain seems to be still on Stevenson's mind later when Jekyll writes that, following the murder of Carew, his career as Hyde is over. He writes: 'Jekyll was now my city of refuge; let but Hyde peep out an instant, and the hands of all men would be raised to take and slay him' (91–92). Dury (*Jekyll*, p. 107) cites

---

1   See Maixner, p. 225.
2   See also the Epistle of St James: 'From whence come wars and fightings among you? come they not hence, even of your lusts that war in your members?' (4.1).

Numbers 35.11 as the origin of 'city of refuge': 'Then ye shall appoint you cities of refuge for you; that the slayer may flee thither, which killeth any person at unawares.' For, 'the hands of all men would be raised to take and slay him', he cites Genesis 16.12: 'And he [Ishmael] will be a wild man; his hand will be against every man, and every man's hand against him.' However (despite the tempting mention of the wild man), a more likely source – given Stevenson's theme, the context of the Carew murder, and the murder in Numbers – is Cain's complaint after the murder of Abel:

> And Cain said unto the LORD, my punishment is greater than I can bear.
> Behold, thou hast driven me out this day from the face of the earth; and from thy face I shall be hid; and I shall be a fugitive and a vagabond in the earth; and it shall come to pass, that every one that findeth me shall slay me (Genesis. 5.13–14).

Cain and Abel are not the only warring brothers in the Bible. Stevenson's language evokes an even more closely joined pair of siblings. Jekyll, having fondly dreamt of separating his unjust self from the just, laments:

> It was the curse of mankind that these incongruous faggots were thus bound together – that in the agonised womb of consciousness these polar twins should be continuously struggling (82).

In Genesis we learn that Isaac's wife Rebekah is with child:

> And the children struggled together within her; and she said, If it be so, why am I thus? And she went to inquire of the LORD.
> And the LORD said unto her, Two nations are in thy womb, and two manner of people shall be separated from thy bowels; and the one people shall be stronger than the other people; and the elder shall serve the younger.
> And when her days to be delivered were fulfilled, behold, there were twins in her womb.
> And the first came out red, all over like an hairy garment; and they called his name Esau.
> And after that came his brother out, and his hand took hold on Esau's heel; and his name was called Jacob (25.22–26).

We now have two sets of warring siblings: Cain slays Abel (4.8); Jacob extorts Esau's birthright (25.29–34); Jacob steals Esau's paternal blessing (27.1–40); Esau vows to kill Jacob (27.41).[3]

These siblings – physical embodiments of the war in the members – could hold the clue to Stevenson's thought processes in constructing the figure of Hyde. The theme of man's dual nature had been exercising him in the period leading up to *Jekyll and Hyde*. In his dream he saw a man in peril swallow a drug and turn into someone else. The dream also gave him the idea of the change becoming involuntary. Here, then, are the three central ingredients of the story, which, when fused, provide one figure who is divisible into two; who is at war with himself; and who loses the battle for domination of his body. The rivalry of the two competing selves suggests both the fratricidal struggle between Cain and Abel – in which Cain slays Abel and is cursed for it – and that of Jacob and Esau, whose struggle for inheritance (a constant motif in *Jekyll and Hyde*) commences even in the womb. The smoothness of Jacob and the hairiness of Esau are reflected in the smoothness of Jekyll (43) and the hairiness of Hyde. If Hyde is a true representation of Esau, then he is 'hairy all over, like an hairy garment', which lends strength to the argument about him being a Wild Man, and would also be appropriate to him being apelike. From this, the Darwinian association would inevitably follow, as well as the need for an accurate description of a suitable ape, namely, a chimpanzee.

Jekyll, of course, is keen to distinguish between himself and Hyde from the start, and lapses into more biblical language as he does so, referring to Hyde as 'the unjust', and himself (rather optimistically) as 'the just [who] could walk steadfastly and securely on his upward path' (82) – an allusion to Proverbs 20.7: 'The just man walketh in his integrity.'

The warring sibling theme is obvious enough, but what is Stevenson saying about Jekyll and Hyde at a deeper level? Jekyll writes that Hyde's form and countenance are 'the expression [...] of lower elements in [his] soul' (83); and refers to his body as a 'tabernacle' (83), echoing the words of St Paul: 'our earthly house of this tabernacle' (II Corinthians 5.1), and

---

3   In defiance of all expectations, Jacob and Esau reconcile (Gen. 33.1–4).

St Peter: 'as long as I am in this tabernacle' (II Peter 1.13). Jekyll's complaint therefore is that part of his indwelling soul is sinful, and it is that part which tends to lead his members astray. Thus the problem is one not so much of bestial tendencies, as of sinful tendencies. Whence, then, comes this sin? G.K. Chesterton, assessing Stevenson as an author, writes:

> [I]f he could bear no witness to the Resurrection, he was continually bearing witness to the Fall (224).

This witness began at an early age. Stevenson writes of his childhood:

> I would lie awake [in bed at night] declaiming aloud to myself my views of the universe in something that I called singing although I have no ear and in a measure of my own although at that time I can have known nothing of verse. One of these *Songstries*, for so I named my evening exercises, was taken down by my father from behind the door, and I have seen it within the last few years. It dealt summarily with the Fall of Man, taking a view most inimical to Satan.[4]

He continues, with an observation, and a question whose relevance will become apparent in our final chapter:

> [B]ut what is truly odd, it fell into a loose, irregular measure with a tendency toward the ten-syllable heroic line. This, as I am sure I can then have heard little or nothing but hymn metres, seems to show a leaning in the very constitution of the language to that form of verse; or was it but a trick of the ear, inherited from 18th century ancestors?[5]

Jekyll and Hyde not only bears witness to the Fall, it re-enacts it.[6] And, it would seem, it does so while employing language derived from both the Bible and *Paradise Lost*. I am not suggesting that Stevenson based his

4   'Memoirs of Himself', *Works*, XXVI, 203–37 (p. 215). Stevenson wrote these memoirs 'alone in San Francisco' (205) in January 1880.
5   Ibid.
6   Paul Fayter, while regarding *Jekyll and Hyde* as a work of 'evolutionist science fiction', nevertheless interprets it as 'an explicitly biological metaphor for the Fall'. See 'Strange New Worlds of Space and Time: Late Victorian Science and Science Fiction', in *Victorian Science in Context*, ed. by Bernard Lightman (Chicago and London:

story on *Paradise Lost*, but rather that the original conception suggested the Biblical and Miltonic parallels to one who, by this time, had restored his belief in God. Katherine Linehan outlines Stevenson's method:

> Intertextual allusions typically operate as a ghostlike presence in the fiction of Robert Louis Stevenson. [...] He habitually left echoes of predecessor texts to be recognized – or not – through such trace effects as an association-laden proper name, a foreign phrase, a teasingly familiar-sounding turn of phrase, or a déjà vu sensation recalling an important scene in a well-known work.
>
> I doubt that any work of Stevenson's, however, can match his most famous spook story, [*Jekyll and Hyde*], for suitability and subtlety of function involved in just such shadowiness of allusion.[7]

Linehan's argument is that,

> While Stevenson worked at top speed to produce a piece of sensation fiction geared to popular accessibility, he laid up an additional store of mind-teasing, shock-inducing reading pleasure through knowing his intertextual sources so intimately that he could draw on them with ease to create what amounts to a coded layer of signification for readers who share a knowledge of those sources.[8]

The biblical allusions in *Jekyll and Hyde* therefore arise naturally from the language and symbolism which Stevenson imbibed while he was growing up; and, I would argue, the Miltonic parallels both grow out of, and in their turn serve to inform, Stevenson's dramatic arc. It has been mentioned that Stevenson burned his first draft, apparently because, according to his wife, he had not seen the allegory. I would suggest that the Miltonic layer may be Stevenson's remedy, because, once it is seen, it provides an obvious – and consistent – allegorical subtext. Milton was one of Stevenson's favourite authors. His mother gave him an edition of Milton's works for his eighteenth birthday.[9] He discussed Milton with J.A. Symonds during

---

University of Chicago Press, 1997), pp. 256–80 (pp. 262–63). Aaron Perkus writes, 'The "Fall of man" motif is ingeniously repeated in the text of *Jekyll and Hyde*' (40).

7   'The Devil can cite Scripture', p. 5.
8   Ibid., p. 6. Linehan makes no mention of *Paradise Lost*.
9   *RLS Letters*, I, 168, n4.

his stays in Davos.[10] When Edmund Gosse was selecting material for his anthology *English Odes* (1881), Symonds and Stevenson suggested Milton's 'Time' and 'Solemn Music'.[11] In his letters Stevenson quotes from Milton's 'Hymn on the Morning of Christ's Nativity';[12] 'Areopagitica';[13] 'On Time' and 'L'Allegro';[14] 'Lycidas';[15] and, of course, *Paradise Lost*.[16] The obvious biblical language and references, and (if my argument is correct) the less obvious but thematically consistent Miltonic allusions, therefore lift *Jekyll and Hyde* beyond a mere story about humanity's lingering animal self, and turn it into an examination of a creature at war with itself in a moral universe. Optimistic Darwinism suggests that mankind will in the fullness of time rise above its primitive origins and shake off its bestial limitations. Henry Jekyll's statement that 'the doom and burthen of our life is bound for ever on man's shoulders' (83) suggests that mankind's problem is one of more than mere biology.

Hyde is associated throughout with Satan. Enfield tells Utterson that the trampling of the girl was 'hellish to see' (31), and that afterwards Hyde behaves 'like Satan' (32). Utterson reads 'Satan's signature' (40) in Hyde's face. Jekyll calls him his 'devil', who contains 'the spirit of hell' (90); 'that child of Hell' (94); and a 'fiend' (36; 85) – a term used by Milton for Satan in *Paradise Lost* (II.677; III.430; IV.1013; XI.101). In order to drive home the association of Hyde with Satan, Stevenson invokes the Book of Job:

> And the LORD said unto Satan, Whence comest thou? Then Satan answered the LORD, and said, From going to and fro in the earth, and from walking up and down in it (1.7).

10   *RLS Letters*, letter 743 to Sidney Colvin, November 1880, III, 120.
11   *RLS Letters*, letter 762 to Edmund Gosse, December 1880, III, 144. Their first choice was Tennyson's 'Duke of Wellington' (143).
12   *RLS Letters*, letter 72, I, 168.
13   *RLS Letters*, letter 146, I, 326.
14   *RLS Letters*, letter 1126, IV, 146.
15   *RLS Letters*, letter 1257, IV, 276.
16   *RLS Letters*, letter 2176, VI, 311.

Stevenson cleverly uses Satan's words, but spaces them apart, and presents them in the same order. On the final night, as Utterson and Poole wait outside Jekyll's cabinet door, listening to the sounds of Hyde within, they hear 'the sound of a footfall moving to and fro along the cabinet floor' (68). Ten minutes later the 'patient foot' is 'still going up and down, up and down' (69). In Jekyll's Statement he relates how, waiting for the hours to pass until Hyde can rendezvous with Lanyon, he hails a cab and is 'driven to and fro about the streets' (94). As he finishes his Statement Jekyll pictures himself once more and irretrievably Hyde, a prisoner in his cabinet, pacing 'up and down this room' (97).

The first description of Jekyll's house is from the back – the area from which Hyde comes and goes. The narrator's perspective places it 'on the left hand' (30). In St Matthew's gospel Hell is on the left hand:

> Then shall he [the King] say also unto them on the left hand, Depart from me, ye cursed, into everlasting fire, prepared for the devil and his angels (25.41).

Milton also places Hell on the left hand. After the Fall Sin and Death construct a bridge from Earth to Hell:

> With Pinns of Adamant
> And Chains they made all fast, too fast they made
> And durable; and now in little space
> The Confines met of Empyrean Heav'n
> And of this World, and on the left hand Hell
> With long reach interpos'd.   (X.318–23)

Milton relates the fall of Satan and the birth of Sin and Death. He then parallels and re-enacts the same process in the Fall of Adam and Eve. Satan, escaping Hell in order to pervert mankind, happens upon two deformed and monstrously ugly creatures, whom he does not recognize. Sin addresses him:

> Hast thou forgot me then, and do I seem
> Now in thine eye so foul, once deemd so fair
> In Heav'n, when at th'Assembly, and in sight
> Of all the Seraphim with thee combin'd

> In bold conspiracy against Heav'n's King,
> All on a sudden miserable pain
> Surpris'd thee, dim thine eyes, and dizzie swumm
> In darkness, while thy head flames thick and fast
> Threw forth, till on the left side op'ning wide,
> Likest to thee in shape and count'nance bright,
> Then shining heav'nly fair, a Goddess armd
> Out of thy head I sprung.   (II.747–58)

Note that Sin has sprung from the left side of Satan's head.

Compare the painful and disorienting experience of Satan with that of Jekyll after he drinks his potion:

> The most racking pains succeeded: a grinding in the bones, deadly nausea, and a horror of the spirit that cannot be exceeded at the hour of birth or death (83).

Sin relates what happened when she made her first appearance:

> amazement seis'd
> All th'host of Heav'n; back they recoild affraid
> At first, and called me *Sin*, and for a Sign
> Portentous held me; but familiar grown,
> I pleas'd, and with attractive graces won
> The most averse, thee chiefly, who full oft
> Thy self in me thy perfet image viewing
> Becam'st enamourd, and such joy thou took'st
> With me in secret, that my womb conceiv'd
> A growing burden.   (II.758–67)

Here Milton expands the archetypal pattern which he will repeat in Adam and Eve. Satan finds the perfect image of himself in Sin; likewise, so does Adam with Eve. God causes a deep sleep to fall on Adam, who yet remains conscious and observes as the Divine form,

> stooping op'nd my left side, and took
> From thence a Rib, with cordial spirits warme,
> And Life-blood streaming fresh; wide was the wound,
> But suddenly with flesh filld up and heald:
> The Rib he formd and fashond with his hands:
> Under his forming hands a Creature grew,

> Manlike, but different sex, so lovely faire,
> That what seemd fair in all the World, seemd now
> Mean, or in her summd up, in her containd,
> And in her looks, which from that time infus'd
> Sweetness into my heart, unfelt before,
> And into all things from her Aire inspir'd
> The spirit of love and amorous delight.   (VIII.465–77)

Note that the extraction of the rib from the left side of Adam is a Miltonic device not found in the Bible.[17] Milton has introduced it for thematic symmetry: Eve springs from the left of Adam just as Sin springs from the left of Satan. After the Fall, as we shall see, Milton darkens this conceit by replacing 'left' with its more formal and archaic equivalent, 'sinister', and all of its negative connotations.

Stevenson, on the other hand, introduces Jekyll's house by using 'left' and 'sinister' in the same sentence (30), thereby associating them both at the beginning, and thereby loading the neutral 'left' with a darker overtone. Hyde may not have sprung, like Sin, from the left side of Jekyll's head; nor, like Eve, from the left side of Jekyll's body; but he is associated with the left-hand side. The court leading to the back of Jekyll's house – from which Hyde comes and goes – is on the left (30). After Jekyll involuntarily turns into Hyde in Regent's Park he writes to Lanyon for help, writing that he would sacrifice his 'left hand' (74) to help Lanyon if he were in trouble. Commentators point out that the phrase is usually, to sacrifice one's *right* hand.[18] Hyde writes to Lanyon that the transforming chemicals are to be found in a press 'on the left hand' (74) in Jekyll's cabinet.[19] Hyde is also associated with 'sinister'. The back of Jekyll's house – the Hyde part – is 'sinister' (30); and Utterson regards the inexplicable terms of Jekyll's will as arising from 'the sinister suggestion of the man Hyde' (59).

---

17   This fact has also been noted recently in *Paradise Lost*, ed. and intro. by David Scott Kasdan (Indianapolis and Cambridge: Hackett, 2005), p. 253.

18   See, e.g., Veeder, *100 Years*, p. 138.

19   Noted in Robert Louis Stevenson, *The Annotated Dr Jekyll and Mr Hyde*, ed., intro. and notes by Richard Dury, 2nd edn, rev. (Genoa: Edizioni Culturali Internazionali Genova, 2005), p. 152. (Hereafter Dury, *Annotated*.)

Stevenson, of course, was not reliant on Milton (or any one particular author) for the commonplace association of 'left' and 'sinister'. But Stevenson's text suggests that (just as Spenserian language and imagery permeated Kingsley's imagination when he was writing *The Water-Babies*), so Stevenson naturally reflected biblical mythology in one of its highest literary expressions – the poetry of Milton – when dealing with such a fundamental issue as the presence of evil in mankind.

Adam, having parted with his rib, wakes infatuated and obsessed with finding the lovely vision from his dream. He sees her coming towards him. He speaks:

> I now see
> Bone of my Bone, Flesh of my Flesh, my Self
> Before me; Woman is her Name, of Man
> Extracted; for this cause he shall forgoe
> Father and Mother, and to his Wife adhere;
> And they shall be one Flesh, one Heart, one Soule.   (VIII.494–99)

Sin is the 'perfet image' (II.764) of Satan. Likewise, Adam's, 'my Self/ Before me', proclaims that Eve is the 'image' of Adam. Yet when she sees him she retreats in apprehension. Adam calls after her, and reassures her in words that call to mind Jekyll's description of Hyde as

> a second form and countenance [...], none the less natural to me because they were the expression, and bore the stamp, of [...] *elements in my soul* (83). [my emphasis]

Acknowledging Eve as both himself and from himself, yet apart, Adam says:

> Return fair *Eve*,
> Whom fli'st thou? whom thou fli'st, of him thou art,
> His flesh, his bone; to give thee being I lent
> Out of my side to thee, nearest my heart
> Substantial Life, to have thee by my side
> Henceforth an individual solace dear;
> *Part of my Soul* [my emphasis] I seek thee, and thee claim
> My other half.   (IV.481–88)

Satan sees himself in Sin. This is the self projected by his pride and ambition. Adam sees himself in Eve. She is the self provided for him by the Lord in order to complement and fulfil Adam's existence. The Lord tells the lonely and incomplete Adam:

> What next I bring shall please thee, be assur'd,
> Thy likeness, thy fit help, thy other self,
> Thy wish, exactly to thy hearts desire.   (VIII.449–51)

All of this could with equal justification be said about Hyde. Eve is the likeness of Adam, yet a dissimilar one; Hyde is Jekyll, yet unrecognizably so. Hyde is created to be Jekyll's fit help in his secret depravities; he is his other self, his wish, and, when Jekyll finally sees him, exactly to his heart's desire.

Eve continues the established pattern of self-observation. Adam wakes after his creation, as if from sleep (VIII.253); and again sleeps (though conscious) during the creation of Eve. Eve wakes after her creation, as if from sleep (IV.450). She tells Adam that she followed the sound of water,

> and laid me downe
> On the green bank, to look into the clear
> Smooth Lake, that to me seemd another Skie.
> As I bent down to look, just opposite,
> A Shape within the watry gleam appeerd
> Bending to look on me, I started back,
> It started back, but pleasd I soon returnd,
> Pleasd it returnd as soon with answering looks
> Of sympathie and love; there I had fixt
> Mine eyes till now, and pin'd with vain desire,
> Had not a voice thus warnd me, What thou seest,
> What there thou seest fair Creature is thy self,
> With thee it came and goes.   (IV.457–69)

Adam (formed from the dust of the ground by the Lord), and Eve (formed from Adam's rib by the Lord), both awake as if from a gentle sleep; and each awakes as if from a gentle sleep, to see an other which they come to realize as their self.

Jekyll, however, like Satan, experiences racking pains, deadly nausea, and a horror of the spirit which he associates with both birth and death – a prophetic choice of words, because the birth of Hyde signals the death of Jekyll. During this period of confusion and disorientation he changes, unaware, into Hyde. Still referring to himself as the 'I' who drank the potion, he writes:

> Then these agonies began swiftly to subside, and I came to myself as if out of a great sickness. There was something strange in my sensations, something indescribably new and, from its very novelty, incredibly sweet. I felt younger, lighter, happier in body (83).

Jekyll experiences for the first time what it is to be Hyde. He writes:

> I knew myself, at the first breath of this new life, to be more wicked, tenfold more wicked, sold a slave to my original evil; and the thought, in that moment, braced and delighted me like wine (84).

Stevenson's language suggests that Jekyll's sensations correspond to those of Adam and Eve after eating the apple: Satan, in the body of the serpent, tempts Eve to eat the fruit, whereby she too is delighted as if with wine. Eve,

> Intent now wholly on her taste, naught else
> Regarded, such delight till then, as seemd,
> In Fruit she never tasted, whether true
> Or fansied so, through expectation high
> Of knowledg, nor was God-head from her thought.
> Greedily she ingorg'd without restraint,
> And knew not eating Death: Satiate at length,
> And highth'nd as with Wine.   (IX.786–93)

Likewise, Adam is also sold a slave to original evil, and is delighted as if with wine:

> Nature gave a second groan,
> Skie lowr'd, and muttering Thunder, som sad drops
> Wept at compleating of the mortal Sin
> Original; while *Adam* took no thought,

> Eating his fill, nor *Eve* to iterate
> Her former trespass feard, the more to soothe
> Him with her lov'd societie, that now
> As with new Wine intoxicated both
> They swim in mirth, and fansie that they feel
> Divinitie within them breeding wings
> Wherewith to scorn the Earth.   (IX.1001–11)

But Jekyll has in fact changed into Hyde. In other words, he has changed from the Satan who conceived Sin, into Sin herself. And as Satan saw himself in Sin, and Adam saw himself in Eve, and Eve saw herself in her reflection in the water, so it is with Hyde and his reflection. Curious to see his new form, he steals from Jekyll's cabinet to stand before the mirror in Jekyll's bedroom. Jekyll writes, in that curiously fluid blending of personalities that characterizes his Statement:

> Even as good shone upon the countenance of the one,[20] evil was written broadly and plainly on the face of the other. Evil besides (which I must still believe to be the lethal side of man) had left on that body an imprint of deformity and decay. And yet when I looked upon that ugly idol in the glass, I was conscious of no repugnance, rather of a leap of welcome. This, too, was myself (84).[21]

20   Jekyll views himself in a better light than the narrator, who describes him as, 'a large, well-made, smooth-faced man [...], with something of a slyish cast perhaps' (43).

21   Alan Sandison also makes the connection between Eve first seeing herself and Hyde first seeing himself. See *Robert Louis Stevenson and the Appearance of Modernism* (London: Macmillan; New York: St Martin's Press, 1996), p. 260. Although he speculates on one other, less certain, reference to *Paradise Lost* (268, n48), he finds no more parallels between the two texts. However, he finds that in *The Master of Ballantrae* 'references to *Paradise Lost* are widespread' (314). Barbara Hannah in her Jungian analysis of *Jekyll and Hyde* writes: '[T]his is perhaps one of the finest descriptions in literature of a man meeting his shadow and recognizing him fully as his own' (46). Hannah explains that the shadow 'comes from our dark, completely unknown side, and is related to the serpent who first confronted Eve with the problem of evil and thus led to the expulsion from Eden' (17). I do not quote this observation in order to claim Stevenson as a proto-Jungian, but simply to provide another example of the universality of Stevenson's text.

Viewed in a Miltonic context, this becomes a very complex moment. Jekyll, recalling the incident much later, considers the image of Hyde in the mirror, and writes, 'This, too, was myself', as if he were Satan observing Sin, or Adam observing Eve. The scene at the time, however, involves not Jekyll observing Hyde, but Hyde observing his own image; and being (if one may use the word here) charmed by it, in the same way that Eve is charmed by her image.[22] But, since it is the Adamic Jekyll's narrative, it is his moment of recognition – expressed in the use of 'I' – that concerns us here.

Whereas Satan after his fall happily continues to acknowledge his relationship with Sin, Adam after his fall rejects the one whom he had formerly found so dear. When Eve presents him with her offence, Adam, not realizing the implications of what he is about to do, elects to follow her example, and reiterates their indissoluble bond:

> However I with thee have fixt my Lot,
> Certain to undergoe like doom; if Death
> Consort with thee, Death is to mee as Life;
> So forcible within my heart I feel
> The Bond of Nature drawe me to my owne,
> My own in thee, for what thou art is mine;
> Our State cannot be severd, we are one,
> One Flesh; to loose thee were to loose my self.   (IX.952–59)

But after the Fall he turns on her in shame, frustration, accusation, and despair, and tries to dissociate himself from her:

> But for thee
> I had persisted happie, had not thy pride
> And wandring vanitie, when lest was safe,
> Rejected my forewarning, and disdaind
> Not to be trusted, longing to be seen
> Though by the Devil himself, him overweening

---

22   Eve's origin must have appealed to Stevenson. In a letter to W.E. Henley he writes: 'I am reading hard for my work on *The Transformation of the Scottish Highlands*, which has grown, like Eve, out of one rib in *Scotland and the Union*' (*RLS Letters*, letter 764, 21 December 1880, III, 146–48 (p. 148)).

To over-reach, but with the Serpent meeting
Fool'd and beguil'd, by him thou, I by thee,
To trust thee from my side, imagind wise,
Constant, mature, proof against all assaults,
And understood not all was but a shew
Rather then solid vertu.   (X.873–84)

Jekyll also, finding himself unable to control his sinful nature, now turns on the self which he created in order to indulge it. In a final attempt to justify himself and place all the blame on Hyde, he writes:

> He had now seen the full deformity of that creature that shared with him some of the phenomena of consciousness, and was co-heir with him to death: and beyond these links of community, which in themselves made the most poignant part of his distress, he thought of Hyde, for all his energy of life, as of something not only hellish but inorganic. This was the shocking thing; that the slime of the pit seemed to utter cries and voices; that the amorphous dust gesticulated and sinned; that what was dead, and had no shape, should usurp the offices of life. And this again, that that insurgent horror was knit to him closer than a wife, closer than an eye; lay caged in his flesh, where he heard it mutter and felt it struggle to be born (95).

We have already examined this passage from the Darwinian viewpoint of most modern commentators, in which the dust and the slime are interpreted as a pre-biological and a biological state. However, Stevenson's biblical imagery elsewhere in the text allows one to regard the dust as that which went to form Adam and all his children.[23] This reading takes us back to the origins of life; but it suggests that, although sin and evil may be a fundamental property of existence, it is not a biological problem, it is a spiritual problem. The pairing of 'hellish' and 'inorganic', however, raises an interesting point about Hyde's origins, as Jekyll immediately equates him with 'the slime of the pit'; which could be either Ur-Schleim in some primaeval Darwinian swamp, or Milton's 'asphaltic slime' (X.298) in the 'Pit', a Miltonic synonym for Hell (I.91) deriving from the Bible.[24] At a level

---

23   Dury (*Annotated*, p. 184) quotes Genesis 3.19: 'For dust thou art, and unto dust shalt thou return.'
24   Numbers 16.30, 33. Job 17.16.

beyond the Darwinian, Stevenson could be taking the scientific process of inorganic matter evolving into organic life, and transferring it back into an archetypal beginning in Hell, a place of

> Fens, Bogs, Dens, and shades of death,
> A universe of death, which God by curse,
> Created evil, for evil onely good,
> Where all life dies, death lives, and Nature breeds,
> Perverse, all monstrous, all prodigious things,
> Abominable, inutterable, and worse
> Then Fables yet have feignd, or fear conceiv'd,
> *Gorgons* and *Hydra's*, and *Chimera's* dire.   (II.621–28)[25]

If this be the case, then when Jekyll calls Hyde a 'child of Hell' he is being exact: Satan may have been exiled to Hell because of his crime, but Hyde has sprung deformed from Hell's natal mud.

The 'amorphous dust' that 'was dead, and had no shape' could be the dust of the earth which was formed into the first man and, by extension, the first woman. After the Fall Adam tells Eve:

> we are dust,
> And thither must return and be no more.   (XI.199–200)[26]

Why is Hyde 'knit to [Jekyll] closer than a wife'? This is both an appropriate and a curious image for Stevenson to use. The use of 'knit' is a highly appropriate adoption of a term familiar from the Bible, in which hearts, souls, individual bodies, and groups of bodies are joined together as one.[27]

---

25   Stevenson was well aware of this passage. In a letter to Sidney Colvin (admittedly, of 1889), he refers to 'gorgons and chimaeras dire' (*RLS Letters*, letter 2176, VI, 310–13 (p. 311)).

26   In Stevenson's philosophy, Adam's fear of being no more is unfounded. As we shall see in the final chapter, part of each generation continues to live on in its descendants.

27   'So all the men of Israel were gathered together against the city, knit together as one man' (Judges 20.11). '[T]he soul of Jonathan was knit with the soul of David, and Jonathan loved him as his own soul' (I Samuel 18.1). 'If ye be come peaceably unto me to help me, mine heart shall be knit unto you' (I Chronicles 12.17). 'That their hearts might be comforted, being knit together in love' (Colossians 2.2).

The use of 'wife', however, is curious. There is only one example of 'closer than' in the Bible; and it would seem to suit Stevenson's purpose exactly:

> A man that hath friends must shew himself friendly: and there is a friend that sticketh closer than a brother (Proverbs 18.24).

Given that Stevenson has introduced the themes of Cain and Abel and Jacob and Esau; and Jekyll has written 'in the agonised womb of consciousness these polar twins should be continuously struggling' (82); and that he goes on to reprise the image by writing that he can feel Hyde 'struggle to be born' (95); and given all of the other biblical references; why does Stevenson not maintain the sibling imagery at this crucial point? Why does he instead elect to shift the focus to 'wife'? Perhaps Stevenson is wanting to remind the reader that, despite Jekyll's attempt to distance himself from Hyde ('He, I say – I cannot say, I' (94)), they are, in fact, like man and wife, one flesh.

It could be that the sudden association of Hyde with 'wife' at this point indicates a deliberate Miltonic association on Stevenson's part. We have seen that the forbidden fruit intoxicates Adam and Eve like wine (IX.793; 1008); and that Jekyll's first draught of his potion delights him like wine (84). We have seen that Eve (VIII.465) and Hyde (30; 74) are both associated with the left. Adam is initially pleased with Eve; Jekyll is initially pleased with Hyde. Adam and Eve both sin together; Jekyll, despite his protestations, sins along with Hyde. After the Fall Adam turns on Eve and wants to reject her; eventually Jekyll turns on Hyde and wants to reject him. It is at this point that Hyde becomes 'closer than a wife' – symbolically, the wife being Eve. This is not to say that Hyde should be consistently identified with Eve, but in this passage Jekyll's language betrays him as the guilty fallen Adam (now 'co-heir [...] to death' with Eve), turning in hypocritical righteous indignation and blaming his fellow sinner for the mess. Jekyll's changing relationship with Hyde appears to follow

---

'[T]he body is of Christ. Let no man beguile you [...], not holding the Head, from which all the body by joints and bands having nourishment ministered, and knit together, increaseth with the increase of God' (Colossians 2.17–19).

Adam's changing relationship with Eve. Before the Fall, Adam tells her how the Lord, 'stooping op'nd my left side and took/ From thence a Rib' (VIII.465–66). More lovingly he tells her, '[T]o give thee being I lent/ Out of my side to thee, nearest my heart/ Substantial Life' (IV.483–85). When he first sees her he says, 'I now see/ Bone of my Bone, Flesh of my Flesh/ Before me' (VIII.494–96). Likewise, Jekyll, recalling his first sight of Hyde, writes, 'This too, was myself' (84).

However, when Adam turns on Eve, he regrets that she was ever created, and laying a darker connotation on her association with the left, denigrates and belittles her as

> all but a Rib
> Crooked by nature, bent, as now appears,
> More to the part sinister from me drawn,
> Well if thrown out, as supernumerarie
> To my just number found.   (X.884–88)

Hyde also, with his nameless deformity, is crooked by nature. He too is physically bent in his deformity, as well as bent both towards and on that which is sinister. He is drawn from the sinister 'lower elements' (83) of Jekyll's soul; and physically emerges first from the sinister aspect of Jekyll's house. In the 'slime of the pit' passage presently under discussion, Jekyll first regards Hyde as dust, which is generally accepted as (among others) an Adamic reference. Jekyll then writes that Hyde is knit to him closer than a wife; and nothing could be closer, since man and wife are one flesh – another biblical allusion centred around Adam and Eve. Next he writes that Hyde 'lay caged in his flesh' (95), as if they were separate. Hyde is associated with beasts, therefore being caged is a natural image to use. But there may be some other word association going on here: 'caged' could well carry the double associations of both 'caged beast' and 'rib-caged' – the rib again reinforcing the association at this point of Hyde with Eve. This would not be an isolated instance in Stevenson's writings. Sir Walter Raleigh (1861–1922), commenting on Stevenson's use of wordplay, writes:

> Sometimes [...] this subtle sense of double meanings almost leads to punning. In *Across the Plains* Stevenson narrates how a bet was transacted at a railway-station, and subsequently, he supposes, '*liquidated* at the bar'. This is perhaps an instance

of the excess of a virtue, but it is an excess to be found plentifully in the works of Milton.[28]

There remains but one more Miltonic character to examine. We recall that Satan became enamoured of Sin, and coupled incestuously with her, whereupon her womb conceived a growing burden. Sin tells Satan:

> Pensive here I sat
> Alone, but long I sat not, till my womb
> Pregnant by thee, and now excessive grown
> Prodigious motion felt and rueful throes.
> At last this odious offspring whom thou seest
> Thine own begott'n, breaking violent way
> Tore through my entrails, that with fear and pain
> Distorted, all my nether shape thus grew
> Transformd: but hee my inbred enemie
> Forth issu'd, brandishing his fatal Dart
> Made to destroy: I fled, and cry'd out *Death*.   (II.777–87)

St James writes:

> Then when lust hath conceived, it bringeth forth sin: and sin, when it is finished, bringeth forth death (1.15).

Jekyll's sin, like Satan's, is pride. He has an 'imperious desire to carry [his] head high' (81). Even after all he has done as Hyde – including the murder of Carew – he still feels superior to his fellow men. Sitting on the bench in Regent's Park he has one last 'vainglorious thought', which produces symptoms resembling those which afflicted the rebellious Satan at the birth of Sin. Jekyll writes:

> [A] qualm came over me, a horrid nausea and the most deadly shuddering. These passed away, and left me faint (92).

---

28   *Robert Louis Stevenson* (London: Arnold, 1927), p. 36. Raleigh is not suggesting that Stevenson picked up this habit from Milton, merely that Stevenson is in good company.

He changes into Hyde, and from then on can no longer maintain the identity of Jekyll for more than a short period of time. Sin has gained the ascendant, and Death is on the wing.

Milton's Death offers a possible solution to one of the great verbal mysteries in Stevenson's story. On the night of Hyde's death Poole persuades Utterson to come to Jekyll's house. Jekyll is apparently missing, and someone is prowling about inside his cabinet. Poole explains that Jekyll had been writing desperately to his chemist for new ingredients. The chemist's name is Maw (65; 66). Why? What does it mean?[29]

After the Fall Satan hurries back to Hell, to spread the good news. On the way he meets Sin and Death. He sends them on towards the Earth, where he tells them to

> Dominion exercise [...],
> Chiefly on Man, sole Lord of all declar'd,
> Him first make sure your thrall, and lastly kill.[30]   (X.400–02)

They speed on, and survey the Earth. Sin asks Death how he likes their new empire. He replies:

> To mee, who with eternal Famin pine,
> Alike is Hell, or Paradise, or Heaven,
> There best, where most with ravin I may meet;
> Which here, though plenteous, all too little seems
> To stuff this Maw.   (X.597–601)

Meanwhile the fallen Adam and Eve ponder their lot, and the misery which they have brought on all the generations yet unborn. Adam, despairing, says to Eve:

---

29   'Maw' is not a word that occurs often in Stevenson's writing. In a letter to Henry James he writes: 'It is terrible how little everybody writes, and how much of that little disappears in the capacious maw of the Post Office' (*RLS Letters*, letter 2288, 29 December 1890, VII, 64–66 (p. 64)). In *Catriona* David Balfour recalls a satirical ditty which contains the words 'satiate my maw' (*Works*, X, 240).

30   This of course is what they do with Jekyll.

> Childless thou art, Childless remaine: So Death
> Shall be deceav'd his glut, and with us two
> Be forc't to satisfie his Rav'nous Maw.   (X.989–91)

The chemist's strange name could be a signal – in Stevenson's mind, at least – that Death's maw is waiting; and the end is near for Jekyll and Hyde.[31]

One can find Miltonic parallels even in the final moments of Jekyll/Hyde. Jekyll, trapped in his cabinet, writes of the mutual hatred between himself and Hyde:

> and indeed, had it not been for his fear of death, he would long ago have ruined himself in order to involve me in the ruin (96).

Likewise, at her first meeting with Satan as he is escaping Hell, Sin reflects on the relationship between herself and Death:

> Before mine eyes in opposition sits
> Grim *Death* my Son and foe, [...],
> And mee his Parent would full soon devour
> For want of other prey, but that he knows
> His end with mine involvd; and knows that I
> Should prove a bitter Morsel, and his bane,
> When ever that shall be.   (II.803–09)

Milton expands on the association between a bitter taste and death, to show how they are the direct consequence of transgressing the law of God. The Lord shows Adam all of the fruits of Paradise, which he may freely eat, but warns him:

> But of the Tree whose operation brings
> Knowledg of good and ill, which I have set
> The Pledge of thy Obedience and thy Faith,
> Amid the Garden by the Tree of Life,

---

31   Veeder provides a Freudian interpretation of 'Maw' (*100 Years*, pp. 128–29).

> Remember what I warne thee, shun to taste,
> And shun the bitter consequence: for know,
> The day thou eat'st thereof, my sole command
> Transgrest, inevitably thou shalt dye.   (VIII.323–30)

As Poole and Utterson break down the door to Jekyll's cabinet, Hyde swallows poison. They find him lying dead on the floor:

> and by the crushed phial in the hand and the strong smell of kernels that hung upon the air, Utterson knew that he was looking on the body of a self-destroyer (70).

The smell of kernels tells us that Hyde has taken cyanide, which has an unmistakable smell of bitter almonds. His last morsel – the final consequence of his transgression – has been bitter indeed.

Jekyll's death is inevitable, and determined by the relationship between Sin and Death. Immediately after the Fall, Sin, who has been awaiting within the gates of Hell the outcome of Satan's adventure, grows impatient to follow her father. She addresses her son:

> Methinks I feel new strength within me rise,
> Wings growing,[32] and Dominion giv'n me large
> Beyond this Deep; whatever drawes me on,
> Or sympathie, or som connatural force
> Powerful at greatest distance to unite
> With secret amity things of like kinde
> By secretest conveyance. Thou my Shade
> Inseparable must with mee along:
> For Death from Sin no power can separate.   (X.243–51)

Jekyll's disobedience, like that of Milton's Adam and Eve, brings death into the world with the first mortal taste of his potion. He likens his first transformation to dying (83). When Hyde takes the draught in front of Lanyon, Lanyon reports that Jekyll was 'like a man restored from death'

---

32   Cf. Adam and Eve's feeling of wings after eating the apple (*PL*, IX.786).

(80). Death, as commentators have observed, is an inherent part of the process of transformation. Hogle, for example, writes of 'Jekyll/Hyde's primordial "change" moving *into* death's blackness while also recalling a death from which it seems to emerge'.[33] But as well as discerning the state or condition of death in Jekyll/Hyde's 'change', one might also discern Milton's Death in Lanyon's description of the dark and shadowy figure who stares out fleetingly from the metamorphosing visitor. Lanyon writes:

> There came, I thought, a change – he seemed to swell – his face became suddenly black, and the features seemed to melt and alter (80).

Milton describes Death:

> The other shape,
> If shape it might be calld that shape had none
> Distinguishable in member, joint, or limb,
> Or substance might be calld that shadow seemd,
> For each seemd either; black it stood as Night. (II.666–70)

Like the Fall of Adam and Eve, Jekyll's transgression brings death not only on himself, but on others as well. Lanyon's death continues the archetypal pattern employed by Milton:– Satan, Sin, Death; Adam, Eve, Death. The prideful Satanic Jekyll 'gives birth' to Hyde, and their ongoing union brings about their death. The Fall pattern is re-enacted in the temptation of Lanyon, in which the 'serpentine'.[34] Hyde – motivated by the serpentine Jekyll – plays on the curiosity of Lanyon and lures him to his doom. Hyde/Jekyll offers Lanyon 'a new province of knowledge and new avenues to fame and power' (79); but the fruit of this knowledge is too bitter for Lanyon, and as he begins his descent into the grave he tells Utterson, 'I sometimes think if we knew all, we should be more glad to get away' (57). The Fall, then, is not a single event; it is an ongoing process, and each of us, whether we will or no, continues to re-enact it, and to die.

33   *100 Years*, p. 190.
34   Irving S. Saposnik, *Robert Louis Stevenson* (Boston: Twayne, 1974), p. 92.

CHAPTER TEN

The Platonic Hyde

Stevenson begins his story with a paradox. The narrator describes Gabriel Utterson as 'a man of rugged countenance, that was never lighted by a smile; cold, scanty and embarrassed in discourse; backward in sentiment; lean, long, dusty, dreary, and yet somehow lovable' (29). What makes such a character lovable? He is 'austere with himself' (29), which is commendable; he has 'an approved tolerance for others' (29), which could imply either Christian charity or a lack of discrimination; he is 'modest', and 'of good-nature' (29). But the fact remains that he is still cold and dreary. What makes him lovable is the fact that at 'friendly meetings, and when the wine [is] to his taste, something eminently human beacon[s] from his eye' (29). This eminently human beacon is the light of his soul which, being essentially good, is also beautiful. But if his soul is beautiful, and 'soule is forme and doth the body make', why is Utterson himself not better looking? After all, as Spenser puts it in his 'Hymne in Honour of Beautie':

> Therefore where ever that thou doest behold
> A comely corpse, with beautie faire endewed,
> Know this for certaine, that the same doth hold
> A beauteous soule, with faire conditions thewed,
> Fit to receive the seede of vertue strewed.
> For all that faire is, is by nature good;
> That is a signe to know the gentle blood.   (134–40)

Spenser of course is not unaware of this Uttersonian paradox among the ladies of his day, some of whom are exemplars of all the virtues, and yet far from beautiful. The explanation is that their souls, on their journey from the realms of spirit to the material world, found only inferior matter with which to clothe themselves. Spenser continues:

Yet oft it falles, that many a gentle mynd
Dwels in deformed tabernacle drownd,
Either by chaunce, against the course of kynd,
Or through unaptnesse in the substance fownd,
Which it assumed of some stubborne grownd,
That will not yield unto her formes direction,
But is perform'd with some foule imperfection.   (141–47)

Utterson is in good company, his most notable predecessor for our purposes being none other than Plato's hero Socrates himself. In the *Symposium* the drunken Alcibiades sets out to praise Socrates before the other party-goers:

> And now, my boys, I shall praise Socrates in a figure which will appear to him to be a caricature, and yet I speak, not to make fun of him, but only for the truth's sake. I say, that he is exactly like the busts of Silenus,[1] which are set up in the statuaries' shops, holding pipes or flutes in their mouths; and they are made to open in the middle, and have images of gods inside them. I say also that he is like Marsyas the satyr. You yourself will not deny, Socrates, that your face is like that of a satyr. Aye, and there is a resemblance in other points too.
>
> [...] And then again he knows nothing and is ignorant of all things—such is the appearance which he puts on. Is he not like a Silenus in this? To be sure he is: his outer mask is the carved head of the Silenus; but, O my companions in drink, when he is opened, what temperance there is residing within! [...] I saw in him divine and golden images of such fascinating beauty that I was ready to do in a moment whatever Socrates commanded: they may have escaped the observation of others, but I saw them (215a–217a).

The introduction of Utterson in this manner raises an important point. Obviously Utterson is not foul and deformed in the way that Hyde is; yet the lawyer is not at first sight a figure whom one would approach socially with many hopes of an agreeable outcome. But having done so, one is illumined in the glow of his soul beaconing from his eyes. The narrator refers to it as 'something eminently human' (29); and these words are well

---

1   A son of Pan, and father of the satyrs. With his ivy-twined staff and rough appearance he was a typical Wild Man. This classical figure continued to exercise the Victorian imagination. See, e.g., Thomas Woolner's poem *Silenus* (1884).

chosen, because by contrast Hyde, according to Jekyll, 'had nothing human; nothing lived in him but fear and hatred' (94). Fear and hatred – the two dominant emotions felt by people in Hyde's presence.

When Hyde tramples on the child, Enfield apprehends him, but tells Utterson that Hyde 'gave [him] one look, so ugly that it brought out the sweat on [him] like running' (31). The doctor who arrives turns 'sick and white with the desire to kill' Hyde (31). The womenfolk of the girl's family become 'as wild as harpies' (32). 'I never saw a circle of such hateful faces', says Enfield (32).

The trampling of the girl, who is 'not much the worse' (31) for the experience, has not, in itself, been enough to provoke such extreme reactions. Nor, as Enfield makes clear, is Hyde's physical appearance:

> There is something wrong with his appearance; something displeasing, something downright detestable. I never saw a man I so disliked, and yet I scarce know why. He must be deformed somewhere; he gives a strong feeling of deformity, although I couldn't specify the point. He's an extraordinary-looking man, *and yet I really can name nothing out of the way* (34). [my emphasis]

Utterson experiences the same reaction upon meeting Hyde for the first time, and, as he walks home, ventures a theory to account for it:

> Mr Hyde was pale and dwarfish; he gave an impression of deformity without any namable malformation, he had a displeasing smile, he had borne himself to the lawyer with a sort of murderous mixture of timidity and boldness, and he spoke with a husky, whispering and somewhat broken voice, – all these were points against him; but not all of these together could explain the hitherto unknown disgust, loathing and fear with which Mr Utterson regarded him. 'There must be something else,' said the perplexed gentleman. 'There *is* something more, if I could find a name for it. God bless me, the man seems hardly human! Something troglodytic, shall we say? or can it be the old story of Dr Fell? or is it the mere radiance of a foul soul that thus transpires through, and transfigures, its clay continent? The last, I think; for, O my poor old Harry Jekyll, if ever I read Satan's signature upon a face, it is on that of your new friend!' (40).

Utterson feels fear and loathing; he notes the impression of deformity. But then he advances our awareness of Hyde's inner condition: the 'eminently human' Utterson is shocked to find that Hyde seems hardly human.

This is the strongest point against him so far, and it is reinforced by the word 'troglodytic', Stevenson's first reference to the Hyde who occupies the twilit area between man and beast. *Troglodyte* can apply equally to a cave-man, or any of the primitive 'sub-human' races encountered by earlier travellers (as we saw in the chapter on *Gulliver's Travels*), or a chimpanzee. Hyde is thus at once human, sub-human, and not human – like a Yahoo. Also like a Yahoo he is deformed. Gulliver's first observation about the Yahoos is that their shape is 'very singular and deformed' (193). One might imagine that Hyde's deformity remains 'unexpressed' (50) because he has clothes on, whereas the Yahoos are naked. However, when Gulliver is able to observe a Yahoo at close range, he is shocked to find 'a perfect human Figure; [...] We were] the same in every Part of our Bodies, except as to Hairiness and Colour' (199). The deformity of the Yahoos, like that of Hyde, therefore arises from, as Utterson surmises about his new acquaintance, the 'radiance of a foul soul that [...] transpires through, and transfigures, its clay continent' (40).

Reactions to Hyde, as we have seen, are also the same as Gulliver's reaction to the Yahoos. Gulliver writes:

> Upon the whole, I never beheld in all my Travels so disagreeable an Animal, or one against which I naturally conceived so strong an Antipathy (193).

He regards them as 'abominable', and concludes:

> I never saw any sensitive Being so detestable on all Accounts; and the more I came near them, the more hateful they grew, while I stayed in that Country (199).

Hyde and the Yahoos both inspire disgust and loathing; but Hyde alone excites fear as well. Why is this? Henry Jekyll writes in his Statement:

> I have observed that when I wore the semblance of Edward Hyde, none could come near to me at first without a visible misgiving of the flesh. This, as I take it, was because all human beings, as we meet them, are commingled out of good and evil: and Edward Hyde, alone, in the ranks of mankind, was pure evil (85).

The Yahoos are embodiments of sin; Hyde is the embodiment of evil.

Jekyll's inference, however, like most of his discoveries, turns out to be incomplete. He is correct; but that is not the full story. Lanyon considers the matter more deeply; and in his letter to Utterson writes of his meeting with Hyde, and of his reaction to this embodiment of evil:

> I was struck [...] with the odd, subjective disturbance caused by his neighbourhood. This bore some resemblance to incipient rigor, and was accompanied by a marked sinking of the pulse. At the time, I set it down to some idiosyncratic, personal distaste, and merely wondered at the acuteness of the symptoms; but I have since had reason to believe the cause to lie much deeper in the nature of man, and to turn on some nobler hinge than the principle of hatred (77).

In order to illuminate this rather obscure passage, we must turn again to Spenser – in particular, Una in Book I of the *Faerie Queene*. J.S. Harrison writes:

> Spenser presents in Una the personification of truth or wisdom.
> But he does more than this; he presents her not only as wisdom, but as true beauty. Spenser is so thoroughly convinced of the truth of that fundamental idea of Platonic ethics, that truth and beauty are identical, that he shows their union in the character of Una, in whom, as her name signifies, they are one.[2]

Harrison continues, showing the power of beauty on the beholder:

> Plato had taught that the highest beauty which the soul can know is wisdom, which, though invisible to sight, would inflame the hearts of men in an unwonted degree could there be a visible image of her. In his 'Phædrus' he had stated that 'sight is the most piercing of our bodily senses; though not by that is wisdom seen; her loveliness would have been transporting if there had been a visible image of her'.[3]

Spenser constantly insists on the remarkable power and influence of Una's beauty. The mere sight of her is enough to tame a hungry savage lion (I.3.5–9). She enchants a wild horde of satyrs and nymphs (I.6.9–19). When

---

2   John Smith Harrison, *Platonism in English Poetry of the Sixteenth and Seventeenth Centuries* (Macmillan, 1903; repr. New York: Columbia University Press, 1930), pp. 3–4.

3   Harrison, p. 4. *Phædrus*, 250, Jowett's translation.

she finally removes the veil which has hidden her face from the Red Cross
Knight, he does 'wonder much at her celestiall sight' (I.12.23).[4]
Harrison continues:

> Spenser has taken the greatest care to show that the source of Una's influence over
> those that come into her presence lies in the power exerted by her beauty; but this
> is the beauty of her whole nature, a penetrating radiance of light revealing the soul
> that is truly wise.[5]

Harrison's language is very close to Utterson's 'radiance of a foul soul that
thus transpires through, and transfigures, its clay continent' (40). Just as
the beauty of Una is the beauty of her whole nature, so the ugliness of
Hyde is the ugliness of his whole – or, rather, single – nature. Hyde is, in
effect, an anti-Una. Therefore, whereas Una excites love, Hyde excites fear
and hatred.

Una is the personification of truth and wisdom, but what is truth? – or,
more to the point, who is Wisdom? Spenser conveys some of her greatness
in 'An Hymne of Heavenly Beautie':

> There in his [God's] bosom *Sapience* [Wisdom] doth sit,
> The soveraine dearling of the *Deity*,
> Clad like a Queene in royall robes, most fit
> For so great powre and peerelesse majesty.   (183–86)

Wisdom is distinct from God, but hardly separable. Enid Welsford
writes:

> Spenser's Wisdom has been identified with the Second Person of the Trinity, the
> Holy Spirit, the Virgin Mary, the Schekina of the Cabala, the Angelic Mind of the
> Neo-Platonists, and even with the most obvious prototype, the personified Wisdom
> of the Old Testament and Apocrypha.[6]

4   The only one unmoved by Una's heavenly beauty is Sansloy – a paynim (I.6.2–6).
5   Harrison, p. 5.
6   *Fowre Hymnes Epithalamion: A Study of Edmund Spenser's Doctrine of Love*, ed. by
     Enid Welsford (Oxford: Blackwell, 1967), p. 170.

Spenser tells how Wisdom's beauty – both innate and reflected from God's presence – is beyond description (lines 204–10). He then goes on to describe the effect of her beauty on the beholder:[7]

> But who so may, thrise happie man him hold,
> Of all on earth, whom God so much doth grace,
> And lets his owne Beloved to behold:
> For in the view of her celestiall face,
> All joy, all blisse, all happinesse have place,
> Ne ought on earth can want unto the wight,
> Who of her selfe can win the wishfull sight.
> [...]
> None thereof worthy be, but those whom shee
> Vouchsafeth to her presence to receave,
> And letteth them her lovely face to see,
> Whereof such wondrous pleasures they conceave,
> And sweete contentment, that it doth bereave
> Their soule of sense, through infinite delight,
> And them transport from flesh into the spright. (239–59)

Hyde, on the other hand, as the embodiment of the infernal presence, elicits an equally strong but opposite response. Beholders, reading Satan's signature on Hyde's face, instinctively recoil from him. His deformed body and nasty character invoke fear; and his devilish soul invokes a powerful reaction from normal people, whose natural inclination is towards God.

Those who behold Sapience enjoy wondrous pleasures, sweet contentment, and infinite delight. Those who behold Hyde experience quite the opposite: Enfield comes out in a sweat (31); Poole feels something in his marrow, 'kind of cold and thin' (68); Jekyll notes that people feel 'a visible misgiving of the flesh' (85); Lanyon remarks on 'the odd, subjective disturbance caused by [Hyde's] neighbourhood [which] bore some resemblance to incipient rigor, and was accompanied by a marked sinking of the pulse' (77); and Utterson suffers a profound spiritual unease – a 'hitherto

---

7   In this instance the witness is beholding Wisdom with the eyes of his soul, not his body.

unknown disgust, loathing and fear' (40), a 'shudder in his blood, [...] a nausea and distaste of life; and [...] the gloom of his spirits' (41).

Here is the key to Lanyon's obscure musings, quoted above, in which he concludes the cause of all these reactions to lie 'in the nature of man, and to turn on some nobler hinge than the principle of hatred' (77). Hyde stands alone in the world as the visible image of Satanic will; as such he inflames the hearts of men (and women) in an unwonted degree with fear, hatred, disgust, loathing, and – Satan's greatest weapon – despair. These are the negative qualities which radiate out from Hyde's foul soul; and the beholders' consequent negative emotions arise because these negative quali-ties overwhelm the fragile balance of the normal human souls in Hyde's path, depriving them of all joy, happiness, and contentment. But coupled with this negative response is the positive impulse in the nature of man – as Lanyon suggests – to resist the Devil.

Meanwhile, what does Henry Jekyll think he has done? Some read-ers, focusing on the powders instead of the transformation, conclude that he has been scientific, and that the powders involve – in Eigner's phrase – 'what we would now call the science fiction aspect of the story' (35). At least one contemporary reviewer shared this assessment:

> In our impatience we are hurried towards the dénouement, which accounts for everything upon strictly scientific grounds, though the science be the science of prob-lematical futurity. [...] For we are still groping by doubtful lights on the dim limits of boundless investigation; and it is always possible that we may be on the brink of a new revelation as to the unforeseen resources of the medical art.[8]

This view has survived into more recent times. According to Donald Lawler:

> Even though in *Jekyll and Hyde* Stevenson does not try to explain or even theorize about how Jekyll is metamorphosed into Hyde, he makes it clear that the trick is done with chemicals. It may seem more like alchemy than pharmacology or chemistry [...]. Nevertheless, Stevenson's choice of chemicals rather than spells was critical because

---

8   Unsigned review, *The Times* (25 January 1886), p. 13. Quoted in Maixner, pp. 205–06. Here we see an example of Stevenson's success in creating a sense of reality.

the substances remove the logic of the story from the realm of the fantastic into the scientific. The probabilities change.[9]

How do they change? Stevenson's use of chemicals would seem to give the story an appearance of reality; but ultimately they fail in their purpose. Jekyll's chemicals are no more scientific than those of the eponymous hero of Godwin's *St Leon* (1799). St Leon (not unlike Jekyll) has discovered an elixir which will restore him to youth. On the run from the Spanish Inquisition, he hides in the house of an old Jew named Mordecai, who agrees to help him, and to procure clothes and 'certain medical ingredients [...],' together with his chafing-dish of coals to prepare them'.[10] St Leon continues, with an intriguing mixture of precision and vagueness:

> I unfolded the papers [Mordecai] had brought me; they consisted of various medical ingredients I had directed him to procure; there were also two or three vials, containing syrups and essences. I had near me a pair of scales with which to weigh my ingredients; a vessel of water; the chafing-dish of my host, in which the fire was nearly extinguished; and a small taper, with some charcoal to relight the fire, in case of necessity (282).

These are the necessities for an alchemist; yet when Lanyon looks at Jekyll's chemicals he finds much the same thing. He writes:

> I found what seemed to me to be a simple crystalline salt of a white colour. The phial, to which I next turned my attention, might have been about half-full of a blood-red liquor, which was highly pungent to the sense of smell, and seemed to me to contain phosphorus and some volatile ether. At the other ingredients I could make no guess (76).

9   'Reframing *Jekyll and Hyde*: Robert Louis Stevenson and the Strange Case of Gothic Science Fiction', in *100 Years*, pp. 247–61 (p. 250).

10   William Godwin, *St Leon: A Tale of the Sixteenth Century, Collected Novels and Memoirs of William Godwin*, ed. by Mark Philp and others, 8 vols (London: Pickering, and Chatto, 1992), IV, 280. Cf. Jekyll's 'certain agents' (82), 'a particular salt' (83), and 'the medicine' (95).

This gives us no scientific information. Nor does Lanyon's description of the chemicals' reaction, even though it sounds very scientific:

> [Hyde] measured out a few minims of the red tincture and added one of the powders. The mixture, which was at first of a reddish hue, began, in proportion as the crystals melted, to brighten in colour, to effervesce audibly, and to throw off small fumes of vapour. Suddenly, and at the same moment, the ebullition ceased, and the compound changed to a dark purple, which faded again more slowly to a watery green (79).

We know that the reaction has worked; but we do not know how or why. This is in direct contrast to a work such as Mary Shelley's *Frankenstein* (1818), whose premise is based firmly on the writings and experiments of Erasmus Darwin, and the Bolognese physiologist Luigi Galvani.[11] Shelley *begins* her tale with the science, and the rest of the story grows out of it; and the science in the novel is extrapolated from current scientific knowledge and theory.

Where, then, is the science in *Jekyll and Hyde*? Jekyll writes that his scientific studies led 'steadily nearer to that truth by whose partial discovery [he has] been doomed to such a dreadful shipwreck: that man is not truly one, but truly two' (82). Is this a Huxleyan sense of organic dualism? Not really; because he goes even further:

> I say two, because the state of my own knowledge does not pass beyond that point. [...] I hazard the guess that man will be ultimately known for a mere polity of multifarious, incongruous and independent denizens (82).

This is hardly a novel insight; it could have come to Jekyll from reading Matthew Arnold – '[T]he divine Plato tells us that we have within us a many-headed beast and man'[12] – or the divine Plato himself, who, in the

---

11   For details of the scientific background to *Frankenstein*, see: Mary Shelley, *Frankenstein*, ed., intro. and notes by Marilyn Butler (London: Pickering, 1993); Anne K. Mellor, *Mary Shelley: Her Life, Her Fiction, Her Monsters* (New York and London: Routledge, 1988). For a description of Galvani's ghastly experiments – in one of which a dead body sat up – see Mellor, pp. 104–06.

12   'Numbers', a lecture delivered in America in October 1883, and published in the *Nineteenth Century* (April 1884). *The Complete Prose Works of Matthew Arnold*,

Republic, is recalling Socrates describing an image of the soul of an unjust man:

> An image like the composite creations of ancient mythology, such as the Chimera or Scylla or Cerberus, and there are many others in which two or more different natures are said to grow into one.
> [...]
> Then do you now model the form of a multitudinous, many-headed monster, having a ring of heads of all manner of beasts, tame and wild, which he is able to put forth and metamorphose at will.
> [...]
> Suppose now that you make a second form as of a lion, and a third of a man; but let the first be far the largest, and the second next in size.
> [...]
> And now join them into one, and let the three somehow grow together.
> [...]
> Next fashion the outside of them into a single image, as of a man, so that he who is not able to look within, and sees only the outer case, may believe the beast to be a single human creature (IX, 588c–e).

Jekyll's science, then, does not involve a discovery of the dual nature of mankind, but is simply directed towards 'the separation of these elements'. But how? He writes:

> I was so far in my reflections when, as I have said, a side light began to shine upon the subject from the laboratory table. I began to perceive more deeply than it has ever yet been stated, the trembling immateriality, the mist-like transience, of this seemingly so solid body in which we walk attired (82).

This, we feel, *is* science, and it apparently derives from the same scientific discoveries still plaguing Stevenson when he writes in 'Pulvis et Umbra':

> Of the Kosmos, in the last resort, science reports many doubtful things and all of them appalling. There seems no substance to this solid globe on which we stamp:

---

ed. by R.H. Super, 11 vols (Ann Arbor: University of Michigan Press, 1960–77), X [1974], 160.

nothing but symbols and ratios. Symbols and ratios carry us and bring us forth and beat us down; gravity that swings the incommensurable suns and worlds through space, is but a figment varying inversely as the square of distances; and the suns and worlds themselves, imponderable figures of abstraction, NH_3 and H_2O. Consideration dares not dwell upon this view; that way madness lies; science carries us into zones of speculation, where there is no habitable city for the mind of man.[13]

Here we see the logical end of contemporary reductionist science: where the physical basis of life is protoplasm; where protoplasm is a compound of chemicals; where chemicals are aggregates of atoms; and where atoms are finally resolved into mathematics.

Or do we? Jekyll's science is not that of his fellow scientists. Lanyon calls it 'unscientific balderdash' (36). Jekyll refers to it as 'mystic and transcendental' (81); and derides Lanyon for being 'bound to the most narrow and material views' (80). The material and the transcendental are at war not only in the persons of Lanyon and Jekyll; Ralph Waldo Emerson – a transcendentalist – declares:

> What is popularly called Transcendentalism among us, is Idealism; Idealism as it appears in 1842. As thinkers, mankind have ever divided into two sects, Materialists and Idealists; the first class founding on experience, the second on consciousness; the first class beginning to think from the data of the senses, the second class perceive that the senses are not final, and say, The senses give us representations of things, but what are the things themselves, they cannot tell.[14]

And he continues, in language very like that of Jekyll and his 'mist-like transience':

> The materialist, secure in the certainty of sensation, mocks at fine-spun theories, at star-gazers and dreamers, and believes that his life is solid, that he at least takes nothing for granted, but knows where he stands, and what he does. Yet how easy is it to show him that he also is a phantom walking and working amid phantoms, and

---

13   *Works*, XII, 284.
14   'The Transcendentalist: A Lecture read at the Masonic Temple, Boston, January 1842', *The Works of Ralph Waldo Emerson*, 12 vols, The Riverside Edition, vol.1, *Nature, Addresses, and Lectures* (London: Routledge, 1903), pp. 311–39 (p. 311).

that he need only ask a question or two beyond his daily questions to find his solid universe growing dim and impalpable before his sense.[15]

Lanyon suddenly finds his solid universe growing dim and impalpable, and it kills him.

The Transcendentalists, being Idealists, were by definition Platonists; and one can find the origins of Jekyll's claims for the insubstantial body, in the works of Plotinus, who writes:

> I prefer to use the word phantasm as hinting the indefiniteness into which the Soul spills itself when it seeks to communicate with Matter.[16]
>
> [A]ll that is allowed to it [i.e., Matter] is to be a Potentiality, a weak and blurred phantasm, a thing incapable of a Shape of its own.[17]

'There are', writes Plotinus, 'no atoms; all body is divisible endlessly.'[18] Matter itself has no size, or shape, or colour, or smell, or touch; it is not hot, or cold, or moist, or dry.[19] It only acquires these properties by virtue of the soul 'bestowing Form' on it.[20] In other words, soul is form and doth the body make.

Jekyll is quite specific on this point. He writes:

> Enough, then, that I not only recognised my natural body for the mere aura and effulgence of certain of the powers that made up my spirit, but managed to compound a drug by which these powers should be dethroned from their supremacy, and a second form and countenance substituted, none the less natural to me because they were the expression, and bore the stamp, of lower elements in my soul (83).

15   Emerson, p. 313. It is interesting to compare this with Kingsley's letter to Revd Maurice in which he promotes his doctrine that 'souls secrete their bodies, as snails do shells'. Kingsley ends this overtly Platonic letter with, 'Whereby you may perceive that I am not going astray into materialism as yet' (*CKL*, II, 171–72).

16   *The Six Enneads*, trans. by Stephen MacKenna, 3rd edn, rev. by B.S. Page (New York: Pantheon, [n.d.]), II.4.11.

17   *Enneads*, II.5.5.

18   *Enneads*, II.4.7.

19   *Enneads*, II.4.12.

20   *Enneads*, II.4.10.

But Jekyll's drug – the powders which are the outcome of years of scientific research – is never explained, nor is the theory behind its action. In fact, as Jekyll admits, in the end even he does not know the identity of the active ingredient (83; 96). There is a good reason for Jekyll's ignorance: the powders came to Stevenson in his dream, and are unconnected with any branch of science. They are simply, as Douglas Thorpe aptly puts it, 'an improbable bit of Gothic machinery' (17), literally dreamt up as a mechanism for the transformation. To inquire into them is both futile and unnecessary. Unlike Mary Shelley, Stevenson can offer nothing from contemporary science to explain his mechanism. He may have been wise not to do so. Maixner writes: 'Countless readers – Henry James included – objected to the transformation by chemical means, which they felt was too material an agency' (24).[21] This suggests that readers were regarding the story not as a speculation on the possibilities of scientific inquiry, but as a meditation on the influence of evil on the soul. Andrew Lang seems most in sympathy with Stevenson's intentions, when he refers to Jekyll's draught as 'the mystic potion.'[22] The only aspect of Jekyll's theory available to the reader lies in the Platonism behind his transcendental medicine. And it is Platonism which confirms Utterson's conjecture about Hyde's 'foul soul'; Hyde conforms precisely to the type described by Plotinus:

> Let us then suppose an ugly Soul, dissolute, unrighteous: teeming with all the lusts; torn by internal discord; beset by the fears of its cowardice and the envies of its pettiness; thinking, in the little thought it has, only of the perishable and the base; perverse in all its impulses; the friend of unclean pleasures; living the life of abandonment to bodily sensations and delighting in its deformity.[23]

Hyde's appearance and eventual ascendancy fulfil all Platonic expectations. Not only does his ugliness reflect his evil soul, but he is 'much smaller, slighter, and younger than Henry Jekyll' (84), which Jekyll puts down to the fact that he has had little opportunity in the past to express his baser side. However, as Hyde's career progresses Jekyll notices an ominous change:

---

21   For responses by F.W.H. Myers and Henry James, see Maixner, pp. 216; 309.
22   Letter to *The Athenaeum* (12 January 1895), p. 49.
23   Plotinus, I.6.5.

> That part of me which I had the power of projecting had lately been much exercised and nourished; it had seemed to me of late as though the body of Edward Hyde had grown in stature, as though (when I wore that form) I were conscious of a more generous tide of blood (88–89).

This is an important point. If Hyde were a pure Darwinian figure, and if the story were one of Darwinian degeneration, then Hyde should become progressively more ape-like. But he does not. He remains the same, but grows larger as he becomes more dominant. This is Platonic: the more that Jekyll partakes vicariously in the adventures of Hyde, the more tainted becomes the upright part of his soul. Hyde is not growing because of his own activities; he is growing because Jekyll's entire soul is becoming more foul. Therefore when Hyde manifests, he progressively represents a larger portion of foul soul; hence he grows larger. Not only does he bear the stamp of lower elements in Jekyll's soul, but he also embodies their steadily increasing amount.

Following the murder of Carew, Jekyll can no longer appear anywhere as Hyde; nor does he wish to. He puts away the powders, and throws himself into doing good works; but, still 'cursed' with his 'duality of purpose', he gives way to temptation as 'an ordinary secret sinner' (92). In arguably the most chilling sentence in the story he writes:

> There comes an end to all things; the most capacious measure is filled at last; and this brief condescension to my evil finally destroyed the balance of my soul (92).

We should take this as a literal statement of fact. Jekyll's soul now becomes predominantly evil, and therefore he looks evil. Just as Tom the water-baby's body became all prickly because his soul became all prickly, so Jekyll's body becomes Hyde-ish because his soul has become Hyde-ish. Whenever he sleeps his powers of self-control relax and he wakes up as Hyde. As he writes:

> In short [...] it seemed only by a great effort as of gymnastics, and only under the immediate stimulation of the drug, that I was able to wear the countenance of Jekyll (95).

It is only by an act of will that he can now force his body into a counterfeit representation of his soul – one which, significantly, he refers to as if it belonged to someone else.

Jekyll's drug – which he now refers to as 'the medicine' (95) – no longer provides more than temporary relief. Why? Jekyll writes that it

> had no discriminating action; it was neither diabolical nor divine; it but shook the doors of the prison house of my disposition (85).

The drug originally worked both ways: it allowed Jekyll to turn into Hyde, and it allowed Hyde to turn back into Jekyll. However, when Jekyll's sins (vicariously accumulated in the body of Hyde) have destroyed the balance of his soul, and his disposition is just as depraved, corrupt, and sinful as Hyde's, what can the drug do? Jekyll barely exists anymore; he has given most of his soul over to Hyde. He declares that, whereas Hyde is 'express and single', he himself is 'imperfect and divided' (84), and 'commingled out of good and evil' (85). Hyde therefore always remains Hyde; but the divided Jekyll is a mixture of Jekyll and Hyde; and when the Hyde aspect comes to dominate his soul, then his body must come to reflect his inner condition. Lasting return to the Jekyll body is no longer possible; the Hyde body takes over. Soul is form and doth the body make; in Jekyll's case the principle operates too well.

PART FIVE

The Inheritance of Evil

One could reasonably anticipate that an examination of *Jekyll and Hyde* would end with the focus totally on *Jekyll and Hyde*. But the text itself does not provide us with all of the information necessary for a complete understanding of Edward Hyde. We have seen that he is the Platonic embodiment of the lower elements in Jekyll's soul; that these lower elements are the satanic impulses fuelling the war in Jekyll's members; and that these lower satanic impulses spring from a lingering brutishness in civilized humanity, a remnant of our former primitive condition. But even when one takes all of the above into account, one is still uncertain what to make of Jekyll's great tragic cry:

> [H]e thought of Hyde, for all his energy of life, as of something not only hellish but inorganic. This was the shocking thing: that the slime of the pit seemed to utter cries and voices; that the amorphous dust gesticulated and sinned; that what was dead, and had no shape, should usurp the offices of life. And this again, that that insurgent horror was knit to him closer than a wife, closer than an eye; lay caged in his flesh, where he heard it mutter and felt it struggle to be born (95).

To understand this passage fully is to understand Edward Hyde and to see finally how all the elements we have been examining come together. And to understand this passage fully we must turn to 'Olalla', written almost immediately after *Jekyll and Hyde*, in which Stevenson deals explicitly with the inheritance of evil.

CHAPTER ELEVEN

Olalla and Hyde: Kinship with the Dust

The theme of inheritance is strong in *Jekyll and Hyde* – Utterson spends most of his time fretting about Jekyll's crazy will, only to find himself in the end the beneficiary – and its cornerstone presence in such works as *Kidnapped* and *The Master of Ballantrae* shows that it exercised Stevenson's mind a great deal. Heir to his father's fortune – and for a time in peril of being denied it – Stevenson knew the worldly benefits of inheriting wealth and property. Heir also to chronic ill health and a highly strung disposition, he knew the awful misfortune of inheriting his parents' and grandparents' physical and psychological failings. Heir also, from his cradle, to a fire-and-brimstone biblical tradition, he knew the burden of sin which he had inherited from his forebears, as God visited their iniquity 'upon the children, and upon the children's children, unto the third and to the fourth generation.'[1] He knew, as Kingsley puts it:

> of races; of families; of their wars, their struggles, their exterminations; of races favoured, of races rejected; of remnants being saved, to continue the race; of hereditary tendencies, hereditary excellencies, hereditary guilt.[2]

Heir also to a world now irretrievably altered by Darwin's theory of natural selection, he knew – again, as Kingsley puts it:

> the importance of hereditary powers, hereditary organs, hereditary habits, in all organized beings, from the lowest plant to the highest animal.[3]

---

1   Exodus 34.7.
2   *Westminster Sermons*, p. xvii.
3   *Westminster Sermons*, p. xvi.

Thus, as we shall see, Stevenson, like Kingsley, saw heredity having as much influence on character as on physique; and the biblical and Darwinian dance about each other, each coming centre-stage in turn in answer to the requirements of the moment. In a lighter mood Stevenson writes of:

> a certain low-browed, hairy gentleman, at first a percher in the fork of trees, next (as they relate) a dweller in caves, and whom I think I see squatting in cave-mouths, of a pleasant afternoon, to munch his berries—his wife, that accomplished lady, squatting by his side: his name I never heard, but he is often described as Probably Arboreal [...]. Each has his own tree of ancestors, but at the top of all sits Probably Arboreal; in all our veins there run some minims of his old, wild, tree-top blood; our civilised nerves still tingle with his rude terrors and pleasures; and to that which would have moved our common ancestor, all must obediently thrill.[4]

Stevenson here is using two terms employed by Darwin: 'probably arboreal' and 'common ancestor'. He is at once drawing attention to our animal origin; while at the same time reminding us that we still carry our primitive animal tendencies and responses within us; and moreover that none of us is exempt from this inheritance.

But Stevenson is also aware that our common ancestor munched on more than nuts and berries:[5] he – and his wife – munched on fruit more bitter:

> [S]ome old Adam of our ancestors, sleeps in all of us till the fit circumstance shall call it into action.[6]

According to Stevenson, then, we have present within us both a biological common ancestor, from whose primitive drives and instincts we may distance ourselves, but whom we may never quite discard; and an existential common ancestor – fallen and full of sin – whose presence in us is even stronger, and potentially more dangerous. This sinful ancestor

---

4   'Pastoral', *Works*, XII, 81–82. Further references are given after quotations in the text.
5   Lucretius describes the natural man subsisting on acorns and berries (*On the Nature of Things*, V, lines 939–42).
6   *Weir of Hermiston*, *Works*, XVIII, 209–408 (p. 299).

bequeaths his sinfulness to the next generation, who in turn bequeath both it and their own to the next, and so on, sin begetting sin, and accumulating down through the generations, until each succeeding generation is crushed beneath the load. The Darwinian common ancestor survives vestigially in our blood; the Adamic common ancestor lives on in our blood, along with all the generations between him and us. One can see this dual process at work in 'Olalla', which Stevenson wrote around the time he was writing *Jekyll and Hyde*, and which throws some light on its more famous companion.

'Olalla' presents the reader with an ancient noble House in Gothic decline, two of whose members are a Wild Man and a Child of Nature living in a traditional Wild natural environment. The narrator – a handsome Scottish officer recovering from wounds sustained fighting in Spain – goes to the mountains to convalesce in the residencia of an impoverished noble family consisting of the mother – the last high-born member of the line – and her son and daughter, whose father may have been a muleteer or smuggler who may or may not have married their mother. Felipe, the dim-witted son, conveys the officer in a cart drawn by a mule. The landscape conforms to the Wild type:

> The country through which we went was wild and rocky, partially covered with rough woods [...] and frequently intersected by the beds of mountain torrents.[7]

Felipe on first appearance conforms to the type of the Noble Savage:

> He was superlatively well-built, light, and lithe and strong; he was well-featured (178).

But he is more truly a Wild Man, displaying one of the Wild Man's defining characteristics: he is 'of a dusky hue, and inclined to hairiness' (178). His occupation also belongs to one type of the Wild Man: he spends his days working in the garden of the residencia (186). However, he is also beginning to display some of the behaviour of an ape. He chatters (177);

---

7   'Olalla', *Works*, XI, 173–239 (p. 177). Further references to this edition are given after quotations in the text.

and when, some days later, the officer takes him on a walk in the woods surrounding the residencia:

> He leaped, he ran round me in mere glee; he would stop, and look and listen, and seemed to drink in the world like a cordial; and then he would suddenly spring into a tree with one bound, and hang and gambol there like one at home (187).

Felipe could simply be expressing more than most the wild tree-top blood of our common ancestor; indeed at this point he has the same naive innocence as one of Stevenson's Lucretian natural men.[8] But immediately afterwards, impelled by some vein of darker blood, Felipe catches a squirrel and begins to torture it. The enraged officer turns on him, and Felipe begs for forgiveness:

> 'Oh, I try so hard,' he said. 'Oh, commandante, bear with Felipe this once; he will never be a brute again!' (188).

Here we have an individual whose line is degenerating. He is beginning to assume ape-like qualities, and his human self is fighting a constant battle with his emerging beast self. He is a fairly familiar figure.

Felipe's sister Olalla is a Child of Nature. She dwells amid the wild beauty which we have come to expect from *Fleetwood* and *Melincourt*:

> The residencia stood on the crown of a stony plateau; on every side the mountains hemmed it about [...]. The air in these altitudes moved freely and largely; great clouds congregated there, and were broken up by the wind and left in tatters on the hill-tops; a hoarse and yet faint rumbling of torrents rose from all round; and one could there study all the ruder and more ancient characters of nature in something of their pristine force (189).

---

8   Ed Block equates Felipe with Hyde in his hairiness, and with Probably Arboreal in his sylvan pursuits. See *Rituals of Dis-Integration: Romance and Madness in the Victorian Psychomythic Tale* (New York & London: Garland, 1993), p. 148. (Hereafter Block, *Rituals*.) Kenneth Graham sees Felipe as a Child of Nature. See 'Stevenson and Henry James: A Crossing', in *Robert Louis Stevenson*, ed. by Andrew Noble (London and Totowa: Vision and Barnes & Noble, 1983), pp. 23–46 (pp. 38; 39).

Her private chamber, 'ascetic to the degree of sternness', faces 'to the north, where the mountains [are] most wildly figured' (203). Whereas Anthelia Melincourt seeks romantic nourishment in Italian poetry, Olalla seeks redemption in books 'devotional, historical, and scientific, but mostly of a great age and in the Latin tongue' (203). She is beautiful (208); and, of course, associated with flowers (209; 211). Finally, her body is a true Platonic representation of her soul:

> It was a lovely body, but the inmate, the soul, was more than worthy of that lodging (211).

So, curiously, is her mind. Whereas Felipe is 'half-witted' (209), and his mother the Señora directs a 'blankly stupid' (192) gaze on the officer, Olalla has escaped this mental retardation. How? Simply, it would seem, by virtue of being a Child of Nature, who, by definition, 'imbibes beauty, innocence and an unerring moral sense from the scenery which surrounds her.'[9] It would appear that Stevenson was relying on his readers' familiarity with the type in order to make further explanation unnecessary. Olalla therefore represents, in part at least, a triumph of environment over heredity.

The Señora, whose blood is entirely noble and degenerate, has sunk into some kind of feline existence: she spends her days in the court of the residencia 'seated in the sun against a pillar, or stretched on a rug before the fire' (192); if she moves it is only to keep herself in the sun (191); her eyes are large and golden (192); and the officer remarks, 'I never knew her to display the least spark of energy beyond what she expended in brushing and re-brushing her copious copper-coloured hair' (193) – an activity analogous to a cat grooming itself.

Stevenson had obviously spent some time observing cats dozing in the sun while keeping one eye open for birds. The officer tells how he would stop and greet the Señora on the way out for his walk and on the way back. He relates:

9   Fairchild, p. 366.

Now she would speak of the warmth in which (like her son) she greatly delighted; now of the flowers of the pomegranate trees, and now of the white doves and long-tailed swallows that fanned the air of the court. The birds excited her. As they raked the eaves in their swift flight or skimmed sidelong past her with a rush of wind, she would sometimes stir, and sit a little up, and seem to awaken from her doze of satisfaction. But for the rest of her days she lay luxuriously folded on herself and sunk in sloth and pleasure (193).

But within this large placid pussy cat there lurks a being far more dark and terrible. One day an unsettling high wind begins to blow about the residencia. The officer's nerves begin to unravel, as do those of Felipe and the Señora. In the middle of the night the officer is awakened from an uneasy sleep by

an outbreak of pitiable and hateful cries. [...] Now they would dwindle down into a moaning that seemed to be articulate, and at these times I made sure they must be human; and again they would break forth and fill the house with ravings worthy of hell (199).

The officer runs to his door, but finds that he has been locked in. Not knowing that the cries are coming from the Señora, all he can do is wonder at their source:

Who was the author of these indescribable and shocking cries? A human being? It was inconceivable. A beast? The cries were scarce quite bestial; and what animal, *short of a lion or a tiger*, could thus shake the solid walls of the residencia? (200). [my emphasis]¹⁰

---

10   This scene probably has its origins in Silverado: 'Again late at night we heard from up the cañon three strange squalls or screams; like, but somewhat different from, those I had attributed to a wild cat, on our first arrival. In our usually silent cañon, they made a great effect. One thought it was an eagle; [...] another was sure it was a California lion; a third was once more in favour of the wild-cat theory' ('The Silverado Diary', *Works*, II, 581–608 (p. 606)). By the time the diary appears in print, the cries are definitely coming from a wild cat: 'Away up the cañon, a wild cat welcomed us with three discordant squalls' (*The Silverado Squatters* (1883), *Works*, II, 439–578 (p. 546)).

Here Stevenson is establishing a definite link between the 'domestic' feline Señora and her wild feline progenitors. He goes on in a later scene to make this link overt. The officer cuts his wrist, and, with his other hand covering the wound, goes down into the courtyard looking for assistance. Finding the Señora dozing before the fire, he asks for help:

> She looked up sleepily and asked me what it was, and with the very words, I thought she drew in her breath with a widening of the nostrils and seemed to come fully alive.
>
> 'I have cut myself,' I said, 'and rather badly. See!' And I held out my two hands from which the blood was oozing and dripping.
>
> Her great eyes opened wide, the pupils shrank into points; a veil seemed to fall from her face, and leave it sharply expressive and yet inscrutable. And as I still stood, marvelling a little at her disturbance, she came swiftly up to me, and stooped and caught me by the hand; and the next moment my hand was at her mouth, and she had bitten me to the bone. [...] I beat her back; and she sprang at me again and again, with bestial cries, cries that I recognised, such cries as had awakened me on the night of the high wind (221).

Some commentators feel that in this scene the Señora is revealing 'the strain of vampirism' that runs in the family.[11] Julia Briggs regards her as a werewolf,[12] as does Michael Hayes.[13] Stevenson's language, however, gives no indication of vampirism or lycanthropy, but is directed towards degeneration and Wildness. Ed Block sees the attack as indicative of 'primitive behaviour';[14] and Edwin Eigner attributes it to 'the wild animal in her

---

11 Irving Massey, 'The Third Self: *Dracula, Strange Case of Dr Jekyll and Mr Hyde* and Mérimée's *Lokis*', *Bulletin of the Midwest Modern Language Association*, 6 (1973), 57–67 (p. 62). See also Robert Mighall, *A Geography of Victorian Gothic Fiction: Mapping History's Nightmares* (Oxford: Oxford University Press, 1999), p. 158. Julia Reid (87) quotes Mighall approvingly. In his edition of *Jekyll and Hyde* Mighall suggests that the scene may have influenced Dracula's attack on Jonathan Harker (172).

12 *Night Visitors: The Rise and Fall of the English Ghost Story* (London: Faber, 1977), p. 68.

13 *The Supernatural Short Stories of Robert Louis Stevenson*, ed. and intro. by Michael Hayes (London: Calder, 1976), p. 10.

14 Block, *Rituals*, p. 152.

nature'[15] – correct, but not specific enough. The Señora's cries are 'bestial' (221) and 'savage' (222). The family has a 'savage and bestial' strain running through it (223). The Señora was 'wild' when she was young, and even 'wilder' as she grew older (176).[16] The old Padre who ministers to the family refers to her as a 'wild lamb' (232), a reference both to her Wild inner condition and to the lost sheep of Luke 15.4 which has wandered from the flock. And, in this defining moment, as Olalla shields the officer with her body while Felipe tries to drag the Señora away, the officer lies on the floor listening to 'the yells of that catamount' (222). 'Catamount' is a contraction of 'cat-a-mountain' – a traditional term for a Wild Man. Shakespeare used it;[17] and in *Westward Ho!* the English sailors refer to the Wild girl Ayacanora as a 'cat-a-mountain' (443). But all of the feline imagery surrounding the Señora also comes together at this moment. In the United States a catamount is a puma or cougar (*OED*); Stevenson may have encountered this usage during his stay at Silverado. 'Cat-a-mountain' is also a term for a leopard, panther, ocelot, 'or other Tiger-cat' (*OED*). During her attack the Señora emits the cries previously associated with a lion or a tiger (200). The Señora, therefore, is not only a Wild woman, but is a large, wild cat, strongly identified with a tiger.

In 'Olalla' Stevenson is interweaving two main themes: degeneration, and inheritance. Felipe and the Señora represent the degeneration theme, and Olalla represents the inheritance theme. This, as we shall see, is something of a simplification, but it provides a platform on which to proceed.

On his first night in the residencia the officer is both beguiled and repelled by the image of an ancestral lady in a portrait in his room. When he first meets the Señora he is 'reminded of the miracle of family descent' (192); but whereas the beautiful face in the portrait is 'marred by a cruel, sullen, and sensual expression' (183), the Señora's face is 'devoid of either good or bad—a moral blank expressing literally naught' (192). After observing Felipe and the Señora for some days the officer concludes:

15   *Robert Louis Stevenson and Romantic Tradition* (Princeton, N.J.: Princeton University Press, 1966), p. 203.
16   Henry Jekyll was also 'wild when he was young' (41).
17   *The Merry Wives of Windsor*, II,ii,27.

The family blood had been impoverished, perhaps by long in-breeding, which I knew to be a common error among the proud and the exclusive. No decline, indeed, was to be traced in the body, which had been handed down unimpaired in shapeliness and strength; the faces of to-day were struck as sharply from the mint as the face of two centuries ago that smiled upon me from the portrait. But the intelligence (that more precious heirloom) was degenerate (195).

Here Stevenson has begun to introduce the underlying principle of the family's long degeneration; and it falls to Olalla to articulate this principle in words which echo strongly the words of Kingsley's Mrs Bedonebyasyoudid and the story of the Doasyoulikes. As we have seen, the fairy tells Tom and Ellie:

Folks say that I can make beasts into men [...]. Whatever their ancestors were, men they are; and I advise them to behave as such, and act accordingly. But let them recollect this, that there are two sides to every question, and a downhill as well as an uphill road; and if I can turn beasts into men, I can, by the same laws [...], turn men into beasts (177).

When Ellie asks, 'But could you not have saved them from becoming apes?', Mrs Bedonebyasyoudid replies:

At first, my dear; if only they would have behaved like men, and set to work to do what they did not like. But the longer they waited, and behaved like the dumb beasts, who only do what they like, the stupider and clumsier they grew; till at last they were past all cure, for they had thrown their own wits away (176–77).

Likewise Olalla's ancestors have thrown their own wits away through the same process. Olalla tells the officer:

My fathers, eight hundred years ago, ruled all this province: they were wise, great, cunning, and cruel; they were a picked race of the Spanish [...]. Presently a change began. Man has risen; if he has sprung from the brutes, he can descend again to the same level. The breath of weariness blew on their humanity and the cords relaxed; they began to go down; their minds fell on sleep, their passions awoke in gusts, heady and senseless like the wind in the gutters of the mountains; beauty was still handed down, but no longer the guiding wit nor the human heart; the seed passed on, it was wrapped in flesh, the flesh covered the bones, but they were the bones and the flesh of brutes, and their mind was as the mind of flies (228).

Eight hundred years ago Olalla's house was wise, great, cunning, and cruel. Now it is merely cunning and cruel. Each generation is in the slow and painful process of losing its human soul, and replacing it with an animal soul. It is significant, therefore, that in this moral descent Felipe and the Señora should be identified with an ape and a tiger, the two animals which Tennyson has told us we must overcome if we are to achieve full humanity:

> Arise, and fly
> The reeling Faun, the sensual feast;
> Move upward, working out the beast,
> And let the ape and tiger die.   (*In Memoriam*, CXVIII, 25–28)

The beautiful pious Olalla, trapped in a decaying mansion with an ape and a tigress, is a potent symbol of the pure soul trapped in its clay continent with the bestial urges of the flesh. Olalla has the same blood in her veins as her mother and brother, but she possesses the discrimination which they have lost, and her mind and soul both yearn towards God. Meanwhile Felipe's mind is 'like his body, active and swift, but stunted in development' (180) – a case of the body reflecting the mind rather than the soul). Likewise the Señora 'live[s] in her body; and her consciousness [is] all sunk into and disseminated through her members, where it luxuriously dwell[s]' (212). Olalla is therefore 'dwelling in a great isolation of soul with her incongruous relatives' (204). But, as we shall see, this unfortunate domestic arrangement is but the physical reflection of a deeper inner torment.

Stevenson explores the theme of inheritance through the portrait in the officer's room, and its resemblance to the present members of the family. The officer gazes on it for the first time:

> Her figure was very slim and strong, and of a just proportion; red tresses lay like a crown over her brow; her eyes, of a very golden brown, held mine with a look; and her face, which was perfectly shaped, was yet moved by a cruel, sullen, and sensual expression. Something in both face and figure, something exquisitely intangible, like the echo of an echo, suggested the features and bearing of my guide [Felipe]; and I stood a while, unpleasantly attracted and wondering at the oddity of the resemblance (183).[18]

18   Kenneth Graham regards the woman in the portrait as 'feline', but not so the Señora, whom he regards as 'something of a vampire'. See Graham in *Robert Louis Stevenson*, ed. by Noble, pp. 39; 43.

After meeting the Señora for the first time the officer returns to his room and compares her with the image in the portrait:

> I was again reminded of the miracle of family descent. My hostess was, indeed, both older and fuller in person; her eyes were of a different colour; her face, besides, was not only free from the ill-significance that offended and attracted me in the painting; it was devoid of either good or bad—a moral blank expressing literally naught. And yet there was a likeness, not so much speaking as immanent, not so much in any particular feature as upon the whole (192).

When the officer finally meets Olalla, although she neither moves nor speaks, he is struck with her liveliness:

> I beheld this maiden on whom God had lavished the richest colours and the most exuberant energies of life, [...] and in whose great eyes he had lighted the torches of the soul (209).

When he returns to his room he looks again at the portrait; but now there is a difference:

> It had fallen dead, like a candle after sunrise; it followed me with eyes of paint. I knew it to be like, and marvelled at the tenacity of type in that declining race; but the likeness was swallowed up in difference (210).

Although Olalla continues the family likeness, there is a quality about her which sets her apart from her fellows.

But Stevenson is interested in the inheritance of more than physical likeness. The officer wanders through the residencia and finds many ancestral portraits in the empty rooms. He is of course taken by the family likeness:

> Never before had I so realised the miracle of the continued race, the creation and re-creation, the weaving and changing and handing down of fleshly elements (202).

There is nothing new here. But he goes on to introduce the next strand of the inheritance theme – the inheritance of physical behaviour:

> That a child should be born of its mother, that it should grow and clothe itself (we know not how) with humanity, and put on inherited looks, and turn its head with the manner of one ascendant, and offer its hand with the gesture of another, are wonders dulled for us by repetition (202).

The looks and the gestures are wonders enough, but they are mere curiosities; the great mystery lies in the inheritance of character. 'Now I often wonder', writes Stevenson in 'The Manse', 'what I have inherited from this old minister [grandfather].'[19] He lists their shared fondness for preaching; their love of Shakespeare; their taste in food and wine; and their infirmities. He goes on:

> I would much rather have inherited his noble presence. Try as I please, I cannot join myself on with the reverend doctor; and all the while, no doubt, and even as I write the phrase, he moves in my blood, and whispers to me, and sits efficient in the very knot and centre of my being (88–89).

The ancestors live on, not just in looks, gestures, and even in character, but as residual memory which can be awakened at any moment. In 'Pastoral', writing about literature, Stevenson writes:

> The fortune of a tale lies not alone in the skill of him that writes, but as much, perhaps, in the inherited experience of him who reads; and when I hear with a particular thrill of things that I have never done or seen, it is one of that innumerable army of my ancestors rejoicing in past deeds (80).

In 'The Manse' he traces back through the innumerable army of his ancestors, beginning with those known to family history, and ends with a passage which we have already seen:

> And away in the still cloudier past, the threads that make me up can be traced by fancy into the bosoms of thousands and millions of ascendants: [...] and, furthest of all, what face is this that fancy can see peering through the disparted branches? What sleeper in green tree-tops, what muncher of nuts, concludes my pedigree? Probably arboreal in his habits (92–93).

Thus every aspect of each individual's existence – looks; physique; mannerisms; character; tastes; even dormant memories – every aspect is determined by hereditary factors. And so it is with Olalla. She shares the family likeness with Felipe and the Señora. She has the 'lightness and swiftness' of Felipe (209); and, even though she lives like a virtual anchoress

---

19   *Works*, XII, 88. Further references are given after quotations in the text.

within the residencia, she dresses with 'something of her mother's coquetry, and love of positive colour' (211). But the burden of inheritance lies heavily on her. 'Have you', she asks the officer,

> seen the portraits in the house of my fathers? Have you looked at my mother or at Felipe? Have your eyes ever rested on that picture that hangs by your bed? She who sat for it died ages ago; and she did evil in her life. But look again: there is my hand to the least line, there are my eyes and my hair. What is mine, then, and what am I? (226).

What, indeed? Is she Olalla, an individual made up of an amalgam of all her ancestors? Or is she, as Henry Jekyll writes that he is, 'a mere polity of multifarious, incongruous and independent denizens' (82), one of whom is Olalla? In her opinion she is the latter; and she tells the officer so after the Señora has bitten him. As he lies on his bed she takes his hand and places it on her heart.

> 'There!' she cried, 'you feel the very footfall of my life. It only moves for you; it is yours. But is it even mine? It is mine indeed to offer you, [...] as I might break a live branch from a tree, and give it you. And yet not mine! I dwell, or I think I dwell (if I exist at all), somewhere apart, an impotent prisoner, and carried about and deafened by a mob that I disown' (225).

Here Stevenson is moving beyond the benign image of his grandfather handing on his arthritic knuckles, or his taste for port; or beyond even the equally benign image of Probably Arboreal chattering away in the old man's brain as he sits in his study composing a sermon. In Olalla we find an individual under siege, and in constant danger of defeat, by the blood which bred her. In fact she has accepted defeat:

> The hands of the dead are in my bosom; they move me, they pluck me, they guide me; I am a puppet at their command; and I but re-inform features and attributes that have long been laid aside from evil in the quiet of the grave (226–27).

But her inherited features are an asset; and she could either rise above her attributes, or at least keep them under control by a mixture of outdoor exercise, cold showers, good works, and prayers before bed. Why, then, this defeatism? The reason is twofold.

First, her passion for the officer is immediate and overwhelming, and of a nature that bothers even him:

> Was this love? or was it a mere brute attraction, mindless and inevitable, like that of the magnet for the steel? [...] I thought how sharp must be her mortification, that she, the student, the recluse [...], should have thus confessed an overweening weakness for a man with whom she had never exchanged a word (214–15).

Before the end of the tale he will come to view this brute attraction in a different light. The fact remains, however, that Olalla is powerless before this influence (whatever it is), and, whereas Henry Jekyll's response to his troublesome passions is to separate himself physically from the passions themselves, Olalla's only remedy is to separate herself physically from the object of her awakened passion, and to send the officer away.

The second reason for Olalla's defeat lies not with her body but with her mind, or, more precisely, with her understanding of the process of inheritance. She has stood apart from herself, and viewed her own existence as a mere drop in the biological ocean that is her family, or 'race'. In 'The Manse' Stevenson approaches this process from the point of view of the individual. He writes that he (Stevenson) was present at significant moments in the lives of his ancestors, but has simply forgotten. 'I have forgotten, but I was there all the same' (90), he writes, meaning that he is made up of all of his ancestors; and although their looks, tastes, and mannerisms continue to manifest themselves in him, their history needs to be recovered consciously through stories, histories, and literature. He continues:

> But our ancestral adventures are beyond even the arithmetic of fancy; and it is the chief recommendation of long pedigrees, that we can [...] be reminded of our ante-natal lives (91).

But then he shifts suddenly from the point of view of the individual, to an assessment of the individual's place in the process which produced him:

> Our conscious years are but a moment in the history of the elements that build us (91).

Put that way, it sounds rather grand – that, just as we have been fashioned over centuries by the romantic, or adventurous, or exotic, or quaint, or wonderful lives of those who went before us and continue to live in us, so we in our turn will remit our bodies to the dust, but continue to live on in our descendants, thus achieving a kind of immortality. It is as if there were some kind of purposive intelligence moving ever forward through the generations.

Put another way, it is a nightmare. Having declared herself a puppet in the hands of her ancestors, Olalla asks the officer:

> Is it me you love, friend? or the race that made me? The girl who does not know and cannot answer for the least portion of herself? or the stream of which she is a transitory eddy, the tree of which she is the passing fruit? The race exists; it is old, it is ever young, it carries its eternal destiny in its bosom; upon it, like waves upon the sea, individual succeeds individual, mocked with a semblance of self-control, but they are nothing (227).

If the race is the true ongoing entity, and the individual nothing, what is the status of the body of the individual? We gain our first clue with the officer's musings on the dark lady of the portrait. He recognizes the evil in her face, but he is seduced by her beauty:

> Day after day the double knowledge of her wickedness and my weakness grew clearer. She came to be the heroine of many day-dreams, in which her eyes led on to, and sufficiently rewarded, crimes. She cast a dark shadow on my fancy; and when I was out in the free air of heaven, taking vigorous exercise […], it was often a glad thought to me that my enchantress was safe in her grave, her wand of beauty broken, her lips closed in silence, her philtre spilt. And yet I had a half-lingering terror that she might not be dead after all, but re-arisen in the body of some descendant (184).

Is this reincarnation? Yes; but who, or what, is reincarnating? The dark lady? Or the family? Olalla provides the answer. She tells the officer:

> Individual succeeds to individual, mocked with a semblance of self-control, but they are nothing. We speak of the soul, but the soul is in the race (227).

As far as the race-soul is concerned, then, the body is simply a vehicle which it fashions for itself over and over again in order to achieve its purpose:

in the case of the women it fashions beautiful and sensual bodies in order to snare men. Stevenson appears to have regarded the soul as a thing dynamic, able to project itself like an aura, and able to influence other souls in its vicinity. Hyde's presence causes others to feel rage, disgust, loathing, fear, depression, and hatred. Likewise the race-soul of Olalla – which in the image of the dark lady of the portrait has filled the officer's mind with daydreams worthy of the basest villain – fastens on the soul of the officer like some kind of burrowing parasite. At first he feels simply the magic and wonder of his first meeting with Olalla:

> Surprise transfixed me; her loveliness struck to my heart; she glowed in the deep shadow of the gallery, a gem of colour; her eyes took hold upon mine and clung there, and bound us together like the joining of hands; and the moments we thus stood face to face, drinking each other in, were sacramental and the wedding of souls (208).

However, when he returns to his room and remembers the moment, he realizes that he has not fallen in love with Olalla so much as been overcome by the power of her soul:

> The thrill of her young life, strung like a wild animal's, had entered into me; the force of soul that had looked out from her eyes and conquered mine, mantled about my heart and sprang to my lips in singing. She passed through my veins: she was one with me (209).

But whereas the decadent soul of the race is strong in Olalla, and ever-watchful for the opportunity to reincarnate itself, the love of God is equally strong, leaving Olalla even more divided than Henry Jekyll. Rather than surrender to the brute passion that has grown between them, she determines to send the officer away. As she approaches the officer, Stevenson yet again stresses her intense vitality:

> She seemed in her walking a creature of such life and fire and lightness as amazed me; yet she came quietly and slowly. Her energy was in the slowness (216).

She sends him away; but when he holds out his arms and calls her name she rushes back and embraces him. The ensuing sequence reads much like the sequence in which Jekyll takes the potion for the first time.

Following the drinking of the draught Jekyll feels elation. So too does the officer, following the passionate embrace. Jekyll writes:

> There was something strange in my sensations, something incredibly new and, from its very novelty, incredibly sweet. I felt younger, lighter, happier in body (83).

The officer writes:

> I stood and shouted to the mountains; I turned and went back towards the residencia, walking upon air. [...] And once more the whole countenance of nature [...] began to stir before me and to put on the lineaments of life and wear a face of awful joy (218).

However, Jekyll's sweet new sensations are tainted:

> [W]ithin I was conscious of a heady recklessness, a current of disordered sensual images running like a mill race in my fancy, a solution of the bonds of obligation, an unknown but not an innocent freedom of the soul (83).

And the officer is beginning to burst with passions more akin to those of a Wild Man:

> I felt a thrill of travail and delight run through the earth. Something elemental, something rude, violent, and savage, in the love that sang in my heart, was like a key to nature's secrets; and the very stones that rattled under my feet appeared alive and friendly. Olalla! Her touch had quickened, and renewed, and strung me up to the old pitch of concert with the rugged earth, to a swelling of the soul that men learn to forget in their polite assemblies (218–19).

Hyde stands 'exulting' (84) in the new sensation of being undivided evil; but the officer exults in the wildly divergent passions which the divided Olalla's embrace has unleashed. His own better part responds to her purity; but his own lower self responds violently to the primitive forces at work within her:

> Love burned in me like rage; tenderness waxed fierce; I hated, I adored, I pitied, I revered her with ecstasy. She seemed the link that bound me in with dead things on the one hand, and with our pure and pitying God upon the other; a thing brutal and divine, and akin at once to the innocence and to the unbridled forces of the earth (219).

In both instances Hyde and the officer are responding to the mysterious force that lies at the heart of *Jekyll and Hyde* and 'Olalla' – a force that
is at once vital to a degree unknown to modern civilized humanity, and
yet at the same time evil. Jekyll describes an 'unknown but not an innocent freedom of the soul' (83); and the officer declares of Olalla: 'I could
not doubt but that I loved her at first sight, and already with a quivering
ardour that was strange to my experience' (209). What is this strange and
unknown force? In Hyde it is 'the raging energies of life' (95); in Olalla it
is 'the most exuberant energies of life' (209).

Whatever it is, it accumulates. The old Padre tells the officer that the
Señora was more normal in her younger days, although already exhibiting
traits observable in her father and his forebears. 'But', he adds, 'these things
go on growing, not only in the individual but in the race' (232).[20] That
which is handed on, constantly growing as each new generation inherits
part of all the lives before it, is the inherited experience of the race, all the
way back to Probably Arboreal. In 'Pastoral' Stevenson presents this process with a child-like wonder:

> [I]n all our veins there run some minims of his old, wild, tree-top blood; our civilised
> nerves still tingle with his rude terrors and pleasures; and to that which would have
> moved our common ancestor, all must obediently thrill (81–82).

But in *Jekyll and Hyde* he shows it in its full horror. Jekyll describes
the existence of Hyde, who contains nothing but negative qualities:

> I would leap almost without transition [...] into the possession of a fancy brimming
> with images of terror, a soul boiling with causeless hatreds, and a body that seemed
> not strong enough to contain the raging energies of life (95).

One could argue that Hyde's 'images of terror' are simply 'the terrors of
the scaffold' (91), which in part they would be. But they could also be the
'rude terrors' of Jekyll's ancestors which live on in his more primitive self.
Likewise Hyde's 'causeless hatreds' could be inherited, since, as they are
causeless, nothing in Jekyll's life has prompted them. The 'raging energies

---

20   This is the same process at work in the Yahoos.

of life' could be the desires and impulses inherited from countless ancestors, both brute and human.

Olalla likewise describes her predicament from her own viewpoint:

> I dwell, or I think I dwell (if I exist at all), somewhere apart, an impotent prisoner, and carried about and deafened by a mob that I disown (225).

Overwhelmed by the presence of her clamouring ancestors, Olalla is driven to the realization that everything she is – in looks, in gestures, in attitudes – everything belongs to them. She shares her body with her ancestors. 'And shall I—', she cries,

> I that dwell apart in the house of the dead, my body, loathing its ways—shall I repeat the spell? Shall I bind another spirit, reluctant as my own, into this bewitched and tempest-broken tenement that I now suffer in? (228).

Here is the paradox: that Olalla, this 'creature of such life and fire' (216), and 'the most exuberant energies of life' (209), is so strongly associated with the dead. The officer writes, 'She seemed the link that bound me in with dead things' (219). And indeed she is. She tells him:

> The hands of the dead are in my bosom; they move me, they pluck me, they guide me; I am a puppet at their command (226).

Hyde also like Olalla contains 'the raging energies of life' (95); and also like Olalla is definitively associated with the dead. Jekyll thought of Hyde,

> for all his energies of life, as of something not only hellish but inorganic. This was the shocking thing; that the slime of the pit seemed to utter cries and voices; that the amorphous dust gesticulated and sinned; that what was dead, and had no shape, should usurp the offices of life (95).

Commentators respond to this passage variously. Leonard Wolf takes the biblical approach:

> The 'slime of the pit' refers to the biblical tar pits known as the Vale of Siddim (Genesis 14.3,8,10). Finally, we note that the 'amorphous dust [that] gesticulated and

sinned' describes Adam, who was made from dust (see Genesis 4.7) and therefore, by extension, describes what all the rest of humanity is made of.[21]

Wolf has identified the biblical flavour in Stevenson's language, but, in mentioning the tar pits in the Vale of Siddim, 'which was full of slimepits' (Genesis 14.10), he has failed to grasp Stevenson's intentions. It would seem that Wolf has focused on 'slime'; whereas the real focus (as we shall see) should be on 'pit'.

Other commentators take the evolutionary approach. Lawler, for example, writes:

> [T]here is no doubt that Hyde represents pre-evolved man in his atavistic, degenerated physical and psychological state. Jekyll himself goes even further:
>   [Quotes passage.]
> Hyde appears to Jekyll so primitive as to be primordial, a lost link between the pre-animate and animate life of the mind (*100 Years*, 252).

Julia Reid sees Jekyll's horror as twofold:

> Jekyll's account is a devolutionary narrative. He portrays Hyde as atavistic [...]. Indeed, he imagines Hyde as having regressed even further down the evolutionary ladder, describing him as 'inorganic' [...]. This imagery resonates with contemporary evolutionist visions of the origins of life. [...] Interestingly, it is evolutionary progress as much as degeneration that is seen as grotesque: the 'slime of the pit ... utter[ing] cries', the inorganic becoming organic (97).

Thus we find two readings of the passage – the biblical and the scientific. Each is valid, and each complements a reading of the other. Either reading, or both together, assumes that Jekyll is thinking of Hyde as originating either at the Fall, or at the moment when the first organic material formed. Stevenson's language in both *Jekyll and Hyde* and 'Olalla' makes it clear that he intended a complementary reading. But his language in 'Olalla' makes it clear that he intended more; and suggests that he intended more in *Jekyll and Hyde* as well. Hyde is 'not only hellish but inorganic' (95), that

---

21   *The Essential Dr Jekyll and Mr Hyde*, illust. by Michael Lark (New York: Plume, 1995), p. 135, n79. Wolf's reference to *Genesis 4.7* should be 'Genesis 2.7'.

is, there are two aspects to his being: the physical and the evil. In his evil aspect he equates with the strain of evil that lurks in Olalla's family from generation to generation; an evil which is both familial and personal. In other words, one is not excused simply because one's evil is inherited – it is still one's own, even though it derives from ancestors.

The biblical and the biological readings, however, lead one to conclude that Jekyll is thinking of Hyde in his manifested form; that in the 'slime' and the 'dust' he is referring to Hyde's origins, and nothing more. That, however, may not be the case. Let us examine Stevenson's use of 'the pit'. In his letters he uses it exclusively in the biblical sense, which can at times incorporate the grave, perdition, and Hell. To Sidney Colvin he writes:

> O when shall I find the story of my dreams, that shall never halt nor wander nor step aside, but go ever before its face and ever swifter and louder, until the pit receives it, roaring?[22]

From Strathpeffer Spa he writes to James Cunningham:

> I must flee from Scotland. It is, for me, the mouth of the pit.[23]

Commenting on Edmund Gosse's biography of his father, he quotes Flaubert – 'prose is never done'. He continues:

> [I]t is *never done*; in other words, it is a torment of the pit, usually neglected by the bards who (lucky beggars!) approached the Styx in measure. I speak bitterly at the moment, having just detected in myself the last fatal symptom, three blank verses in succession – and I believe, God help me, a hemistich at the tail of them: hence I have deposed the labourer, come out of hell by my private trap, and now write to you from my little place in purgatory. But I prefer Hell: would I could always dig in these red coals.[24]

---

22   *RLS Letters*, letter 353, [14 January 1875], II, 106–07 (p. 107).
23   *RLS Letters*, letter 720, [September 1880], III, 99–100 (p. 100). Cf. Psalm 69.15: 'and let not the pit shut her mouth upon me.'
24   *RLS Letters*, letter 2313, April 1891, VII, 104–07 (p. 105).

Later in the same letter he refers to the Samoan rainy season,

> which is really a caulker for wind, wet and darkness – hurling showers, raving winds, pit-blackness at noon.[25]

In a letter to Henry James he writes:

> I am writing – trying to write in a Babel fit for the bottomless pit.[26]

And in one of his prayers written at Vailima he refers to the pit as if it were a Bunyanesque moral slough. He prays to God:

> Help us to look back on the long way that Thou hast brought us [...]; on the pit and the miry clay, the blackness of despair, the horror of misconduct, from which our feet have been plucked out.[27]

Jekyll's 'slime of the pit' has nothing to do with pits of slime: it is slime which is in the Pit, in this instance, the grave, whose Hellish connotations reinforce the sense of Hyde's evil.[28] If we look again at Olalla's speeches to the officer we see that she regards her body as 'the house of the dead' (228), in which she is 'carried about and deafened by a mob' (225); and that she simply re-informs 'features and attributes that have long been laid aside from evil in the quiet of the grave' (226–27). Jekyll's body too is a house of the dead – although, whereas Olalla regards hers as a 'tenement' (228), Jekyll prefers to think of his as a more dignified 'tabernacle' (83). Olalla is deafened by the mob of her evil ancestors, dating all the way back to their brutish state. Jekyll is deafened by the cries and whispers of his inherited evil – the slime of the pit, or the bodies of his ancestors going all the

---

25   Ibid., p. 106.
26   *RLS Letters*, letter 2374, 7 December [1891], VII, 209–11 (p. 210). The term 'bottom-less pit' occurs seven times (and nowhere else in the Bible) in the Book of Revelation, where it is used to refer specifically to Hell (9.1,2,11; 11.7; 17.8; 20.1,3).
27   'For the Family', *Works*, XXVI, 153.
28   Dury regards 'the slime of the pit' as 'the repulsive contents of Hell' (*Annotated*, p. 184, n2).

way back to Adam or Probably Arboreal.[29] These bodies have rotted and decomposed back into their constituents, and returned to the earth and slime from which they have arisen. 'The hands of the dead are in my bosom', laments Olalla, acknowledging them, 'they move me, they pluck me, they guide me; I am a puppet at their command' (226). Likewise Jekyll, still denying Hyde, laments that 'the amorphous dust gesticulated and sinned' (95). Earth to earth, ashes to ashes, dust to dust. God made Adam from the dust of the ground, and all of our ancestors have returned to dust: this is the dust that causes Jekyll's body to gesticulate and sin in the form of Hyde.[30] Olalla laments, 'I but re-inform features and attributes that have long been laid aside from evil in the quiet of the grave' (226); and Jekyll is shocked 'that what was dead, and had no shape, should usurp the offices of life' (95). Hyde is both hellish and inorganic. His elements lie in the pit of the grave with the dust and the slime; and his evil dwells in the pit of Hell where it constantly 'struggle[s] to be born' (95) into another body.

The image that we are left with, then, is a powerful blending of the biblical and the evolutionary, in which the slime (either the foamy scum of the Ancients which brings forth monstrosities; or the decomposed corpses of generations going back to the dawn of time) of the pit (either Hell or the grave; or a combination of both) calls commandingly to the one living tenant in the house of the dead; in which the amorphous dust (either the inorganic matter which has become organic; or Adam; or the dust of the dead which has returned to the earth) assembles itself again into a living body which gesticulates (like a puppet) and sins; in which the dead and shapeless (either the clay of the earth; or the features and attributes of the evil ancestors) comes to life of its own volition.

29   We should also remember that Stevenson heard his grandfather's voice: 'he moves in my blood, and whispers words to me, and sits efficient in the very knot and centre of my being' ('The Manse', p. 89).
30   Dury glosses 'amorphous dust' as, 'the remains of a dead body' (*Annotated*, p. 184, n3); and quotes Genesis 3.19: 'For dust thou art, and unto dust shalt thou return.' He regards Hyde as 'a symbol of death and decay' (*Annotated*, p. 60). See also *Annotated*, p. 184, n6.

There is a sense in which the body – and its impulses – is the dominant agent, and the conscious self a mere spectator. We can see this most clearly in a scene between Olalla and the officer in which he attempts to persuade her (with breathtaking inconsistency) that their love is more than a physical attraction. He begins by telling her,

> [W]here the body clings, the soul cleaves; body for body, soul to soul, they come together at God's signal; and the lower part (if we can call aught low) is only the foot-stool and foundation of the highest (226).

She replies that her body has been cobbled together from parts of all her ancestors, and they all inhabit it with her. 'We speak of the soul,' she says, 'but the soul is in the race' (227).

He insists that their attraction is in response to 'the common law, [...] the voice of God' (227). And here again we have that curious blending of the divine and the biological that we find in Kingsley, in which all of nature's laws are governed by God's will. Note the movement of the images: from their joined hands; to her heart; to their separate and then combined elements; to the clay of the earth; to the stars in space; all, as Stevenson well knew (and expressed earlier in 'Pulvis et Umbra'), composed of the same dust:

> Your hand clings to mine, your heart leaps at my touch, the unknown elements of which we are compounded awake and run together at a look; the clay of the earth remembers its independent life and yearns to join us; we are drawn together as the stars are turned about in space, or as the tides ebb and flow, by things older and greater than ourselves (227).[31]

This curious example of Scottish wooing would hardly set Olalla's mind at rest; the officer is simply repeating all of her fears back to her, but viewing them in a positive light; and, despite the nod in God's direction, the

---

31   The officer relates an earlier scene in which the biblical, the Platonic, and the natural are all brought together in a Kingsleyan moment: "'Nature,' I told her, "was the voice of God, which men disobey at peril; and if we were thus dumbly drawn together, ay, even as by a miracle of love, it must imply a divine fitness in our souls'" (217).

picture which he paints is one of mindless organisms impelled by cosmic forces. The 'unknown elements' which compound them consist on the one hand of the features, attributes, memories, and inclinations passed down through the generations;[32] but they also consist of the physical elements that make up their bodies. Both senses are present, but the dominant one is the physical, which then leads into the 'clay of the earth'. The clay of course is loaded with biblical meaning; and here it – and not the soul – is the active agent in this cosmic marriage. Here the clay – like Jekyll's 'slime of the pit' and 'amorphous dust' which struggle 'to be born' – remembers its independent life: it remembers the countless times in which it has moved and sensed and been aware as part of a body, no matter whether animal or human. The clay – which is a malignant presence in both *Jekyll and Hyde* and 'Olalla' – 'yearns to join' Olalla and the officer. 'Join' here is an ambiguous word: it can mean that the clay simply wishes to commune with them and partake vicariously in their existence. But given the context, the meaning is clear – the clay wants them to join in sexual union, to produce another organism in which the clay may once again enjoy its independent life. Olalla's reply renders this meaning unequivocal:

> And shall I—I that dwell apart in the house of the dead, my body, loathing its ways— shall I repeat the spell? Shall I bind another spirit, reluctant as my own, into this bewitched and tempest-broken tenement that I now suffer in? Shall I hand down this cursed vessel of humanity, charge it with fresh life as with fresh poison, and dash it, like a fire, in the faces of posterity? (228).

At this point Olalla is fighting on two fronts in a very complicated battle for her body. We recall that when the officer first sees the portrait of the dark lady, he is attracted by her beauty but repelled by the aura of evil about her. But over the next few days he begins to be seduced by, and to dwell upon, the lure of that very evil. Having been given a taste for it in his fancy, he immediately responds to it in the flesh of Olalla; and the portrait loses its hold on him. One should not, however, overlook the fact

---

32   'Our conscious years are but a moment in the history of the elements that build us' ('The Manse', p. 91).

that, while the officer is falling in love with Olalla, the more potent attraction is between their respective 'unknown elements' which have awoken to each other: she is not the only one with a long ancestry. Nor is she the only puppet living with a mob in the house of the dead.

The officer is besotted with Olalla, but equally repelled by the savagery and madness in her blood. However, he allows his infatuation to overrule his judgment. Having had his elements awakened, he unwittingly becomes their puppet in his attempts to seduce Olalla away from her resolve. She thus has to struggle to subdue not only her own demons, and her feelings for the officer, but also the passionate advances which her own dark nature has inspired. Besotted though she may be with the officer, she is more horrified by the evil in her blood. With Christ as her example, and, at the end literally, her support, she chooses a life of celibate renunciation: 'the race shall cease from off the earth' (228).

At the end Olalla and the officer stand together at the foot of a life-size crucifix on the rocky ledge of a hill overlooking the residencia. By now we know that the line is tainted, and that the taint keeps on growing both in the line and in each individual during his or her lifetime; therefore Olalla herself is likely to deteriorate as she ages (although this possibility is not mentioned in the text). Still the officer importunes her yet again. She places her hand upon the cross. 'Behold', she tells him,

> the face of the Man of Sorrows. We are all such as He was—the inheritors of sin; we must all bear and expiate a past which was not ours; there is in all of us—ay, even in me—a sparkle of the divine. Like Him, we must endure for a little while, until morning returns bringing peace. Suffer me to pass on upon my way alone; it is thus that I shall be least lonely, counting for my friend Him who is the friend of all the distressed, it is thus that I shall be the most happy, having taken my farewell of earthly happiness, and willingly accepted sorrow for my portion (238).

The officer gazes up at the crucifix:

> The face looked down upon me with a painful and deadly contraction; but the rays of a glory encircled it, and reminded me that the sacrifice was voluntary. It stood there, crowning the rock, [...] an emblem of sad and noble truths; that pleasure is not an end, but an accident; that pain is the choice of the magnanimous; that it is best to suffer all things and do well. I turned and went down the mountain in silence; and

when I looked back for the last time before the wood closed about my path, I saw Olalla still leaning on the crucifix (239).

Olalla has come in for some criticism for her stand. Eigner writes that her theology is 'twisted' (211); Block writes that her 'interpretation of Christ is idiosyncratic' (*Rituals*, p. 158); Reid finds her version of Christianity 'warped' (88).[33] Likewise, no one is very happy with the officer. Block finds him 'almost indifferent', and 'passive' (*Rituals*, p. 160); Reid thinks that he 'acts fairly unheroically' (88). What, then, is going on in this crucial final scene?

By the time that Olalla and the officer come to stand on the hill by the crucifix, they are highly ambiguous figures. She is the virgin penitent embodiment of an evil and decadent line. He is the thrall to an aura of sin, bent on drawing her unwillingly deeper into its power so that it can pass itself on to another generation.

Olalla's invocation of Christ serves a double purpose. Her first point is, 'We are all such as He was—the inheritors of sin' (238). By this she is not seeking to identify with Christ, but to cite him as an example – the only example – of the point which she wishes to make: by incarnating, Christ took on sin which was not his. Olalla's sin is not hers (because she did not incur it herself), and yet it becomes hers (because she shares her body with it; in fact it makes up her body). Sin and evil (whether from the Fall or from our bestial ancestry) is a fact of our existence. It lives inside us, as Hyde lives in Jekyll. Having become hers, it then goes on to make her sin further. From this it follows that 'we must all bear and expiate a past which was not ours' (238). We must acknowledge the wrong done by our ancestors, and acknowledge our potential to repeat it. We must bear the burden of our collective individual taint, and endeavour to expiate it by curbing its appetites at all times, until the vessel that holds it returns to the dust and sets the suffering individual free. Jekyll provides an example of what happens when we unleash the evil; Olalla provides an example of self-containment through abandonment to a higher power.

---

33 For their complete arguments on this point, see Eigner (210–11); Block (*Rituals*, pp. 157–60); Reid (88).

Viewed in this light, we can see the officer's 'passivity' as a genuine acceptance and approval of her position. Admiring her resolve and her faith in Christ's example, he quietly departs, leaving her in communion with her saviour.

There is, of course, another way of viewing the scene. If we step back and regard the iconography which Stevenson establishes, we see Christ on the cross on a hill, flanked by two sinners, one of whom is penitent, and one of whom is not. Can it be that, in the officer, Stevenson has given us another narrator whose witness is just as unreliable as Henry Jekyll's? If Olalla is identified with the good thief, and the officer is identified with the bad thief, then 'Olalla' becomes the story of the self-deluded officer's fall from grace, and subsequent perdition.

If we look at the narrative arc we see the officer's bestial side being awakened by the dark lady of the portrait. Later when he meets Olalla he loves her 'at first sight [...] with a quivering ardour [...] strange to [his] experience' (209). After their first embrace he feels within himself 'something elemental, something rude, violent, and savage' (219). As he is drawn further into this elemental vortex, his attitude towards his feelings changes. He is 'unpleasantly attracted' (183) by the dark lady's portrait, but, as he writes: 'its beauty crept about my heart insidiously, silencing my scruples one after another' (184). After his first meeting with Olalla, despite falling in love with her, his soul is 'besieged by cold and sorrowful considerations' (209). At their second meeting, although he is drawn to her 'like a magnet', he is held back by 'something yet more imperious' (211). But by now he is in thrall, and as he considers their situation afterwards, he comes to a decision: 'All side considerations fell off from me; were she the child of Herod I swore I should make her mine' (212). After their third intense, silent, and unfulfilling meeting he has a moment of petulant vanity as he dwells on the nature of their relationship:

> Of me, she knew nothing but my bodily favour; she was drawn to me as stones fall to earth; the laws that rule the earth conducted her, unconsenting, to my arms; and I drew back at the thought of such a bridal, and began to be jealous for myself. It was not thus that I desired to be loved (215).

But then, at their next meeting, when she unexpectedly tells him to go away, he pours out a succession of desperate lovelorn promises, 'And then, strongly commanding [him]self, [he] change[s] the note' (217). He then attempts to win her around by using exactly the same argument which he has recently found so personally offensive:

> 'Nature,' I told her, 'was the voice of God, which men disobey at peril; and if we were thus dumbly drawn together, ay, even as by a miracle of love, it must imply a divine fitness in our souls; we must be made,' I said—'made for one another. We should be mad rebels,' I cried out —'mad rebels against God, not to obey this instinct' (217).

The officer's infatuation thus makes him sophistically attribute to God the very process which he has always found so questionable.

Olalla is then left to choose between the officer's God of nature, and her own God of Heaven. It is, after all, nature that she is trying to overcome. Again she looks to Christ as an example: by his suffering he overcame death. She, by her renunciation of happiness, will overcome the dead, who, paradoxically, live again through the living. But the officer is now in thrall to the dead, and can gain only 'some sense' (239) of Christ's importance. Whereas Olalla apprehends all of Christ's religious significance for the sinner, the officer can only appreciate him as a noble example of a life well-lived.

Olalla's rejection of the officer signifies more than a triumph over the flesh; she has, in a sense, broken the family curse. The officer is not the first to be drawn into the family's clutches. Just before Olalla's arrival at the crucifix, the officer has been talking with an old friend of Olalla's father, who describes their last fateful meeting at the residencia many years before:

> I took him by the arm, Señor, and dragged him to the gate; I conjured him, by all he loved and respected, to go forth with me; I went on my knees before him in the snow; and I could see he was moved by my entreaty. And just then she came out on the gallery, and called him by his name; and he turned, and there was she standing with a lamp in her hand and smiling on him to come back. I cried out aloud to God, and threw my arms about him, but he put me by, and left me alone (235).

In this moment of high melodrama we see the pattern emerge of generational temptation by the women of the house, and the corruption, degeneration, and eventual destruction of their hapless consorts. The Señora employs her sensuality willingly, and the clay fashions itself into more vessels for the dead to share with the willing. The men, once drawn in, lack the strength to resist; and only Olalla has the power to break the cycle, overcoming both her own sensual impulses, and the increasingly desperate urgings of her victim-turned-pursuer, whose life she has probably saved, but whose soul he has probably lost.

Whatever its final meaning, 'Olalla' shows us that Hyde embodies the clamorous residue of Jekyll's ancestry, both moral and biological. Paradoxically, the 'energies of life' (95) which Hyde contains are in fact the seemingly immortal accumulated memories and experiences of the dead which survive in the living; and since by their very nature they represent the most intense memories and experiences, they constitute the more vital part of the individual. Jekyll's insight, 'the doom and burthen of our life is bound for ever on man's shoulders' (83), is true, because each new generation inherits it. But Jekyll is just an ordinary middle-aged urban professional, who is keen to indulge his sensual side, while anxious to preserve his public image. Olalla, however, is a Child of Nature – the symbol and embodiment of purity and virtue. We recall Fairchild's definition: the Child of Nature

> is born and grows to maturity in the heart of some wild region untouched by civilization, and [...] imbibes beauty, innocence and an unerring moral sense from the scenery which surrounds her (366).

In the Platonic system beauty is indicative of a pure soul; therefore Olalla's soul is pure, as Anthelia Melincourt's soul is pure. But Olalla's pure soul has incarnated along with the oppressive baggage of her evil ancestors; and she shares her body with them. Olalla's case is therefore the most extreme example possible of the duality which afflicts Stevenson's characters. If even she, a long-established symbol of innocence and purity, is found to be infected with the curse of ancestral sin, then none can escape.

Jekyll comes to recognize that Hyde is the embodiment not of an individual self, but of the compound presence of Jekyll's ancestors. This compound presence is composed of two aspects: the physical and the moral. Hyde is 'much smaller, slighter, and younger' (84) than Jekyll. Jekyll explains this by saying that Hyde had been relatively dormant. However, Hyde also exhibits signs of 'decay' (84). There is, then, something about Hyde that is both young and old. Olalla says, 'The race exists; it is old, it is ever young [...]. We speak of the soul, but the soul is in the race' (227). Jekyll shares his body with his race-soul and its accumulated evil. This race-soul is what Jekyll refers to as 'lower elements in [his] soul' (83). Hyde is the Platonic 'expression' (83) of these elements.

Hyde's troglodytic appearance reflects the increasingly ape-like presence of Jekyll's early ancestors. This presence is not necessarily a bad thing. In 'The Manse' and 'Pastoral' Stevenson presents Probably Arboreal as a pleasant enough fellow. Likewise, in 'Olalla', when the officer takes Felipe for a walk in the woods, Felipe scampers about like a monkey. The officer reports:

> I have rarely enjoyed more stirring company; the sight of his delight was a continual feast; the speed and accuracy of his movements pleased me to the heart (187).

But when Felipe proceeds to torture a squirrel, and the officer turns on him in anger, Felipe begs for mercy and forgiveness:

> Oh, commandante, bear with Felipe this once; he will never be a brute again! (188).

Here we find a clear distinction between behaving like a primitive man, and behaving like a brute; between natural behaviour and evil behaviour.

An examination of *Jekyll and Hyde* in the light shed by 'Olalla' allows a fuller understanding of both the origins and the persistence of the living force which manifests itself as Hyde. His hairiness signifies the presence of ancient inherited characteristics and tendencies which, although they might be primitive or Wild, are not necessarily evil, and can be exhilarating. His disquieting aspect is not his Darwinian apishness, but his Platonic unspecified deformity, which arises, as it does with the Yahoos, from his moral turpitude. He is thus at once both archaic and evil; at once both Darwinian and Christiano-Platonic. He is Probably Arboreal and he is Adam; and he is their combined dust which frets impatiently to be born in each new generation.

Conclusion

Stevenson's copious supper of bread and jam proved to be a nourishing meal indeed, fuelling as it did his sleeping imagination, and giving him the germ of his most famous story. The publication of *Jekyll and Hyde* brought him popular success, critical acclaim, and enough money to liberate himself from his father's oppressive benevolence. The success of *Jekyll and Hyde* has led to stage productions; films; radio and television adaptations; retellings and variations on the theme; and it has led to 'Jekyll and Hyde' becoming a proverbial expression throughout the world. It has also, of course, provided fruitful soil for scholars.

In producing a tale which explores the duality of the human condition, Stevenson has left popular culture with a great 'shilling shocker', and left scholars in many fields with a text whose depths reward serious analysis.

But in the popular imagination what remains of Stevenson's original conception, beyond the smoking potion and the evil self? Each new adaptation, each new retelling serves merely to dilute the original – to distort it somewhat, in much the same way that in the parlour game the message, 'The General is going to advance, send reinforcements', becomes, 'The General is going to a dance, send three-and-fourpence.' Hyde, disconnected from the signifiers which Stevenson attached to him, can now be represented in any way, and given any meaning that the latest adaptation requires. He has, for example, emerged as 'a flamboyant ladykiller', 'a sexy, self-possessed knockout of a woman, with dark hair and high cheekbones', and 'a towering, bald-headed ghoul'.[1] He has also – in a 'characterization based on Dean Martin' – appeared as 'handsome but vulgar'.[2]

---

[1]   Linehan, *Jekyll*, pp. 172; 173; 174. See *Robert Louis Stevenson's The Strange Case of Dr Jekyll and Mr Hyde*, dir. by Charles Jarrott (USA/Canada, 1968); *Dr Jekyll and Sister Hyde*, dir. by Roy Ward Baker (UK, 1971); *Jekyll and Hyde*, dir. by David Wickes (UK, 1990).

[2]   Dury, *Annotated*, p. 199. See *The Nutty Professor*, dir. by Jerry Lewis (USA, 1963).

One could argue that the meaning of the story – no matter how corrupted a new version may be – always remains essentially the same, namely, that we have an evil self within us, and if we allow it licence it will become uncontrollable. This is true enough; but it is hardly an original insight, and its impact has been somewhat dampened for the modern reader by the events of the twentieth century.

Scholarship on *Jekyll and Hyde* has been extensive, far-ranging, and formidable, and shows no signs of either flagging, or declining in insight or originality of thought. Stevenson's contemporaries analysed it from within their own cultural milieu, using the resources available at the time. The modern scholar may legitimately and fruitfully analyse it as a text which reveals Stevenson's personality, or the society of his day, using scientific, sociological, psychological, political, and theoretical frameworks which were not available to him. In so doing, the scholar not only interprets Stevenson's text, but is able also to employ the text as a resource to illuminate concerns relative to it, rather than central to it.

The aim of this book, however, has been to return to an understanding of the figure of Edward Hyde as he would have appeared to the readers of Stevenson's time – a figure of evil, certainly, but a figure of evil whose apelike appearance invoked Darwin's theory of natural selection; whose deformity drew ultimately on the Platonic tradition; and whose evil was contextualized by the use of biblical language.

Those scholars who address such matters (apart from the exceptions noted previously) tend to approach Hyde from either a Darwinian or a biblical viewpoint, arguing that Darwinism is antagonistic to religious belief, therefore Hyde belongs to either one or the other camp. Meanwhile the Platonism underlying Stevenson's conception has remained largely unexamined. We should not forget that Darwinism is also antagonistic to the Platonic science which dominated evolutionary debate in the nineteenth century; therefore, again, Hyde should be either Darwinian or Platonic. Nor should we forget that, although Christianity has absorbed some key Platonic concepts regarding the soul, it has also rejected others of equal importance – one being the belief in reincarnation. Yet a clergyman like Donne happily employs this concept in a poem which begins in the Garden of Eden. A compartmentalized approach cannot comprehend either the origin or the meaning of Hyde, because Stevenson, like Kingsley before him, ignores any perceived contradictions, and creatively blends these themes to arrive at a conception which incorporates all three.

Hyde is hairy: but is it because he represents Probably Arboreal; or because he represents Esau? Hyde is amorphous dust: but is it because he is as old as inorganic matter; or because he is as old as Adam? Hyde is deformed: but is it because he has departed from the image of God; or because he is the Platonic reflection of a foul soul; or because he is simply shaped more like an ape than a human? The answer of course is that he is at once Probably Arboreal and Esau; he is inorganic matter and Adam (and, for that matter, Eve); and his deformity can be explained in all the ways just mentioned. Thus Hyde appears as a baffling and unsettling figure, whose origins remain mysterious and conjectural precisely because they embrace so many possibilities – possibilities which are at once both cumulative and oppositional. He is greater than the sum of his parts precisely because those parts, like Jacob and Esau, were continually struggling in the agonized womb of Stevenson's consciousness,[3] and that of the readers of his day.

Stevenson was neither a scientist, a philosopher, nor a theologian. He read science, philosophy, and the Bible; but he used them to feed his writing. This review also has been neither scientific, philosophical, nor theological; it has proceeded from an examination of some of the literature which precedes and throws light on *Jekyll and Hyde*.

The greatest light which must be shed, however, is Stevenson's use of Platonism to explain Hyde. Jekyll's science is Platonic; Hyde's presence in Jekyll is Platonic; his deformity is Platonic; his effect on other people is Platonic; his physical growth over time is Platonic; and the eventual dominance of his form is Platonic. Platonism therefore not only lies at the heart of *Jekyll and Hyde*, but it determines the narrative as well.

Hyde is a violent Wild Man. He is primitive and apelike, yet sophisticated in his tastes and behaves like a gentleman when the need arises. He is thoroughly evil, yet possesses the discretion to curb his malice in public (most of the time). All of his impulses are towards self-gratification at the

3   See *Jekyll and Hyde*, p. 82.

expense of others; yet on most occasions he must keep them under control. In his own way he is as divided as Henry Jekyll. In his Statement Jekyll writes that 'man is not truly one, but truly two' (82). But he immediately qualifies that proposition: 'I hazard the guess that man will be ultimately known for a mere polity of multifarious, incongruous and independent denizens' (82). Hyde is not simply one of these denizens; he is 'the expression' of 'lower elements' in Jekyll's soul (83). In other words, as Stevenson's other writings – especially 'Olalla' – make clear, he is a compound presence. Hyde is composed of the residue of all of Jekyll's ancestors, going all the way back to the beginnings of life. Not only is he the biological residue of Jekyll's ancestors, but Stevenson's essays make it clear that he is also their psychological and cultural residue as well, living on and accumulating from generation to generation.

T.H. Huxley begins one of his essays with a quotation which is applicable to the present argument:

> It has been well said that 'all the thoughts of men, from the beginning of the world until now, are linked together into one great chain'.[4]

The image of course relies on the reader's familiarity with the Great Chain of Being. Instead of visualizing a chain in which a succession of discrete thoughts are joined together, Huxley envisages a continuous flow of thoughts which interact and blend with each other, as organisms on the Great Chain share aspects of each other in their upward and downward progression. And so it is with Edward Hyde, whose link in the great chain of Stevenson's thought is not discrete, but related to all the other links which came before it.

---

4   'On Descartes' "Discourse Touching the Method of Using One's Reason Rightly and of Seeking Scientific Truth"', *Method and Results, Collected Essays*, I, 166–98 (p. 166). Huxley gives no reference for this quotation. I have been unable to locate his source.

Bibliography

Agar, Herbert, *Milton and Plato* (Gloucester, Mass.: Princeton University Press, 1928; repr. Smith, 1965)

Anon., 'Secret Sin', *The Rock* (2 April 1886), 3

—— Unsigned review of *Jekyll and Hyde*, *The Times* (25 January 1886), 13

Arata, Stephen D., 'The Sedulous Ape: Atavism, Professionalism, and Stevenson's *Jekyll and Hyde*', *Criticism*, 37 (1995), 233–59

Arnold, Matthew, *The Complete Prose Works of Matthew Arnold*, ed. by R.H. Super, 11 vols (Ann Arbor: University of Michigan Press, 1960–77)

Bage, Robert, *Hermsprong: or, Man as He Is Not*, ed. and intro. by Vaughan Wilkins (London: Turnstile Press, 1951)

Bald, R.C., *John Donne: A Life* (Oxford: Clarendon Press, 1970)

Baldwin, Anna, and Sarah Hutton, eds, *Platonism and the English Imagination* (Cambridge: Cambridge University Press, 1994; repr. 2004)

Bartra, Roger, *The Artificial Savage: Modern Myths of the Wild Man*, trans. by Christopher Follett (Ann Arbor: University of Michigan Press, 1997)

Beeckman, Daniel, *A Voyage to and from the Island of Borneo, in the East Indies* (1718), In *A General Collection of the Best and Most Interesting Voyages and Travels in All Parts of the World*, ed. by John Pinkerton, 17 vols (1808–14) (London: Longman and others, 1812), XI, 96–158

Beer, Gillian, *Darwin's Plots: Evolutionary Narrative in Darwin, George Eliot and Nineteenth-Century Fiction* (London: Routledge & Kegan Paul, 1983)

Bennett, George, *Wanderings in New South Wales, Batavia, Pedir Coast, Singapore, and China: Being the Journal of a Naturalist in Those Countries, during 1832, 1833, and 1834*, 2 vols (London: Bentley, 1834)

Bennett, Josephine Waters, 'Spenser's Venus and the Goddess Nature of the *Cantos of Mutabilitie*', *Studies in Philology*, 30 (1933), 160–92

—— 'Milton's use of the Vision of Er', *Modern Philology*, 36 (1939), 351–58

Bernheimer, Richard, *Wild Men in the Middle Ages: A Study in Art, Sentiment, and Demonology* (New York: Octagon, 1970)

Bibby, Cyril, *Scientist Extraordinary: The Life and Scientific Work of Thomas Henry Huxley* (Oxford: Pergamon Press, 1972)

Bisset, Archibald, 'Personal Reminiscences of the University Life of Robert Louis Stevenson', in *I Can Remember Robert Louis Stevenson*, ed. by Rosaline Masson (Edinburgh and London: Chambers, 1922), pp. 48–56

Block, Ed. Jr, 'James Sully, Evolutionist Psychology, and Late Victorian Gothic Fiction', *Victorian Studies*, 25 (1982), 443–67

—— *Rituals of Dis-Integration: Romance and Madness in the Victorian Psychomythic Tale* (New York and London: Garland, 1993)

Bloom, Allan, 'An Outline of *Gulliver's Travels*', in *Ancients and Moderns: Essays on the Tradition of Political Philosophy in Honour of Leo Strauss*, ed. by Joseph Cropsey (New York: Basic Books, 1964), pp. 238–57

Bloomfield, Anne, 'Muscular Christian or Mystic? Charles Kingsley Reappraised', *International Journal of the History of Sport*, 11 (1994), 172–90

Brantlinger, Patrick, and Richard Boyle, 'The Education of Edward Hyde: Stevenson's "Gothic Gnome" and the Mass Readership of Late-Victorian England', in *Dr Jekyll and Mr Hyde after One Hundred Years*, ed. by William Veeder and Gordon Hirsch (Chicago: University of Chicago Press, 1988), pp. 265–82

Briggs, Julia, *Night Visitors: The Rise and Fall of the English Ghost Story* (London: Faber, 1977)

Bulger, Thomas, 'Platonism in Spenser's *Mutabilitie Cantos*', in *Platonism and the English Imagination*, ed. by Anna Baldwin and Sarah Hutton (Cambridge: Cambridge University Press, 1994; repr. 2004), pp. 126–38

Butler, Marilyn, *Peacock Displayed: A Satirist in his Context* (London: Routledge & Kegan Paul, 1979)

Canfield, J. Douglas, 'Corruption and Degeneration in *Gulliver's Travels*', *Notre Dame English Journal*, 9 (1973), 15–22

Cannon, Walter F., 'Darwin's Vision in *On the Origin of Species*', in *The Art of Victorian Prose*, ed. by George Levine and William Madden (New York, London, Toronto: Oxford University Press, 1968), pp. 154–76

Carlyle, Thomas, *Past and Present* (London: Oxford University Press, 1960)

Chaucer, Geoffrey, *The Works of Geoffrey Chaucer*, ed. by F.N. Robinson, 2nd edn (London: Oxford University Press, 1966; repr. 1974)

Chesterton, G.K., *Robert Louis Stevenson*, 3rd edn (London: Hodder and Stoughton, 1929)

Chitty, Susan, *The Beast and the Monk: A Life of Charles Kingsley* (London: Hodder and Stoughton, 1975)

Clifford, James L., 'The Eighteenth Century', *Modern Language Quarterly*, 26 (1965), 111–34

Cloyd, Emily L., *James Burnet* [*sic*]: *Lord Monboddo* (Oxford: Clarendon Press, 1972)

Cockburn, Henry, *Lord Cockburn's Works: Vol 2, Memorials of His Time* (Edinburgh: Black, 1872)

Cropsey, Joseph, ed., *Ancients and Moderns: Essays on the Tradition of Political Philosophy in Honour of Leo Strauss* (New York: Basic Books, 1964)

Cruse, Amy, *The Victorians And Their Books* (London: Allen & Unwin, 1962)

Dale, Mrs, 'Fresh Side-Lights on R.L.S.', in *I Can Remember Robert Louis Stevenson*, ed. by Rosaline Masson (Edinburgh and London: Chambers, 1922), pp. 6–12

Darwin, Charles, *The Origin of Species and The Descent of Man* (New York: The Modern Library, 1927)

Darwin, Erasmus, *Zoonomia*, 2nd edn, 2 vols (London: Johnson, 1796)

Dawson, Carl, *His Fine Wit: A Study of Thomas Love Peacock* (London: Routledge & Kegan Paul, 1970)

Day, Clarence, *The Best of Clarence Day* (New York: Knopf, 1948; repr. 1956)

Dickson, Arthur, *Valentine and Orson: A Study in Late Medieval Romance* (New York: Columbia University Press, 1929; repr. New York: AMS Press, 1975)

Donne, John, *The Sermons of John Donne*, ed., intro. and critical apparatus by Evelyn M. Simpson and George R. Potter, 10 vols (Berkeley and Los Angeles: University of California Press, 1958; repr. 1962)

—— *The Elegies, and the Songs and Sonnets*, ed., intro. and commentary by Helen Gardner (Oxford: Clarendon Press, 1965)

——*John Donne: The Satires, Epigrams and Verse Letters*, ed., intro. and commentary by W. Milgate (Oxford: Oxford University Press, 1967)

—— *The Complete English Poems*, ed. by A.J. Smith (London: Allen Lane, 1974)

Dudley, Edward and Maximillian E. Novak, eds, *The Wild Man Within: An Image in Western Thought from the Renaissance to Romanticism* [Pittsburgh], (University of Pittsburgh Press, 1972)

Eigner, Edwin, *Robert Louis Stevenson and Romantic Tradition* (Princeton, N.J.: Princeton University Press, 1966)

Emerson, Ralph Waldo, *The Works of Ralph Waldo Emerson*, 12 vols (London: Routledge, 1903)

The Epic of Gilgamesh, intro. by N.K. Sandars (Harmondsworth: Penguin, 1972; repr. 1975)

Fairchild, Hoxie Neale, *The Noble Savage: A Study in Romantic Naturalism* (New York: Russell and Russell, 1928; repr. 1961)

Fayter, Paul, 'Strange New Worlds of Space and Time: Late Victorian Science and Science Fiction', in *Victorian Science in Context*, ed. by Bernard Lightman (Chicago and London: University of Chicago Press, 1997)

Frantz, R.W., 'Swift's Yahoos and the Voyagers', *Modern Philology*, 29 (1931), 49–57

Frye, Northrop, *The Secular Scripture* (Cambridge, Massachusetts, and London: Harvard University Press, 1976)

——*Myth and Metaphor: Selected Essays, 1974–1988*, ed. by Robert D. Denham (Charlottesville and London: University Press of Virginia, 1990)

Frye, Roland M., 'Swift's Yahoo and the Christian Symbols for Sin', *Journal of the History of Ideas*, 15 (1954), 201–17

Funnell, William, *A Voyage round the World* (1710), in *A Collection of Voyages* (London: [n. pub.], 1729)

Furnas, J.C., *Voyage to Windward: The Life of Robert Louis Stevenson* (London: Faber, 1952)

Gaughan, Richard, 'Mr Hyde and Mr Seek: Utterson's Antidote', *Journal of Narrative Technique*, 17 (1987), 184–97

Godwin, William, *Collected Novels and Memoirs of William Godwin*, ed. by Mark Philp and others, 8 vols (London: Pickering and Chatto, 1992), IV, *St Leon: A Tale of the Sixteenth Century*; V, *Fleetwood: or, The New Man of Feeling*

Graham, Kenneth, 'Stevenson and Henry James: A Crossing', in *Robert Louis Stevenson*, ed. by Andrew Noble (London and Totowa: Vision and Barnes & Noble, 1983), pp. 23–46

Graves, Robert, *The Greek Myths*, 2 vols (Harmondsworth: Penguin, 1966–67)

Hall, Donald E., ed., *Muscular Christianity: Embodying the Victorian Age* (Cambridge: Cambridge University Press, 1994)

Hannah, Barbara, *Striving Towards Wholeness* (London: Allen & Unwin, 1972)

Harman, Claire, *Robert Louis Stevenson: A Biography* (London: Harper Collins, 2005)

Harper, George Mills, *The Neoplatonism of William Blake* (Chapel Hill: University of North Carolina Press, 1961)

Harrison, John Smith, *Platonism in English Poetry of the Sixteenth and Seventeenth Centuries* (Macmillan, 1903; repr. New York: Columbia University Press, 1930)

Hart, Jeffrey, 'The Ideologue as Artist: Some Notes on *Gulliver's Travels*', *Criticism*, 2 (1960), 125–33

Harth, Phillip, *Swift and Anglican Rationalism: The Religious Background of A Tale of a Tub* (Chicago and London: University of Chicago Press, 1969)

Heath, Stephen, 'Psychopathia Sexualis: Stevenson's *Strange Case*', *Critical Quarterly*, 28 (1986), 93–108

Henkin, Leo, *Darwinism in the English Novel 1860–1910: The Impact of Evolution on Victorian Fiction* (New York: Russell and Russell, 1963)

Herbert, Sir Thomas, *Some Years Travels into Divers Parts of Asia and Afrique* (London: [n. pub.], 1638)

Hogle, Jerrold, 'The Struggle for a Dichotomy: Abjection in Jekyll and His Interpreters', in *Dr Jekyll and Mr Hyde after One Hundred Years*, ed. by William Veeder and Gordon Hirsch (Chicago: University of Chicago Press, 1988), pp. 161–207

Hopkins, Gerard Manley, *The Letters of G.M. Hopkins to Robert Bridges*, ed. by Claude C. Abbott, 2nd edn, rev. (London: Oxford University Press, 1955)

Horace, *Odes*, trans. by Edward Bulwer Lytton (London and New York: Routledge, 1872)

Huxley, Thomas Henry, *Collected Essays*, 9 vols (London: Macmillan, 1894) (Hereafter *CE*.)

—— 'The Connection of the Biological Sciences with Medicine', *Science and Education*, *CE*, III, 347–73

—— 'Evolution in Biology', *Darwiniana*, *CE*, II, 187–226

—— 'On the Physical Basis of Life', *Method and Results*, *CE*, I, 130–65

—— 'Science and Pseudo Science', *Science and Christian Tradition*, *CE*, V, 90–125

—— 'The Struggle for Existence in Human Society', *Evolution and Ethics*, *CE*, IX, 195–236

—— *Man's Place in Nature*, intro. by Ashley Montagu (Ann Arbor: University of Michigan Press, 1971)

Inge, William Ralph, *The Platonic Tradition in English Religious Thought* (London: Longmans, Green, 1926)

—— *The Philosophy of Plotinus*, 3rd edn, 2 vols (London: Longmans, Green, 1948)

Irvine, William, *Apes, Angels and Victorians* (London: Readers Union, Weidenfeld and Nicholson, 1956)

James, Henry, *Partial Portraits* (London: Macmillan, 1888; repr. 1919)

Janson, Horst W., *Apes and Ape Lore in the Middle Ages and the Renaissance* (London: Warburg, 1952; repr. Nendeln/Liechtenstein: Kraus, 1976)

Kelman, John, *The Faith of Robert Louis Stevenson* (Edinburgh and London: Oliphant Anderson and Ferrier, 1907)

Kendall, Guy, *Charles Kingsley and His Ideas* (London: Hutchinson, 1947)

Kingsley, Charles, *Alexandria and Her Schools* (Cambridge: Macmillan, 1854)

—— *Westminster Sermons* (London: Macmillan, [1874]; repr. 1894)

—— 'Joseph', in *The Gospel of the Pentateuch and David* (London: Macmillan, 1885), pp. 91–103

—— *Alton Locke, Tailor and Poet* (London: Macmillan, 1889)

—— 'How to Study Natural History', in *Scientific Lectures and Essays*, 2nd edn (London: Macmillan, 1890), pp. 289–310

—— 'The Natural Theology of the Future', in *Scientific Lectures and Essays*, 2nd edn (London: Macmillan, 1890), pp. 313–36

—— 'The Wages of Sin', in *The Water of Life, and other Sermons* (London: Macmillan, 1890), pp. 40–55

—— *Westward Ho!* (London: Dent, 1906; repr. 1960)

—— *The Water-Babies: A Fairy-Tale For A Land Baby*, illust. by Rosalie K. Fry (London: Dent, 1973)

Kingsley, Frances E., *Charles Kingsley: His Letters and Memories of His Life*, 2 vols (London: King, 1877)

—— *Charles Kingsley: His Letters and Memories of His Life* (London: Macmillan, 1883; repr. 1904)

Knight, William, *Lord Monboddo and Some of His Contemporaries* (London: Murray, 1900)

Kreitzer, Larry, 'R.L. Stevenson's *Strange Case of Dr Jekyll and Mr Hyde* and Romans 7.14–25: Images of the Moral Duality of Human Nature', *Journal of Literature and Theology*, 6.2 (June 1992), 125–44

Lang, Andrew, Review of *Jekyll and Hyde*, *Saturday Review*, 61 (9 January 1886), 55–56

—— Letter to *The Athenaeum*, 3507 (12 January 1895), 49

—— Letter to *The Athenaeum*, 3511 (9 February 1895), 187

Lawler, Donald, 'Reframing *Jekyll and Hyde*: Robert Louis Stevenson and the Strange Case of Gothic Fiction', in *Dr Jekyll and Mr Hyde after One Hundred Years*, ed. by William Veeder and Gordon Hirsch (Chicago: University of Chicago Press, 1988), pp. 247–61

Levine, George, and William Madden, eds, *The Art of Victorian Prose* (New York, London, Toronto: Oxford University Press, 1968)

Liebregts, Peter, and Wim Tigges, eds, *Beauty and the Beast: Christina Rossetti, Walter Pater, R.L. Stevenson and their Contemporaries* (Amsterdam: Rodopi, 1996)

Lightman, Bernard, ed., *Victorian Science in Context* (Chicago and London: University of Chicago Press, 1997)

Linehan, Katherine, 'The Devil can cite Scripture: Intertextual Hauntings in *Strange Case of Dr Jekyll and Mr Hyde*', *Journal of Stevenson Studies*, 3 (2006), 5–32

Lovejoy, Arthur O., *The Great Chain of Being* (Cambridge, Massachusetts: Harvard University Press, 1936; repr. 1961)

Lucretius, *On the Nature of Things*, trans, by H.A.J. Munro [1860] (London: Routledge; New York: Dutton, [1907])

Mack, Douglas S., 'Dr Jekyll, Mr Hyde, and Count Dracula', in *Beauty and the Beast: Christina Rossetti, Walter Pater, R.L. Stevenson and their Contemporaries*, ed. by Peter Liebregts and Wim Tigges (Amsterdam: Rodopi, 1996), pp. 149–56

McLynn, Frank, *Robert Louis Stevenson: A Biography* (New York: Random House, 1993)

Maixner, Paul, ed., *Robert Louis Stevenson: The Critical Heritage* (London: Routledge & Kegan Paul, 1981)

Manlove, Colin N., *Modern Fantasy: Five Studies* (Cambridge: Cambridge University Press, 1975)

Massey, Irving, 'The Third Self: *Dracula, Strange Case of Dr Jekyll and Mr Hyde* and Mérimée's *Lokis*', *Bulletin of the Midwest Modern Language Association*, 6 (1973), 57–67

Masson, Rosaline, ed., *I Can Remember Robert Louis Stevenson* (Edinburgh and London: Chambers, 1922)

Mellor, Anne K., *Mary Shelley: Her Life, Her Fiction, Her Monsters* (New York and London: Routledge, 1988)

Mighall, Robert, *A Geography of Victorian Gothic Fiction: Mapping History's Nightmares* (Oxford: Oxford University Press, 1999)

Mills, Kevin, 'The Stain on the Mirror: Pauline Reflections in *The Strange Case of Dr Jekyll and Mr Hyde*', *Christianity and Literature*, 53 (2004), 337–48

Milton, John, *The Poetical Works of John Milton*, ed. by Helen Darbishire (London: Oxford University Press, 1958; repr. 1960)

——*Paradise Lost*, ed. and intro. by David Scott Kasdan (Indianapolis and Cambridge: Hackett, 2005)

Monboddo, James Burnett, Lord, *Antient Metaphysics: or, The Science of Universals. With an Appendix, containing an Examination of the Principles of Sir Isaac Newton's Philosophy*, 6 vols (London: Cadell; Edinburgh: Balfour, 1779–99)

——*Of the Origin and Progress of Language*, facsimile repr. of 1st edn (London: Cadell; Edinburgh: Balfour, 1773–92), 6 vols (Menston: Scolar Press, 1967)

Montagu, Ashley, 'Tyson's *Orang-Outang Sive Homo Sylvestris* and Swift's *Gulliver's Travels*', *PMLA*, 59 (1944), 84–89

Moore, James R., *The Post-Darwinian Controversies: A Study of the Protestant Struggle to Come to Terms with Darwin in Great Britain and America 1870–1900* (Cambridge: Cambridge University Press, 1979)

More, Henry, *Henry More: The Complete Poems*, ed. by Alexander B. Grosart (Edinburgh University Press, 1878; repr. Hildesheim: Olms, 1969)

——*Philosophical Poems of Henry More: Comprising Psychozoia and Minor Poems*, ed., intro. and notes by Geoffrey Bullough (Manchester: Manchester University Press, 1931)

More, P.E., *Platonism* (Princeton: Princeton University Press, 1917)

Morton, Peter, *The Vital Science: Biology and the Literary Imagination, 1860–1900* (London: Allen & Unwin, 1984)

Noble, Andrew, ed., *Robert Louis Stevenson* (London and Totowa: Vision and Barnes & Noble, 1983)

Noble, James Ashcroft, review of *Jekyll and Hyde*, *Academy*, 29 (23 January 1886), 55

Novak, Maximillian, 'The Wild Man Comes to Tea', in *The Wild Man Within: An Image in Western Thought from the Renaissance to Romanticism*, ed. by Edward Dudley and Maximillian E. Novak (University of Pittsburgh Press, 1972), pp. 183–221

Oken, Lorenz, *Elements of Physiophilosophy*, trans. by Alfred Tulk (London Ray Society, 1847)

Osborn, Henry Fairfield, *From the Greeks to Darwin: An Outline of the Evolution Idea* (New York and London: Macmillan. 1894)

Ovington, John, *A Voyage to Surat* (1696) ed. by H.G. Rawlinson (London: [n. pub.], repr. 1929)

Paradis, James, *T.H. Huxley: Man's Place in Nature* (Lincoln and London: University of Nebraska Press, 1978)

Passman, Dirk F., 'Degeneration in *Gulliver's Travels*: Excavations from Brobdingnag', *Swift Studies: The Annual of the Ehrenpreis Centre*, 1 (1986), 46–50

Peacock, Thomas Love, *The Novels of Thomas Love Peacock*, ed., intro., and notes by David Garnett (London: Hart-Davis, 1948)

—— *The Works of Thomas Love Peacock*, ed. by H.F.B. Brett-Smith and C.E. Jones, the Halliford edn, 10 vols (New York: AMS Press, 1967), I, *Biographical Introduction and Headlong Hall*; II, *Melincourt*

Perkus, Aaron, 'Dr Jekyll Hydeing in the Garden of Eden', *Mythos*, 6 (1996), 35–43. Revised chapter from *Where the Wild Things Are: The Male Uterus and the Creation of Monsters* (unpublished doctoral dissertation: Binghamton University, 1994)

Persak, Christine, 'Spencer's Doctrines and Mr Hyde: Moral Evolution in Stevenson's "Strange Case"', *Victorian Newsletter*, 86 (1994), 16–18

Pizer, Donald, 'Evolutionary Ideas in Late Nineteenth Century English and American Literary Criticism', *Journal of Aesthetics and Art Criticism*, 19 (1961), 305–10

Plato, *The Dialogues of Plato*, trans. and ed. by Benjamin Jowett, 4th edn, 4 vols (Oxford: Clarendon Press, 1953)

—— *Complete Works*, ed., intro. and notes by John M. Cooper (Indianapolis: Hackett, 1997)

Plotinus, *The Six Enneads*, trans. by Stephen MacKenna, 3rd edn, rev. by B.S. Page (New York: Pantheon, [n.d.])

Pope, Alexander, *Pope's Essay on Man*, intro. and notes by F. Ryland (London: Bell, 1898)

—— *Pope's Iliad of Homer*, ed. and intro. by A.J. Church, illust. by Wal Paget (London: Cassell, 1910)

Prickett, Stephen, *Victorian Fantasy* (Sussex: Harvester Press, 1979)

Punch, 'Monkeyana' 40 (18 May 1861), 206

—— 'The Maniac–Man– Monkey' 87 (27 December 1884), 305

Punter, David, *The Literature of Terror: A History of Gothic Fictions from 1765 to the Present Day* (London: Longmans, 1980)

Raleigh, Sir Walter, *Robert Louis Stevenson* (London: Arnold, 1927)

Reichert, John F., 'Plato, Swift, and the Houyhnhnms', *Philological Quarterly*, 47 (1968), 179–92

Reid, Julia, *Robert Louis Stevenson, Science, and the Fin de Siècle* (Basingstoke and New York: Palgrave Macmillan, 2006)

Robe, Stanley L., 'Wild Men and Spain's Brave New World', in *The Wild Man Within: An Image in Western Thought from the Renaissance to Romanticism*, ed. by Edward Dudley and Maximillian E. Novak (University of Pittsburgh Press, 1972), pp. 39–53

Roche, Thomas P., Jr, *The Kindly Flame: A Study of the Third and Fourth Books of Spenser's Faerie Queene* (Princeton: Princeton University Press, 1964)

Roe, John, 'Italian Neoplatonism and the Poetry of Sidney, Shakespeare, Chapman and Donne', in *Platonism and the English Imagination*, ed. by Anna Baldwin and Sarah Hutton (Cambridge: Cambridge University Press, 1994; repr. 2004), pp. 100–16

Rogers, Woodes, *A Cruising Voyage Round the World* (London: [n. pub.], 1712; 2nd edn, 1726)

Roppen, Georg, *Evolution and Poetic Belief: A Study in Some Victorian and Modern Writers* (Oslo: Oslo University Press, 1956)

Rosen, David, 'The Volcano and the Cathedral: Muscular Christianity and the Origins of Primal Manliness', in *Muscular Christianity: Embodying the Victorian Age*, ed. by Donald E. Hall (Cambridge: Cambridge University Press, 1994)

Roston, Murray, *The Soul of Wit: A Study of John Donne* (Oxford: Clarendon Press, 1974)

Sandison, Alan, *Robert Louis Stevenson and the Appearance of Modernism* (London: Macmillan; New York: St Martins Press, 1996)

Saposnik, Irving S., *Robert Louis Stevenson* (Boston: Twayne, 1974)

Savage, Thomas, 'Observations on the External Characters and Habits of the *Troglodytes Niger*', *Boston Journal of Natural History*, 4 (1843–44), 362–86

Scott, Dr Thomas Bodley, 'Memories', in *I Can Remember Robert Louis Stevenson*, ed. by Rosaline Masson (Edinburgh and London: Chambers, 1922), pp. 212–14

Scott, Walter, *The Works of Jonathan Swift, D.D.*, 19 vols (Edinburgh: Constable, 1814)

—— *Count Robert of Paris* (London and Edinburgh: Black, 1894)

Shaftesbury, Anthony Cooper, 3rd Earl of, *Characteristics of Men, Manners, Opinions, Times, etc.*, ed., intro. and notes by John M. Robertson, 2 vols (Gloucester, Massachusetts: Smith, 1900; repr. 1963)

Shelley, Mary, *Frankenstein*, ed., intro. and notes by Marilyn Butler (London: Pickering, 1993)

Sheridan, Thomas, *The Life of the Rev. Dr Jonathan Swift, Dean of St Patrick's, Dublin*, vol. I of *The Works of the Rev. Dr Jonathan Swift, Dean of St Patrick's, Dublin*, arranged, revised, and corrected, with notes, by Thomas Sheridan, A.M., 17 vols (London: Bathurst, Strahan, and others, 1784)

Showalter, Elaine, *Sexual Anarchy: Gender and Culture at the Fin de Siècle* (New York: Viking, 1990)

Sigstedt, Cyriel Odhner, *The Swedenborg Epic: The Life and Works of Emanuel Swedenborg* (New York: Bookman, 1952)

Simmons, Clare A., 'A Man of Few Words: The Romantic Orang-Outang and Scott's *Count Robert of Paris*', *Scottish Literary Journal*, 17.1 (May 1990), 21–34

Smith, A.J., ed., *John Donne: The Critical Heritage* (London and Boston: Routledge & Kegan Paul, 1975)

Smith, William, *A New Voyage to Guinea* ([n.p.: n.pub.], 1744)

Spencer, Herbert, 'A Criticism on Prof. Owen's Theory of the Vertebrate Skeleton', in *The Principles of Biology*, rev. and enlarged, 2 vols (London: Williams and Norgate, 1898), II, 548–66. (first publ. in *British & Foreign Medico-Chirurgical Review* (October 1858))

—— *The Principles of Biology*, rev. and enlarged, 2 vols (London: Williams and Norgate, 1898)

—— *First Principles*, 2 vols (London: Williams and Norgate, 1910)

Spenser, Edmund, *Edmund Spenser: The Fowre Hymnes*, ed. by Lilian Winstanley (Cambridge: Cambridge University Press, 1907)

—— *Works: A Variorum Edition*, ed. by Edwin Greenlaw and others, 11 vols (Baltimore: Johns Hopkins Press, 1932; 3rd repr. 1961)

—— *Fowre Hymnes Epithalamion: A Study of Edmund Spenser's Doctrine of Love*, ed. by Enid Welsford (Oxford: Blackwell, 1967)

—— *Edmund Spenser's Poetry*, ed. by Hugh Maclean (New York: Norton, 1968)

—— *The Faerie Queene*, ed. by A.C. Hamilton (London and New York: Longman, 1977)

—— *The Yale Edition of the Shorter Poems of Edmund Spenser*, ed. by William A. Oram and others (New Haven: Yale University Press, 1989)

Stevenson, Robert Louis, *The Works of Robert Louis Stevenson*, Vailima edn, 25 vols (New York: Scribner, 1921; repr. AMS Press, 1974)

—— 'The Body-Snatcher', *Works*, VII, 457–88

—— *Catriona, Works*, X

—— 'Lay Morals', *Works*, XXIV, 167–240

—— 'Macaire', *Works*, VI, 259–313

—— 'The Manse', *Works*, XII, 84–93

—— 'Memoirs of Himself', *Works*, XXVI, 203–37

—— 'The Merry Men', *Works*, XI, 11–87

—— 'Olalla', *Works*, XI, 173–239

—— 'Pastoral', *Works*, XII, 72–83

—— 'Pulvis et Umbra', *Works*, XII, 283–92

—— 'The Silverado Diary', *Works*, II, 581–608

—— *The Silverado Squatters, Works*, II, 439–578

—— *Weir of Hermiston, Works*, XVIII, 209–408

—— *The Supernatural Short Stories of Robert Louis Stevenson*, ed. and intro. by Michael Hayes (London: Calder, 1976)

—— *Dr Jekyll and Mr Hyde and Other Stories*, ed. and intro. by Jenni Calder (London: Penguin, 1979)

—— *The Letters of Robert Louis Stevenson*, ed. by Bradford A. Booth and Ernest Mehew, 8 vols (New Haven and London: Yale University Press, 1995)

—— *The Strange Case of Dr Jekyll and Mr Hyde and Other Tales of Terror*, ed., intro. and notes by Robert Mighall (London: Penguin, 2002; repr. 2003)

—— *Strange Case of Dr Jekyll and Mr Hyde*, ed. by Katherine Linehan (New York and London: Norton, 2003)

—— *Strange Case of Dr Jekyll and Mr Hyde*, ed. by Richard Dury (Edinburgh: Edinburgh University Press, 2004)

—— *The Annotated Dr Jekyll and Mr Hyde*, ed., intro. and notes by Richard Dury, 2nd edn, rev. (Genoa: Edizioni Culturali Internazionali Genova, 2005)

Swearingen, Roger G., *The Prose Writings of Robert Louis Stevenson* (Hamden, Connecticut: Archon, 1980)

Swedenborg, Emanuel, *Angelic Wisdom Concerning the Divine Providence* (London: Swedenborg Society, 1934)

—— *The Delights of Wisdom Concerning Conjugial Love*, trans. by Alfred Acton (London: Swedenborg Society, 1953)

Swift, Jonathan, *Prose Works of Jonathan Swift*, ed. by Herbert Davis, 14 vols (Oxford: Blackwell, 1957–68)

—— *The Poems of Jonathan Swift*, ed. by Harold Williams, 2nd edn, 3 vols (Oxford: Clarendon Press, 1958)

—— *Gulliver's Travels*, ed. by Robert A. Greenberg (New York: Norton, 1961)

—— *The Correspondence of Jonathan Swift*, ed. by Harold Williams, 5 vols (Oxford: Clarendon Press, 1963–65)

Symonds, John Addington, *The Letters of John Addington Symonds*, ed. by Herbert M. Schueller & Robert L. Peters, 3 vols (Detroit: Wayne State University Press, 1967–69)

Tennyson, Alfred, Lord, *In Memoriam*, intro. and notes by Kingsley Hart (London: Folio Society, 1975)

Thorpe, Douglas, 'Calvin, Darwin, and the Double: The Problem of Divided Nature in Hogg, MacDonald, and Stevenson', *Newsletter of Victorian Studies Association of Western Canada*, 11.1 (Spring 1985), 6–22

Tropp, Martin, 'Dr Jekyll and Mr Hyde, Schopenhauer, and the Power of the Will', *Midwest Quarterly*, 32 (1991), 141–55

Turner, Frank M., *The Greek Heritage in Victorian Britain* (New Haven and London: Yale University Press, 1981)

Tuveson, Ernest, ed., *Swift: A Collection of Critical Essays* (Englewood Cliffs, N.J.: Prentice-Hall, 1964)

——'Swift: The Dean as Satirist', in *Swift: A Collection of Critical Essays*, ed. by Ernest Tuveson (Englewood Cliffs, N.J.: Prentice-Hall, 1964), pp. 101–10 (first publ. in *University of Toronto Quarterly*, 22 (1953), 368–75)

Valentine and Orson, trans. by Henry Watson [1503–05?], ed. and intro. by Arthur Dickson (London: Oxford University Press, 1937; repr., New York: Kraus, 1971)

Veeder, William, 'Children of the Night: Stevenson and Patriarchy', in *Dr Jekyll and Mr Hyde after One Hundred Years*, ed. by William Veeder and Gordon Hirsch (Chicago: University of Chicago Press, 1988), pp. 107–60

Veeder, William and Gordon Hirsch, eds, *Dr Jekyll and Mr Hyde after One Hundred Years* (Chicago: University of Chicago Press, 1988)

Voltaire, Jean François Marie Arouet de, *Candide: And other Tales*, intro. by H.N. Brailsford (London: Dent, 1937; repr. 1967)

Webster, C.M., 'Notes on the Yahoos', *Modern Language Notes*, 47 (1932), 451–54

Wedgwood, Julia, Review of *Jekyll and Hyde*, *Contemporary Review*, 49 (April 1886), 594–95

White, Andrew D., *A History of the Warfare of Science with Religion in Christendom*, [1896] 2 vols (New York: Dover, 1960)

Willey, Basil, *The Seventeenth Century Background: Studies in the Thought of the Age in Relation to Poetry and Religion* (London: Chatto and Windus, 1967)

Williams, Kathleen, *Jonathan Swift and the Age of Compromise* (Lawrence: University of Kansas Press, 1959)

——ed., *Swift: The Critical Heritage* (London: Routledge & Kegan Paul, 1970)

Wilson, James, 'Swift, the Psalmist, and the Horse', *Tennessee Studies in Literature*, 3 (1958), 17–23

Wolf, Leonard, *The Essential Dr Jekyll and Mr Hyde*, illust. by Michael Lark (New York: Plume, 1995)

Wright, Daniel L., '"The Prisonhouse of my Disposition": A Study of the Psychology of Addiction in *Dr Jekyll and Mr Hyde*', *Studies in the Novel*, 26 (1994), 254–67

Yates, Frances A., *Giordano Bruno and the Hermetic Tradition* (London: Routledge & Kegan Paul, 1964)

Index